VIOLENCE AGAINST WIVES

VIOLENCE AGAINST WIVES

A Case Against the Patriarchy

R. Emerson Dobash

Russell Dobash

THE FREE PRESS
A Division of Macmillan Publishing Co., Inc.
NEW YORK

The Free Press
A Division of Macmillan Publishing Co., Inc.
866 Third Avenue, New York, N.Y. 10022

Collier Macmillan Canada, Inc.

First Free Press Paperback Edition 1983

Printed in the United States of America

printing number paperback
   3 4 5 6 7 8 9 10

printing number hardcover
3 4 5 6 7 8 9 10

Library of Congress Cataloging in Publication Data

Dobash, R. Emerson.
  Violence against wives.

  Bibliography: p.
  Includes index.
  1. Wife abuse. 2. Patriarchy. 3. Social history.
1. Dobash, Russell, joint author. II. Title.
HV6626 D6 1979   362.8'2   79-7181
ISBN 0-02-907320-0
ISBN 0-02-907810-5 pbk

For all women who struggle individually and collectively against the violence and oppression from which they suffer.

CONTENTS

PREFACE

The use of physical violence against women in their position as wives is not the only means by which they are controlled and oppressed but it is one of the most brutal and explicit expressions of patriarchical domination. The position of women and men as wives and husbands has been historically structured as a hierarchy in which men possessed and controlled women. There were numerous legal, political, economic and ideological supports for a husband's authority over his wife which included the approval of his use of physical force against her. The legal right of a man to beat his wife is no longer explicitly recognized in most western countries but the legacy of the patriarchy continues to generate the conditions and relationships that lead to a husband's use of force against his wife. Patriarchal domination through force is still supported by a moral order which reinforces the marital hierarchy and makes it very difficult for a woman to struggle against this, and other forms of domination and control, because her struggle is construed as wrong, immoral, and a violation of the respect and loyalty a wife is supposed to give to her husband. Despite this, women do continue to struggle against their husbands' specific oppression as well as against the 'morality' that forces a woman to remain silent or to seek fault in herself for her husband's violence. Women struggle against all odds—against cultural ideals that still require a woman to submit to almost any form of treatment that her husband considers appropriate and against the policies and responses of various social agencies which often demonstrate direct or indirect support for the husband's authority and his use of violence.

The fact that violence against wives is a form of a husband's domination is irrefutable in the light of historical evidence. Such evidence constituted a starting point in our own development of a comprehensive explanation and understanding of wife beating. We think that any approach to the understanding of a social problem must include a consideration of history, biography, institutional processes and cultural beliefs and ideals. Thus, not only did we look closely at the violence in specific families and consider the factors associated with its emergence and continuation, we also sought to understand the relationship between community reactions and the continuation of that violence. This form of analysis took us beyond the narrow and false boundaries that all too often needlessly restrict social researchers. Such boundaries often confine the inquiry only to violent individuals or to specific violent families and lead to the partialling out of those individuals or families from the wider social, economic and political world. We avoided this narrow approach by embedding our analysis of individual violent behavior in the wider social and cultural context. This was done by exploring the manner in which economic and social processes operate directly and indirectly to support patriarchal domination and the use of violence against wives. This method sharply contrasts with the bulk of social science research which attempts to abstract and isolate social problems and social processes from the wider social context in which they occur.

Our initial training in the social sciences primarily emphasized, above all else, issues relating to abstract research, measurement, hypothesis testing and survey research. This background certainly prepared us to deal with the technical problems that must be addressed in all research endeavors. However, it was also narrow and constraining as we found ourselves confronted by many crucial issues and problems which required that we go beyond the confines of a narrow and technical empiricism. We began to work on an alternative form of social science which would go beyond the usual simplistic statistical research that is so often seen as the only, or at least the superior, form of 'scientific' research. We did this while holding on to the goals of social science as we see them—the production of systematic and verifiable evidence which will provide a sound basis for explanation and understanding.

Another major goal in conducting and presenting our work was to retain our commitment to social action. We do not separate our social and political lives from our intellectual lives. We do not stand apart or aloof from our research and its presentation. We do not seek to adopt that arid, sterile, and artificial stance of supposed 'objective' neutrality that now permeates much of social science. This book is the outcome of a continual process of working on a form of social science which is aimed at explaining social issues, not just measuring them and at providing evidence which relates to social action. This process engages us in going beyond the narrow concerns of most technical and academic research, requiring us to consider not only how one conducts better research but also how one's research relates to the wider social, economic, and political world which it will enter as part of the continuing intellectual and political discourse.

ACKNOWLEDGMENTS

This book would not have been possible without the cooperation and assistance of many women. We owe an inestimable debt of gratitude to the women living and working in refuges. This book would not have been as meaningful nor would it have had a purpose if it had not been for all the women who so generously opened up their lives and relived very painful experiences in order that such information might be used to help countless other women in the same position. In recounting their stories, we have changed all personal and place names.

We would like to express our gratitude to the dedicated and hard working women of the Scottish Women's Aid Federation and the National Women's Aid Federation in England both for their efforts in working with battered women and for the support and assistance they have given us throughout the research. Initially we were introduced into the newly opened refuges for battered women in Edinburgh and Glasgow by Margo Galloway and Maura Butterly. During the course of the research numerous Women's Aid workers helped and supported us in various ways, but we would especially like to thank Lee Harris, Lois Hobbs, Judi Hodgkins, Kathy Kerr, Mary O'Donnell, Sue Robertson, and Fran Wasoff for their assistance regarding the interviews in Scotland. Jo Sutton and Lou Lavender of the National Women's Aid Federation in England painstakingly read drafts of our papers (in a tent during their holidays) and constantly served as critics and educators. Jalna Hanmer invited us to become members of the Anglo-French Exchange on Violence Against Women, where we met Dominic Poggi and Yves Dezalay and were exposed to new ideas and criticisms of some of our early ideas and methods which were both painful and threatening yet contributed to our development of a more meaningful and useful approach. Lisa Slot-Anderson and Nora van Crevel introduced us to the refuge in Amsterdam and to the problems of battered women in the Netherlands. Marjory Fields, Del Martin, Eleanor Kremen and Betsy Warrior, who are working in diverse ways for and with battered women in America, have always had time to discuss and exchange information with us regarding the problems confronting battered women. All of these women, as well as many others, have contributed greatly to our in-

sight into and our awareness of the problems and issues surrounding battered wives.

We both conducted interviews but the majority were eventually carried
out by our two hard-working research assistants and co-workers Kath
Cavanagh and Monica Wilson. Without their sensitive, sympathetic, yet
rigorous interviewing, and their hours of transcribing, coding, and analysis
the research would never have been completed. Our colleagues at the
University of Stirling, Jim Young, Stewart Butts, and David Wilson, and
Dick Ogles of the University of Colorado, read various sections of the
manuscript and offered critical suggestions and useful references. Susan
Reid spent untold hours reading numerous drafts of the entire manuscript
and suggesting helpful changes and additions. She served as an intellectual
critic offering valuable insights and suggestions and gave personal support
and encouragement throughout the preparation of this book. Maggie
Rhodes transcribed and typed the recorded interviews, and Eleanor Bruce
was patient enough to transform our numerous drafts into a polished
manuscript.

We are grateful to the Scottish Home and Health Department for providing a grant and to the Glasgow and Edinburgh police and court officials
for allowing access to their records. Of course, the ideas expressed herein
are our own and do not necessarily reflect the views of the Scottish Home
and Health department. The Carnegie Trust provided a small grant for
travel within the United States. We would also like to thank The Free Press
for editorial assistance and especially Charlie Smith, who urged us to write
about people rather than statistics.

CHAPTER I

VIOLENCE AGAINST WIVES: A CASE AGAINST THE PATRIARCHY

THE STRUGGLE WAS BEGUN by five hundred women and children and one cow. On a spring afternoon in 1971 this unlikely group marched down the streets of an English town and unknowingly began a movement that was to grow to international proportions within the next few years. Some of the women were members of a local women's liberation organization who, like many women at that time, had decided to put their feminist principles into practice by working on various community problems. This particular group began with a compaign against rising food prices in the local shops and soon organized a march protesting a proposed reduction in free milk for schoolchildren. The cow served as an apt symbol of their protest, and the sight of the beast casually strolling down the middle of the main street in the company of hundreds of women and children no doubt provided quite an amicable spectacle and drew even greater attention to their cause.

Despite their efforts, the march was not a direct success. Unconditional free milk for all schoolchildren was not retained, but the solidarity created among the women by the march resulted in their successful effort to set up a community meeting place for local women. The local council made a derelict house available to them for the annual rent of one peppercorn, and by November 1971, Chiswick's Women's Aid was open.[1] The center was to belong to all women in the community; they could go there to talk and share ideas, to escape from loneliness and isolation, or to seek help with their problems, ranging from poor housing to alcoholism.[2]

During some of these discussions at Chiswick's Women's Aid a few women began to reveal that they had been systematically and severely beaten by their husbands for many years.[3] The women gave detailed accounts of the pain and fear that filled their lives, accounts like those that now fill the newspapers and like those that we have heard and read since 1973 during hundreds of hours of in-depth interviews with battered women and in our detailed search through the evidence from nearly a thousand police and court cases of assaults against wives.

The type and severity of the violence experienced by women at the hands of their husbands vary considerably. One woman told us how she

1

broke her back after leaping out of a first story window in order to escape the beating she was receiving from her husband. Another revealed that she was dragged up and down a flight of stone stairs by her hair and then whipped with a wire spring belt. Another had her hair literally pulled out by the roots and was left with a permanent bald spot. Countless others suffered black eyes, split lips, broken teeth, and bruised throats, shins, and spines.

Despite the current exposure of such cases, only a very few of them ever become public—covered by the media or brought to court. Most go unnoticed or unmentioned as the women hurry about their business in shops and at work, successfully concealing their wounds under scarves, long sleeves, or trousers or unsuccessfully under heavy makeup or behind dark glasses. Thus, it was quite by accident that the problem of battered women was discovered as a few victims began to reveal their private problems to others. Once discovered, however, this became the sole focus of Chiswick's Women's Aid and of the numerous other independent Women's Aid groups that formed during the following months and years.[4]

In 1971, almost no one had heard of battered women, except, of course, the legions of women who were being battered and the relatives, friends, ministers, social workers, doctors, and lawyers in whom some of them confided. Many people did not believe that such behavior actually existed, and even most of those who were aware of it did not think that it affected sufficient numbers of women or was of sufficient severity to warrant wide-scale concern. There was very little press or television coverage, and it was almost by word of mouth that women all over Britain began to hear about battered women and began to try to organize their own groups and set up shelters for women and children in their own areas.

In the beginning this was a very slow, almost haphazard, process. At the British Women's Liberation Conference held in Edinburgh in June 1974, a special session on the issue of battered wives was attended by only 20 women. A few of the latter were already helping to run the very few refuges that were then open and the rest were trying to open similar shelters. Also present to listen and give advice was the newly appointed national coordinator for Women's Aid—a very grand-sounding title for the head of a fledgling federation of a very few diverse, relatively powerless, and resourceless groups. We talked about numerous issues and problems including those of our research project, which had begun some months earlier. There was a great deal of interest and concern among this small group: the following year a similar session was held at the conference and the room, which was meant to hold several hundred people, was filled to overflowing. In the space of that year, public interest and concern had grown enormously, to a great extent because Women's Aid groups had secured media support. The press were especially enthusiastic. Once they had also discovered the issue of battered women, they launched an all-out campaign, which although sensationalist at times was usually supportive. This helped not only to raise public awareness and sympathy for women who were being beaten, but it also helped Women's Aid groups to increase in number, expand in membership, and gain moral and financial support in their efforts to provide more refuges for battered women and their children.

There was an explosion of activity. Groups were forming all over England, Scotland, and Wales, and they were usually struggling against great odds in order to open their own refuge. The House of Commons appointed a Select Committee on Violence in Marriage in 1974,[5] which began to take evidence on violence against wives and children. Legislation in this area was soon proposed. Similar activity began on the Continent, in Australia, and in North America.

The 1970s were not, however, the first time that wife beating had been discovered by the public and taken up as an issue of general concern rather than remaining hidden as a personal tragedy only specific to the women involved. That had happened at least twice before, in the latter part of the nineteenth century and in the early part of this century. In addition to these two short lived periods of public concern history is dotted with cases of individual women who struggled virtually alone against the violence of their husbands, and also of influential reformers who stood almost completely apart from their colleagues in their attempts to help women by trying to institute changes in their traditional status. These reformers believed that only through such changes could women be freed from some of the numerous legal, economic, educational, political, and physical abuses deemed appropriate to their secondary status in society and particularly to their position in marriage. However, the periodic concern of the public or of reformers has been only a fleeting elaboration of the continual struggles of isolated women against their husbands' abuses.

Some examples of one means men used to try to control their wives and the way in which women struggled against it were featured in the 1976 Bicentennial exhibition on Women in America from 1750 to 1815, held in Plymouth, Massachusetts. Displayed were advertisements in Colonial newspapers illustrating the attempts of husbands to deny their wives any reasonable means of escape from marriage. In 1764, one John Wilson placed the following advertisement in the *South Carolina Gazette*:

ADVERTISEMENT FOR A RUNAWAY WIFE
Lydia, the wife of John Wilson, having eloped from her husband; he hereby forbids all persons to give her any credit in his name, being determined not to pay any debt of her contracting, from this 28th day of October, 1764. He likewise forbids the harbouring or entertaining his said wife, on pain of prosecution.[6]

Although such advertisements were run quite commonly, all was not necessarily what it appeared to be. Many women published replies to clarify their reasons for running away and attempted to clear their names and protect their credit. For example, in 1776 one Sarah Cantwell issued her own declaration of independence.

RETORT FROM A RUNAWAY WIFE
John Cantwell has the Impudence to advertise me in the papers, cautioning all Persons against crediting me; he never had any credit till he married me: As for his Bed and Board he mentioned, he had neither Bed nor Board when he married me. I never eloped, I went away before his face when he beat me.[7]

The same exhibition displayed the famous letter written in 1776 by Abigail Smith Adams to her husband, John Adams, asking him to "Remember the Ladies" in this new society that he was helping to create. The plea from this influential woman was that all women be freed from the unlimited power traditionally given to husbands and thus be assured of at least some protection from the potential "cruelty and indignity" that could be inflicted upon them.

. . . and by the way in the new Code of Laws which I suppose it will be necessary for you to make I desire you would Remember the Ladies, and be more generous and favourable to them than your ancestors. Do not put such unlimited power into the hands of the Husbands. Remember all Men would be tyrants if they could: If particular care and attention is not paid to the Ladies, we are determined to foment a Rebellion, and will not hold ourselves bound by any Laws in which we have no voice, or Representation.
That your Sex are Naturally Tyrannical is a Truth so thoroughly established as to admit of no dispute, but such of you as wish to be happy willingly give up the harsh title of Master for the more tender and endearing one of Friend. Why then, not put it out of the power of the vicious and the Lawless to use us with cruelty and indignity and impunity. Men of Sense in all Ages abhor those customs which treat us only as the vassals of your Sex.[8]

Nevertheless, the ladies were forgotten. In fact, they are still struggling to have an equal rights amendment added to the Constitution of the United States. But, in at least one sense, the men were forgotten as well. In the case of marital chastisement, the husband's traditional right to beat his wife, established under English and European law, was neither confirmed nor denied in the United States. That omission, however, was eventually remedied. In 1824 wife beating was made legal in Mississippi. Court cases in several other states reaffirmed the traditional right of a man to beat his wife and did so in language identical to that of the English common law.[9]

Such laws, and of course the practices they protected, became the subject of rather widespread public concern and protest in both Britain and America in the latter part of the last century and again in the early part of this one.[10] During the 1870s Parliament took evidence concerning the nature and incidents of brutal assaults against wives and considered the use of flogging as a punishment for recalcitrant husbands.[11] Against objections that the sanctity of marriage was being violated, laws were passed that gave women meager protection against cruelty and allowed divorce on this ground. In America a few laws of chastisement were revoked in 1871.[12] With these actions taken, the issue disappeared from public view in both countries and once again became the concern only of those individuals directly involved.

Wife beating was taken up by the British and American suffragettes, who made it a part of their early platform, which was directed at sweeping changes in every sphere of women's lives.[13] This subject soon receded into obscurity, however, as the suffragettes concentrated increasingly upon achieving the vote, which they saw as the means of acquiring sufficient political power to solve all of the other problems affecting women.

In fact, in 1935 Bertrand Russell wrote a short newspaper article entitled "Rights Husbands Had Once," in which he assumed that the issue of violence against wives had been completely and amicably resolved. He claimed that husbands had become a "downtrodden race." Referring to the loss of a husband's traditional right to beat his wife, Russell cited the case of Susannah Palmer, who in 1878 became something of a national heroine because of what she had endured.

> Her husband was a drunken costermonger, who took to thieving and tried to induce her to do likewise. He turned her out into the streets at night, in order to make room for another woman; in the morning he gave her two black eyes and knocked out five of her teeth. After a repetition of such scenes she left him, taking the children with her; but he pursued her, took her earnings from her, and sold her bed, all of which he had a legal right to do. At last she took a knife and slightly wounded him. She had previously applied to the law for protection, but had been told that the law could do nothing, as her husband had not deserted her. For assaulting her husband she was sent to Newgate prison, where she expressed perfect contentment, because her husband could not get at her. Charitable persons took charge of the children, and it seems that, by at last breaking the law, she secured some of the relief which the law had refused her.[14]

Russell was not maintaining that the loss of the husband's legal right to chastise his wife should be mourned. On the contrary, he argued that there should be equality in marriage and that this could occur only when men and women had equal rights as well as equal duties. He argued that an illogical mixture of old and new ideas about the status of women had resulted in gains in women's right to be free from the traditional control of their husbands, including the use of physical force, but in little or no change in their economic dependence upon them. Since women still "earned their livelihood through marriage," they could not be said to take an equal share in the duties of marriage. It was because of what Russell saw as this equality of spouses' rights coupled with the imbalance of duties, that he referred to husbands as downtrodden. Moreover, he saw no possibility of changes that would equalize the financial contributions of husbands and wives under an economic system predicated upon a certain amount of unemployment.

Though we do not disagree with the latter part of Russell's argument, it is important to note that he assumed that at least as far as physical chastisement was concerned the issue of equal rights for husbands and wives had been resolved. He was, of course, premature in accepting that a husband's traditional right to beat his wife had ceased to be exercised simply because it had ceased to be legal. The case of Jean Collins, reported in 1976, bears an uncanny resemblance to the one of Susannah Palmer (1888) cited by Russell.

> Mrs Jean Collins, a mother of four, deliberately stole £19 from her gas meter and then went to the police and begged them to lock her up—so that she could escape the violence of her husband. . . . Mrs Collins admitted: "I only did it to be locked away because my husband keeps beating me". Police took her and her children to a battered wives' hostel . . . [and after pleading guilty] she was given a conditional discharge for a year.[15]

It is even more difficult to understand Russell's idea when one considers that not more than six years prior to the writing of that article, Marie Stopes, in her well-known campaign for birth control, had published scores of letters from women who recounted in horrific detail the daily burdens of poverty and endless childbearing; these letters also contained many accounts of husbands who were physically violent to their wives. Although Russell's sentiments may have been supportive, his apparent assumption that women no longer were beaten by their husbands stands as a monument to his ignorance about the beliefs and behaviors in the world around him. This ignorance was widespread, of course, and Russell might be forgiven for it because at least he saw wife beating as a serious problem that should be resolved in favor of women. That sentiment alone separated him from the indifference and antagonism expressed by most others before and after his time.

Until recently, battered wives and influential people like Abigail Adams, John Stuart Mill, Frances Power Cobbe, Marie Stopes, Lucretia Mott, Elizabeth Cady Stanton, and Mary Wollstonecraft stood almost alone in asserting that women should be freed from a whole variety of abuses and oppression including physical abuse. In so doing they opposed a long patriarchal tradition in which indifference and antagonism toward changes in the status of women reflected cultural beliefs about the "natural" hierarchical relationship between husband and wife. This subordination of women was explicitly established in the institutional practices of both the church and the state and supported by some of the most prominent political, legal, religious, philosophical, and literary figures in Western society, for instance, Rousseau, Hegel, Kant, Fichte, Blackstone, Saint Augustine, John Knox, Calvin, and Martin Luther. In one way or another, they each advocated a patriarchal relationship between men and women and especially between husbands and wives. They believed that men had the right to dominate and control women and that women were by their nature subservient to men. This relationship was deemed natural, sacred, and unproblematic and such beliefs resulted in long periods of disregard or denial of the husband's abuses of his economic, political, and physical power.

In this century at least, numerous ideas about the nature of the family and the marital relationship also left women to struggle alone against oppression. Belief in the sanctity of the family was closely associated with belief in personal privacy and with the rejection of outside intervention in family affairs. An almost dogmatic adherence to such ideas meant that the family was analogous to a fortress, closed off almost completely from the outside world—considered a good arrangement because it purportedly allowed family members to be nurtured in an ambience of security and happiness and at the same time protected from the evils of the outside world. The cult of domesticity and beliefs in family harmony and bliss made the idea of outside intervention in domestic affairs seem a needless violation of the sanctity and privacy of the home.

In Western societies, the ideas of peace and security and harmony are still so strongly associated with the institution of the family that it has been exceedingly difficult to deal with the fact that many people are horribly abused within the home. Today, most people are frightened of the dangers that may lurk outside their front door, in ill-lit streets, and down dark alleyways. Massive campaigns have been conducted against crime in the streets. Everyone's sense of well-being is to some extent affected by the fear of such crimes, and this fear often dictates many of one's daily movements such as which route to take home late at night. There can be no doubt that being assaulted or raped by a stranger in some dark alleyway is frightening, humiliating, painful, and perhaps fatal, but are such things any less horrific if they happen within the home and at the hands of a relative? The fact is that for most people, and especially for women and children, the family is the most violent group to which they are likely to belong. Despite fears to the contrary, it is not a stranger but a so-called loved one who is most likely to assault, rape, or murder us.

Despite overwhelming evidence to challenge it, the myth of family bliss and security survives almost totally intact. The official statistics, which have long been available, clearly show the high incidence of violence among family members; yet these figures have usually been ignored or given scant notice or treatment (especially when compared with the concern about violence in other settings). It is almost as though we have averted our eyes from violence in the family because we do not want it to happen and believe that it should not happen. When forced to acknowledge its existence, we attempt to deny that it is widespread or severe or that it happens between "normal" people. We wish to believe that a beating from a member of the family is somehow less serious, less painful, or less harmful than one from a stranger. Such is the strength of the myth of family bliss and of the desire to preserve it.

It is not surprising, therefore, that violence against wives had to be rediscovered in the 1970s. An issue was unearthed which had long been known to many but had been ignored by all but a few. And long-standing public indifference or acceptance meant that when wife beating was rediscovered, very little was known about it. There was little systematic information about what actually happens during violent episodes or how they affect a couple's relationship. There was little known about what wife beating means in the wider society and how it is supported or rejected by various social institutions and agencies.

In order to provide the foundation upon which meaningful proposals for solutions might be based, it is necessary to develop an explanation and to have an understanding of violence directed against wives. But to begin, as is often done, by examining almost all forms of physical violence and aggression together and treating them in a similar fashion[16] will not achieve this end. Considering violence or aggression as a single abstraction is often done in an attempt to create theoretical models which it is mistakenly thought will provide overall explanations for many, if not all, forms of violence. What this in fact does is to obscure or ignore the very real and significant differences between various forms of violent behavior, and this results in confusion rather than clarity. At least two very serious errors are made. First, there is the tendency to define almost all acts involving physical force by a single term such as "violence." This means that a statement about violence could include such diverse behaviors as a slap or shove, a blinding punch in the face, a crushing kick in the stomach or spine, or a wound from a knife or bullet. Second, there is the tendency to lump together all acts of violence performed in a wide variety of settings and by very different types of people. Thus, abstract explanations of violence and general statements about it are based upon information on the use of diverse forms of physical force (slapping, beating, or wounding) in a wide variety of settings (homes, streets, or battlefields) and by disparate categories of peoples (spouses, parents and children, gang members, or political enemies). This approach is about as useful as a geologist's referring to everything on the moon simply as rocks.

The folly of attempting to seek explanations for a wide variety of behaviors occurring in diverse settings and within different categories of people becomes patently obvious when one compares three acts that by this technique might all be referred to as violence. Consider striking a child's bottom, wounding someone while robbing them, or killing an opponent in war. All three of these acts contain some element of physical force, but common sense tells us that in almost every other respect they differ. To place these acts together in an effort to seek some overall explanation for them would simply miss the point because such an exercise would fail to deal with the physical, interpersonal, and social differences that enable us to make sense of them. As has already been stated, there are obvious differences in the degree of physical force used and the severity of the injuries sustained. At the interpersonal level, there are also differences in the nature of the relationship between the individuals involved, the motivation behind the use of force, the material or personal gains to be had from its application, and the degree of intimidation involved in the act. Socially, these acts vary in terms of the setting in which they occur, the degree of legitimacy accorded them, the institutional and moral supports for them, and their meaning in the wider society.

If, for instance, we consider merely the degree of legitimacy accorded each of these three acts of violence, the differences are both vast and obvious. Although it is usually deemed legitimate, and even laudable, to kill an opponent in war, such legitimacy, not to mention regard, rarely attaches in the case of 'merely' wounding a fellow citizen while robbing him. On the other hand, most parents who hit their children, and this includes almost everyone, usually see themselves—and are seen by others—as acting for the child's 'own good' and would be horrified at the suggestion that what they are doing could be referred to as violent. Yet, had they slapped or struck a neighbor or a police officer, they might have been called before the courts on a charge of assault. Similar statements of difference could be made about each of the other aspects of these three episodes, but the point is that violence cannot be conceived of as a single entity. We must think in terms of 'violences' and each type must be examined and explained by reference to its unique social, historical, and interpersonal characteristics.

Just as there are numerous forms of violence outside the family, there are also numerous forms that can occur within it, and it would be equally misleading, inaccurate, and uninformative to refer to all uses of physical force between family members simply as 'family' violence or all uses of physical force between husbands and wives simply as 'marital' or 'spousal' violence. It is, of course, possible for all family members (male or female, adult or child) to use various forms of physical force against each other. Parents, children, spouses, and siblings have all been known to hit, beat, or kill one another and examples can be cited of every possible form and degree of physical force being used between every possible combination of relatives. These incidents, however, do not occur with the same frequency or severity between all family members and they do not have the same meaning in the wider society or to the individuals involved. Violence against wives must therefore be studied in its own right and solutions to this problem can be found only if they are based upon an understanding of this issue's complexities and subtleties.

This task is not a process of narrowing but one of expansion. Once a concrete form of violence has been chosen for analysis, it then becomes necessary to examine it in its widest context. It is insufficient either to concentrate solely upon its history, its place in contemporary society, or its manifestation in the daily lives of particular people or to give any of these areas a superficial treatment. Each aspect of the phenomenon must be considered in detail and their interrelationships examined.

Proposing that each type of violence be studied in its own right does not mean that there are no similarities among them or that an understanding of one cannot provide insights into another. An extensive knowledge of one form of violence can, in fact, sometimes be used heuristically when beginning to examine another form. In this respect a brief discussion of violence against children provides a useful analogy for beginning an examination of violence against wives.

Children are the most frequent targets of what might be referred to as casual or legitimate applications of physical force. They are smacked and slapped quite frequently in what is defined by almost everyone as the normal practice of child rearing. Hitting a child is considered to be a necessary part of the process by which the experienced adult teaches the inexperienced child the correct way to behave. From the parent's point of view at least, this is seen as a beneficial and natural part of his or her relationship with the child. The parent is in a position of authority with respect to the child and has responsibility for insuring that the child behave in accord with widely accepted, general ideals, as well as in accord with his or her specific wishes or demands. Violation, or suspected violation, of these parental demands results in the child's becoming the focus of various mechanisms calculated to achieve compliance and bring him or her under control. Included in this arsenal of compliance-gaining techniques is a certain amount of shaking and slapping and other forms of mild chastisement. The right to hit a child is guaranteed and justified by the differential status, authority, and responsibility deemed to reside with parents, who are universally acknowledged to be the senior members in a hierarchical relationship with their children. The only restraints placed upon them are vague limits concerning how far they might go in exercising this parental right. The parent who is too zealous in meting out physical punishment may himself be punished, but such sanctions (unless the violence is extreme or life-threatening) always pose a dilemma between supporting the parent's rights and authority and protecting the child from the abuses of such power and authority.

The relationship between husbands and wives was once almost identical to that between parents and children. The husband's use of physical force against his wife was similarly an expression of the unequal status, authority, and power of marital partners and was widely accepted as appropriate to the husband's superior position. The husband was legally vested with responsibility for the control and management of his wife's behavior because she was generally acknowledged to be naturally less capable and responsible than her spouse. However, because of various socioeconomic changes, the marital relationship is no longer characterized by such gross inequalities, and the understanding of the problem of wife beating now requires consideration of numerous complex and contradictory factors.

The recent increase in efforts to redress many of the traditional inequities in the relationships between men and women, and for some the mistaken belief that this goal has been achieved, has given rise to some erroneous speculations about the causes of wife beating. On the one hand, it has been maintained that many men are now struggling to maintain what they believe to be their rightful position of authority and dominance over their wives; thus, when the woman's challenges of the husband's authority become too frequent or too excessive, he reasserts his authority and beats her into submission. Some of the proponents of this idea stand on the side of tradition and quietly root for the husband. Crudely put, the position is something like this: when a man's wife gets uppity, he puts her in her place and gives her the beating she deserves. Others cite this same idea as evidence of how deep-rooted the inequities between husbands and wives really are and of how difficult it will be to eliminate them without massive changes at all levels of society. Both accept the fact that the inequities remain, but differ concerning their desirability. On the other hand, there are those who maintain that because women are now equal with men, they are equally as likely to be the perpetrators of violence against their husbands as they are to be the recipients of it. Contentions of this nature make sense, and doubtful sense at that, only if one adopts a definition of physical violence that is so gross as to be trivial, including everything down to the once in a lifetime shove or push. Minor physical incidents probably occur in most marriages, and they are, of course, most regrettable, but we do not consider them to be indicative of a violent relationship nor should we speak of battered wives or battered husbands in such cases—especially when these terms imply the systematic, frequent, and brutal use of physical force. Throughout this book we will be focusing upon the persistent direction of physical force against a marital partner or cohabitant, and we will focus upon women as wives, who are, in fact, the most frequent targets of such violence.[17]

As part of the very laudable and long overdue attempt to redress some of the inequalities between men and women there has been another, equally laudable, move to eliminate the inequalities reflected in our language. For example, words like chairman have been replaced by words like chairperson. But just as such new terms can help overcome the mental images that contribute to inequality, they can also obscure some of the inequalities that continue to exist. The use of neutral, or equalitarian, terms like 'marital violence' or 'spouse assault' do exactly that. These terms imply that each marital partner is equally likely to play the part of perpetrator or victim in a violent episode, that the frequency and severity of the physical force used by each is similar; and that the social meaning and consequences of these acts are the same. None of this is true. In the case of marital violence, it is the husband who is most likely to be the perpetrator and his wife the victim. For this reason we do not subscribe to twists of equalitarian terminology that mask centuries of oppression of women and contribute to their further oppression by neutralizing the very word that describes the continued practice of wife beating.

Although women are by far the most frequent victims of the systematic use of physical force between marital partners or cohabitants, it is interesting that the first question invariably raised on the subject of battered wives is, "What about battered husbands?" This question usually evokes comments such as the following: "They must have deserved it." "They obviously like it." "They must need it." "There isn't a problem. It only happens to the poor and it is accepted by them as part of their way of life." "If I were married to her, I would beat her, too." "Never mind the women, what about the children?" From a different audience come these comments: "He must be sick." "She must be sick and in turn making him sick." Still another audience will ask, "Why does she stay?" "How can she put up with that?" "Why don't they punish these men more severely and help women get away from them?" "Why doesn't somebody do something?" "What can we do?"

We have given talks and presented papers throughout Britain, on the Continent, and in North America and we have consistently heard these comments and been asked these questions. They are all relatively similar and predictable because they represent the rather well established ideas, perspectives, and points of view held by certain individuals and by various types of organizations and interest groups. All such comments and questions are important and must be addressed. Some of them raise complex and far-reaching issues that are difficult to formulate, much less grapple with; others pose threats to beliefs that are so strongly held that they could almost be called sacred; others reveal prejudices that may never have been recognized by the asker; and some expose myths that can no longer be upheld and should be dispelled.

If we are to attempt to solve the problem of wife beating, then we must understand it. That understanding cannot be achieved by compiling personal and family statistics on those who happen to fall into the public eye or those who are willing to share their private lives and troubles with scrutinizing social scientists, doctors, or lawyers or with friendly neighbors. What is required is in-depth information about the violence itself and the relationship in which it occurs, as well as an analysis of the society in which wife beating occurs and the cultural beliefs and institutional practices that contribute to this pattern.

It is the spirit of C. Wright Mills's dictum that a social phenomenon can be understood only through a serious and thorough treatment of its history, biography, and culture that this analysis has been undertaken.[18] This comprehensive method will aid in overcoming the artificial and damaging separation between science and practice. The Women's Aid movement has succeeded in making the "private troubles" of battered women into a "public issue".[19] Thorough research will help provide the foundation for bringing about meaningful and permanent social changes that will positively affect the lives of women who are now being battered and those who without these changes are destined to become the victims of such violence.

Wives as Victims: Evidence and Explanations

A GREATER UNDERSTANDING OF violence will be achieved through a careful consideration of the nature of the social settings and situations in which it occurs. Investigations that attempt to abstract physical violence out of its social setting and focus primarily on the backgrounds or personal characteristics of individuals are not likely to lead to an elucidation of interpersonal violence. As Toch has written, "Violent acts, and violent interactions, do not make sense when viewed in isolation."[1] Violent encounters arise in socially constructed situations such as confrontations between adolescent street corner groups[2] and athletic events such as ice hockey games.[3] Social scientists are beginning to recognize that certain institutions encourage or provoke the use of physical force for specific socially constructed purposes. This patterning of violence is what makes it intelligible and explicable. What might first appear as random or senseless behavior begins to make sense when it is placed in its social and cultural context. The seemingly senseless violent acts of an otherwise nonaggressive juvenile gang member become understandable when his behavior is placed in the context of the situation that is socially constructed by the gang members, their backgrounds, and the history and meanings attached to such settings.[4] This approach can be profitably applied to the investigation of violence directed at women within the home.

Social scientists have been slow to recognize the violent aspects of the family even though criminologists have uncovered overwhelming evidence of the widespread use of physical force in the family setting. The research reports of criminologists only recently have begun to receive the attention of social investigators interested in the family, social scientists who have traditionally been more interested in stressing the idealized, nonviolent aspects of the family rather than the actual nature of this institution.

The first task of this chapter is to explore the existing reports relating to violence in the home. In unraveling these diverse reports two significant conclusions emerge: the first is that violence in the home is a frequent occurrence in contemporary society; the second is that the use of force be-

14

tween adults in the home is systematically and disproportionately directed at women.[5] Recent interpretations of these reports often mention the first finding but usually fail to recognize or emphasize the direction of the violence and to grasp the significance of both of these findings. The second task of this chapter is to explore and critically examine the nature of 'theoretical' statements relating to violence in the family and to propose an alternative. We find most of these theoretical arguments inadequate and even erroneous. These errors arise from several sources, the major ones being a failure to consider violence in its social and cultural context, a failure to grasp the significance of existing research reports, and inadequate and muddled conception of violence(s), an extremely narrow focus on interacting couples and a corresponding emphasis on deviant or aberrant factors in violent families, and, most important, a faith in an abstracted, generalized, and ahistorical approach to the study of the family and the use of violence within it.

We propose that the correct interpretation of violence between husbands and wives conceptualizes such violence as the extension of the domination and control of husbands over their wives. This control is historically and socially constructed. The beginning of an adequate analysis of violence between husbands and wives is the consideration of the history of the family, of the status of women therein, and of violence directed against them. This analysis will substantiate our claim that violence in the family should be understood primarily as coercive control, but before we proceed to a historical analysis of violence in the home, it is important to identify what it is that requires explanation. The subsequent review of existing research reports will indicate that it is not marital violence that demands explanation but violence that husbands direct at their wives.

Wives as Victims

HOMICIDES

Criminologists interested in patterns of homicide have produced important data that provide clues to the nature of violence between men and women though later research has tended to ignore these clues. Mac-Donald's perusal of criminal statistics covering the late nineteenth and the early twentieth century in several countries indicated that men were much more likely to commit murder than women and that "a large number of murders by men are wife murders."[6] In England and Wales for the years 1885–1905, out of the 487 murders committed by men, more than a quarter of the victims, 124, were women murdered by their husbands; another substantial proportion, 115, were mistresses or sweethearts of their assailants.[7] Over 50% of all murder victims were women with long-standing relationships with the male murderer. Clearly, these results should alert us to the importance of the status and position of women relative to men in society and in the home. Von Hentig's investigation of crime in Germany during the 1930s also revealed that women were more likely to be killed by intimates, and in 1931 62% of the women murdered by intimates were killed by their husbands.[8] The closer the relationship between women and men, the greater the probability of murder of women. As Von Hentig observed, "when a woman is killed, [look] for her relatives, mainly the husband and after that her paramour."[9]

Von Hentig also pointed to a historical phenomenon that underlines the importance of the status of women in the home. He noted that regardless of the country, all showed a high rate of female victims in the domestic services.[10] This is another indication of the importance of the subordinate status of women as a factor in violence in the home. Though the status of domestic servants has altered in the twentieth century, and they no longer significantly contribute to the homicide statistics, wives still do.

The work of Wolfgang in Philadelphia during the 1950s provided additional evidence relating to the relationship between gender and violence. As Wolfgang indicated, "There is a significant association between sex and criminal homicides, since males outproportion females as murderers."[11] He cited numerous studies from diverse cultures that found a substantial difference in male and female homicide rates.[12] As have other researchers, Wolfgang emphasized that homicide is directly related to "relatively close, intimate, personal, and direct [relationships]—in short, primary contacts."[13] Primary group relationships accounted for 65% of all victim-offender relationships in Wolfgang's research. This pattern was clearest in the statistics relating to homicide in the home, with female victims usually being married to their assailant. He reported that "significantly" the number of wives homicidally assaulted by their husbands constituted 41% of all women who were killed. Husbands murdered by their wives made up only 10% of all the men who were killed.[14]

In an analysis of the nature of the killings Wolfgang found that family homicides were much more likely to be severe than homicides in other settings, that is, involving numerous stab wounds or severe beatings; also these brutal murders were much more likely to be of wives.[15] He concluded that the home was the most frequent setting for severe violence. In the area of "victim precipitated" homicides, husbands were much more likely to have physically provoked their wives than wives to have provoked their husbands. Of the 47 cases of female defendants, 28 husbands were judged to have "strongly provoked" their wives whereas physical provocation was recognized in only 5 cases in which husbands murdered their wives.[16] Boudouris's work in Detroit revealed a similar pattern. In discussing murder by nonwhite females he argued that they could be explained as a "result of the woman's act of self-preservation when attacked by . . . her spouse."[17] Thus, when wives kill their husbands there is strong indication that they are responding to physical attacks from them.[18] Wolfgang's important study suggested rather systematic differences in the rates, direction, intensity, and motivation of homicides committed by and between men and women.

Similar results were published in two comprehensive surveys of official reports of murder in England and Wales during two periods, 1957–1968 and 1967–1971. Gibson and Klein's study of homicides occurring between 1957 and 1968 revealed that most murders of women occurred in the home.[19] They reported that of all female victims, "wives (including common-law wives) were usually the most frequent victims."[20] For example, in 1962, 63% of all murdered women were married to their murderer and for the years from 1967 to 1971, of all female victims of murder and manslaughter over the age of 16, 58% were killed by their husband or lover. Yet, very few women were murderers. The number of female murderers was extremely small over the 14-year period. Providing corroboration of Wolfgang's research, Gibson concluded that the patterns for 1967–1971 were strikingly similar to those discovered in the 1957–1967 period, with most victims, especially women, being closely associated with the murder suspect and women being a great deal less likely to commit homicide than men.[21]

Boudouris's study of police records for the years 1948–1952 revealed that 51.5% of all homicides involved "family members or close friends," whereas 24.3% of the homicides involved only "family relationships."[22] More recent American research has also revealed that men were much more likely to commit murder than women[23] and that when women were killed they were very likely to be killed by intimates. In a replication of Wolfgang's research in Chicago Voss and Hepburn found in 1965 that only 38% of male homicide victims were slain in the home whereas 62% of all female victims were killed in the home.[24] When women were killed in the home they were most likely to be slain by a member of the family or by a close friend; 60% of the nonwhite and 79% of the white females were killed by a close friend or by a family member.[25]

The important conclusions to be drawn from the research relating to homicides is that the home is the location of an extraordinary proportion of killings and that women are much more likely than men to be slain in their position as wives or intimates of men than are men in their position as husbands. Additional evidence of this pattern has come from studies of police records and divorce cases focusing on less lethal forms of violence in the family and in the wider society.

ASSAULTS

McClintock's research into all criminal offenses in England and Wales revealed similar patterns in data on assaults.[26] Comparing the rates and patterns of violent offenses for 1950 and 1960. McClintock discovered that over 30% of all violent offenses occurred within the home in what he described as "domestic disputes." Most of the attacks occurring within the home, almost 90%, were attacks by males against females.[27] A survey of police reponses to family disputes in Hamilton, Ontario, during 1974 and 1975 showed that 84% of them involved assault; 95% of these assaults involved attacks on wives.[28] In one of the early self-report studies of crime within the general population, Ennis reported additional American evidence relating to the importance of long-standing relationships and the family setting for understanding interpersonal violence.[29] In the crimes against the person category (assaults, robberies) his respondents reported that they knew the offender in 45% of the cases. A closer examination of these violent offenses revealed that 70% of the female respondents who reported being assaulted were assaulted in or near the home, though very few men reported being assaulted near the home.[30]

An additional avenue for gathering information regarding violence in the home has been the analysis of divorce cases.[31] O'Brien's research into divorce in a midwestern American town revealed that 28 of the 150 individuals interviewed spontaneously reported overt violence. The majority of this violence was directed at women and was a recurring feature of the relationship. He summarized by stating that "the most commonly reported form of violence was that the husband was physically abusive of his wife."[32] Levinger concluded after his study of 600 couples who applied for divorce in Cleveland, Ohio, "that wives complained 11 times more frequently than husbands about physical abuse."[33] An examination of over fifteen hundred divorce cases in a large English city for the years 1966–1968 revealed that physical abuse by the husband was the most frequently cited reason for seeking a divorce.[34] Over 90% of the women mentioned physical abuse as at least one of the reasons for divorce and the majority of these women indicated that violence was a recurring aspect of the relationship.[35] Whitehurst, using various techniques to elucidate the nature of violence in the family, also investigated divorce cases appearing before the courts in an American city.[36] Again, the direction of this violence was clear. Men were more likely to assault their wives than wives were to assault their husbands, and Whitehurst suggested "that nearly all families suffer from violence at some point in their life-cycle development."[37] Three English researchers estimated, after a 1976 study of divorce petitions in southern England, that 70% of English "wives who petition for divorce each year . . . suffer from serious brutality."[38]

Gelles's study, which was specifically designed to examine marital violence, found patterns similar to those cited above.[39] In his sample of 80 couples, 54% used physical force and the bulk of the violence was directed at wives. Gelles pointed out that husbands were much more likely to be violent than wives and a quarter of the violent husbands in his sample assaulted their wives on a regular basis.[40] Some women in his study did strike their husbands but there was an important qualitative difference between the types of violence used by men and women. Women used a rather restricted range of physical force whereas husbands employed a wide range of techniques and were much more likely to use severe forms of violence, such as choking.[41] Gelles also found that men often used the threat of violence as a means of controlling their wives' actions yet such a technique was never employed by women. These results are quite interesting and we would argue that they point in an unequivocal direction, but unfortunately Gelles failed to grasp their significance. Although he emphasized that violence seemed to be a rather common occurrence in many homes, a frequently noted observation, he noted but failed to emphasize and understand the significance of a second and, to our minds, just as clear pattern: the use of physical force between adults within the family was not randomly distributed between husbands and wives but was systematically directed at women.

INTERPRETATIONS OF VIOLENCE

These various research efforts into homicide and assault in the wider society and in the family provide strong evidence that the domestic setting is fraught with violence. They further suggest that homicide and assault in the home constitute a sizable proportion of all homicides and assaults, that the position of women in the family is important in the patterning of violence, and that the most likely female victims are wives of offenders.[42] The above findings, we would argue, also provide irrefutable evidence that severe recurring violence between adults in the home is most often directed at wives. This conclusion contradicts the view, sometimes implicitly held, that husbands and wives are equally violent.

Social scientists have made numerous errors in their conception of violence between husbands and wives. Often they have failed to distinguish qualitatively different types of physical force between various family members. They have mistakenly inferred that attitudes toward the use of violence are equivalent to its actual occurrence,[43] and they have erroneously attempted to explain away the greater use of violence by husbands by arguing that men and women have an equal potential for violence. For example, three American researchers, Straus, Gelles, and Steinmetz, have suggested that findings that indicate greater and more severe violence on the part of men in the family arise "only because women are on average weaker than their husbands and hence have more to lose by such acts."[44] The implication of this statement is clear: women could or would be just as violent as men but because they are different (weaker) they are less violent. Interestingly, this argument suggests its own refutation. Women, in their view, are not as violent as their husbands for various reasons, the primary one being anticipation of failure as a result of their inferior strength. The argument that women could be or might be just as violent as men is irrelevant. We are not interested in explaining what is with what might be, and their supposition that women could be just as violent as men is not supported by any evidence. As Lystad concluded after an extensive examination of the literature relating to violence between spouses, "The occurrence of adult violence in the home usually involves males as aggressors towards females."[45] In our own analysis of 3,020 cases of violence occurring in two Scottish cities in 1974 (see Appendix C), we found that assaults against wives was the second most common violent offense. The largest category was violence between unrelated males (39%), second to that was assault of wives (26%). Of the 3,020 violent offenses, 1044 involved family members. And a closer scrutiny of the violence among family members revealed that 76% was husbands assaulting their wives and 1% was wives assaulting their husbands (see Appendix B, Tables 4 and 5). The fact that violence between adults in the family is directed at women is clearly the 'social fact' that requires explanation and provides us with the clue to understanding violence between spouses. Thus, the concern is not to explain marital or spousal violence in general but to explain violence against wives. In so doing we will gain important insights into the contemporary family.

Sociologists who propose that "violence in the family affects just about everyone" or that "the marriage license is a hitting license"[46] are not specific enough and miss the point. They ignore or fail to consider what most of the general public knows and what research reports indicate: physical force between adults in the family is overwhelmingly directed at women. The home is a dangerous place for women (and children) and markedly less dangerous for men. This is the crucial point. This is what requires understanding and has been overlooked by many social scientists. The above examination and reinterpretation of existing research rectifies this shortcoming, leading us to a clearer view of what is happening, but we must go further if we wish to know why violence against wives takes place.

Theoretical Treatments of Violence in the Home

The emerging interest in violence occurring within the home has resulted in the development of various abstract, generalized models of family violence. Efforts to develop general theories that include all forms of family violence are not likely to be useful for the understanding of the use of physical force against women since these proposals lead to the blurring of crucial differences in the violence that occurs between various family members. Before we proceed to an explication of an alternative approach to husband and wife violence, an approach that leads to a clearer understanding of this behavior, we will evaluate existing perspectives.

An early article concerned with the use of physical force in the family is Goode's interesting and heuristic work.[47] He rightly argued that the family, like all other social institutions, rests "to some degree on force or its threat"[48] and that it is husbands and fathers who are most likely to use such force. These observations should alert us to the idea that the use of physical force is an integral part of the institution of the family and is one of the means used to achieve control therein. Coercive forms of social control are often obscured in everday life.[49] For example, just as it is difficult to see the nature of coercion in industrial settings until workers rebel against oppression and the owners or the state uses force against them, it is also difficult to perceive the nature of oppression directed at women within contemporary families unless this oppression becomes overt. Goode's insights regarding the family are obscured, however, because of his attempt to hinge his analysis on an abstracted conceptual model (exchange theory) through which he tried to account for violence between all family members in a similar fashion.

Goode further argued that his analysis alerts us to the many diverse "mandates and restrictions on *all of us* in our family roles, which are ultimately backed by force [emphasis added]."[50] His abstract and generalized approach to family violence led him to slight the systematic differences in these physical restrictions and to see this use of force in preserving roles as a benign, even beneficial, aspect of families. If force did not exist, he argued, the structure of the family system would be destroyed.[51] But social processes, such as the use of force, do not operate for the benefit of social systems, they operate for the benefit or detriment of human beings acting within historically generated institutions. The family historically has operated and continues to operate for the benefit of men and the state and rarely for women. The advantages enjoyed by husbands and the restrictions on the rights and activities of wives were once legally specified. Goode apparently assumed that since these legal prescriptions no longer exist, there is no longer a differential in the position occupied by the restrictions operating on husbands and wives. He even seems to have accepted the enforcement of these restrictions by the use of force. Taken to its logical extension this view considers it acceptable to use physical force against women because violence is crucial to the maintenance of the family.

Another idea that is sometimes offered as a possible explanation for wife beating is the theory of the subculture of violence. Wolfgang and Ferracuti argued that violence is the result of subcultural patterns existing in certain societal groups and that violent responses are seen as normative in such groups.[52] This normative acceptance of violence results in variation in the rates of violence across societal groups. The subculture of violence thesis has received an extraordinary amount of attention in the literature on violence. Various attempts have been made to establish the existence of norms and patterns of behavior leading to a disproportionate amount of

violence in different regions in the United States[53] and among certain
groups such as the working class, racial minorities, or the police.[54] Unfortunately, some of these research efforts have focused on violent individuals
who do not belong to a common group (e.g., men who are incarcerated for
violent offenses) and thus could not be said to come from a common subculture.[55] These studies usually have attempted to correlate the attitudes
and values of a group of disparate individuals with their violent behavior
in order to substantiate or refute the subculture of violence thesis. Such
studies can tell us nothing about subcultural aspects of violence. To
substantiate the subculture of violence thesis it is necessary to establish a
structural and cultural interrelatedness between violent individuals and to
locate them within historically specific communities or identifiable
subareas within society.[56] This form of contextual analysis is what makes
certain aspects of the work of Wolfgang and Ferracuti so compelling since
they have explored violent behavior within specific cultural areas.

Because violence against wives is so widespread and transcends the
bounds of any particular social group we do not consider the subculture of
violence thesis an adequate explanation for this problem. Moran's assertion
that men represent a subculture of violence confuses the issue since if all
men are the bearers of aggression and violence producing norms then these
are not subcultural but are dominant cultural patterns learned by all men.
Men are socialized into aggression, taught directly or indirectly that it is an
appropriate means of problemsolving and of demonstrating authority in
certain situations. As Whitehurst concluded after his study of divorce
cases, men are "heavily socialized in instrumental and aggressive ways"[57]
and they are likely to use these behaviors in maintaining or attempting to
enforce control and domination within the family. Men are also more
likely to be sensitive to affronts to their authority and explicitly to learn
violent techniques. This willingness to use force is coupled with a set of
beliefs and standards regarding the appropriate hierarchical relationship
between men and women in the family and the rightful authority of
husbands over wives. Thus, all men see themselves as controllers of
women, and because they are socialized into the use of violence they are
potential aggressors against their wives.

Social scientists often have conceptualized criminal behavior as learned
behavior[58] and this conception has been implicitly incorporated into
sociological and social-psychological thinking on violence. The learning
view of violence as something socially 'normal' and integral to certain
learning contexts, e.g., the family, has become widely accepted in the
psychological literature on violence;[59] this view implicitly incorporates
sociological perspectives on violence that emphasize its normative
character. The use of violence is a learned response, learned in the company of others, such as in an adolescent gang, or by policemen as a technique for enforcing authority, or within the family itself. Human beings are

the products of socially structured institutions, institutions that often reward and encourage aggression in certain circumstances and settings. The learning conception of violence against wives is inconsistent with alternative views of violence in the family, like those of psychiatrists who emphasize the pathological or deviant aspects of violent individuals or family structures.

We have two examples of this perspective in the works of Schultz[60] and Snell, Rosenwald, and Robey.[61] Using extremely small samples of violent husbands and their wives, these researchers proposed that the source of such violence is unfulfilled childhood experiences and deviant marital relationships. Schultz argued that the four violent men he interviewed had "domineering, rejecting mother relationships" resulting in "a submissive, passive individual."[62] The work of Snell, Rosenwald, and Robey focused almost exclusively on the other side of the marital dyad. Wives of wife assaulters are, according to Snell, "aggressive, efficient, masculine and sexually frigid," with a "strong need to control the relationship"[63]—in short, deviant in the eyes of these researchers. The sociological variant of this method of seeking the explanation for violence in terms of deviance is represented by Straus's[64] emphasis on deviant authority structures as the source of violence in families and O'Brien's[65] focus on economic problems of the husband that result in his lower status in the family. Based upon the results of his quasi-experimental study of a few families and the results of a survey of high school graduates' perceptions of violence between their parents, Straus argued that "the level of violence is greatest when the wife is dominant in decisions."[66] This "deviant" family structure leads to violent confrontations according to both O'Brien and Straus. The implication of these psychiatric and sociological perspectives is quite clear; if these deviant situations did not exist and men, for example, had higher status than their wives (the usual pattern), violence would not occur.

We do not need to seek the explanation of family violence in deviant or pathological individuals or family structures. Seeking the causes and sources of violence and crime through an emphasis on pathological individuals or deviant relationships has been an important activity of those who would ignore the simple fact that violence is endemic to modern Western societies. The evidence on collective violence has indicated the folly of this approach. Tilly's exhaustive and penetrating research into the French rebellions of the eighteenth and nineteenth centuries clearly demonstrated that the members of violent 'mobs' were not the disenfranchised or deranged members of society but were, rather, normal citizens attempting to bring about changes in their society.[67] As Tilly argued, "collective violence should not be seen as a disruption, a deviation or a last resort—when it is one of the most common forms of political action."[68]

The conception of violence as a result of the usual and normal functioning of institutions can be profitably applied to interpersonal violence. The use of physical force against wives should be seen as an attempt on the part of the husband to bring about a desired state of affairs. It is primarily purposeful behavior and not the action of deviant or aberrant individuals or the prerogative of deviant or unusual families. Investigators adopting an approach that emphasizes deviance, individual or structural, often reveal more about their own prejudices than they do about the nature of the behavior they are investigating. They also adopt the fallacious view that "evil is always caused by evil," that behavior we deplore, such as wife beating, is generated by antecedants that are also bad, such as alcoholism, drug abuse, or lack of parental love.[69] Although such factors may be associated with the problem of violence against wives, they are not crucial to the explanation of that violence. Rather, men who assault their wives are actually living up to cultural prescriptions that are cherished in Western society—aggressiveness, male dominance, and female subordination—and they are using physical force as a means to enforce that dominance.

Another approach followed in the pursuit of an understanding of marital violence is the multifactor approach.[70] Investigators using this method seek to list[71] or to discover[72] various factors related to violence in the family. This inductive, abstract empiricism assumes an atheoretical and objective approach to social reality whose positivistic rationale is erroneous. These naturalists of the social sciences always begin with certain presuppositions regarding the phenomena about which they are collecting facts.[73] One could not begin to collect facts without a theory and a method that enabled one to perceive those facts. Often these investigators are unaware of their own theories or prejudices though they become very apparent when the collected facts are presented. For example, Gayford gathered various facts from battered women about their backgrounds.[74] Since he did no more than list these items—e.g., the onset of menstruation, premarital sexual experience, and the use of contraception—it is impossible to see their relevance. A method that is intent on specifying the ingredients of marital violence but ignores their significance is likely to lead to a maze of confusing results and unanswered questions. If such an analysis has any utility, it becomes apparent only when these factors are considered or explored in concrete social settings. This establishes both their interrelatedness and their relative importance.

The generalized inductive approach to violence in the home is mirrored by the generalized deductive activities of social scientists interested in constructing abstract laws of social behavior. Attempting to adhere in a programmatic manner to the blueprint of natural science provided by the logical positivists[75] these social scientists assume that advances in the physical sciences can be matched in the social sciences by mechanically adopting their procedures.[76] Faith in these procedures results in a social science that is ahistorical and oriented primarily to technical problems relating to theory testing and to measurement. Recently we read of a crisis in sociology,[77] a crisis related at least partially to the efforts of the logical positivists in the social sciences to emulate the procedures of the physical sciences. These protestations and cries of alarm and dismay have gone relatively unheeded by many sociologists—sociologists who seemingly have lost their way. The goal of understanding society is forgotten and ignored: the major preoccupation of the logical positivists is the development of standardized measuring techniques to test hypothetical statements, an activity unlikely to lead to an understanding and explanation of social problems and behavior and events that occur in historically structured institutions.

This search for general laws and abstract theories is aptly illustrated in the general systems approach to society, the family, and family violence.[78] Family sociologists who adopt this perspective argue that we should replace existing approaches to the family with the general systems approach. The promise of general systems theory is, according to its proponents, that it can be applied to any type of system, human, mechanical, or biological. Following this methodology Straus presented data relating to husband-wife violence that emphasized power and dominance.[79] Reviewing his evidence, which pointed to greater violence in families in which the wife was dominant, he conjectured that these families were deviating from accepted norms of male dominance. This deviant situation supposedly leads to dissatisfaction on the part of the male and to the use of violence.[80] Following the general systems perspective, he maintained that "the same principles can be applied to all role relationships in the conjugal and perhaps also to the extended family."[81] And what are these principles? Straus produced flow charts of the sequences he considered important in the initiation and amplification of family violence. These charts include everything from precipitating factors to goal orientation through labeling and violent self-images. This model is so abstract and generalized as to be of little use in the analysis of any particular type of violence between family members, even excluding the usual sociological accounts of differential roles and activities of husbands and wives.

The general systems model removes people from the family setting, human beings with historically shaped motives, values, and intentions, and relates abstract concepts to other concepts, ignoring the historical and interactive aspects of the family. When one examines Straus's model or any other systems model, one sees that it is preeminently a metaphysical argument in the sense that an analysis lacking in substantive content is an analysis of relationships between abstractions and is little more than relationships between words. We reject this extremely abstract method and think that the more general and abstract the approaches to interpersonal violence become, the less useful they are in the understanding of violence.

We prefer explicitly to adopt the general methodology of Weber and Marx, which emphasizes historical and contemporary contexts.

An Alternative Approach

Weber argued that an analysis of social phenomena becomes useful and scientific only "when it is accompanied by a substantive predicate."[82] The more general and abstract social laws become, the less they contribute to the understanding of "individual" phenomena and more indirectly "to the understanding of the significance of cultural events."[83] The meaning or significance of cultural (social) phenomena can be ascertained only through a historical analysis that places contemporary phenomena in their historically given context. The meaningfulness of events or phenomena "does not coincide with scientific laws" and "the more general the law the less the coincidence."[84] Weber argued that general laws or models are useful, if at all, only in a heuristic sense and that such a general analysis is a mere independent preliminary to additional, historically based procedures.

In a broad sense Weber's methodology corresponds with Marx's in adopting a historical stance and in rejecting a social science based on general, abstracted laws.[85] Marx's methodology rejects the analysis of social facts in an isolated and ahistorical manner.[86] He argued that classical economists engaged in a superficial analysis of capitalist society; by not going beyond the obvious features of capitalism in their analysis of wages, markets, and prices, they failed to grasp the essence of these phenomena. Only when we penetrate beneath or beyond the immediately given nature of social facts, as Marx did in his analysis of value and use-value in the context of capitalist societies, will we grasp their significance. In order to get beyond these surface manifestations it is necessary to establish the historically given character of the social problem under study.

Social scientists who are attempting to follow the procedures of the physical sciences as translated, albeit incorrectly,[87] by the logical positivists are intent on developing abstract theory devoid of substantive content. Actually, nothing could be further from scientific activity, assuming the aim of science is explanation and understanding. The failure to consider the historical character of social phenomena and human relationships results in a barren and totally unscientific social science.[88] Becker indicted the social scientist and questioned the outcome of supposedly 'scientific' sociology.

> Measured against the needs of the times there is nothing remotely resembling a science of man: there are only mountains of disciplinary journals, and hordes of busy specialists . . . most of the disciplinary activity in the social sciences represents trivial work. True, it is hard-working, certainly well-intentioned, at times deeply hopeful and anxious—but still somehow very much beside the point.[89]

In order to understand and explain violence between husbands and wives we must go beyond the interacting couple, the isolated and abstracted social relationship, and place the violent behavior in its proper historical and contemporary setting. Such an analysis will result in the contradiction of prevailing views that emphasize the deviant and pathological character of violence against wives, perspectives that have resulted from a myopic, inadequate, and abstracted empiricism. The exploration of the problem in its historical context is the first step in an analysis that leads us to the discovery of the significance and meaning of violence against women in the home. As Marx wrote, such a historical analysis "would be superfluous if the outward [immediate] appearance of things coincided with their essence."[90] This is the only method that will lead us to a sounder understanding of social phenomena. A methodology that proceeds from a historical analysis to an integration of the isolated and seemingly unconnected aspects of social life is the only one that can "hope to become knowledge of reality."[91] This method will also provide direction for the amelioration of social problems. Abstracted social science—lost in the exploration, collection, and collating of abstracted facts and intent on creating timeless universal theories of society in general—has failed to provide direction for the alleviation of social problems such as violence against wives. The more abstract and ahistorical our models and procedures become, the less they will direct our concern and action.[92] A historical analysis must be followed by an examination of the problem of wife beating in its specific contemporary manifestation. The contemporary analysis must not, however, narrowly focus on the violence, abstracting it out of the social institution of the family and the cultural ideals that provide ideological support for the man who attacks his wife. What is needed is a research technique that provides an integrated analysis of social phenomena of various levels of analysis. The best method for achieving this goal is the context specific approach to concepts and research.

The Context Specific Method

Several researchers have used a context specific approach to develop a fuller explanation[93] and understanding of specific social problems or issues. For example, Wegnar proposed that social scientists adopt a context specific approach to alienation. He defined alienation as "a personal orientation involving negative feelings and cynical beliefs toward a special social context."[94] He argued against conceptualizing alienation as a general negative feeling toward the total society and against the construction of abstract measuring devices meant to apply to diverse substantive contexts.[95] The procedure he would employ involves the careful specification of concepts embedded in propositions referring to specific social domains (such as factories and communities), which are then coupled with research techniques that explore "the dynamics underlying the relationship between social contexts and individuals."[96] It makes little sense, he argued, to speak of alienation in general since one could be alienated from one's work but be well integrated into family or community.

The comprehensive and important work on gang delinquency conducted by Short and Strodtbeck[97] employed a context specific approach, though not labeled as such, as one technique in determining the dynamics of juvenile gang activity in Chicago. Their research was concerned with "on-going group relations" and attempted to provide "a clearer understanding of the precipitation of episodes within delinquent gangs."[98] To this end they explored the relationship between acts of gang members and their norms and values relative to specific interaction settings. Using diverse techniques to gather data, such as gang workers' accounts and structured interviews, they explored the operation of these norms in various violent episodes. They discovered that norms relating to status conferral and status affirmation operated with other, more situational processes and factors, such as aleatory factors, in determining the outcome of encounters between gangs and police or other adults. The outcome of such encounters, often involving aggression or violence, can be explained and understood only through consideration of the backgrounds brought to these settings and the operation of these factors in specific contexts.

Parker's study of adolescents in Liverpool was also guided by a context specific method.[99] Parker conceived of context in a broader sense than Short and Strodtbeck. His participant observation research considered the community and institutional settings in which boys found themselves, settings that generate various types of activities some of which could be described as delinquent. But Parker also looked at a wider context than the immediate neighborhood of the boys, arguing that "The delinquency of the boys is minimal in the context of their other behaviour and when placed in the context of deviance in the wider society—their delinquency is mundane, trivial, petty—and very little threat to anyone."[100] This form of analysis, which interrelates numerous situational factors leading to a given behavior and places that behavior in the wider societal context, is less likely to lead to errors of exaggeration in the differences in behavior such as violence.

Another research effort employing a context specific approach was Faulkner's[101] insightful study of violence between ice hockey players. Arguing against a conception of violence as a breakdown of the social order, Faulkner maintained that "situations are to be found where the practice of violence can be considered as the successfully constructed product of social control rather than its demise."[102] As he indicated, most studies of violent behavior attempt to explore the socio-demographic background of violent individuals; thus, "we will lack information on the context of uses and situations"[103] relating to interpersonal violence. He argued that "scholars have paid periodic but only fleeting attention to the cultural interpretations given to violent action, or equally important, to the types of social contexts in which it regularly occurs."[104] Faulkner's work was an attempt to rectify this situation. He focused on the control features of aggression and violence in the context of a hockey player's establishment and maintenance of an essential occupational quality, the ability to handle himself physically. This process was explored relative to the expectations and normative standards of the game and of colleagues and opponents. Fighting and "fighting well" established an important feature of a player's occupational role and was "a resource for the establishment and regulation of [players'] control over others."[105]

Cicourel has argued the most consistently for the consideration of contexts in understanding social behavior and in the conduct of research.[106] In *Method and Measurement in Sociology*, following the work of Schutz, he stressed "the importance of constructing models of social action which specify typical motives, values and course-of-action types within the context of objects with various sense properties."[107] Cicourel used this methodology in a research effort to determine the taken for granted procedures employed by probation officers in making decisions about juvenile offenders.[108] This research sought to place the practical decisionmaking of probation officers in the context of their everyday activities and background experiences, while taking into account the operation of other relevant agencies within the community context.

In his analysis of Argentine fertility, Cicourel widened his consideration of context to analyze more explicitly the role of the observer (interviewer) in the research setting, attempting to consider and chart the changing nature of the situational content of interviewing.[109] The research attempted to determine the impact of the overall context of family relationships and activities on fertility patterns, as well as to assess the relationship between the context of the interviewing process and the meanings attached to that process by both interviewers and respondents. Interviewers were encouraged to consider the social context of the interview and provide descriptions of this context in their field reports. This procedure allowed the interviewer to "make sense of the respondents' utterances."[110]

Cicourel's recent work is almost totally concerned with the methodology of research. However, much of his work has been devoted to determining the patterns of behavior, activities, and intentions that result in the production of bureaucratic structures or official statistics relating to delinquency[111] and rates of fertility.[112] Cicourel explicitly employs a technique that considers the intentions and actions of people in the context of the institutions in which they live and work.

Toch also has employed a technique that explicitly considers human behavior (violence) relative to the settings in which it occurs.[113] His interviews with violent men were designed to explore the sequential processes leading to a violent episode and the meanings attached to the resultant behavior by the participants while placing "such encounters in the broader context of the person's previous relationship to others."[114] This procedure enables one to determine the shape and form of violence and establish in what sort of "restricted life situations" (contexts) it is most likely to occur. It also leads, as Cicourel would argue, to an understanding of the meaning the violent act has to the individual in everyday settings.

Our review of studies that followed the context specific approach illustrates its importance in social research. This method contrasts with the many sociological research techniques intent on developing abstracted measuring devices devoid of specific substantive content.[115] The essence of the context specific approach is that the social world can be understood only by exploring human behavior in the settings in which it occurs.

We employed the context specific technique in our research as part of a more general methodology—methodology that emphasizes the need for a historical analysis of the problem of wife beating and leads to consideration of the problem in the specific social contexts in which it now occurs; at the same time it was necessary to take into account the biographical background of individuals studied and the wider social setting. (See the Study, Appendix C.) This unified approach takes us beyond the immediate appearance of phenomena and integrates the specific problem in a totality of social processes and problems. As Lukács wrote: "The history of a particular problem turns into the history of problems."[116]

CHAPTER 3

THE LEGACY OF THE "APPROPRIATE" VICTIM

THE AGE OF CHIVALRY is remembered almost exclusively in terms of knights in shining armor saving damsels in distress and the code of behavior that prescribed special treatment of women. A fifteenth-century English translation of the "Knight of La Tour Landry" indicated the "special" and correct treatment for a "scolding" wife.

> He smote her with his fist down to the earth, and then with his fist he struck her in the visage and broke her nose, and all her life after she had her nose crooked that she might not for shame show her visage it was so foul blemished. . . . Therefore the wife ought to suffer and let the husband have the word, and be the master.[1]

So much for the illusion of knights in shining armor. But, can this be true? How is it possible that this gruelling description of wife beating could appear during the age of chivalry? Surely, a chivalrous French knight did not really end an argument with his damsel or wife by punching her in the face and breaking her nose. This entry in a popular handbook of the day would indicate that he did. In fact, such treatment was not appropriate for one's damsel but only for one's wife. It is impossible to say who first declared that wives could and should be beaten by their husbands or when this practice began; it is equally difficult to find any historical period in which there were no formulas stating the form such beatings should take and specifying the conditions under which a wife was deserving of a good clout.

Woman's Place in History: A Singular and Subordinate Status

Although there are very few historical references to women as important, powerful, meaningful contributors to the life and times of a people,[2] history is littered with references to, and formulas for, beating, clubbing, and kicking them into submission. Women's place in history often has been at the receiving end of a blow. This history is a long and sad one—sad because of the countless women who have been browbeaten, bruised,

bloodied, and broken and sad because the ideologies and institutional practices that made such treatment both possible and justifiable have survived,
albeit somewhat altered, from century to century and been woven into the
fabric of our culture and are thriving today.

It is not possible to understand wife beating today without understanding its past and the part the past plays in contemporary beliefs and
behaviors. The essence of wife beating cannot, however, be distilled merely
from a description of ancient wife beating practices or from a reiteration of
the laws specifying chastisement. Understanding requires an account of
how wife beating fits into the family and into the entire society. It also requires an examination of the individual and institutional factors that reveal
why wives, and not husbands, were beaten.

Legal, historical, literary, and religious writings all contribute to
understanding the unique status of women, a status that composes the
kernel of the explanation of why it is they who have become the "appropriate" victims of 'marital' violence. Almost all of the writings about
women discuss them in only one type of relationship, their personal relationships with men. The only roles truly allowed women in the real or the
imaginary world have been those of wife, mother, daughter, lover, whore,
and saint. Although the focus is almost always upon women in their so-
called special and exclusive status as wives, mothers, daughters, and
lovers, the artist, the historian, the legislator, and the clergyman give differing forms and meaning to this status. Virginia Woolf noted the curious
and contradictory position of women in the imaginary world of literature
and the more realistic world as noted by the historian.

> A very queer, composite being thus emerges. Imaginatively she is of the
> highest importance; practically she is completely insignificant. She pervades
> poetry from cover to cover; she is all but absent from history. She
> dominates the lives of kings and conquerors in fiction; in fact she was the
> slave of any boy whose parents forced a ring on her finger. Some of the most
> inspired words, some of the most profound thoughts in literature fall from
> her lips; in real life she could hardly read, could scarcely spell, and was the
> property of her husband.
>
> It was certainly an odd monster that one made up by reading the
> historians first and poets afterwards—a worm winged like an eagle; the spirit
> of life and beauty in a kitchen chopping up suet. But these monsters,
> however amusing to the imagination, have no existence in fact.[3]

In reality, women rarely had an identity apart from that given them as
wives, mothers, and daughters, and departure from that identity was
discouraged and punished. Rarely in historical or religious writings has a
woman been named and discussed as an individual except in terms of an exceptional ability or inability to fulfill family obligations. For example,
biblical references to Ruth, the Virgin Mary, as well as various named and
unnamed whores,[4] and historical references to women like Josephine and

Cleopatra, all describe women in terms of their relationships with men and their membership in families. Women were rarely remembered as individuals, even when they did something memorable.[5] They were nameless, undifferentiated, undistinguished, and indistinguishable. They were considered to be all alike; they were merely the members of some man's family. As such, there was little or nothing the historian thought he could write about any particular one of them.

Since the historian was not interested in a group of people who were seen as merely family members, they ignored women. On the other hand, writers and artists found the imaginary woman compelling. The contradictory and unrealistic picture of what it meant to be a woman may be found in literature and history, but something that was much closer to reality was reflected in laws and religion. Within legal and religious institutions, the only legitimate position for women in most Western societies has been in the family. Women have been relatively isolated and segregated in the home and socialized primarily for this position. Numerous mechanisms, moral and legal, have been developed to render women relatively unwilling or unable to leave or to change either the institution of the family or the particular family of which they were a member.

The status of women was not only separate and singular but also subordinate, and this subordination was institutionalized primarily in marriage and the family. In the family, the parameters of a woman's behavior were set, her undifferentiated nature reiterated, her relationships with men defined, her subordination taught, and her deviations controlled. Saint Augustine wrote that in marriage "woman ought to serve her husband as unto God, affirming that in no thing hath woman equal power with man . . . affirming that woman ought to be repressed."[6]

Although some women escaped this monolithic and secondary status, the pressures to enter marriage were great, alternatives few, and those who did not marry lost the only completely "legitimate" and therefore socially unproblematic position open to them. It is significant that Augustine used the word woman in place of wife: it was almost inconceivable for an adult woman to be anything other than a wife, and he had no need to differentiate between a woman's gender and her marital status. Since women were usually deprived of alternatives to marriage and subordinated within it, they were completely trapped in inferiority. To be a wife meant becoming the property of a husband, taking a secondary position in a marital hierarchy of power and worth, being legally and morally bound to obey the will and wishes of one's husband, and thus, quite logically, subject to his control even to the point of physical chastisement or murder.

The seeds of wife beating lie in the subordination of females and in their subjection to male authority and control. This relationship between women and men has been institutionalized in the structure of the patriarchal family and is supported by the economic and political institutions and by a belief system, including a religious one, that makes such relationships seem natural, morally just, and sacred. This structure and ideology can be seen most starkly in the records of two societies that provided the roots of our cultural legacy, the Romans and the early Christians.

The Roman Legacy

The Romans have been credited with exceptionally good treatment of women. Women were educated, played an essential part in religious celebrations, could inherit property, and during some periods had limited rights of divorce.[7] But this was the Rome after the Punic Wars of the second century B.C. This Rome had undergone considerable economic, political, social, and familial change and was quite different from the patriarchal society of the early Empire.

On the other hand, the early Roman family was the cornerstone of society and was one of the strongest patriarchies known.[8] The family was a religious, educational, economic, and legal institution commonly spanning three generations and presided over by a male head, who was priest, magistrate, and owner of all properties, both material and human, and who had absolute power over everything and everyone. The patriarch decided whether a newborn child was to be allowed to live and join the family or be put in the street to die. He could choose marriage partners for his children, divorce them without their consent, sell them into bondage, and punish or kill them for any wrongdoing.[9]

There was a very clear and undisputed family hierarchy. The head of the household owned and controlled everything and obviously held the highest status in both his own family and the rest of the society. The training of children from a very early age reflected the fact that boys were to lead, to own, and to control and that girls were to be their subordinates, and there was a marked parental preference for male children, who would continue the family line, its property, and its religion.[10] Name giving also reflected differential worth: males were given three names, designating the individual, the clan, and the family, females usually were given only two names. The one dropped was the first name, which denoted the individual; instead, she was called *maxima* or *minor*, *secunda* or *tertia*.[11]

Children usually were educated informally by their parents. Special emphasis was placed upon morals, reverence of gods and the law, obedience to authority, and self-reliance.[12] Girls were educated almost entirely by their mothers, whereas at the age of seven boys accompanied their fathers into the field or to the forum and were tutored in agriculture, business, or government. When a boy reached manhood, about seventeen, this was marked by an important celebration that included a procession to the forum, a feast, a religious sacrifice, and the adoption of the toga of a man.

There was no celebration when a girl reached womanhood,[13] and she was given in marriage as young as twelve years of age.[14]

The separation of the male and female roles was extreme. The singular role to be allocated to women, that of wives, was reflected in the girl's education. This contrasted with the more complex and worldly training of the boy. The subordination of the girl and her subsequent lack of importance were reflected in everything from her name to the conditions of her marriage. At marriage the guardianship of a woman was transferred from her father to her husband.

It is said that the first law of marriage was proclaimed by Romulus, the legendary founder of Rome (753 B.C.): "The law was to this effect, that a woman joined to her husband by a holy marriage should share in all his possessions and sacred rites."[15] This dramatic statement of equality is not unlike our modern community property laws and would certainly seem to negate the idea that women were dependent and controlled within marriage. But the initial impression of equality soon vanishes as the particular aspects of the law are explored in greater detail: "This law obliged the married women, as having no other refuge, to conform themselves entirely to the temper of their husbands and the husbands to rule their wives as necessary and inseparable possessions."[16] Since there was no place in Roman society for detached persons, the wife had nowhere else to go. She had few, if any, alternatives outside marriage, and she was a piece of property within it.

Several types of marriage were practiced by the ancient Romans, all of them specifying who had power over the wife and who took possession of her property. Only in the case of 'free marriage,' a later development, did a woman not pass into the power of her husband. But even in this marriage she was certainly not free. Such marriages usually were contracted in order to retain her family's property by preventing the husband from gaining control over the wife's share, and the woman simply remained within the power of her father. In all other types of marriage, the woman passed into *manus*, or her husband's power.[17] This could be done by *use*, by *coemption*, or by *confarreatio*. In marriage by use, the woman came into the hand of her husband[18] when he had possessed and used her for one year, i.e., they had lived together for a year. Marriage by coemption was marriage by symbolic sale in which the man purchased the woman in front of five witnesses. Confarreatio was the most solemn form of marriage. A woman came into her husband's hand in front of ten witnesses in a ceremony that included the speaking of certain solemn words and was marked by the offering of a cake as a sacrifice to Jupiter.[19] The entire process began with the betrothal celebration, in which the man gave the woman a ring to wear on the third finger of her left hand, and ended when he carried her over the threshold.[20]

The ideal wife was described by Dio Cassius in A.D. 9.

> For is there anything better than a wife who is chaste, domestic, a good housekeeper, a rearer of children; one to gladden you in health, to tend you in sickness; to be your partner in good fortune, to console you in misfortune; to restrain the mad passion of youth, and to temper the unseasonable harshness of old age?[21]

Certainly the ideal wife was desired and appreciated for both her affections and her services, and the obedient wife enjoyed rewards, respect, and influence within the domestic sphere.

> Accordingly, if a wife was virtuous and in all things obedient to her husband, she was mistress of the house to the same degree as her husband was master of it, and after the death of her husband she was heir to his property in the same manner as a daughter was to that of her father.[22]

ENFORCING THE PATRIARCHAL ORDER

Obedience, however, was something a wife could not withhold without serious consequences. It was the legal right of a husband to require that his wife obey him. She was his property and subject to whatever form of control was necessary for achieving obedience and what was deemed by himself and by the law to be appropriate behavior. The laws specified the types of behavior that were to be controlled, the legitimate means by which such control could be effected, and who had the right to control.

During the early patriarchal period, adultery and the drinking of wine were the gravest offenses a wife could commit and were punishable by divorce or death. Romulus considered adultery "a source of reckless folly and drunkenness a source of adultery."[23] The severity of the punishment for the adultress remained during later reforms, although its enforcement decreased. Drunkenness later became a less serious offense, punishable merely by divorce. Counterfeiting the household keys, making poison, abortion, attending public games without the husband's permission, and appearing unveiled in the streets also became punishable by divorce.[24]

In all of these cases, it was the wife who was the offender and the husband the offended. In all cases it was the husband who had the right to control, the wife the obligation to obey. Whether the offense was small:

> C. Sulpicius Gallus . . . repudiated his wife because she had been seen out of doors with her face uncovered. The sentence was harsh but based on reason. 'The Law', he could have said to her, 'bids you seek to please no one but me. It is for me that you must be attractive. For me that you must adorn yourself. To me that you must confide the secrets of your beauty. In sum, I am to be the judge of your charms. *Any other glance which you attract to yourself, even innocently, can only render you suspect of entertaining some criminal disign'.*[25]

Or great:

> Romulus instituted certain laws one of which is somewhat severe, which suffers not a wife to leave her husband but grants a husband power to turn off

his wife [divorce her] either upon poisoning her children [abortion], or counterfeiting his keys, [to the wine cellar], or for adultery.[26]

A husband was allowed to leave his wife if she committed any of these offenses, but, until later reforms, she was prohibited from leaving him even if he engaged in the same behavior. For him, such behavior was not defined as an offense, and he was therefore not liable for punishment.

Husbands and fathers could put a woman to death without recourse to public trial. Although such legally prescribed executions were rarely carried out,[27] it seems reasonable to conjecture that these statutes reflected general acceptance of physical abuse of women and legitimized their subjugation through force. This subjugation is illustrated in a speech delivered by Cato the Censor in which he indicated the correct response of husbands and wives to marital indiscretion: "If you should take your wife in adultery, you may with impunity put her to death without a trial—but if you should commit adultery or indecency, she must not presume to lay a finger on you, nor does the law allow it."[28]

Roman husbands had the legal right to chastise, divorce, or kill their wives for engaging in behavior that they themselves engaged in daily. But it did not take something as extreme as marital infidelity to rouse the man of the house to raise club and boot—or sandal—to the erring wife. If she were caught tippling in the family wine cellar, attending public games without his permission, or walking outdoors with her face uncovered,[29] she could be beaten.

The double standard in the law seemed directed at protecting the rights and authority of men (after all, they were the lawmakers) and controlling and oppressing women. The husband was given full powers: "When a husband puts away his wife . . . he judges the woman as a censor would, and has full powers if she has been guilty of any wrong or shameful act."[30] And it was agreed that this situation was right despite the consequences. This is aptly illustrated by the case of Egnatius Metellus, a Roman husband

> who beat his wife to death because she had drunk some wine; and this murder, far from leading to his being denounced was not even blamed. People considered that her exemplary punishment had properly expiated her offense against the laws of sobriety; for any woman who drinks wine immoderately closes her heart to every virtue and opens it to every vice.[31]

Adultery, suspected infidelity, and sexual jealousy over women were mentioned most frequently in marital laws, and the punishment for sexual offenses was always severe. The reason was not so much thwarted love but loss of control and damage to a possession. Women were the chattels of their husbands, and as pieces of property it was important that they remain under the control of, and in the possession of, their owner. The stress placed upon chastity and fidelity was also related to the idea that women were property who produced other property (especially male children), who would in turn inherit the property of the head of the household. It was important that the transfer of property from father to son not be obstructed by doubts about paternity.

Control of wives was of the utmost importance to the Romans, and it was expected that this task be carried out by the husband in the privacy of his own home rather than become a public matter. Accordingly, lawmakers and public officials preferred not to interfere in domestic affairs.[32] Of course, not all women accepted private and public subordination without protest and struggle, but such struggles were met with strong resistance and sanctions by Roman men. The importance of maintaining control and the strong reaction to insubordination were expressed in a speech by a consul outraged by a group of women who publicly protested against a law that restricted their wearing apparel.[33] After pushing his way through the crowd of women, he expressed his anger, disgust, and fears.

> Romans, if every married man had made sure that his own wife looked up to him and respected his marital authority, we should not have half this trouble with women in general. But now, having let female insubordination triumph first in our homes, we find our privileges trodden and trampled on in the public forum. We have failed to control each woman individually, and we find ourselves quailing before a body of them. As to the outrageous behavior of these women . . . I do not know whether it reflects greater disgrace on you, tribunes, or on us the consuls: on you if you have brought them here to incite to sedition; on us, if we allow laws to be imposed on us by demonstrating women as done formerly by a secession of the common people. It was not without strong feelings of shame that I pushed my way through an army of women on my way here. I should have asked them, "What do you mean by coming out in public in this unheard of fashion and calling out to other women's husbands? Could you not have raised all these matters at home and with your own husbands?" . . . Woman is a violent and uncontrolled animal, and it is useless to let go the reins and then expect her not to kick over the traces. You must keep her on a tight rein. . . . Women want total freedom or rather—to call things by their names—total licence. If you allow them to achieve complete equality with men, do you think they will be easier to live with? Not at all. Once they have achieved equality they will be your masters.[34]

His fear and concern were not misplaced because this was a time when family organization was changing from an absolute patriarchy to one in which women were struggling for and winning greater freedom.

The Punic Wars ended in 202 B.C. They had lasted a long time and brought about conditions that resulted in many changes in the family. The long absences of men meant that women had assumed many of men's responsibilities and had been freed from some traditional controls.[35] The sex ratio changed in favor of female predominance, and many adults did not marry. There was a rise in wealth brought through levies on conquered lands, and this meant an increase of the idle rich and of slaves. Property began to be individually controlled, prohibitions upon female inheritance were diminished, and a class of wealthy women arose. This change in the status of propertied women brought departures from the sole pursuits of wife and mother, and many upper-class women engaged in traditional male pursuits: politics, philosophy, attending military maneuvers, and joining new religious movements.[36]

There was a departure from the severe sexual code, and the single code of the past gave way before a proliferation of laws concerning the distinctions among various types of infidelity, fornication, and adultery. The severity of a specific offense and its punishment varied with the sex, social class, and marital status of the participants. The old double standard and the emphasis on family heritage could still be seen in laws that specified that a married man had not committed adultery if he had intercourse with a slave, but that a wife could be killed if she did the same. Chastisement was also still possible though in a somewhat mediated form.

> If a man should beat his wife with a whip or a rod, without having been induced to do so for one of the reasons which we have stated to be sufficient [i.e., where the woman is blameworthy enough to justify divorce]. We do not wish [the marriage] to be dissolved on this account; but the husband who has been convicted of having, without such a reason, struck his wife with a whip or a rod shall give her by way of compensation for an injury of this kind a sum equal in value to the amount of the antenuptial donation to be taken out of his other property.[37]

By the fourth century A.D., excessive violence on the part of either party, husband or wife, constituted a sufficient ground for divorce, but so did a wife's attendance at public games without her husband's permission. The grounds for divorce were enlarged and now included certain types of 'illegitimate' violence against women, but only for those who were freeborn.

> If a woman should ascertain that her husband is an adulterer, a homicide, a poisoner, or one who is plotting anything against Our government; or has been convicted of perjury or forgery; or is a violator of sepulchres, or has stolen anything from sacred buildings; or is a robber or a harbourer of robbers, a cattle thief or a kidnapper; or, in contempt of his house and for her, or in her presence, has consorted with dissolute women (which is especially exasperating to females who are chaste); or if he has attempted to deprive her of life by poison, or by the sword, or in any other way; *or if she should prove that he had beaten her (which is not allowed in the case of freeborn women)*, We then grant her permission to avail herself of the necessary aid of repudiation, and to present legal reasons for divorce [emphasis added].[38]

A woman no longer had to remain her husband's property despite his behavior, but he had to be a pretty despicable character before she was allowed to leave him. In the case of women who were beaten, only the accident of freeborn status allowed them to seek a divorce. These advances made toward the "emancipation" of women were great, but women were still not equal and they still had no redress from chastisement unless they were rich.

Most of the reforms affected only the ruling group; the practices of other groups changed less dramatically. The poor were more likely to cling to the patriarchal traditions and to be scandalized by the new-found freedom of women and the anticipated instability of marriage. It was just such a class of people who became the nucleus of a religious sect known as the Christians. In the first century their domestic mores did not form a unified Christian doctrine but reflected the traditional patterns of common people, Jewish, Greek, and Roman; yet, conflict with, and persecutions by, the ruling elite and attempts to eliminate their sect soon brought a more unified doctrine that rejected many of the practices and reforms of the ruling class of Rome.[39]

The Law of God

In some ways, the early Christians rejected the existing hierarchies and oppression of Rome and posited the very revolutionary principle of equality of all people (all souls were equal before God, husband and wife were helpmates). In other ways, they rejected the reforms of later Rome, which had given greater freedom to women and challenged the absolute patriarch, and they reaffirmed the earlier principles of marital hierarchy and inequality between husband and wife. This contradiction may be best summarized in the later writings of Paul, that great "admirer" of women, who wrote that wives were to be subordinate to their husbands and "let the wife see that she fear her husband."[40] This so-called Christian attitude toward women, which surely reinforced their subjugation through force, did not differ dramatically from the law of the early Romans.

Christian principles have had a most profound influence upon the cultural beliefs and social institutions of Western society. With respect to the relationship between husband and wife, it was not the revolutionary principles of equality but the retrogressive principles of patriarchy that were taken up most enthusiastically and vehemently by later Christians and that have largely prevailed. The ancient right of the husband to control his wife was incorporated into the new "nonbarbaric, humanistic" religion and the *Decretum* (c. 1140), one of the early and enduring systematizations of church law, gave this principle precedence over egalitarianism: "Women should be subject to their men."[41] Once again women were relegated to the home, and their subordinate and inferior status was reaffirmed.

The Christian account of creation is particularly instructive concerning the separate, singular, and subordinate position of women. Woman was created after man; indeed, she was a by-product of him. And she was created in response to man's needs.

And the Lord God said, It is not good that a man should be alone; I will make a helpmate for him.[42]

And the rib, which the Lord God had taken from man, made he a woman, and brought her unto the man. And Adam said, This is now bone of my bones, and flesh of my flesh: she shall be called Woman, because she was taken out of Man.[43]

No sooner had woman been created than she was deceived and outwitted. She acquiesced in evil and implicated her husband in her offense. Man proclaimed his innocence and the guilt of his new piece of property.

And the man said, The woman whom thou gavest to be with me, she gave me of the tree, and I did eat.[44]

Nevertheless, God meted out eternal punishments for all. To the serpent, for deceiving the woman:

Thou art cursed above all . . . Upon thy belly shalt thou go, and dust shalt thou eat all the days of thy life.[45]

To Eve, for deceiving her husband:

Unto the woman he said, I will greatly multiply thy sorrow and thy conception; in sorrow thou shalt bring forth children; and thy desire shall be to thy husband.[46]

To Adam, for listening to his wife and thus being deceived:

And unto Adam he said, Because thou has harkened unto the voice of thy wife, and hast eaten of the tree, of which I commanded thee, saying, Thou shalt not eat of it: cursed is the ground for thy sake; in sorrow shalt thou eat of it all the days of thy life.[47]

So it is that chapter 2, verse 22, of Genesis woman is created out of man and given to him in order that she might save him from loneliness. Within twenty subsequent verses she brings—because of her weak nature—devastation and curses to all. She destroys paradise, illustrates to man the dangers of listening to his wife, and is punished for all eternity by being made subject to the rule of her husband.

The New Testament, with all its changes, brought little or no relief to women. Emphasis was again placed upon her subordination and rightful subjection to man. It was written that woman was created after man and for his needs.[48]

For Adam was first formed, then Eve. For the man is not of the woman; but the woman of the man.[49]

Neither was the man created for the woman; but the woman for the man.[50]

The order of the creation somehow seemed to represent the religious and matrimonial hierarchy.

But I would have you know, that the head of every man is Christ; and the head of the woman is the man.[51]

For a man . . . is the image and glory of God: but the woman is the glory of the man.[52]

Women's nature was believed to be weak; thus she was lured into disobedience and persuaded man to follow.[53]

And Adam was not deceived, but the woman being deceived was in transgression.[54]

The subjugation of wives was the punishment for Eve's wrongdoing, and husbands were advised not to listen to their wives for they might cause further transgressions.[55]

Silence was demanded of women and all authority taken from them.

Let the woman learn in silence with all subjection. But I suffer not a woman to teach nor to usurp authority over the man, but to be in silence.[56]

Let your women keep silence in the churches: for it is not permitted unto them to speak; but they are commanded to be under obedience, as also saith the law.[57]

And if they will learn any thing, let them ask their husbands at home; for it is a shame for women to speak in the church.[58]

The biblical laws of marriage[59] and the prescriptions of conjugal duties[60] follow these principles but are stated in terms of love and obedience for wives and of the husband's duty to love and yet to rule his household well by keeping everyone in subjection.[61] Since purity of the spirit was sought, which was seen to be in opposition to the base desires of the flesh expressed in sex and marriage, marriage was initially considered to be a most undesirable state, to be entered into only by those who were unable to control their sexual appetites.

But if they cannot contain, let them marry: for it is better to marry than to burn.[62]

It was a very long time before marriage and married love were sanctified and became a sacrament of the church.[63] It was, however, considered important that those who did enter the lesser state of marriage not defile themselves still further by behaving badly. Once married, husbands and wives were to remain married[64] and were to abide by the scripture that defined the relationship between them.

These scriptures provided a moral ideology that largely denigrated women and made their inferiority and subjugation to their husbands appear natural, just, and sacred. Although other scriptures were contradictory and espoused equality, they were not so enthusiastically embraced. This is perhaps not surprising considering the roots of early Christianity and the fact that the church itself was later to organize along hierarchical principles. The relationship between cleric and parishioner was almost identical to that of husband and wife (or children). The belief in the power, wisdom, and authority of one figure over others is, after all, fundamental to Christianity. God is the head and there are tiers of followers who more or less approximate Him and are given powers over their "inferiors." It is this religious ideology that was translated into the organization of the church, with its layers of authority: God, the clergy, the flock. Within the flock, and in accordance with the same hierarchical beliefs, the male head of household was the "Godhead"; his wife and children were his "flock." He was believed to be responsible for them, to have authority over them, and ultimately to control them and keep them in subjection. The law of God provided a sacred and moral ideology to uphold the existing patriarchical structure of the family.

The Nature of the Patriarchy and Its Maintenance

The patriarchy is comprised of two elements: its structure and its ideology.[65] The structural aspect of the patriarchy is manifest in the hierarchical organization of social institutions and social relations, an organizational pattern that by definition relegates selected individuals, groups, or classes to positions of power, privilege, and leadership and others to some form of subservience. Access to positions is rarely based upon individual ability but is institutionalized to such an extent that those who occupy positions of power and privilege do so either because of some form of ascribed status or because of institutionalized forms of advantage that give them the opportunity to achieve status. It is this institutionalized nature of the hierarchical structure that predetermines which individuals or groups will prevail and which ones will be subservient. It is also through such institutionalized differentials that those who have accrued power and privilege are able to acquire still further power and privilege for themselves and for those they have selected to inherit their positions.

One of the means by which this order is supported and reinforced has been to insure that women have no legitimate means of changing or managing the institutions that define and maintain their subordination. Confining women in the home, banning them from meaningful positions outside the family, and excluding them from the bench and the pulpit is to deny them the means of bringing about change in their status. The best they can hope for is a merciful master both inside and outside the home.

The maintenance of such a hierarchical order and the continuation of the authority and advantage of the few is to some extent dependent upon its 'acceptance' by the many.[66] It is the patriarchal ideology that serves to reinforce this acceptance. The ideology is supportive of the principle of a hierarchical order, as opposed to an egalitarian one, and of the hierarchy currently in power. It is a rationalization for inequality and serves as a means of creating acceptance of subordination by those destined to such positions.

The ideology insures that internal controls regulate the complaints of most subordinates. Socialization into an acceptance of the "rightful" nature of the order and its inequities can, if successful, allow such inequities to go unquestioned and unchallenged or to make challenges seem unnatural or immoral. Such a general acceptance of the hierarchical structure means that any challenges to it (from those who are not internally controlled by the idea of its rightfulness) will be met by external constraints in the guise of social pressures to conform (from those who do believe in its rightfulness) and by legitimate intervention both to prevent and to punish deviance. When the ideology legitimizes the order and makes it right, natural, and sacred, the potential conflict inherent in all hierarchies is more likely to produce conflict within the individual and less likely to emerge as overt resistance.

In this respect women in general and wives in particular largely have been denied the means to struggle effectively against their subordination. Although individual women do dissent—and their struggles could pose considerable personal difficulties for the husband faced with a wife who does not know her place—women usually have been sufficiently removed from power and influence as to pose no challenge to the laws or common practices. The development of a legitimate hierarchy based upon acceptance and genuine compliance has meant a far more secure and less problematic order for those in control. The successful socialization of men and women for their positions within marriage has provided a mechanism for both the legitimation and the reinforcement of the marital hierarchy.

Christianity, as well as most other religions, has provided the ideological and moral supports for patriarchal marriage, rationalized it, and actively taught men and women to fit into this form of marriage. On the other hand, the state has codified this relationship into law, and it regulates both the marital hierarchy and access to the opportunities to institute change in the hierarchy. The history of the patriarchal family shows the integration of the family in society and the way in which the family, the church, the economic order, and the state each have influenced and supported one another in maintaining their own hierarchies.

The Patriarchal Family and Control and Chastisement of Women

The patriarchal structure of the family and the ideology that supported it continued almost completely intact after the Roman empire had fallen and the early Christians ceased to be a minority "protest group." Patriarchal principles were not immutable, but vestiges of the structure and remnants of the ideology can be followed throughout time to the present date. Modifications can be seen, but the essence of the patriarchal family and of the hierarchical relationship between husband and wife has not been eliminated. It continues to be the foundation of male supremacy and of the subordination of women in society and in marriage; thus, it forms the foundation of wife beating. The complex patterns of any society during any particular epoch will, of course, vary from those of another time or place. But no new historical period is completely new. Patterns of behavior, social arrangements, and ideologies often emerge with modified meaning and consequences in a new period. Some patterns and ideologies are completely revolutionized and the old disappears; others remain almost intact, changing only temporarily or superficially. The position of women in marriage, although certainly not unchanging or immutable, fits this latter pattern more closely than most other social arrangements.[67] It behooves us, therefore, to examine our cultural heritage very closely in order to see exactly what impact it has had on subsequent epochs—what has remained, what has changed, and what had disappeared.

THE MEDIEVAL HOUSEHOLD

Throughout the Middle Ages the large kin group remained the organizing institution for all society. Political organization was based upon large families, which controlled agriculture and the distribution of goods.[68] To a great extent the elite families were the rulers of separate societies within a larger society. A few large and powerful households[69] formed their own realms, and each one had its own social order and fortified itself against the possibility of being taken over by a more powerful family.[70]

In a world made up of large fortified households vying with each other for domination, the women of the feudal lords served as commodities and as symbols of the power and honor of men. They were exchanged in order to increase wealth or influence, to solidify bonds, or to serve as traders of peace.[71] Once married, the woman and all her goods became the property of her husband and his family. She was transferred from one patriarch to another for mutual benefit, economic or political gain, and became the object of efforts to protect and regulate her property value. Chastity before marriage and fidelity after were important aspects of these male property rights and were also outward signs that the master was in control.[72]

Because the selection of a marriage partner had such large consequences for the entire kin group, children, and especially daughters, had little or no say in the choice of their own marital partner and could be beaten if they refused to marry. Marriages were arranged for the benefit of larger kin groups and in accordance with the wishes of the male heads of household.[73]

Marital affection did, of course, exist but personal fulfillment was not the primary purpose of marriage. Consequently, there was a separation between the object of one's affection and one's spouse, a separation between love and marriage. Love was given to one person and duty and obligation to another.

During this era, the concept of courtly love emerged and reflected this separation.[74] There is some dispute about whether courtly love was ever widely accepted or practiced,[75] but it is said that the idea was begun by wandering French troubadours, who sang of chivalry and of love between those who were forced by their families to marry one person but had affection for another. The troubadours sang the praises of beautiful women who were loved and worshiped from afar. Since chastity and fidelity were important commodities in the feudal household and were jealously guarded even to the point of locking women in chastity belts during their lord's absence, courtly love was not meant to be sexual but only affectional in nature. This ideal, however, applied only to the propertied women of the castles and not to those of the cottages, who saw a great deal of lusty lovemaking, infidelity, and deception.[76] The glorification of women and of romantic love contributed mightily to the subordination of wives and daughters, who became objects to be admired, enjoyed, and coveted, at least as long as they were young or attractive. Accordingly, women had to be controlled and protected from the claims of other men as long as they might be considered desirable to them. Note that the characteristics that made women admirable or desirable or worthy of love or glorification were defined by men. Thus, in the process of being idealized by men, women became even more dependent upon them and subject to their desires and demands.[77] It has been noted that a sentimental ideology such as this is closely associated with the prevalence of the use of male force.[78] The separation between love and marriage and the commodity status of women's chastity and fidelity certainly meant that wives were guarded jealously and could be punished severely for violations of duty while the damsel remained the object of tender love and affection. Indeed, a husband was expected to chastise his wife for misbehaviors and might himself be punished by neighbors if he failed to do so.[79]

For women, adultery was a grave property offense committed against her "owner" and was punished severely. For example, in 1240, a Spanish woman who committed adultery could be killed with impunity by a husband or fiancé.[80] The Italian adultress was "severely flogged through the city streets . . . and exiled for three years."[81] It was legal for a Frenchman to beat his wife when she wronged him by committing adultery, or by preparing to do so, or by refusing to obey him.[82] The English husband was enjoined not to inflict bodily damage other than that which "pertains to the office of a husband for lawful and reasonable correction."[83] In medieval

France a compassionate decree was proposed to a synod of rabbis pleading for all wives.

> The cry of the daughters of our people has been heard concerning the sons of Israel who raise their hands to strike their wives. Yet who has given a husband the authority to beat his wife?[84]

The decree was not adopted. But then such a proposal could not be expected to have much chance of success in an era in which the city of Siena instituted rules of marriage that specified the control of wives through force.

> When you see your wife commit an offense, don't rush at her with insults and violent blows; rather, first correct the wrong lovingly. . . . But if your wife is of a servile disposition and has a crude shifty spirit, so that pleasant words have no effect, scold her sharply, bully and terrify her. And if this still doesn't work . . . take up a stick and beat her soundly, for it is better to punish the body and correct the soul than to damage the soul and spare the body. But you shouldn't beat her just because she doesn't get things ready exactly as you would like them, or for some other unimportant reason or minor failing. You should beat her . . . only when she commits a serious wrong; for example, if she blasphemes against God or a saint, if she mutters the devil's name, if she likes being at the window and lends ready ear to dishonest young men, or if she has taken to bad habits or bad company, or commits some other wrong that is a mortal sin. Then readily beat her, not in rage but out of charity and concern for her soul, so that the beating will redound to your merit and good.[85]

Despite the secondary position of wives during the Middle Ages and the acceptability of using force against them, women did enjoy various forms of power and influence and their position was in fact much higher than it was to be in the following periods. In McNamara and Wemple's analysis, "The Power of Women through the Family in Medieval Europe,"[86] they maintained that women's rights in public and private spheres varied in ancient Roman and Germanic cultures (in the ancient Roman empire women had some private rights but no public rights and in the ancient Germanic culture they occupied an exceptionally important place in public life but had little power in private life) and that the power of women in aristocratic families of Germany rose during the fifth and the sixth century.[87] Married women also had higher status under Anglo-Saxon law in the latter part of the fifth century than they were to have for the next fifteen hundred years.[88]

CHAPTER 4

THE NUCLEAR FAMILY AND THE CHASTISEMENT OF WIVES

AT THE CLOSE OF THE MIDDLE AGES numerous changes were taking place that were to affect all aspects of society. The modern state was emerging out of and replacing the large feudal households as the main organizing institution of society; mercantilism and the early forms of capitalism were replacing the feudal economy; Protestantism was challenging Catholicism; and the nuclear family was taking precedence over the family line.[1] These dramatic changes in political, economic, religious, and family institutions were all interrelated and basically eroded the position of women and strengthened the husband's authority over his wife.[2] The authority of the male head of each conjugal unit was increased while wives became more dependent and subject to control and chastisement and lost many of the means that traditionally had afforded them some opportunity, albeit very limited, to resist or struggle against subordination. As the French historian Petiot put it:

> Starting in the fourteenth century, we see a slow and steady deterioration of the wife's position in the household. She loses the right to take the place of the husband in his absence or insanity. . . . Finally, in the sixteenth century, the married woman is placed under a disability so that any acts she performs without the authority of her husband or the law are null and void. This development strengthens the power of the husband, who is finally established as a sort of domestic monarch.[3]

The State, the Nuclear Family, and the Husband's Authority

In order for the state to emerge as the dominant institution of power in society, it had to displace the large feudal households as the main political and economic institutions of society. The large fortified household posed a threat to the emerging state and the state's preeminence depended to a large extent upon subordinating the traditional loyalties to aristocratic kinship to those of patriotism and obedience to the crown.[4] Stone has argued that the

48

two means of strengthening the state in England included the destruction of the power and authority of, and loyalty to, aristocratic kinship and the deliberate fostering of the "increase of power of the husband and father within the conjugal unit . . . a strengthening of the patriarchy."[5] This was meant to displace power and loyalty inward toward the smaller, less powerful nuclear family and outward toward the crown while at the same time continuing to encourage hierarchical beliefs and patterns of organization. For although the large fortified households posed a threat to the state, the patterns of authority and deference within them were believed to be the very patterns of mind and habit necessary to achieve obedience and allegiance to the state.[6]

Thus, in sixteenth-century England, when the state began to assume more powers of justice, punishment, military protection, and regulation of property, there was waged a massive propaganda campaign in support of the nuclear family and oriented toward encouraging subservience, obedience, and loyalty both to the king and to the husband.[7] The propaganda supported the patriarchal form of authority in the nuclear family and equated loyalty to the patriarch with allegiance to the monarch and to God. It included such statements as that made by James I of England in 1609: "Kings are compared to fathers in families."[8] Obedience to kings was stated in terms of "Honor thy Father"[9] (mother was left out), and in France it was declared that "one makes Kings on the model of fathers."[10] Stone concluded that this propaganda campaign was effective in "generating an internalized sense of obligation and obedience to the absolute sovereign, as well as obedience to the absolute husband and father."[11] A critical view of this achievement was taken by Montesquieu, who maintained that "the servitude of women" and "despotic government" were clearly related.[12]

The structure and ideology of the patriarchal family of the Middle Ages had, of course, formed much of the basic structure and ideology of both the modern state, which emerged out of and superseded that institution, and the smaller, less powerful nuclear family, which was encouraged by the state in order to obtain its own support and security. Thus the state and the nuclear family were inextricably intertwined and mutually supportive; they both grew out of the large medieval households and were largely modeled upon them. Ariès's excellent history of family life, *Centuries of Childhood*, and Foucault's superb history, *Madness and Civilization*, both noted the influence of the patriarchal family upon the development of other social institutions and the continued interrelationship between these institutions. Ariès commented on the nuclear family: "Henceforth a value was attributed to the family which had previously been attributed to the line. It became the social cell, the basis of the State, the foundation of the monarchy."[13] Foucault noted that the family was the cornerstone of the patriarchal society, that it was the model upon which other social institutions were based, and that its order became a moral order, its hierarchy sacred.[14]

These common roots and the interrelationship of the family and other social institutions often have been ignored by historians of the family, and this false separation obscures their mutual supports and the similarity of their goals and practices. Commenting on this false separation between the family and other social institutions, Zaretsky pointed out that historians of the family have focused upon the internal aspects of the family, which are formal and legalistic (laws, inheritance, divorce, social relationships of age and sex), and their theories have conceptualized a slow move from extended kin to nuclear family, which presents a picture of inertia when compared with the economic and political upheavals. This contrast leads to a view "that 'history' is the realm of politics and economics while the family is confined to 'nature.' "[15] He refuted this view and proposed that the changing social basis of the family can be understood only when it is analyzed in terms of its interrelationship with "the organization of production."[16]

Early Capitalism, Increased Dependence of Wives, and Devaluation of Domestic Work

As late as the seventeenth century, there was no sharp distinction between economic and domestic life and the basic unit of production was the household unit. "Economic organization was domestic organization,"[17] and households included not only individuals related through marriage and birth but also individuals with a primarily economic relationship to the head of the household, such as servants and apprentices.[18] Whether the household was oriented to manufacturing or agriculture, all the labor was carried out within the domestic sphere by all members of the household. Wives, children, servants, and apprentices were all subject to the control of the patriarch, and this control included the legitimate use of physical chastisement against them. This hierarchical relationship was based primarily on loyalty to the patriarch though some of the relationships (apprenticeships) were of a quasi-contractual nature.

With the rise of mercantilism and early forms of capitalist production, the primacy of the domestic unit as the major economic unit was eroded.[19] In the wage and commodity society that was emerging, the locus of productive activity began to shift from the family to explicitly economic settings of production such as the factory. Gradually, domestic production for the master of the household gave way to various forms of cottage industry controlled by individual entrepreneurs outside the domestic unit. This process began to weaken the hold of the master over certain members of the household such as servants and apprentices, and the factory system eventually transferred the apprenticeship system out of the domestic unit and into the manufacturing setting. This changed the nature of that social relationship, and by the middle of nineteenth century the relationship between apprentice and master changed from one that was based at least partially on filial ties and enforced by loyalty and chastisement to a relation of employee and employer that was regulated by contract.[20] Of course, this shift from domestic production to industrial production was not linear, with one mode of production and social relationship completely transposing and replacing the other, nor did it completely transform all social relationships, especially that of husband and wife.

An important outcome of the development of modern capitalist forms of production, especially the factory system, was the demarcation of the economic and domestic spheres of life. Wage work was characterized by hierarchical and exploitive relationships established by contract and public negotiation, whereas domestic work was characterized by private, patriarchal forms of subordination and control bolstered by moral prescriptions demanding loyalty from subordinates. Both Zaretsky and Secombe argued that industrial capitalist forms of production split the general labor process and that domestic laborers (wives) were "divorced from the means of production and exchange . . . [and] dependent upon the redistribution of the wage in private without benefit of a contract other than the general marriage contract."[21] This separation resulted not only in the extreme privatization of domestic relationships but also in the greater physical isolation and segregation of women in households.[22] It resulted also in the devaluation of domestic work because in a wage economy it has no value that can be measured by a wage. This, of course, meant devaluation of the domestic worker. The woman continued to be subordinate to her husband; she, unlike the apprentice, did not escape patriarchal control.[23] She was, and still is, subject to domination, oppression, and physical chastisement within the domestic sphere. Under capitalist forms of production, her contacts with the outside world were dramatically constricted and her economic, and to a considerable extent her social, life mediated through her husband. In this respect, Zaretsky maintained that "if we can understand the family as part of the development of Capitalism this can help establish the specific historical formation of male supremacy."[24]

The Rise of Protestantism and the Sanctification of Marital Authority

The rise of the nuclear family, the increase in the husband's authority, and the deepening of the wife's subjection also were related to the rise of Protestantism. With it there was an attempt to bring Christian principles and morality into every home. Emphasis was placed upon individualism, authority, and obedience, and there was a sanctification of marriage and married love. All of this resulted in the flow of greater authority to husbands and a decline in the status of wives, whose obedience became a moral duty.[25]

The medieval idea that marriage is a business contract was rejected by Protestantism; love and marriage ceased to be separated and were sanctified by religion. Marriage became the ideal state rather than an institution for those too weak of the flesh to remain celibate. New emphasis was placed upon the neclear family, loyalty between spouses, and domestic virtue, and the home became the center of Christian life.[26] Stone argued that the most far-reaching consequence of the Reformation in England was the new emphasis upon home and domestic virtue and that to a large extent the parish was replaced by the household as the center of "piety, prayer and moral indoctrination." The head of the household inherited much of the authority and power of the priest, and his increased authority had a moral or sacred quality imparted to it by religious support. The church also supported affective ties between husbands and wives as a means of keeping marriages together, sanctified and glorified married love, and rejected divorce as a means of ending an unsatisfactory relationship.[27] On the face of it, it would seem that the family was indeed changing for the better.

With this revolution in religion, with the new emphasis that was being placed upon the individual, the conjugal pair, and the sacredness of marriage and marital love, it would seem that those scriptures that stressed equality between husband and wife would now preempt those stressing inequality and subjection. Yet, the position of married women was at its lowest ebb during the sixteenth and seventeenth centuries. The idea of married love, which was to have some softening effect on the eighteenth-century family, was glorified but seemed to be stressed more as a "means to other ends of procreation and socialization of children and the channelling of sexual appetite"[28] than for its own sake. It was perhaps less related to affection and more related to supporting the husband's position of greater authority by making obedience to him a matter of sacred love and Christian duty.

The prominent thinkers of the Reformation differed widely in their views of the status of women and wives, but basically they reaffirmed the old ideas rather than wholeheartedly embracing the new. Martin Luther began the Reformation in 1517 and his ideas were to be a major influence upon the development of this religious revolution and, later, upon most of the Western world. His ideas about women, though at times contradictory, were largely supportive and stood in opposition to the extreme misogyny of the time. Unlike others, he was not disgusted by women's bodies or afraid of their sexuality, nor did he approve of their ridicule in public. He went to their defense against the archbishop of Mainz, who had described pudenda as the "stinking, putrid, private parts of women."[29] Luther taught that it was to be remembered that women are God's creatures and he looked upon them as "friendly rivals."[30]

Underlying many of Luther's ideas was the scriptural description of husbands and wives as helpmates, and this would certainly have formed an egalitarian foundation for the sanctification of marriage and the increasing emphasis upon the conjugal pair. These ideas were enlightened, even revolutionary, for their time, but others reaffirmed the old, hierarchical view of marriage. For example, in 1531 Luther expounded on women's "natural" inferiority to men and their "proper" social sphere, using as evidence a description of male and female body types.

> Men have broad shoulders and narrow hips, and accordingly they possess intelligence. Women have narrow shoulders and broad hips. Women ought to stay at home; the way they were created indicates this, for they have broad hips and a fundament to sit upon, keep house and bear and raise children.[31]

The connection between broad shoulders and intelligence or wide hips and domestic work may defy all logic, but Luther seemed satisfied that no further proof was necessary. He maintained that "parts of her body show God's purpose. . . . Therefore let this suffice."[32] So there was not only the 'infallible logic' of biology, it was also God's intention. And who can argue with God or those who speak for Him and are the only transmitters of His ideas or intentions?

The structure of Luther's argument is not uncommon even today, although science is now our god. Such arguments take the form of defining social relationships, which are created by people and are thus quite varied and flexible, as caused by some physiological attribute (which is relatively inflexible). Thus, the social relationship, it is argued, must take on the same natural and relatively immutable and inflexible character as its physical correlate. We may be amused by Luther's contention that broad shoulders and intelligence are correlated or that broad hips determine who should perform domestic work, but the appeal of similar arguments in support of the dominant ideology is always great, and we may well ask about contemporary arguments that define men's and women's social status in terms of genetics or hormone balance.[33]

Luther also reaffirmed the old idea that women are weak in character and need to be controlled: "[Women] are ashamed to admit this, but Scripture and life reveal that only one woman in thousands has been endowed with the God-given aptitude to live in chastity and virginity. A woman is not fully the master of herself."[34] And, in his own marriage, a bit of physical chastisement did not seem inappropriate in maintaining control over his wife, Katie: "when Katie gets saucy, she gets nothing but a box on the ear."[35]

The odd combination of companionate love and marriage and the husband's mastery and domination was also stressed in Calvinism. In Geneva, considered by some to be a "women's paradise," women could participate in the singing of psalms with their husbands, and wife beating was discouraged,[36] but men were reminded that "when he loveth [he] should remember his mastery."[37] The Calvinism of John Knox, unlike the thinking of Martin Luther, was completely uncompromising, seemed not to be aware of the egalitarian scriptures, and held out little or no promise for women. In 1558, John Knox wrote *"The First Blast of the Trumpet Against the Monstrous Regiment of Women."*[38] The blast was actually directed at the female monarchs of the time, who were being criticized for the reigns of terror gripping Europe. By using the logic of stereotyping,[39] Knox attributed the misdeeds of previous male monarchs to individual abuses of power, whereas those of female monarchs were attributed to the inadequacies of their sex. This was the style of argument Knox brought to his *Blast . . . Against the Monstrous Regiment of Women,* and some blast it was.

Armed only with the Bible, religious sermons, and the ideas of Tertullian, Augustine, Ambrose, Paul, Chrysostom, and others, he reviewed and reiterated the old arguments: the natural and irrefutable inferiority of women's character, their sole place in the family, and their rightful subordination to their husbands. Citing Chrysostom, Knox maintained that the character of all women is rash, foolhardy, lacking in right reason and wisdom, imprudent, and easily persuaded to any opinion.[40] Their God given nature is also tender, flexible, soft, and pitiful, suiting them for childbearing[41] and subordination. Knox added a bit of ethology to support this argument of women's natural subordination: "For nature has in all beasts printed a certain mark of dominion in the male, and a certain subjection in the female, which they keep inviolate. For no man ever saw a lion make obedience, and stoupe before the lioness."[42]

Knox maintained that it was woman's distinctive nature that made Eve fall prey to the false persuasions of Satan, and because her husband listened to her he also was led astray. Therefore, women are uniquely suited to be ruled over by men and should be forbidden to teach lest they once again be placed in a position from which they might lead others astray. "[God] hath ordained man to be superior. . . . Because in the nature of all women lurketh such vices, as in good governors are not tolerable."[43]

Knox repeatedly quoted chapter and verse from the Bible to support his case: woman is not in God's image; she should remain in subjection to her husband and should never usurp his authority. "It was a great monster in nature that women should not be tame . . . and have more pleasure [in the activities of men] than to marry and be subject to men."[44] To confirm his argument and to refute those "carnal and worldly men" who might disagree with him, he brought forth the examples of Deborah and Hulda, who did teach and have authority,[45] and maintained that these individual women were merely exceptions to the general rule. If that was not convincing enough, he cited God's commandment: "God hath subjected womankind to man by the order of his creation, and by the curse that he pronounced against her."[46] And, finally, "God by his will revealed, and manifest word stands plain and evident on my side."[47] Knox put the strong religious case for the subordination of all women, even queens, brought all of the Christian writers in on his side, and for the coup de grâce brought in God Himself.

The rules of man were ascribed to a higher authority to which there was no redress. What was manmade, enforced by men, and to the benefit of men was attributed not to men, and therefore amenable to change or to challenge as unjust, but to God, and therefore both just and immutable. Religion was indeed a powerful arm of the patriarchy because it was not defined as political in nature or as manmade. It was an invaluable tool that was used most effectively in achieving what Cato the Roman had pleaded for: that husbands control their wives within the confines of the household and thus save men in general from being publicly confronted with women's pleas for change or their accusations of injustice.

Ideas advocating the total subordination of wives to their husbands were enthusiastically supported by Protestant preachers, moral theologians, and the laity,[48] or at least the male laity, and were actively reinforced by the state. These ideas were disseminated both from the pulpit and in marriage manuals, which were very popular at that time. Two of the most popular manuals, which prescribed means by which these "lofty" principles of subordination could be put into practice, were Cleaver's *A Godly Form of Household Government* (1593)[49] and Gouge's *Of Domesticall Duties: Eight Treatises* (1634).[50] Gough stated the position on wives most succinctly: "The extent of wives subjection both doth stretch itself very far, even to all things."[51] The only exception he made to this claim was the denial of a husband's right to beat his wife.[52] Similar popular attitudes were reflected in Swernam's *The Araignment of Lewd, Idle, Froward and Unconstant Women*, a brutal piece of misogyny that went through ten editions from 1616 to 1634 and aroused four angry rebuttals.[53]

It was, however, the "Homily on Marriage" that was probably the most influential manual, reaching the largest audience for the longest period of time. The inferior character, rights, and status of wives were clearly stated in this document, which was ordered by the crown to be read in church every Sunday from 1562 onward.[54] In it, the wife's subjection and obedience were made a primary necessity for a happy Christian marriage, but husbands were advised, for the sake of domestic peace, not to exercise the right to beat their wives but rather to remember women's weak and inconstant character when dealing with them.[55]

Although there were those who maintained that women were "of a servile nature such as they may be better beaten,"[56] and a popular Gloucestershire saying advocated that "a woman, a spaniel and a walnut tree, the more they are beaten, the better they be,"[57] wife beating was usually discouraged or forbidden by theologians and by the authors of marriage manuals.[58] Religious leaders placed faith in the idea that the subjection of wives, which they supported so strongly, could be achieved by teaching women that it was their sacred duty to obey and by vesting husbands with great authority to control them. The sanctification of marriage made the lowly position of wives a holy one and the idea of married love and loyalty further ensnared wives and supported husbands by making the wife's submission a moral duty.

It should not be forgotten, however, that this age of the increasing importance of the individual was also the "great age of flogging"—extreme brutality and authoritarianism were a part of the school and the home from the sixteenth to the eighteenth century.[59] Flogging was used throughout society as a means of controlling the powerless: children, women, and the lower classes. Female oppression was determined by the birch.[60] Parents "slashed their daughters in order that they were perfect women,"[61] and the new teacher was given the symbol of his office, the birch.[62] Although the theologians used the moral order, social pressure, and fear of eternal damnation to win compliance from wives and discouraged wife beating, it was widespread. Members of the community considered chastisement to be perfectly acceptable and attempted to limit only its severity.

Community Limits and Controls upon Chastisement

Through the seventeenth, eighteenth, and nineteenth centuries, there was little objection within the community to a man's using force against his wife as long as he did not exceed certain tacit limits. The eighteenth-century French belief that "the man who is not master of his wife is not worthy of being a man"[63] was widespread and to a great extent justified beating wives either for various "offenses" against her husband's authority or for failure to live up to his ideals about her work, domestic or otherwise.

> The community [in eighteenth-century France] is unmoved and watches without astonishment a brewer publicly slap his wife who failed to produce the right meal at the right time.[64]

> A carpenter from Query beat his wife with an axe handle and said, "She deserved it" because she was flirting with a soldier. He considered this a just punishment and the community agreed.[65]

Community tolerance of such behavior was great indeed. A woman could be beaten if she behaved "shamelessly" and caused jealousy, was lazy, unwilling to work in the fields, became drunk, spent too much money, or neglected the house. The community agreed that these were offenses that merited, even required, punishment as long as the physical force was restricted to "blows, thumps, kicks or punches on the back if they leave no lasting traces."[66] In short, permissable, or legitimate, violence was that which would be suitable for any inferior, such as a child or a servant. Men were not allowed to use "sharp edged or crushing instruments," that is, weapons, especially cleavers, axes, sickles, or knives. Nor was it considered appropriate to direct blows at the head or sensitive or vital organs (breast or stomach), and "maltreatment by a husband during pregnancy or after a birth was always cited with great indignation."[67] It was the moderate use of physical punishment that separated the "reasonable husband from the brute."[68]

The violence could be quite severe before the community would take collective offense and even then they might not intervene but only express disapproval because to intervene directly was to interfere in the private sphere of family life, which was the rightful arena of the patriarch. The community's stance then, as today, permitted women to be continually subjected to the most extraordinary degree and forms of physical abuse.

> Sieur Alquier, bourgeois of Montaubau . . . prided himself on beating his wife black and blue and on once having beaten her with birch and on chasing her naked with a switch of reeds with which he beat her until the blood flowed and her body was blackened. After which he shut her up without bread . . . threw cold water on her breasts and deprived her of all hot food. As a result of this she fell ill and vomited blood which made the husband decide to put her out of the house. . . . She took this opportunity to have herself cared for in hospital. . . . At four in the morning he burst in with armed bailiffs and made to snatch her from the bed in order to incarcerate her in a convent in the country. Under a hail of blows and dragged by the hair across the room the poor woman fainted and began to vomit blood. The husband maintained that he had the right to take her back by force if necessary, and he should teach her a lesson for asserting her independence.[69]

Even bourgeois women, such as the wife of Sieur Alquier, could not expect much support or intervention from others in the community since the tacit limits were usually more symbolic than real.

Speaking about community response to wife beating in the nineteenth century, Cobbe maintained that there existed a "particular kind of indulgence . . . extended by public opinion."[70] Even English gentlemen, to her horror and chagrin, condoned attacks on wives when they were guilty of nagging or scolding or slatternly behavior.[71] It was even felt that women enjoyed being beaten. As one nineteenth-century wag put it when speaking about Lancashire women, "It has become a truism that our women are like dogs, the more you beat them the more they love you."[72] In nineteenth-century England, as in eighteenth-century France and as today, the state and the community chose not to intervene in the relationship between husband and wife. This dictum was supported by some clergy, as Reverend Harper saw it, "I make bold to believe that if ever I should turn into a wife I shall choose to be beaten by my husband to any extent (short of being slain outright), rather than it should be said a stranger came between us."[73]

These "noble" sentiments echoed those of most members of eighteenth- and nineteenth-century communities. The major occasion for the expression of community disapproval of the "excessive" violence of husbands was during rituals of ridicule that were practiced at certain times of the year.

Public shaming and punishment were an important aspect of community life and were used as a means of setting limits on behavior and of re-emphasizing social bonds. One form of nonjudicial sanction or limit setting was the charivari, which was practiced especially in rural areas throughout the Middle Ages and continued until roughly the close of the nineteenth century. Another was the "conduct of misrule," which might involve various rituals in which the usual hierarchical relationships between husband and wife or youths and adults were temporarily inverted. This occasion served as a means of reducing the tensions felt by subordinates; the "misrule" insured that those tensions and antagonisms were channeled into carefully structured ceremonies and thus did not form any real challenge to the relationship itself.[74] One of the targets of the ritualized mockery of the charivari and misrules was the marital relationship. Men might, for example, be subject to public ridicule for beating their wives. Typically, a group of villagers engaging in raucous and outlandish behavior gathered in front of the offender's house to express the community's dissatisfaction with his actions and to shame him into conforming to the approved pattern.[75] Another form of symbolic ridicule involved the degradation of a straw effigy of the offender: directly affronting the husband might prove difficult and possibly dangerous. These forms of public shaming were called "riding the steng" or "rough music."[76] In Yorkshire and other parts of northern England it was practiced at least as late as 1862 and seems to have been directed at men who beat their wives or were unfaithful to them.[77] Members of the community would appear before the delinquent's house and commence a "serenade with cow's horns, and warming-pans, and tea kettles,"[78] with an orator intoning the following verses:

> There is a man in this place
> Has beat his wife [a pause]
> Has beat his wife! !
>
> 'Tis a very great shame and disgrace
> To all who live in the place etc.[79]

The various forms of public mockery, such as the charivari or "riding the steng," though sometimes directed at husbands who beat their wives, were much more likely to be directed at couples who deviated from the behaviors and demeanor considered appropriate in marriage. As the American historian Shorter pointed out, the French charivari "struck at wife-beaters, if at all, mainly during the month of May. And then, apparently only at men who in fact beat their wives during that month, traditionally considered women's month."[80] Public degradations were directed most frequently at cuckolds, scolds, or henpecked husbands. In societies morally and culturally committed to patriarchal domination the public ridicule of family relations was meant to reinforce the authority of the husband and punish insubordinate wives or, on occasion, to punish husbands who did not preserve their domestic authority.[81] Husbands who did women's work or "permitted themselves to be beaten by their wives (a rare occurrence) were subject to sharp censure."[82] A fourteenth-century Frenchman who showed cowardice, and particularly those beaten by their wives, was made to sit backwards on an ass and hold its tail as a penalty. Men thought to be ruled by their wives might also be subjected to another form of charivari called a "cuckold's court."[83]

Women who did not know their place and were seen to be outside their husband's control were also subjected to public ridicule and degradation. Throughout the Reformation, so-called nagging or scolding women were sentenced to the ducking stool, placarding (as in *The Scarlet Letter*), and whipping.[84] In eighteenth-century Scotland the ducking stool was replaced by the branks as a punishment for scolding women. Although many of the public ridicules discussed above were lighthearted affairs, the use of the branks illustrated that the community meant business in chastising women; a brank was "an iron bridle with a padlock and a spike to enter the mouth, which was forced on the offender." It was a painful gag.[85]

The public chastisement of women who nagged or otherwise verbally abused their husbands had disappeared by the late nineteenth century, but the imagery of the provoking wife remained, as it does today, a powerful justification and rationalization for the physical punishments and degradations meted out by husbands in private. By the close of the nineteenth century, women and men were no longer subjected to public forms of ridicule by the local community; other forms of punishment and legal and judicial remedies had taken their place.

The Laws of Control and Chastisement

"Attitudes towards legal forms of punishment reveal the values that society takes most seriously."[86] Until the Reformation in the sixteenth century, the canon law set the general principles that guided the laws of all Europe on the subject of women,[87] and in the eyes of the law, husbands and wives represented two different categories of individuals with quite varied rights. If a woman killed her husband (or a servant his master) this was treason. If she were found guilty, she could, until the reign of Charles II, receive the worst possible punishment. She would be drawn and burnt alive. If, however, a husband were found guilty of killing his wife, he was guilty merely of murder and could receive what was considered to be the less degrading punishment of being drawn and hanged.[88] Not only was the wife more harshly treated than the husband for committing the same offense, but she was also placed in the same category as a servant, and this depicted her true position relative to her husband (master) and made their relative social worth quite clear. Women had a secondary status and sometimes no legal status at all. Matrimony deprived a woman of her legal rights, set different standards for her behavior, and gave her husband the legal right to inflict corporal punishment upon her.

The term "rule of thumb" purportedly derived from the ancient right of the husband to chastise his wife with a stick no thicker than his thumb.[89] However, this prerogative was not always exercised in such a moderate way. In the fourteenth century, Frenchmen were in many cases to "be excused for the injuries they inflicted on their wives, nor should the law intervene. Provided he neither kills nor maims her, it is legal for a man to beat his wife when she wrongs him."[90] The wrongs that warranted such punishment included adultery, contradicting or abusing one's husband, or refusing, "like a decent woman, to obey his reasonable commands."[91] In these and similar cases, it was the husband's office to be his wife's chastiser. The rule of thumb, or the right to chastise, was *never given to wives.*

It was the law of England that most directly influenced American[92] law, guiding the writing of many contemporary statutes in Britain and North America. Although there were many areas in which English common law actively and overtly discriminated against women and especially married women—who had an inferior legal status to that of their single sisters—it was the laws concerning marriage that were most directly related to the use of physical coercion against them. For it was in their position as wives that women became "special" beings and were stripped of the civil liberties given to other citizens.[93]

Under English common law a distinction was made between married and single women. Commenting on the English common law in 1765, Blackstone maintained that "by marriage the husband and wife are one person in law: that is, the very being or legal existence of the woman is suspended in marriage."[94] The married woman surrendered not only her legal identity to her husband but also her rights to her own property, to personal credit, and to the guardianship of any children she might have. The wife came under the control of her husband and he had the legal right to use force against her in order to insure that she fulfilled her wifely obligations, which included consummation of the marriage, cohabitation, maintenance of conjugal rights, sexual fidelity, and general obedience and respect for his wishes.[95] In 1724, an angry woman summarized the position of married women: "Matrimony to a woman is worse than excommunication in depriving her of the benefit of the law."[96]

Under the older common law the husband was very much lord of all he surveyed and even more. An old enactment thus described a husband's duty:

He shall treat and govern the aforesaid A well and decently, and shall not inflict or cause to be inflicted any injury upon the aforesaid A except in so far as he may lawfully and reasonably do so in accordance with *the right of a husband to correct and chastise his wife*.[97]

It goes without saying that the aforesaid A was one of those special characters in the law otherwise known as wives. Blackstone had this to say on the husband's power to chastise his wife:

The husband also, by the old law might give his wife moderate correction. For, as he is to answer for her misbehaviour, the law thought it reasonable to intrust him with his power of restraining her, by domestic chastisement, in the same moderation that a man is allowed to correct his apprentices or children, for whom the master or parent is also liable in some cases to answer. But this power of correction was confined within reasonable bounds, and the husband was prohibited from using any violence to his wife except in so far as he may lawfully and reasonably do so in order to correct and chastise his wife.[98]

To become a wife meant to take on a special legal status, a status that excluded the woman from the legal process, placed her in the same category as children and servants, demanded surrender and obedience, and elevated her husband to the position of lawmaker, judge, jury, and executioner. In this capacity, the husband was able to punish offenses that in any other setting would clearly not be considered offenses and to use his discretion in determining the severity of punishment. Excesses were not uncommon. Even a blatantly unjust legal system would not have allowed many of the punishments meted out by husbands: broken nose for an unwashed dish or a black eye for a cross word.

Blackstone's repeated references to "moderate chastisements" were sufficiently vague to allow broad interpretation: "The law was, indeed, even worse than might appear from the words of Blackstone. The wife who beared unreasonable violence could, to be sure, bind her husband to keep the peace; but she had no [legal] action against him."[99] Yet, these legal prescriptions were justified on the ground that they were created for the benefit of women. It may be debatable whether the right of chastisement would have been defined by everyone, and especially by women, as beneficial. Blackstone, however, went so far as to say that the female sex was a great favorite of the laws of England.[100]

The consequences of such favoritism were evident both in the old common law of the people and the civil law of the aristocracy. The husband had the same or even greater authority over his wife in civil law: "allowing him for some misdemeanours to give his wife a severe beating with whips and clubs; for others only to apply moderate correction."[101] It was during the reign of Charles II that the husband's "power of correction began to be doubted" and the wife could have security of peace against her spouse.[102] In practice it was noted, however, that the "lower rank" of people, who always had been fond of the old common law, still claimed their ancient privilege, "and the courts of the law will still permit a husband to restrain a wife of her liberty, in case of any gross misbehaviour."[103]

Wife beating was described by some as the "amiable weakness," and it was not just a weakness of the common people. During the reign of Queen Anne (1702–1714) courtly gentlemen were not averse to using the ancient prerogative.

> I cannot deny but there are Perverse Jades that fall to Men's Lots, with whom it requires more than common Proficiency in Philosophy to be able to live. When these are joined to men of warm Spirits, without Temper or Learning, they are frequently corrected with Stripes [a stroke with a whip, scourge, staff, sword, etc.]; but one of our famous Lawyers is of the opinion, That this ought to be used sparingly.[104]

Even Bonnie Prince Charlie, the much eulogized Scottish hero who led a wild and romantic, but doomed, rebellion, has been depicted in his final days as a "drunken wife-beater."[105]

In America, the legal history of chastisement was short and the practice not uniformly regulated, although wife beating was no doubt as old as the colonies. In the seventeenth century, the Puritans forbade husbands and wives to use ill words against each other or to strike each other,[106] but otherwise chastisement was missing from the statutes until 1824, when the supreme court of Mississippi acknowledged the husband's right of chastisement. The court maintained that in cases of "great emergency," a husband should be permitted to moderately chastise his wife "without subjecting himself to vexatious prosecutions for assault and battery, resulting in the discredit and shame of all parties concerned."[107] Similar decisions followed in courts in Maryland and Massachusetts, and the principles stated in these decisions were the same as those in Blackstone's commentaries on English common law. In many cases the wording was identical.[108]

By 1864 a court in North Carolina ruled that the state should not interfere in cases of domestic chastisement. The law "will not invade the domestic forum or go behind the curtain" but prefers to "leave the parties to themselves, as the best mode of inducing them to make the matter up and live together as man and wife should," unless "some permanent injury be inflicted or there be an excess of violence."[109] The principle of noninterference in domestic disputes mirrors the principle laid down in ancient Rome and is followed by law enforcement agencies throughout the Western world today. And this principle continued to be one of the main vehicles by which husbands were, in fact, allowed to continue to beat their wives even after the practice was made illegal.

The Rejection of Laws of Control and Chastisement

Although the husband's *absolute* power of correction did begin to be doubted in England during the seventeenth century, it was not until the nineteenth century that this doubt became sufficiently strong or widespread in England and America to result in a more thoroughgoing rejection of the legal support for various forms of control and chastisement. Let us briefly consider the legal landmarks in the rejection of chastisement and then place these in the more general context of the struggle to change the status of women in society and in marriage.

The first legal rejection of chastisement occurred in England in 1829, when the act that gave a husband the right to chastise his wife was erased from the statute book.[110] This, of course, was a far cry from actually ending such assaults and women still had no real protection from violent husbands and no means of escape from a violent marriage. Relief required much wider changes in the laws concerning cruelty, cohabitation, property rights, separation and divorce, and support, some of which was obtained in the period from 1850 to 1900. For example, in 1853 the Act for Better Prevention and Punishment of Aggravated Assaults upon Women and Children was passed, and extended to women some of the same protection already extended to animals who were cruelly treated. It allowed for a maximum punishment of £20 or six months' imprisonment, and the offender could be bound to keep the peace for six months following his release.[111] The Married Women's Property Act of 1895 added to this and made conviction for assault a sufficient ground for divorce.[112] Upon conviction of the husband, it became possible for a woman to obtain legal separation, custody of the children, and a weekly sum from her husband toward the family maintenance. It was, of course, very difficult to get a conviction for assault and the standard of proof was often so high as to make a conviction almost impossible. A divorce on the ground of cruelty was likely only if the husband's misconduct was persistent and sufficiently serious to "break down her health or render serious malady imminent." Women seeking divorce also faced the problem of the expense and difficulty of actually using the courts.[113] It was not until 1891, in the case of *Reg. v. Jackson*,[114] that the legal right of the English husband to restrain his wife's liberty by physical means may be said to have been completely abolished.

In America, wife beating was made illegal in Alabama and Massachusetts in 1871. It was ruled that "the privilege, ancient though it be, to beat her with a stick, to pull her hair, choke her, spit in her face or kick her about the floor, or to inflict upon her other like indignities, is not now acknowledged by our law."[115] By the end of the nineteenth century, the right of chastisement was expressly rejected. In 1894 the Mississippi court, which had been the first to legalize chastisement, repudiated that earlier decision and described it as a "revolting precedent."[116] Courts declared that "the rule of love superseded the rule of force" and "the moral sense of the community revolts at the idea that the husband may inflict personal chastisement upon his wife, even for the most outrageous conduct."[117] It was reasoned that since the time of Blackstone "learning, with its humanizing influences, has made great progress. . . . Therefore, a rod which may be drawn through the wedding ring is not now deemed necessary to teach the wife her duty and subjection to the husband."[118] The wives of those men who continued to draw the rod through the wedding ring usually were allowed to divorce, and by 1910 only 11 American states still did not allow "absolute" divorce for cruelty.[119] Cruelty, however, was not always clearly defined, and the American laws usually specified "extreme," excessive, or "habitual" assaults, attempted murder, or endangering of life. The addition of superlatives would imply that "ordinary" cruelty did not constitute a ground for divorce, and only excessive cruelty was sufficient to warrant action. As such wife beating had not been made strictly illegal; rather, a legal baseline of tolerance had been established.

Despite this legal maneuvering, wife beating was still quite common at the time the laws were being changed, and in 1910 it was written that wife beating continued to be a flagrantly common offense.[120] Although laws often reflect values and attitudes that are widely held and deeply rooted in a culture, and the changing of laws may be a means to change values and attitudes, there is often great resistance to such changes among police and magistrates as well as among the majority of the population. In many cases there is ignorance of the law and in others flagrant disregard for it. This was especially true in the case of wife beating. After nearly a century and a half of "civilizing" had been added to the comments of Blackstone and wife beating had been made illegal, the spirit of the old common law was still visible on the backs and faces of the women of Britain and America. There were still thousands of women who were "perambulating punching-bags, who knew this and who only wanted to get through life with as few bruises as possible."[121]

Struggles Against Subordination and Repression of Women

Throughout time there have been numerous individual and collective struggles against the various institutional supports for husbands' absolute authority over wives and their right to control them and use physical chastisement against them. Some of these challenges have been directed only at the laws and practice of chastisement; others have been aimed at property rights, divorce, guardianship of children, equal education, and enfranchisement.[122] The most germane and important struggles have been those that have not concentrated solely upon chastisement, or any other single issue, but have been oriented toward eliminating the unequal status of men and women, which is central to the problem of control and chastisement of wives.

One of the most outstanding early contributions to this struggle came from Wollstonecraft, who wrote *The Vindication of the Rights of Women* in 1792.[123] She argued vehemently against Rousseau's idea that women are naturally subordinate to men and should be treated as such both within the institutions of society as well as by individual men. Her primary focus was upon achieving equal education for women so that they would have the opportunity to use their abilities and become something other than the inferior intellectuals they were believed to be and, without benefit of equal education, often became. Her denial that women are naturally inferior to men, her assertion that they have been systematically denied the opportunity to develop and are conditioned to be inferior through various institutions such as the system of education, and her argument that equality is a human right were revolutionary and relatively unpopular ideas that would require dramatic changes both in social institutions and in the dominant ideology if they were ever to be realized. She cautioned, however, that simply allowing women to be educated without making changes in education itself would achieve little. She maintained that since education is oriented toward training men and women into "the opinions and manners of the society they live in," it could be "fairly inferred that, till society be differently constituted, much cannot be expected of education."[124] She hoped for a society in which all people were equal and that was truly a very different world from her own.

Within the next fifty years, very few changes occurred to free women from extreme control. For example, wife sales continued and were recorded in "Sale of Wives in England in 1823"; this practice persisted until the 1890s.[125] Despite the fact that the right of chastisement was erased in 1829, wife beating went on.[126] The First Reform Act of 1832 for the first time explicitly denied women the right to elect members of Parliament.[127] This deprived them of the small share they had in local politics, and between 1832 and 1869 English women had "less direct influence on public life than [at] any other period."[128]

Perhaps of greater importance to women during this period was the fact that more voices were added to that of Wollstonecraft; a debate began about the position of women and women started collectively to struggle for change. In 1825, Thompson entered the debate with a book marvelously entitled *Appeal of One Half the Human Race, WOMEN, Against the Pretensions of the Other Half, MEN, to Retain Them in Political, and Thence in CIVIL AND DOMESTIC SLAVERY.* It was written in answer to James Mill's, John Stuart Mill's father, claim that women are incapable of taking part in politics.[129] Of great significance in the area of women's activism was the trip made to America in 1820 by the Scotswoman Frances Wright; it has been maintained that she actually began the agitation for women's rights during that visit.[130]

Women's voices began to be heard more frequently as they worked for the causes of the oppressed, especially slaves. In 1840, a World Anti-

Slavery Convention was held in London. The presence of women delegates caused a furor among the male "radicals," who relegated the women to the galleries and prohibited them from participating.[131] Perhaps it was this explicit show of discrimination against women even among men dedicated to eliminating the inequities of slavery that ultimately convinced women that they must work vigorously to end their own servitude.[132] In London, the British and American women who were disgruntled with their treatment at the convention discussed the idea of a public meeting concerning women's rights, but it was not until eight years later that one was held in Seneca Falls, New York.

The first Women's Rights Convention produced a document modeled upon the Declaration of Independence. The Declaration of Sentiments began:

> We hold these truths to be self-evident: that all men and women are created equal; that they are endowed by their Creator with certain inalienable rights; that among these are life, liberty, and the pursuit of happiness. . . .
>
> The history of mankind is a history of repeated injuries and usurptions on the part of man toward woman, having in direct object the establishment of an absolute tyranny over her. To prove this, let facts be submitted to a candid world.[133]

A long list of oppressions and grievances followed. For example:

> In the convenant of marriage, she is compelled to promise obedience to her husband, he becoming, to all intents and purposes, her master—the law giving him power to deprive her of her liberty, and to administer chastisement.[134]

The women passed resolutions aimed at gaining greater control over their lives, including such things as control of property and earnings, rights to divorce, and guardianship of children. Women had become a group aware of their collective oppression and oriented toward bringing about far-reaching changes in the society and in the social institutions, especially marriage, that defined and supported the conditions of that oppression and denied them access to the means of ending it. Suffrage was included in the resolutions but it was not unanimously sought because some women were afraid that to demand the vote would make them appear ridiculous.[135]

This movement for women's rights, which was only later to concentrate solely upon suffrage, spread quickly and public opinion both for and against began to grow. Meetings were held, pressures were brought to bear, and some of the demands, often in diluted form, began to be written into law. In the same year as the conference, 1848, New York passed the Property Bill, which was amended in 1860 to give a wife full control of her own property and joint guardianship of her children and to allow her to enter into civil contracts in her own capacity.[136] Indeed, New York was something of a groundbreaker among American states. During the 1850s and 1860s various laws were put into effect throughout America and England that were to improve women's status not just in marriage but also in politics, education, and industry.[137] Of particular importance in Britain was the Matrimonial Causes Act of 1857, which "set up a Court for divorce and . . . made it possible to actually dissolve a marriage in the absence of a costly private Act of Parliament." The grounds included incest, adultery, bigamy, rape, sodomy, bestiality and cruelty. However, this became the jurisdiction of the High Court and magistrates did not begin to hear matrimonial cases until 1878.[138] Some cases overturned older judgments, others increased controls and exclusion.[139] One judgment that was reversed in 1852 involved a very famous English case of 1840 in which a husband's right to require his wife to cohabit with him was affirmed even if it required kidnapping, moderate beating and keeping her prisoner in the house. The defendant, Cecilia Maria Cochrane, had run away from her husband to live with her mother in Paris and after four years had been "forcibly taken captive" by her husband, who kept her "Lest she flee again."[140]

> [The judge ruled:] The question raised in this case is, simply, whether by the common law the husband, in order to prevent his wife from eloping, has a right to confine her in his own dwelling house, and restrain her from liberty, for an indefinite time, using no cruelty. . . . There can be no doubt of the general dominion which the law of England attributes to the husband over the wife; 'the husband hath by law power and dominion over his wife, and may keep her by force, within the bounds of duty, and may beat her, but not in a violent or cruel manner.' On the other hand . . . the courts will interpose their protection whenever the husband attempts to abuse the marital power. . . . [But] the happiness and honour of both parties places the wife under the guardianship of the husband and entitles him . . . to protect her from the danger of unrestrained intercourse with the world, by enforcing cohabitation and a common residence. Mrs Cochrane has lived apart from her husband for nearly four years, without loss of character, but she must allow me to say that her husband, with the highest opinion of her virtue, might yet be excused even by her, if he felt uneasy when he learned, as stated in the return, that she had gone to masked balls in Paris with people whom he did not know . . . he has a right to restrain her from the power to frequent such amusements, unprotected by his presence and without his permission. . . . She has not the right to bring his honour or her own into possible or even imagined jeopardy. It is urged that by refusing to discharge her I am sentencing her to perpetual imprisonment. Cases of hardship will arise under any general rule . . . and I cannot doubt that a greater amount of human happiness is produced in the married state, from the mutual concession and forbearance, which a sense that the union is indissoluble tends to produce, than could be enjoyed in the carelessness and want of self-government which would arise when the tie was held less firm.[141]

Married women always had been controlled and abused by legal loss of their property upon marriage and by the husband's right to exploit their labor and to appropriate their wages, but the Married Women's Property Act of 1857 forbade a husband to "seize his wife's earnings and neglect her and allowed her to keep her own wages after the desertion of her lord. Before that time a husband might desert his wife repeatedly and return from time to time to take away her earnings and sell everything she had acquired."[142] It was not, however, until the Married Women's Property Act of 1882 that the law giving a husband full ownership of all his wife's property by the mere act of marriage was finally abrogated.[143] Abuse in the form of cruel and blatant exploitation of labor as well as frequent and severe beatings is illustrated in the case of Betty Harris, a 37-year-old Victorian woman who worked for her husband in a coal mine as a drawer pulling the wagon through the pit in places too low for horses to pass.

> I have a belt around my waist and a chain passing between my legs, and I go on my hands and feet. The road is very steep. The pit is very wet where I work . . . my clothes are wet through almost all day long. . . . I have drawn till I have had the skin off me; the belt and chain is worse when we are in the family way. My feller [husband] has beaten me many a time for not being ready. I were not used to it at first, and he had little patience. I have known many a man beat his drawer.[144]

Explicit concern over the physical abuse of wives began to be expressed in 1853, and Fitzroy put it to the House of Commons that the country should treat its married women no worse than it treated its domestic animals.[145] In that same year, the Act for Better Prevention and Punishment of Aggravated Assaults upon Women and Children was passed (see p. 63).[146] Four years later, a special court was established for divorce and cruelty became one of the grounds for a judicial separation or divorce.[147] Legal redress was not, however, generally available to the public but was usually reserved for those who could afford to use the courts, and the Matrimonial Causes Act of 1857, like much legislation that was to follow, applied in fact only to extreme cases of cruelty, and exceedingly high levels of proof were demanded, as we noted in our discussion of the 1895 Married Women's Property Act. There was confusion about the legal limits on wife beating and this was reflected in Reverend Cooper's History of the Rod, published in the 1860s.

> Authorities are not agreed as to what constituted a 'moderate castigation', and the instrument wherewith it was to be inflicted . . . though a husband might not by law beat his spouse with a stick of a certain size, he might safely do so with a switch of a certain size or with his hand. Some men, not inclined to be severe, used to restrict the size of the thickness of the rod to the little finger.[148]

Throughout the latter part of the nineteenth century laws that improved the position of women alternated with retrogressive legislation that supported various forms of extreme repression. The Contagious Diseases Act of 1866,[149] one of the most repressive and degrading laws, was widely used to restrict the mobility of all women. It was meant to protect men from contracting venereal diseases from prostitutes and to protect "innocent persons who might be connected with such men."[150] If the police *suspected* any woman of being a prostitute, she could be required to submit to a degrading medical examination and be detained under penal law. The inequality of this law and abuses of it were notorious, and it meant that *most* women had been effectively prohibited from moving about alone or without being in some way visibly under the control or protection of a man who might vouch for her movements and attest to her innocence of prostitution. Chapman maintained that the inequality of this act, along with the Divorce Act, had the happy result of rousing the "consciences of both men and women; the whole cause of the rights of women gained an immense impulse from the crusade for their repeal."[151]

A new voice was added to the struggle in 1869 with John Stuart Mill's pleas in the House of Commons for women's right to equality under the law and with publication of *The Subjection of Women*,[152] an indictment of legal equality and justice as far as women were concerned. Mill pointed out that women were treated like domestic slaves who could be subjected to despotism, violence and all manner of abuse; yet they were not allowed to leave the marriage nor to seek legal redress.[153] He focused upon marriage and upon the power given to husbands.

> The sufferings, immoralities, evils of all sorts, produced in innumerable cases by the subjection of individual women to individual men, are far too terrible to be overlooked. . . . And it is perfectly obvious that the abuse of power cannot be very much checked while the power remains. It is a power given, or offered, not to good men, or to decently respectable men, but to all men; the most brutal and the most criminal. . . . The law of servitude in marriage is a monstrous contradiction to all the principles of the modern world. . . . It is the sole case, now that negro slavery has been abolished, in which a human being in the plentitude of every faculty is delivered up to the tender mercies of another human being, in the hope forsooth that this other will use the power solely for the good of the person subjected to it. Marriage is the only actual bondage known to our law. There remain no legal slaves except the mistress of every house.[154]

In support of his argument, Mill also laid to waste the ideas about women's natural inferiority and the sacred nature of the marital hierarchy, which had long justified their unequal treatment as well as much of the abuse they suffered in the home, in other social institutions, and before the law. He also pointed out the ease with which legislators, as well as others, accepted arguments that fitted in with the dominant ideology and noted the low standard of proof they required in support of such ideas, comparing the latter with the very high standard of proof that the same legislators required in order to reject the dominant ideology or to support any alternative thereto.

Five years after Mill's plea for far-reaching changes in marriage, the issue of assaults on wives once again became the focus of attention. Colonel Egerton Leigh made an appeal to the House of Commons for greater punishment for aggravated assaults on women. "He said that England had been called the Paradise of Women and he brought forward his motion to prevent it from becoming a Hell of Women." A debate ensued in the Commons, and in the heat of this debate Leigh withdrew his amendment authorizing flogging accompanied with a joke about "fair play for the fair sex," which Cobbe described as one of those comments "inexpressibly sickening in connection with this subject."[155] Disraeli then requested that the matter be left to the Home Office and a special parliamentary committee was created to investigate serious assaults on wives and children. A circular was sent to judges, court recorders, magistrates, and sheriffs, asking them to produce figures on the assault cases they dealt with and to consider the adequacy of the punishment for brutal (versus ordinary or trifling) assaults on wives and the introduction of flogging as a punishment.

Figures were collected on brutal assaults reported and subsequently dealt with by the chief constables for all of the counties of England and Wales in the five-year period from 1870 to 1874. During that time, 52 counties reported a total of 15,032 cases; 8,924 (59%) were assaults between men and 6,108 (41%) were assaults of women and children.[156] Although it is impossible to determine exactly how many of the assaults in the latter category were of wives rather than children, at least one estimate of the time was about four-fifths women.[157] "Ordinary" domestic assaults were not included in this survey, and for every offense reported numerous offenses no doubt went unreported. And underreporting was probably as high then as it is today. The greater reluctance to report relatives probably operated then as it does today. This reluctance and fear of retaliation no doubt deflated the figures on brutal assaults of women and children. Even these deflated figures revealed a daily average of over three assaults on women and/or children during the five-year period from 1870 to 1874 compared with an average of almost five assaults between men each day.[158] It cannot be stressed enough that these were only *brutal* assaults, not so-called ordinary ones. Conservative estimates of the number of ordinary cases of daily wife beating could easily increase this figure tenfold, and much higher estimates (based on what we know from our own data) would probably be more realistic.[159]

The replies of constables contained accounts, for example, of a man who "set his dog on his wife after knocking her down repeatedly" and of numerous incidents of kicking and clogging [kicking while wearing clogs] wounding, and sometimes murder. The section entitled "The Lash, and Punishments of Police Magistrates" included letters from magistrates concerning the acceptability of flogging as punishment for brutal assaults on wives. Although the eye-for-an-eye principle of retribution might have been fulfilled by flogging wife beaters, it was indeed a cruel punishment and one that the magistrates and Parliament were not willing to legitimize without some consideration. The majority did agree that the law was not sufficiently stringent and were in favor of flogging,[160] but the language of the responses often revealed considerable acceptance of "ordinary" domestic brutality committed by "noncriminals" especially since wife beating was thought to occur only among the working classes.

> October 27, 1874
>
> Sir,
>
> The popular movement in favour of the lash seems daily to be assuming shape and consistency with reference to prospective legislation as to the punishment of various cowardly classes of offences, and more especially wife-beating. . . . The use of the lash has been introduced in England with marked effect in cases of garrote . . . but these are cases which have to do with a hardened set of offenders. . . . The class, however, with which the legislation now contemplated would have to deal would be a non-criminal class, that is to say, a working class, providing honestly means of the support of themselves and families. . . . Have we not good reason to doubt that the extensive use of the lash as proposed may have the effect of hardening and self-abasing many of the men to whom it was employed, and destroying their usefulness as members of the community? . . .
>
> But while there are considerations to be weighed as against the use of the lash in the usual run of cowardly domestic cases, from time to time we hear of cases so atrocious in their savage cruelty and cowardliness that we feel the lash is their only proper punishment, or rather the necessary adjunct of a proper punishment. For instance, the ruffian who set his dog on his wife after knocking her down repeatedly, as recently reported, richly deserved the repeated infliction of lashes as a part of his punishment. The view which we take of the matter is that the lash should not be awarded in usual and ordinary cases of wife-beating unless two, or at least one, previous conviction has been recorded against the offender. In extraordinary cases of domestic brutality the supreme judges and sheriffs should have the option of awarding it, but that only on conviction by a jury.[161]

Men who earned a wage were less likely to be referred to as criminals and there was great concern that an honest, wage earning wife beater maintain his self-respect and utility as a worker rather than be brought before the courts and made subject to punishment. A punishment likely to damage his self-respect (flogging) was to be considered only when the man had repeatedly been before the courts for assaults that went beyond the ordinary. The self-respect of the wife, which may have been damaged daily or weekly, was not mentioned.

Another letter expressed the oft heard sentiment that the problem was unchanging: only the attention directed to it varied.

> Sir,
>
> Wife beating is unfortunately a crime that has always been prevalent in this country among the lower orders, and the beating, as a rule, has always been done in a brutal manner. It would be difficult to show that it is worse at

the present moment than ever it was, but public attention has been closely fixed upon the offence of late; and whenever an object comes under the public eye, the public eye becomes microscopic, and enlarges it to an enormous extent.[162]

A year after the publication of this parliamentary evidence, a prominent lawyer addressed the National Association for the Promotion of Social Science and commented on the savage brutality toward women, in Liverpool which was "certainly not exceeded in any part of her Majesty's dominions, and nowhere is the ill usage of woman so systematic and so little hindered by the supposed strong arm of the Law."[163] Three years later, 1878, Power wrote her searing account of "Wife Torture in England," noting the time elapsed since the evidence had been presented to Parliament and the failure to make any practical use of it.[164] She estimated, using the judicial statistics, that about 6,000 women had been "brutally assaulted—that is, maimed, blinded, trampled, burned, and in no inconsiderable number of instances murdered outright" during the three-year delay by Parliament.[165] She presented a long list of cases that had occurred during one four-month period.

Michael Copeland, who threw his wife on a blazing fire.

Frederick Knight jumped on the face of his wife (who had only been confined a month) with a pair of boots studded with hobnails.

Richard Scully knocked in the frontal bone of his wife's forehead.

Thomas Richards, a smith, threw his wife down a flight of fourteen steps, when she came to entreat him to give her some money for her maintenance. He was living with another woman.

Charles Bradley . . . set a large bulldog at her, and the dog, after flying at the upper part of her body, seized hold of the woman's right arm, which she lifted to protect herself, and tore pieces out. The prisoner in the meantime kept striking her in the face, and inciting the brute to worry her. The dog dragged her up and down, biting pieces out of her arms, and the prisoner then got on the sofa and hit and kicked her on the breast.

John Mills poured out vitriol deliberately, and threw it in his wife's face, because she asked him to give her some of his wages. He had said previously that he would blind her.

George Ralph Smith, oilman, cut his wife, as the doctor expressed it, 'to pieces', with a hatchet, in their back parlour. She died afterwards, but he was found Not Guilty, as it was not certain that her death resulted from the wounds.

Thomas Harlow, 39, striker, was indicted for the manslaughter of his wife. . . . in an argument which began because she would not give him twopence out of the wages which she had earned that day by hawking all day in the rain. The altercation ended with him striking her a violent blow under the right ear, felling her to the floor. She died in a few minutes afterwards, the cause of death being concussion of the brain. The prisoner subsequently gave himself into custody, and made a statement attributing his conduct to the provocation his wife had given him. The jury found the prisoner guilty, and recommended him to mercy *on account of the provocation* he received. Sentence was deferred.[166]

Cobbe's account of wife beating was the most thorough and well-documented treatment of the subject for almost one hundred years after its writing. Although her tone often was Victorian, she probed most of the same issues, questions, objections, and rationalizations that are heard today: underreporting, nonintervention, drink, blaming the victim, provocation, and nagging[167] are only a few. Perhaps the greatest insight was revealed in her discussion of the cause of wife beating.

> The general depreciation of women *as a sex* is bad enough, but in the matter we are considering, the special depreciation of *wives* is more directly responsible for the outrages they endure. The notion that a man's wife is his *property*, in the sense in which a horse is his property (descended to us rather through the Roman law than through the customs of our Teuton ancestors), is the fatal root of incalculable evil and misery. Every brutal-minded man, and many a man who in other relations in life is not brutal, entertains more or less vaguely the notion that this wife is his *thing*, and is ready to ask with indignation (as we read again and again in the police reports), of anyone who interferes with his treatment of her, 'May I not do what I will *with my own?*' It is even sometimes pleaded on behalf of poor men, that they possess *nothing else* but their wives, and that consequently, it seems doubly hard to meddle with the exercise of power in this narrow sphere![168]

The collective voice of women struggling for better treatment was increasingly being heard, and that same year, 1878, the Matrimonial Causes Act Amendment Bill had a clause tacked on to it that gave protection to a wife suffering at the hands of her husband by allowing her to use cruelty (defined as threat to her future safety and demanding a high level of proof) as a ground for separation, but not divorce, and to gain custody of the children and receive support.[169]

There was considerable controversy among Parliamentarians about this protection and some magistrates declined to act upon this and similar legislation since they thought it might be detrimental to the husband or to the sanctity of marriage. Wife beating was still widespread and yet in the late 1800s there were very few cases of aggravated assault on English wives in litigation every day;[170] the inaction was such that instances of women who attempted to drown themselves in order to escape domestic brutality were not exceptional or uncommon. Pearsall described the experience of Elizabeth Smith, whose attempt to drown herself in 1889 was stopped by a police constable. She pleaded, "Oh, do let me drown myself. My husband has been knocking me about." When the husband complained that he did not know why his wife wanted to commit suicide, she replied, "Yes, you

do. You told me to do it."[171] It was said that the law" [rather than protecting women] actually oppressed them. They were left homeless, helpless
and hopeless."[172] By and large, changes in the law were directed not toward
eliminating domestic assaults but toward setting limits upon how far a man
could go in controlling his wife.

This early legislation did so little to alleviate the problem that wife
beating was taken up as an issue by early 20th century British and
American suffragettes, and the Women's Charter of 1909 contained a section which was explicitly concerned with assaults on women.[173] The suffragettes deplored the lenient manner in which magistrates dealt with such
offenses and demanded that they act more decisively, imposing more fines
and sentences.[174] In 1910 they secured the introduction of the Assaults on
Wives (Outdoor Relief) Act, which if enacted would have given women the
right to claim relief from the parish on the ground of cruelty. But as if to
give credence to their criticisms, five years later, in 1915, a London police
magistrate came up with the wonderfully original opinion that "the husband of a nagging wife . . . could beat her at home provided the stick he
used was no thicker than a man's thumb."[175]

Legislation on women's rights and the responses to these laws were a
reflection of a long history in which the husband had complete authority
over his wife and was given the legal and moral obligation to manage and
control her behavior. The use of physical coercion was simply one of the
"legitimate" means traditionally used to achieve such control. The subordinate position of women in the family and in other social institutions
throughout the 19th century despite their movement into wage work, and
they remained the legitimate victims of domestic chastisement.[176]

The legal, political, and economic institutions were committed to,
benefited from, and reinforced the patriarchal structure and ideology. It
would have been inconceivable for them to have supported any other form
of family relations. All institutions were organized along these lines and all
people were socialized into the supporting ideology, which emphasized
authority, obedience, service, and hard work and rested firmly on the
ideals of love, dedication, and loyalty. These ideals, and their accompanying practices formed the foundations of the subordination and control of
women.

CHAPTER 5

BECOMING A WIFE

IT IS STILL TRUE THAT FOR A WOMAN TO BE BRUTALLY or systematically assaulted she must usually enter our most sacred institution, the family. It is within marriage that a woman is most likely to be slapped and shoved about, severely assaulted, killed, or raped.[1] Thus, it is impossible to understand violence against women without also understanding the nature of the marital relationship in which it occurs and to which it is inextricably related.

The following will examine the nonviolent nature of marriage and the position of husbands and wives and consider how their relationship can lead to the use of physical violence against wives. We will consider contemporary ideals about responsibility, control, and authority in marriage, the expectations for husbands and especially wives, and the socialization of young girls for this ultimate goal. This discussion will form a framework that we will then use in examining the biographic and dynamic aspects of the development of the relationships of the couples we studied as they go through various changes from the beginning of courtship through the first year of marriage and up to the first assault (see Appendix C, The Study). Throughout this discussion, we will consider the ideals and beliefs that are held about the nature of the relationship between wives and husbands and look at the way in which children, and especially girls, are actively socialized to fulfill their role in this relationship. Starting from the point at which the couple begins to develop a somewhat permanent relationship, we will focus upon the specific issues important to them at various stages in the early development of their relationship and note the changes that occur as the couple settles into the married state, wherein husband and wife both try to live up to their own ideals about marriage and at the same time to resolve the daily problems marriage poses to them. Of particular interest are the changes that occur in the separate and joint social activities of the man and woman as they begin to approximate more closely the behavior they each deem appropriate for husbands and wives. This shifting pattern illustrates the man's growing authority over, and possessiveness toward, his wife and his own relative social independence. At the same time it illustrates the woman's decreasing control over her own activities and the radical constriction of her social life as she becomes circumscribed by her role as wife, progressively isolated from outside contact, and increasingly subservient to her husband's expectations and demands. These changes give rise to the conditions under which marital violence emerges.

In subsequent chapters, we will examine the violent attack in some detail and consider the impact that continued violence has upon the marital relationship. We then go beyond the institution of marriage and the relationship of the individual couple and analyze other social institutions in terms of how they contribute to wife beating through a system of direct supports and ambivalent rejections. Let us now begin with the dominant ideology about what it means to be a wife and examine the process of becoming one.

Females are 'born' to be wives. To be a 'real' woman requires becoming a wife and to be a complete wife means being a good mother. Nothing less is really acceptable and little more is tolerated. Women are circumscribed by this, the only truly legitimate status they are allowed, and all of their activities are in some ways restricted by it and defined in terms of it.[2] Women, in their position as wives, become relatively separated from the world and isolated in the home, where they are meant to be subordinate to their husbands and to serve the needs of others.[3] This situation is part of the cultural legacy of the patriarchal family. There have, of course, been numerous historical changes in the status of women and in the institution of marriage: wife beating is no longer strictly legal and an absolute patriarchy can no longer be said to exist. Most of these changes, however, have done little to modify the patriarchal ideals and hierarchical nature of family organization. They continue. The beliefs are taught to all children and there are numerous means by which we institutionalize and legitimate the control that husbands have over their wives.

Most men and women marry, but the importance of this event and the ideals, expectations, and demands attached to marriage are not the same for men as they are for women. Marriage is thought to be of primary importance to women and of secondary importance to men. The ultimate goal is that the woman become a wife and the man become a worker, which usually defines their respective social statuses.[4] For a woman, the expectation is not merely that she become a wife, but that she behave in accordance with the expectations attached to the status and position allocated wives in Western capitalist society. This means assuming the major responsibility for domestic work and child care and providing emotional comfort, psychic support, and personal service to all family members in a spirit of extreme commitment and selflessness.[5] Erikson has maintained that a woman's very identity must remain sufficiently flexible to allow her to adapt to the peculiarities of her future husband and children.[6]

The Little Girl Is Prepared

The process of learning to become a wife is primarily a gentle, per-suasive, and subtle one. From the moment of birth, the little girl is sub-jected to selective and discriminative training from all those around her. Numerous attempts are made to shape and direct her behavior, to define her conceptions of herself, and to constrict her estimation of her potential. The little girl is taught that her major objective is to be married, that her identity is based upon the achievement of a successful marriage, and that the success of this, her only or at least her major, venture rests basically with her. Female children are encouraged to imitate the behavior and at-titudes of adult married females. They are given baby dolls to mother, playhouses, miniature pots, pans, and brooms, and bride dolls to emulate long before they realize what it means to be a little girl.

Conversely, little boys are not actively socialized to become husbands or fathers because this is not thought to be of primary importance in their lives. They are taught to think of themselves in terms of work, financial responsibility, independence, and individual development. Young boys are encouraged to take on as much independence as they can manage, and this is reflected in the freedom of movement they are allowed. The laboratory for life for little boys is the world, but for the little girl it is the home and perhaps a bit of the wider world. Thus, the girl is always more controlled and restricted and her movements more closely supervised. These restric-tions merely reflect the intention of giving her practice with those things that will eventually become her responsibility and of preventing her from straying too far into another world, where she might run the risk of render-ing herself less 'fit,' intellectually or sexually, for marriage.

Belotti's excellent book *Little Girls*[7] recounts with incredible detail the process by which these cultural ideas are put into practice by parents and teachers. Although Belotti was writing about Italian society, the process is basically the same in other Western countries. Belotti maintained that the socialization of children to fit the ideals of masculinity and femininity in-volves numerous methods in constraining and conditioning both boys and girls. This "negative conditioning" represents a "forced" integration of all children into the cultural mold of sex-linked identity.[8] The efforts put into this training are vigorous and include almost all of the behaviors that adults direct at children. Demands, expectations, rewards, and rejections form much of the conditioning that underlies the "daily gestures which generally pass unnoticed, automatic reactions whose reason and ends escape us."[9] Such behaviors are repeated by adults without thought of their meaning or sometimes even without knowledge of their consequences, yet they are the customs of child care based upon "an extremely rigid code" of masculinity and femininity. Thus, the breaking of this chain of conditioning is not easy because it "is linked almost invisibly from one generation to another."[10] The extreme efforts put into the socialization of children are a conscious reflection of the idea that sex role identity will not just develop naturally and that great effort must be exerted in order to prevent any real individual deviation.[11]

Belotti, as well as numerous others, argued that the hierarchy of worth of individuals, based on what they will become as adults, is marked by an overwhelming preference in society for male children.[12] She presented an extensive list of ideas that reflect this preference: an active fetus is a boy; a boy is born more easily than a girl; girls cry more than boys; if a pregnant woman has a good complexion she is carrying a boy, a bad complexion means a girl. It is also known that couples who have children of only one sex will have more children in their attempt to have a boy than they will in order to add a girl to the family.[13] In practice, there is less tolerance of the individual wants and needs of girls. Boys are more willingly breastfed; girls are weaned early. If a girl is a greedy eater, the breast is more likely to be removed in order that she learn not to attack it in an aggressive or self-indulgent manner but to suck in a 'feminine' manner.[14] Boys are also more readily left naked and allowed to play with their genitals, which often become the subject of adult comment, pride, or jesting; exploration among girls is suppressed, modesty is stressed, and the language contains no words to be used in commenting, jesting, or bragging about her sex organs or her sexuality.[15]

Through her analysis, Belotti repeatedly illustrated the preference for males, the tolerance of their behavior, and the ways in which they are encouraged to be active, adventuresome, and independent so that they grow up to fulfill their individual potential and to enter into the world.[16] Mothers indulge little boys, even submit happily to their symbol of authority.[17] Mothers shape the behavior of boys by reacting to them in "the same tolerant, compliant accomplice's attitude which [they maintain] towards adult men." Alternatively, a woman will shape her daughter in accordance with the image of females approved by men:[18] "The female is expected to become an object, and she is valued for what she can give." She must "renounce personal aspirations and suppress her own will so as to allow others to achieve theirs."[19] Thus, demands are made of little girls that train them to be passive, to learn to give, to serve others, to restrict their own ambitions and desires, and to be compliant. The house is always there for the little girls to practice the dull, repetitive, and solitary tasks that will constitute much of her life's work, and there are always brothers and fathers whom she must learn to respect, to take a secondary position to, and to serve.[20]

To some extent this training of girls is successful because it begins when the child is so young that there can be "no conscious struggle against oppression."[21] However, since such behavior does not come naturally to little girls, who are not necessarily suited to this inflexible position, their independent, adventurous behaviors are often actively repressed.[22] This repression may often go unnoticed and unchecked in the responses of adults, but it does not go unnoticed by children, and by the age of three little girls already begin to state that they would rather be little boys.[23] It is not that they want to be males but that they want to have the same independence, privileges, authority, prestige, consideration, and respect accorded their brothers, their male friends, and their father.

The following incidents from the lives of the women we interviewed help to illustrate the ideas parents have about girls and show how the girl's life is shaped and restricted by such ideas. One woman told us of how her mother's illness meant that she had to take over the domestic responsibilities at the age of eight.

> Besides that my dad was the type who thought that "a woman's place was in the house," to do all the work, and my mother had been in the hospital for a while and my dad wouldn't allow me out. I had to stay in and cook and do all the cleaning. I was off school about six months when my sister was only two years old. I had to run the house.

Although this little girl may have had more responsibility than other girls of her age, it is merely a matter of degree. The lives of most young girls are filled with efforts to teach them domestic skills and to afford them opportunities to practice and perfect such skills.

More important, however, is the process of inculcating the attitudes of love, respect, deference, and dependence that will best suit females for the secondary position they will eventually take in the marital hierarchy. This model may be presented through direct teaching of the child and reinforced through the child's observation of the behavior of her parents and other adults, and it is usually practiced in the girl's relationship with her father, her brothers, and her schoolmates. These relationships represent the most direct means by which the girl is taught to combine domestic skills with deference to the authority of those males to be served. But this is not just a lesson for the little girl: it also serves as a lesson for the little boy. He comes to see himself as destined for better things and somehow superior to girls, who are already defined in terms of their domestic role and their deference to males. One woman spoke of how her husband's attitudes toward women had been shaped by such childhood experiences.

> He thinks women are there for men's use.
>
> *Why?*
>
> Because this is what his mother taught him. The two girls had to work in that house, but the boys got let off with everything. She even made the girls clean the boys' shoes and press the boys' trousers.

Boys and girls are socialized into the ideology and the behaviors appropriate for female service and male authority, but the efforts to achieve this end must be directed most systematically at the girl, and it is she who may come up against the very harsh realities of what this process can lead to. The following incident made a lasting impression upon one woman we interviewed and illustrated to her, at the age of seven, that girls could be punished if the quality of their service was not thought to be acceptable.

And what about the kids? Was your father violent toward the children? Toward you or your brothers?

Just me. No, just me. I've got scars on my body to prove it. When I was seven he put me through a glass door. You know a big front door. . . .

What was the reason?

They don't like girls. . . . No, he didn't like me. For some reason. I honest to God don't know why. . . . One time, my mum and dad were fighting and they used to put me in the middle, like, "Tell your father this" and "Tell your mother that." It was a Sunday—I'll never forget it until the day I die. She said, "Go in the front room and give your father his dinner." So I went in and gave him his dinner, and my mother came out and she said, "Go get his plate and give him his pudding." I'll never forget it because it was apple tart and custard. And I went in and I said, "Oh, I need the toilet," and I gave him it. I just gave it to him like that and I ran up the stairs to the toilet. Next thing I heard his voice calling me. Oh and I was shaking as I was going down the stairs, and he took that plate of boiling hot custard and apple tart and smashed it right in my head, and split my head open. I've still got a dent in my head. And that was because I didn't hand it to him right.

In this case, the punishment was extreme, but the lesson was quite ordinary and is constantly taught in a myriad of more subtle ways. Not only must the little girl serve the male authority figure, she must do so with respect. If she does not learn both of these lessons she will not be seen as well suited for marriage. Thus, the process of restricting and orienting her activities begins long before the time when she begins to go out with boys. This ideology is so strong and the social pressure so great that by preadolescence a girl is admired and becomes the subject of pride if she shows signs of attracting boys and developing characteristics of compliance, helpfulness, and obedience, characteristics that will make her more marketable for marriage. The parents of girls who are independent and active or athletic call them tomboys and pray that this will be a temporary state that will pass as soon as they "discover" boys; the parents of exceptionally intelligent girls agonize along with them as they try to resolve the dilemma of being intellectually superior to males but socially 'inferior' to them. Usually a bright girl must either choose between her intellectual prowess and her heterosexual acceptability or learn to conceal her intelligence.[24] The pressure and the propaganda for marriage increase during adolescence and a considerable amount of money is made in readying girls for dating and for marriage.[25] In fact, such effort is put into insuring that girls become wives that by a very early age many of them find it almost impossible to think of themselves in any other way.[26]

The process of socialization is, of course, never completely precise, successful, or predictable; thus girls and boys may not learn to fit into their prescribed roles or may do so only imperfectly. It is also true that there are many contradictions in the ideals presented to children and the expectations held of them. In America, for example, there is a general ideal of equality for all citizens despite sex, race, religion, or age. Although this ideal is not fulfilled, its very existence can present the female child with a vehicle for questioning and possibly rejecting her unequal treatment as a girl.

It is not until a girl begins to go out with members of the opposite sex that the dominant ideology and the years of training and preparation come into direct practice. Thus, the lives of most women can be divided into two parts: being prepared for marriage and being married. The second phase begins when a couple begins to go out together. Although most women go out with several men before beginning the relationship with the individual they will eventually marry or live with, it is this final courtship upon which we will concentrate as we examine the ways in which the couple's life changes and the woman increasingly becomes a wife.

Beginning the Relationship

There is a considerable literature on dating and courtship. Most of it focuses either upon comparing the socio-demographic characteristics of the couple (age, religion, social class, etc.) or upon examining the similarities in their needs and attitudes. Much of this work leaves us with a great deal of information about each of the individuals and with correlations between their backgrounds and attitudes but without much insight into the development of their relationship. Such correlations reveal very little about the dynamic interplay between cultural beliefs and ideals, socialization, and the development of the husband-wife relationship. Yet it is this dynamic process that we must examine if we are to understand the context that may eventually give rise to violence.

In this section we will use material from our interviews with 109 battered women to follow couples from the beginning of their relationship through the first year of marriage and to the first assault (see Appendix C, The Study). We will examine the issues that confront couples at various stages in their relationship, the changes that occur in their social lives, and the patterns of isolation, possessiveness, domination, and control that develop. We will illustrate how these patterns form the basis of the violence that may later emerge. In order to examine this process of changing activities and commitment, we asked the women about the couple's social life and activities prior to marriage, during the first year of marriage, and throughout the remaining years of married life. We also asked about the social lives that the woman and the man had apart from each other during each of these periods. The patterns of these three separate sets of social life during these three stages in the development of the couple's relationship illustrate quite dramatically how the woman is increasingly isolated, controlled, and restricted as the relationship becomes more permanent and as she takes on the status and responsibilities of a wife.

When a couple first begins to go out, the specific question to be resolved by them is whether or not there is ever going to be a relationship. The relationship starts, as would be expected, without commitment from either party and with a greater concern about their individual lives than about their possible future life together. One woman noted this initial lack of commitment when discussing her future husband.

> He asked me out on a Friday night. On the Monday he said he didn't want to see me again. I thought, "Well, that's the end of that," and then the following Sunday I went to mass with my sister. He made inquiries about me at various places. . . . And from then on he wanted to take the relationship up again and go out with me again. And I thought, "Oh, well, he must be keen on me to make an effort to come and find out all about me and take it up from there." And I still wasn't terribly keen. I know that sounds awful but I wasn't really keen whether he went out with me or not.

During the initial stages of going out, couples spend time together in pursuits that lead either to the continuation or termination of the fledgling relationship. They lead separate lives, which consist of sets of relations with their family, a social life with friends of the same and the opposite sex, and a commitment to a job or to continuing their education. As their commitment to each other increases, however, they begin to modify their individual social lives in order to spend more time together and to demonstrate their increasing interest in each other and their desire to continue the relationship. At this point, almost all of the couples (93%) went out together at least once a week (see Appendix B, Table 1). Mostly, they went to movies, pubs, parties, or dances. Some went for walks and a few spent evenings visiting friends and relatives. The women described this as a very enjoyable period. The men were usually kind and attentive and the women felt appreciated and loved. The enjoyment in going out was based almost solely upon these feelings and not upon how often they went out or upon what they did when they went out. Many of the women and men became totally committed to the relationship and had no social life apart from it: 66 of the women and 45 of the men had no separate social life and never spent evenings out with anyone else, even friends of their own sex. The men and women who did have separate social lives were quite active. A little over a quarter (28%) of the women went out with their own friends at least once a week, and almost half (49%) of the men did so (see Appendix B, Tables 2 and 3). The women tended primarily to go to movies with their girlfriends, sometimes they went to a dance together. As the relationship became more serious, the women began to decrease the number of evenings they spent out with female friends. When they did go out they were more likely to engage in activities like movie going in order to insure that there would be no doubt in their boyfriend's mind about whether or not they were seeing other males. More men continued to go out socially with their own friends and to do so much more frequently than the women. The men tended to spend their time primarily in the all-male world of the pub and sometimes in pursuit of other women at dances or parties. There was less concern about engaging in the kinds of activities that would assure their girlfriends that they were not seeing other females.

Most women have been taught to accept this differential pattern of leisure behavior even though they may not approve of it. One woman indicated that her prospective husband would frequently go out drinking with his friends. When asked how she felt about this she said: "I didn't mind. I used to sit in. I didn't go out at all. Men think they have the right to go out on their own."

As courtships progress, couples spend increasingly more time together and the main issue confronting them becomes the degree of commitment they are willing to give to each other and the future they envision for the relationship. Before they agree to some symbolic indication of increased commitment, such as engagement, each person has great uncertainty about the status of the relationship and about the other's desire to continue it. Thus, they show their commitment to each other and their willingness to maintain or even increase that commitment by spending more time together, by expressions of affection, and by periodic displays of sexual jealousy.

Increasing Possessiveness

Incidents of sexual jealously, especially among the men, seemed to be the major source of conflict in couples prior to marriage; yet such incidents were not usually defined by either party as detrimental to the relationship. Instead, jealousy was usually seen by the woman as confirmation that the man was serious about her. When a man and woman have not committed themselves in what they see as a permanent way, such as marriage, displays of jealousy and possessiveness often serve as more powerful evidence that the relationship is serious than do displays of affection (especially since affection may sometimes be complicated by the possible motive of gaining sexual access). Such incidents were not usually accompanied by violence.

Did he ever hit you before you got married?

No. He once got very angry with me. He didn't hit me, but he got very angry. I thought it was because he was fond of me and he was jealous, but I didn't realize until afterwards that it was nothing to do with fondness. It was quite different. He asked me a lot of questions about who I had been out with before I knew him and he made me bring from the house a whole pile of letters and photographs and he stood over me as I stood over an open drain in the road and I had to put them in one by one—tear them up and put them in.

It is the man's sense of possessiveness and exclusivity that seems to develop more strongly during the courtship, and as the relationship moves closer to marriage he has a greater sense of his right to take over the woman and even, as in this case, to try to obliterate, if only in a symbolic sense, all her relationships with anyone other than himself. In fact, in the cases in which women experienced violence prior to marriage (23%), sexual jealousy, usually unfounded, was the precipitating factor. For example, in the following case, unusually severe for this stage, the couple had been going out for two years when a most violent episode occurred after she called off their engagement because of his continued affairs with other women.

I used to find out about him having affairs with other girls, things like this. . . . And this time I just told him, "Look, the engagement's got to get broken off for both our benefits." So I broke off the engagement and that was the night he struck me really bad . . . he kicked me with his steel-tipped boots and bled my eyes.

In this case the man wanted to monopolize the woman but he did not expect her to make the same claims upon him. Another woman described her future husband's violent reaction to his belief that there might be another man in her life.

One night, we were coming home, we had a good night out, too, and we were coming home. It was freezing, it was winter time, and I said to him, "Let's hurry up and get up the road to my mother's and we'll get a cup of tea." And he said, "You're just in a hurry to get your brother's pal." And I said, "Don't be so stupid, you're a liar." And he just had me outside my gate and he had me over the fence and I was screaming.

In the last case the confrontation began because the man was jealous, but it became violent at the point when the woman challenged him by denying the truth of his charge. The two factors of possessing her completely and of maintaining authority over her formed the core of this violent episode.

Most couples in our study did not have violent courtships. Those who did all believed that the violence would disappear once they were married and there was no more reason for jealousy. For those who did not have violent courtships there was no reason to believe that violence would ever enter their lives.

INCREASING ISOLATION

The period before marriage, though not usually characterized by violence, does involve increasing possessiveness toward, and isolation of, women as they come under the exclusive control of the prospective husband. Though in this period a woman may attempt to define the relationship in more egalitarian terms, the parameters of the relationship are largely culturally defined. The woman is encouraged to discontinue her independent social relationships, constrict her network of friends, and become increasingly committed to her future husband. Men are meant to adjust their behavior but not nearly to the same extent as women. Men are supposed to be attentive and to take the women out, but it is also thought to be their right to continue their relationships with friends, although they may reduce these contacts or even eliminate them temporarily. This period is often described by women as the best time of life. They are receiving the attentions of a man who is fond of them; at the same time they are somewhat free from parental control and are not yet subject to a husband's authority. They have few domestic responsibilities and are able to engage in a reasonable range of social activities. For men, this period represents a temporary loss of independence, which is often seen as a slight deviation in order to secure a wife. It is a period of inconvenience that men generally expect to end after marriage.

Marriage

The couples in our study got married or began to live together because they were in love. Love was seen as an indication of their commitment to each other, as a positive evaluation of the courtship, and as the factor that would serve as the underlying motivation to solve all future problems. This is the idea about love that is commonly held in our society, yet it is based upon what happens during courtship, a period characterized by relative freedom from responsibility and by the expectation that each party will make numerous compromises and departures from their past behavior in order to gain favor and further commitment from the other. This affection is not based upon most of the issues and behaviors that are to become a part of married life, and the ideal of love discourages couples from recognizing the real need to prepare for marriage. Thus, the man's and the woman's different ideas and expectations about marriage do not seem to need to be discussed and resolved: love will take care of that. This belief was expressed by three women asked why they married.

> I thought he was going to be steady and good. All the things I admired in a man I thought he would have, and the jealousy bit I thought was alright because that's how a man should feel about a woman if he loves her.

> I thought I was in love. I suppose that's what everybody wants to think.

How long did that last? How long did those feelings last?

> Oh, gee whiz, it's hard to say. I don't think really genuinely, much more than, oh gosh, five years. Really genuine feeling, you know.

> When I got married it was because I thought I was in love and I think because I felt a bit of hero worship for him. . . . It was a wee village and he was the best-looking guy in the village and he picked me. I mean I used to think he was great because he had all the modern style, he was good-looking, everything. I thought he was fantastic, so when he asked me to go out this was something great.

Since the period before marriage is rarely preparatory for marriage but is quite distinct in character, involving different goals and activities, it is to be expected that considerable changes in the lives of the couple will occur with marriage, when questions of financial support, domestic work, reproduction, and child care must be resolved. It is the form and meaning of these changes that tell us about the institution of marriage per se and about the use of violence within it. When a couple first begins to live together, their ideas about marriage are usually based largely upon the ideals that each has learned from parents, friends, school, and the media.

It is during the first year of marriage that we can best see what these cultural ideals are because they have not yet been modified in accordance with the material and personal realities of married life. The ideals about what a husband and wife are expected to be play an important part in the process of working out the form of the couple's daily lives and the nature of their relationship, which in turn forms the foundation of the continuing relationship. In this sense, the initial phase of marriage represents the encounter of cultural ideals and values with concrete issues of daily life. There is, of course, a dramatic schism between the abstract images of marriage as portrayed in women's magazines, men's magazines, marriage manuals, and social science textbooks. These images are often conflicting, presenting an irreconcilable "male" and "female" view of issues such as dominance, authority, control, commitment, egalitarianism, and independence, yet they provide the starting points from which each person's adaptation to their new life must proceed.

THE WIFE'S DIMINISHING SOCIAL LIFE

Becoming married is a process of change, especially for women, and one of the most dramatic changes that occurs is the extreme constriction of the woman's social world. When the social life of the couple and the separate social lives of men and women before marriage are taken as a point of comparison for the first and later years of marriage, the pattern that emerges very clearly illustrates the differing expectations and behavior of men in their position as husbands and for women in their position as wives. The pattern of these differences is not random or subject to a great deal of variation between couples, but rather reflects widely held cultural expectations about the appropriate spheres of husbands and wives.

Immediately after marriage a couple may continue their courtship pattern of going out together. However, usually within a few months there is a reduction in the number of evenings they spend out together and in the number of evenings she spends out with her friends, while there is an increase in the number of evenings he spends out with his own friends (see Appendix B, Tables 1–3). The types of leisure activities they engage in together and separately also change, as does the amount of enjoyment each receives from them.

A 22-year-old civil servant and mother of an infant, who had been married for 19 months, spoke about her social life during the months before she married. She and her prospective husband went out together about six days a week. It was generally accepted that each of them had the right to go out periodically with his or her own friends. Although neither went out frequently on his or her own, neither was restricted in what he or she did, and this was not a source of any problems between them. Soon after marriage, there was a dramatic change both in their activities and in their attitudes.

> When we were first married you couldn't find a nicer person, considerate. He couldn't seem to do enough for you. He really was a nice person then. He used to take me to the late-night cinema on Saturday night at the Odeon; apart from that, a few times out to visit his friends in the evening and never anywhere else. I didn't mind going out to the cinema, but I wasn't keen about going to see his friends [because her husband refused to include her in the conversation and his friends ignored her]. After we were married he would have to almost be forced to take me out for a drink. Twice in all the time that we have been married, he's taken me out for a drink. He just didn't want to take me into a bar. . . .
>
> He saw his friends quite a lot. . . . He used to have two days off and quite often he would say, "I'm just going to see so-and-so for an hour and I'll be back." And it would be more like six or seven hours before he turned up again. [When she told him that she didn't like this, he replied] that this was his only day off and he should get to do what he liked with it. And I pointed out that it was the only day that I see you, too, and surely I should get to see you as much as they do. He said, "You see me every day." But I didn't see

him every day because I left the house at 8:00 in the morning and he was still sleeping [he worked split shifts] and I was out until after 5:00 at night working and when I got home he was either gone or just leaving to go to work.

[Her husband restricted her social life to visiting the wives of his friends.] Well, I got to know another girl . . . I quite liked and I used to go and visit her maybe once a week. But then he decided that he didn't like her and I wasn't to go and see her anymore. Well, just to keep peace, I said okay. . . . I saw my old girlfriends once or twice.

Another woman discussed how their social life together diminished after marriage.

For the first few months we went out pretty regularly. He took me out but always for the same thing, always for a drink. He would never go anywhere else. He never varied it. It was always for a drink. About two or three times a week. . . . I used to say things like "Can't we go to the lakes?" "Yes, we will do," he'd say. "Yes, alright, we will do." We hadn't a car so of course it wasn't easy, but we never went anywhere, only for a drink.

How often did he go out without you?

He started to complain a little bit. He got a bit churlish about it after a few months and he would say things like "A bloke needs to go out on his own." He'd say things like "I think I'll join a snooker club." He joined and he started going to that. He liked that and he was pretty good at it and then he went to the Isle of Man with another man from the pub where he went regularly. . . . I remember being slightly—very—annoyed about that . . . and I was hurt at that but I didn't mind because I thought that men did go to pubs. I used to think that if I complained that I was going to develop into a nagging wife. . . . After about six months he started going out every night, and I was being taken out as a kind of—the reverse if anything. If I got out on a Friday night, it was "I haven't much money left" or "We've got to take it steady" or "We can't keep spending money like this, you know, we've got to watch it." He would say, "When you take a woman out, you have to buy her a drink. It's different when a bloke goes out. He doesn't drink as much." There was always a good reason why it was more feasible to go out on his own or with his friends. He did take me out, but not as often. I didn't like to complain because it was in the first few months of our marriage that I found out what he could be capable of.

In both these cases, as in countless others, the couple's social life was very active and enjoyable before marriage but changed very quickly afterward. The man resumed some or all of the exclusively male activities he had engaged in prior to marriage and spent more and more of his free time with friends (see Appendix B, Table 2). The woman was left at home, was often a second choice for company, and was rarely consulted on what they should do together. Now let us examine the factors associated with this very obvious and dramatic change in the lives of the couples after marriage.

THE RESTRICTING IDEALS ABOUT WIVES

During the first year of marriage, most of the couples did not have children and their financial position was not considerably different from that during their courtship. Thus an explanation of the change in their social lives does not lie in new domestic responsibilities, which might decrease the wife's free time (assuming that those responsibilities were hers), or in financial strain, which would require a cutback in entertainment spending. Rather, the explanation lies in the ideals about married life and especially the husband's ideals.

Once a permanent relationship has been established through marriage, going out together ceases to be the necessary means of seeing each other and a symbol of commitment or the desire to continue the relationship. These issues supposedly have been resolved by marriage, and the social life of the couple now becomes subject to ideas about the appropriate and acceptable behavior of a husband and a wife. These ideas, no matter how liberal, are based upon a patriarchal model and include the issues of differential authority, dependence, responsibility, and individuality. Initially, it is these expectations or ideals, and not the material demands of married life, that underlie the changes in the couple's social life and the struggles for and against these changes.

The man's commitment to marriage is traditionally seen as primarily one of financial support. This is thought to be the only absolute commitment a husband must make. Although men are sometimes not the breadwinner at all and are often not the sole breadwinner in the household,[27] the belief remains that this is his basic responsibility and that certain prerogatives and privileges are consequently his. Authority, independence, and freedom of movement are seen as appropriate for the person who 'represents' the family in the economic world, and entertainment is thought to be both a necessary release from, and a reward for wage work. Hence, the belief in the husband's prerogative to continue his separate social life. In fact, he may feel that he should at least periodically do things on his own or go out against his wife's wishes merely as a public gesture that it is he, and not she, who is in command.

The wife, on the contrary, is neither expected nor allowed to pursue former social interests. It is believed that her commitment to marriage demands an exclusivity not demanded of the husband, and this exclusive commitment to the relationship must be constantly demonstrated.

> You get married and you drop all your friends unless they are married as well and they start coming about. Where I was concerned all my mates, were nae married, and at the beginning they used to come to the house but then when they seen that Ian never spoke to them, they used to just go away. And then you didn't have the same decisions. I mean you couldn't say, "Oh, come on, we'll go for a coffee to the café." You couldn't do something like that, you see. Your life changes completely.

Her individual social activities either cease or are dramatically reduced, and the social life she does have must meet with her husband's approval. For example, she might be allowed to visit relatives, married friends, and sometimes have a "girl's night out." A woman has to change her social life in order to live up to the ideal of a good wife and to confirm without question that she belongs to a man, otherwise the marriage is thought to be violated or threatened. A wife must show her commitment to her husband, which necessarily means her growing isolation and his growing sense of control over her. As one woman put it, "He wouldn't let me out. It was alright for him, not for me." He isolates her in order to prevent her from violating her commitment to him and to keep her available for service: "He likes me in a box and comes when he needs me, but I'm not allowed to have needs."

The desire or the ability of the woman overtly to question her husband's movements is sharply reduced, and sometimes eliminated, after marriage. Those women who question a husband's behavior are liable to the criticism of nagging. The husband, on the other hand, gains 'rightful' authority over all or most of his wife's social movements, and it is not uncommon to hear a woman say, "He ran my life. I had no freedom."

The exclusive commitment that a woman must make to marriage underlies the initial curtailment of her social life and movements and not, as is often stated, the demands of domestic duties. But if in the beginning of marriage, it is the differing ideals about husbands and wives that allow him considerable freedom of movement and authority and contribute to her growing isolation and subordination, in later marriage her responsibility for domestic duties actually begin to take up her time and energy and further restrict her world.

THE RESTRICTIONS AND RESPONSIBILITIES OF DOMESTIC WORK

Child rearing, domestic labor, and personal and psychic service are thought to be the major responsibilities of the wife. Although she may receive some assistance with them, they are deemed her responsibility, and since the demands of household labor, unlike most wage labor, are constant, and have no obvious termination point. Accordingly, a 'good' wife has little time apart from her family and a 'good' mother is bound even more closely to the home: going out means leaving her duties and responsibilities. She must always plan her life around meals and minding the children. When a husband goes out for an evening or attends an afternoon football match or takes a weekend trip, he need not make arrangements for child care or leave sandwiches in the refrigerator, and certainly no feeling of irresponsibility or guilt mars his enjoyment. Thus, to be a good wife means to curtail or eliminate any activities (social, intellectual, artistic, athletic, etc.) that interfere with the fulfillment of domestic responsibilities.

The idea that a woman's place is in the home is often taken to mean that a woman should not work for a wage, yet historical evidence reveals that women have always worked. The contemporary situation, in which a large percentage of women do work for a wage, would seem to indicate that this statement may be only an ideal. The dictum that a woman's place is in the home is much more applicable to what she is supposed to do when she comes home from her job than it is to whether she should go out to work. Thus the idea that a woman's place is in the home does not so much mean that she shall not go out to work but that she should not go out to play. Household responsibilities are not seen as work that could be done by anyone, but represent both a service due the person in authority and a sign of love and loyalty to him. The cleanliness of the house, the preparation of meals, and the care of clothing often serve as symbols that a wife is committed to her husband, that she takes care of him and respects his authority and serves him, and that she has been well prepared for these tasks.

> I'd been brought up to clean and cook and all the rest of it, so I thought it would be great to run after him and cook and clean. . . .

Did you feel able for all this?

> Oh, yeah. I'd been brought from when I was eight years old. I was eight when my wee brother was born so I had to run the house and get up at six o'clock in the morning to get my dad's breakfast. So that's all I was used to. I never went to dancing or nothing. It was all that you expected from life at that age. Well, I never knew there was anything else to it. You know, get married, settle down, have kids, and . . .

The Restrictions and Responsibilities of Child Care

Another factor that causes a dramatic shift in a marriage is the birth of children. Children bring numerous pleasures to their parents in the form of companionship and entertainment, along with the enjoyable responsibilities of teaching them and guiding their development, but they also bring demanding and often unpleasant work such as endless cleaning, washing clothes, changing diapers, and the necessity for constant supervision. Although the care of children is very time-consuming, it is not the tasks per se but the woman's almost total responsibility for child rearing that brings about the change in her life.

The strongest case for the encapsulation of women within the home has been put by those who maintain that anything other than full-time care by the mother will result in developmental problems for the child. The idea is recent in human history and originated largely with Freud, but Bowlby certainly popularized "mumism" by using science not so much to explore behavior as to support the claim that the mother-child relationship must be constant or the child may suffer psychic damage.[28] The father is almost irrelevant in this scheme but the demand for the physical presence of the mother at all times firmly supports the principle that child rearing responsibilities belong to the mother, not to the father or anyone else, for that matter. This idea of so-called scientific fact has been greatly popularized despite the refutation by more sophisticated research,[29] as well as by the experience of hundreds of years of social life. Mumism remains, however, as a powerful ideological tool in segregating women either through institutional arrangements (women are encouraged to quit work when they have children, few day nurseries are available, etc.) or through guilt and fear in mothers of young children and through social pressure from family and friends.

One 19-year-old woman explained that before she and her husband were married, they went out three nights a week and saw each other most nights. He rarely went out without her, and she and her sister went to the movies together once a week. After they were married, he went out two nights a week with his friends and never took her out again. When asked if she minded, she said, "I didn't mind at first, but after a while I did. I used to have to just sit in the house because once Tracy was born he used to say, 'Well, you're the mum, you're the housewife, you don't get out, you have to stay in,' " When she told him that she did not like always staying in he said, "You're the mum. You shouldn't have gotten married." A mother of three spoke about a similar change after the birth of their first child: "And after I had Paul, I would keep on at him, 'Why can we not go out somewhere?' It would always be, 'No, I'm not letting your mother watch the weans. She wouldn't know what she was doing.' That was his side." Most women restrict their own activities because of the children; many husbands expect their wives to abandon all interests outside the home. Even simple and uncostly activities are rejected and refused: "When I got married, I only went out with him. But with the children and that wasn't very often because I thought I was needed in the home. . . . After the children I used to say, 'Let's go for a walk,' but no, the walking was over."

All men and women change their behavior in order to meet the demands of married life, but it is the woman who is most firmly associated with marriage and she who is expected to take on the majority of the responsibilities and make the greatest number of changes in her life-style. Bettelheim summarized the ideological supports for this process when he said, "As much as women want to be good scientists and engineers, they want first and foremost to be womanly companions of men and to be mothers."[30]

When a woman becomes a wife, she must give up most of her activities and aspirations and adjust her identity. She must schedule her work and pastimes around the work and leisure of other family members. She must fit herself into the nooks and crannies which are left after everyone else has been cared for, cleaned, served, fed and nurtured. The woman becomes increasingly isolated and segregated as her husband's sense of possession grows and as household tasks mount and demands for service become greater. These demands are heavily laced with the ideas of duty and morality and they take on an almost religious character. The husband's and wife's expectations may not be in accord and rarely are they truly negotiable. Failures to meet the husband's expectations do not just cause him inconvenience, annoyance, or disappointment: they are seen as affronts to the moral order and to his authority. The moral nature of the wife's obligations is a very powerful mechanism that causes her to suffer guilt if she is unwilling or unable to be the ideal wife. And the moral nature of these obligations means that a husband can rightfully expect and demand compliance from his wife. This places her in a secondary position with respect to him and invests him with the right and indeed the obligation to control her behavior by the various means available to him. Physical coercion is simply one of those means.

The First Violent Episode

The first time a husband hits his wife marks another change in their relationship. However, this event and the change it represents should not be examined in terms of what that relationship becomes after years of violence but in terms of the nature of the relationship at the time it first happens. Although it is not generally thought to be proper or masculine for a man to hit a woman, this constraint does not strictly apply to the treatment of one's wife. It is commonly believed that there are times when every woman needs to be taken in hand. Usually these are occasions when a woman challenges a man's authority, fails to fulfill his expectations of service, or neglects to stay in "her place." On such occasions men will treat women with disdain and use either subtle or obvious means to degrade, isolate, or ignore them. It is almost inconceivable that he would punch her in the jaw, unless, of course, she happened to be his wife.

It cannot be stressed too much that it is marriage and the taking on of the status of wife that make a woman the "appropriate victim" of violence aimed at "putting her in her place" and that differential marital responsibility and authority give the husband both the perceived right and the obligation to control his wife's behavior and thus the means to justify beating her. A social worker told us about a male client who in recounting a heated argument he had had with a woman commented, "I would have hit her, but she wasn't my wife." Countless jokes are told about giving one's wife "the old one-two," Jackie Gleason built a career upon his husbandly "pow—right in the kisser," and Punch has been beating the pulp out of Judy in front of audiences of delighted and impressionable children for centuries. But it is not humorous to read a newspaper account of an incident in which a man seen by a policeman beating his wife in the street and told to stop replied, "I can do what I like, she's my wife."[31] That it is the wife who is the victim of marital violence cannot be denied.[32] (See Appendix B, Tables 4 and 5.)

Of the women interviewed, 77% did not experience violence until after marriage, but most of them had not been married very long when the first incident occurred. One woman we interviewed told us that she was first beaten on her honeymoon and when she cried and protested, her husband replied, "I married you so I own you." Forty-one percent of the women experienced their first violent attack within six months after the wedding, and another 18% within the first year. Another 25% were hit within the next two years, making a total of 84% within the first three years of marriage. Only 8% of the women did not experience their first attack until after five years of marriage. Eisenberg and Micklow found in their study that 90% of the women were beaten in the first year of marriage.[33] The husband's sense of ownership and control is immediate. It comes with the marriage contract, and all the social meanings and obligations associated with the words "love, honor, and obey."[34]

Although both partners feel that marriage allows them to make some demands upon the other, there is a considerable difference in their abilities to achieve their own ends when there is disagreement. A wife's pleas, arguments, or demands that her husband meet his marital obligations as she perceives them may be met with compliance, excuses, indifference, or blows. A man should not be questioned by his wife (or at least not excessively) no matter what the reason. He is to be accorded the respect due his superior position and authority. So even if his wife has quite a legitimate demand, request, or complaint, she cannot go on too much about it because this is an affront to his authority. She must plead, cajole, and beguile and hope that he will be convinced. She is almost never in a position to coerce him by physical means and has neither learned the techniques of violence nor been taught to think in terms of physical control. The husband, on the other hand, feels he has a right to control his wife's behavior and authority over most, if not all, areas of her life; it is these beliefs, coupled with his desire to maintain authority, that lead to his first assault. The more general taboo that it is not correct for man to hit a woman is qualified—"unless she is your wife"—as immediate demands for control supersede demands for propriety.

The first violent episode may mark the change from a relationship involving no violence to one in which there is some form of violence. It is an event that is at the same time dramatic and insignificant. In physical terms, it is often insignificant, that is, compared to what happens later. The first act of violence commonly consists of a single blow that results in little or no injury (36% of the women in our sample reported no injury). Although the event may be insignificant in terms of the physical assault, it is dramatic in terms of the responses of both the man and the woman. Both usually respond with some degree of surprise, shock, shame, and guilt. Many of the men and women (41% and 71%, respectively) had no experience of violence in their homes as children, or in the neighborhood in which they grew up (34% women, 46% men), and simply did not believe that men could or should assault women. Those who had been exposed to violence in the home or were more aware that it does occur and that there is some acceptance of it in society, albeit not in their own family, were nevertheless surprised, shocked, and hurt when the man she loved hit her or when he hit the woman he loved. The awareness that some people hit their wives or even that some people they know hit their wives does not prepare people to expect or accept violence in their own marriage.

Arguments preceding the first attack are primarily associated with the husband's possessiveness and his ideas about his wife's responsibilities to him. These arguments center around sexual jealousy and domestic work but are often set off by what is thought to be a violation of the husband's authority. In our interviews, expectations concerning the preparation and serving of food commonly began the first incident.

> It was just he couldnae bear anything wrong with his food or—he was fanatic about his food—it was alright if he slapped his egg on and made grease all over the place. He could sit and eat it up then, but I was nae allowed to do that. I had to take more care over his food. . . .
>
> I did his breakfast in a hurry, and he complained about the grease on the plate and I probably told him I hadnae time this morning. . . . I think he said he wasnae a pig, he couldnae eat that, and he threw the plate at me. I think I picked up mine and threw mine at him. Then when it hit him, you see, I hurt his feelings more than anything else and he couldn't keep his hand off me. . . . He couldn't bear it and he hit me. . . . He grabbed my arm and pulled my hair. I didn't hit him back, I was too taken aback, you know. I didn't believe, I didn't know, that men could bloody well hit women like that, you know.
>
> I just ran down the road. You know, in the country it's different from the town. I just ran down the road till I got myself back together and by that time he had calmed down and had come doon the road, said he was sorry, and of course all was forgiven. . . .
>
> I remember he said, "Now look, this is not me, you know. I think It's terrible to hit a woman, and my temper got the better of me." And he was sorry and he would try to keep his temper in the future and I said something like, "Oh well, we'll have to stop having greasy eggs in the morning."

The initial violent episode is not treated as though it signals the beginning of a violent relationship. It is treated as an isolated, exceptional event, which is what one would expect it to be treated as. Only in retrospect does the woman begin to examine the first violent act more broadly, seeking signs that "she should have noticed." At the time the man often feels guilt, begs forgiveness, and promises that it will never happen again, and the woman is usually quite willing to forgive him once the initial shock and hurt feelings have passed. The relationship is reconstituted as though the event will never happen again. This reconstitution is based upon evidence, hope, and rationalization.

The evidence is that there never has been any violence before, that the husband rejects this behavior in principle by promising never to do it again, and that the specific issue that gave rise to attack has been resolved. There is no reason to expect the violence to be repeated. Sometimes the husband may attempt to free himself of guilt or shame by justifying his actions and by focusing upon the behavior of his wife, which he maintains provoked his strong response. If he has been drinking, he may deny the behavior or claim that the behavior was really not his but was the "drink talking." Because women have been taught to look to themselves for the cause of their troubles, the woman begins to search her conscience to see how she contributed to her husband's reaction. The idea that a woman does not get hit for nothing and that a wife has certain obligations that must be fulfilled prevails. She may blame herself for 'provoking' her husband and feel ashamed because his behavior seems to be a clear indication that she is not living up to her wifely duties. And she promises herself that she will do better. She attempts to comprehend the violence in terms of her own behavior: to see her own 'guilt', and both to forgive her husband (for perhaps merely overreacting) and to seek a solution by changing her behavior so as to give him no further reason for hitting her. Thus, the first violent episode is played down, isolated, solved, defined as insignificant, and forgotten. But the factors that give rise to it are much wider reaching than a late meal, too much to drink, or an admiring glance, real or imagined, from another man. The first episode clearly illustrates a growing sense of possessiveness, domination, and "rightful" control and these are the factors that lead to the continuation of the violence.

CHAPTER 6

THE VIOLENT EVENT

TO ASSUME THAT A VIOLENT EPISODE can be easily encapsulated in time and space ignores the enduring aspects of relationships that contribute to verbal confrontations and physical violence. Violent episodes occur in the context of the ongoing marital relationship and such episodes are inextricably bound up with the day-to-day activities of the men and women who live together. Thus, taking the beginning point of the violent event as that period immediately preceding it is in some ways artificial and misleading because the events are never ending. The cessation of one episode of violence may constitute the beginning of another, even though the next attack may not occur until considerably later. Unfortunately, social research is more like still photographs than motion pictures: certain aspects of social reality must be suspended in order to capture other selected aspects of that reality. This is merely to argue that it is impossible to consider and study everything at once; therefore, for the sake of presentation, we will treat a violent episode as if it does have an explicit beginning and end.

We will consider a violent episode as a discrete event. The dynamics of a violent event will be explored by using case materials from our interviews with battered women, especially the information relating to first, worst, last, and typical attacks, as well as evidence from other sources (see Appendix C, The Study). In considering the dynamics of a violent episode we will explore the factors leading up to an attack, describe the nature of the physical violence, explore the immediate and long-run reactions and feelings of the husband and wife, and locate these events in time and space. This form of analysis of violence has rarely been attempted, primarily because social scientists have not been able to observe interpersonal violence or to conduct in-depth interviews with participants in violent events. Yet, an analysis of this nature is crucial if we are to understand the dynamics of violence toward wives.

The Beginning of the Violent Episode

Conceptualizing the violent incident as having an explicit beginning requires consideration of the usual antecedents of such events. The research

97

relating to violent events, though admittedly sparse, basically supports the contention that violence between intimates is typically preceded by a verbal confrontation.[1] There is some debate regarding the seriousness of these verbal altercations: some researchers see them as trivial exchanges; others argue that they focus on serious, long-standing issues. After examining police accounts of violent episodes, Hepburn concluded that verbal confrontations that preceded violent attacks related to trivial matters involving various social processes.[2] He argued that violent behavior should "be viewed as behavior that is constructed in a situation . . . which involves accountability and claim-making behavior between intimates."[3] According to Hepburn, intimates like husbands and wives are continually accountable to one another for their actions, and each person is able to claim the attention, interest, and concern of the other partner; it is this claim making that occurs prior to a violent attack.

The events described to us were almost always preceded by a verbal confrontation relating to ongoing aspects of the marital relationship, with the husband or wife making demands on their partner or complaining about various transgressions. The majority of these arguments were not trivial but centered on long-standing contentious issues. Whether it was the first, worst, last, or typical violent incident described by the women, the majority of the disputes that preceded the violence focused on the husband's jealousy of his wife, differing expectations regarding the wife's domestic duties and the allocation of money (see Appendix B, Table 6). This pattern also emerged concerning the most frequent source of confrontations throughout the couple's married life. Forty-four percent of the women reported sexual jealousy (almost always unfounded) as the major source of altercations, followed by disagreements relating to money (16%) and the husband's expectations regarding the woman's homemaking (16%).

Sources of Conflict

Jimmy had assaulted his wife on innumerable occasions because of sexual jealousy.[4] He recounted his story to a reporter and stated that he had started assaulting his wife after only two weeks of marriage. On one occasion, he became so angry over one of his wife's old boyfriends that he viciously assaulted her and left her bedridden for over three weeks. He indicated that he allowed his wife no deviation from the rigid ideal of a perfect woman: "When I think of it, I didn't want her to be a human. I wanted a plaster statue of a saint." His saint could not look at or speak to other men without a severe reprimand from her husband.

Many of the women we spoke to told us of similar reactions from their husbands. One woman described how her husband, like Jimmy, was jealous from the very beginning of their marriage.

From the very start he's always been jealous, if he seen me even speaking to a neighbor and it happened to be a man, it didn't matter if he was nine or ninety, "What are you talking to him for? What can you have to talk to him about?" I mean, you could just be passing the time of day with somebody.

Another woman described her husband's jealous reactions, which began after nine years of a marriage that had never been marred by excessive jealousy or violence. This example aptly illustrates the development of a particularly violent incident that was preceded by a confrontation regarding the husband's jealousy.

If he felt like a break or a rest, he used to just go away on maybe the Friday night and come back on the Sunday. He'd leave me the hotel to run, the bars to look after, the catering and the kids and everything. He came back on the Sunday night and he accused me of having somebody staying with me on the Saturday night, which was not true. I mean if he had reason to believe that it was true I would have faced him with it, you know, but it wasnae true. The barmen were really awful good to me and the kids and knew some of the things he was doing to me and tried to help. He accused me of having one of them to stay on Saturday night.

After we cleared the pub on Sunday night . . . the barmen said, "Well, we better get home," because they both had daytime jobs, and I went down to let them out the door. The barmen went away, and I just locked the door, put the bolts in, and I just turned and he was racing down the stairs at me. He accused me of being with one of them again, you know, and I mean the two of them were standing there together. This is what I don't understand, if one of them had went away, but I mean you only needed to look out the window and he would have seen the three of us all standing there, but he really started, really beating me.

Other women reported that their husbands instigated arguments regarding domestic duties, such as housekeeping or child minding activities. One woman's description of the last assault she experienced during her thirteenth year of marriage illustrates this type of confrontation.

He started accusing me of things, you know, stupid and ignorant things. I'd cleaned the living room maybe and dust in the fireplace for instance, and maybe one of the kids would come in and have a biscuit or something and I would leave what I was doing and go and get them a biscuit, and when I came back naturally you think you've finished dusting the mantelpiece and you just leave it. He would come in and he would say, "Have you done this room today?" And I'd say, "Yes." He'd say "Did you dust?" And I'd say, "Course I dusted." Maybe there was a transistor sitting on the mantelpiece, this is just an instance, and he would say, "Well, you haven't dusted under that then." And I said, "I have done." And he lifted it up and he'd say, "Well look at that." And that's what used to cause fights.

Another woman recounted an argument over food preparation when discussing what usually happened before an assault:

I would be in bed and if he was in that kind of mood, he would pull the bedclothes off and say, "Get out of that fucking bed, come on, get out and get me something to eat." He might start on about my family or friends—it could be anything that would set him off—he would say, "Pull your face straight, you miserable bugger," or "There's never anything in this bloody house to eat. Is that all you've got?" I said we might have a bit of boiled ham or something. He said, "Right, put that on a sandwich." Or if there's cheese, "There's never anything but bloody cheese, cheese, cheese, cheese, all the time." So you'd get it, and then I might just answer back, and I'd say, "Well it's good enough for me, cheese, and it's good enough for the children. What's wrong with a cheese sandwich?" It would start off with him being angry over trivial little things, a trivial little thing like cheese instead of meat on a sandwich, or it might be the way your face just looked for a second at him, or something, and then he'd just give you one across the face, always across the face.

The other common focus of disputes leading to attacks was the expenditure of money. The women told us that their requests for housekeeping money and their husband's expenditure of money on his individual pursuits, such as a night out at the pub or gambling, led to verbal confrontations and violence. Money was also found to be a major source of disputes between husbands and wives in a Yorkshire village studied by Dennis, Henriques, and Slaughter.[5] They found, as did O'Brien in the United States, that financial matters were much more likely to lead to arguments than any other issue and these "rows," as they were called in the village, often ended in physical attacks. In describing the last time her husband used violence against her, one woman recalled the specific verbal exhange about money that led to the attack.

Well, I had friends in and he went away out and he came in the scullery and says to me, "Can I get ten bob for the bookies?" And I says to him, "I've no got very much money." So he went out and there was nothing said. The next thing my sister saw him walking back in the living room and she says to me, "He is coming back in, and he's in a hell of a temper. You can see it on him." So next thing we heard the scullery getting smashed up, you see, so I went in and I says to him, "What's wrong?" "Don't you f——ing ask me what's wrong," he says. I says, "What is it? What have I done?" So he slapped me across the face.

Although confrontations usually precede violent attacks, confrontations do not necessarily involve verbal exchanges. Some of them may involve only a one-word or one-sentence accusation made by either partner, which is immediately followed by a punch or a kick; other violent events begin without any words having been uttered. For example, Eisenberg and Micklow[6] and Martin[7] talked to women who were attacked while they were asleep. James Bannon, field commander of the Detroit Police Department, substantiated this process: "The provocation may be as non-verbal and non-physical as failure to keep the house clean or failure to make the breakfast."[8] A number of women told us of such episodes, and the following account illustrates a violent reaction regarding food preparation that began without a verbal confrontation.

> He had come home from work and he'd been drinking. He was late and I'd started cooking his meal, but I put it aside, you know, when he didn't come in. Then when he came in I started heating it because the meal wasn't ready. I was standing at the sink, and I was sorting something at the sink, and he just came up and gave me a punch in the stomach. I couldn't get my breath. He'd punched me and the wind was knocked out of me. I just sort of stood there, and I couldn't get my breath. I held on to the sink for ages, and the pain in my stomach and trying to get my breath, and that was the first time I remember that he ever touched me. It was only because his tea wasn't ready on the table for him.

Men who repeatedly attack their wives often do so because they perceive, as in the preceding example, that their wives are not providing for their immediate needs in a manner they consider appropriate and acceptable. These chastisements are sometimes not prefaced by an argument. In the following case a woman was peeking into her child's Christmas present prior to an attack. This behavior annoyed and upset her husband, who set upon her; only afterward did he verbally chastise her for her supposed failure to meet his expectations.

> He just saw me opening the present and he just flew into the room and just landed one at me. He always used to do that, then the arguments and reasons would come in later.

Gelles presented two uncannily similar episodes involving children's birthday parties. Both demonstrate the reaction of men who thought that their needs and desires should take precedence over those of all other members of the family.

> We were having a birthday party and my father was there. . . . Well, I had my son blow out the candles and make a wish and then help make the first cut. I had him give the first piece to my father because he had to go to work. My husband stormed out of the house. . . . He came back loaded that night simply because my father had the first piece of birthday cake instead of him. . . . That was the first time he broke my wrist.[9]

The antecedents of this episode related to the failure of the wife to meet her husband's perceived immediate needs, a failure that threatened his conception of himself as the head of the household.

A fuller understanding and explanation of confrontations like the above would lead far beyond their immediate and specific antecedents, such as a late meal, a piece of birthday cake, or a verbal accusation. They can be understood only in the context of the authority hierarchy and wider expectations of the men and women living in a violent relationship. One can sustain the contention that these altercations are trivial only if one examines and considers just their superficial appearance. The specific factor or factors preceding the violence may seem insignificant and the violent response totally unrelated to the context in which it occurs when the confrontations are analyzed without due consideration of the ongoing relationship. It is imperative, therefore, that we seek an understanding and explanation of verbal encounters preceding violent episodes in the wider patterns of subordination and domination in the marriage and in the expectations of the men and women involved. In a violent episode it is not necessarily the specific issue that is being contested but the relationship between the husband and wife. Couples usually argue over the same issues during their marriage and though these problems may not explicitly arise prior to a violent episode, they are the background factors that shape the marriage and its violence.

Had you argued about food or items of meals before, in the past?

Yes, I used to get annoyed because I'd have a meal ready for him and he wouldn't come in.

How had you usually solved the problem before?

We just argued about it. It was never, ever solved because he never improved. He still came in late for meals.

The violent men Toch interviewed might wait days to avenge a perceived affront to their authority or masculinity (one waited six months),[10] collecting evidence of the victim's continual transgressions, or attempting to contrive a conflict situation, or manipulating the victim into a position of perceived moral disadvantage.[11] A disadvantage, real or imagined, meant to establish that the victim had been unfaithful or had failed to live up to her obligations as a wife and mother. As one woman told us: "Imagination played a big part because he could imagine things about imaginary men. I think he felt guilty in himself and he had to try and get something on me."

Toch noted that this temporal and perceptual backdrop to a verbal confrontation and violent incident also included the man's assumption that his "wishes must invariably prevail"[12] against the claims of others. Toch aptly illustrated this sort of situation through a case in which a man reacted violently to his wife's protestations regarding his sexual transgression.[13] He became "very upset" and indignant that his wife should be annoyed when she discovered him in bed with another woman. According to him she should not be annoyed because he could do what he liked and her views were unimportant.

The husbands of the women we interviewed, like those described by Toch, did not like their actions, opinions, and beliefs questioned during a verbal confrontation and quickly responded to such challenges with force.

And how long was this after the argument began that he hit you?

It was just minutes. He came up the stair after me and we said what we had to say about it. He had his say and I had mine and he didn't like my attitude so I got it. It was as simple as that. You know, it really was.

Women were required to agree with their husbands and accept their position of authority regardless of its merit. If they did not, they might be summarily silenced through the use of force.

We were having an argument about something. I think it was money. I'm no exactly sure but probably because we didn't have the money for him to go out—that was what usually caused all the arguments. It was the first time he really hit me. It wasn't just a slap, you know, he didn't give me a black eye at first, but it was really a sore one, you know, a punch. Before then he used to shout and bawl messages, you know; I wouldn't answer back, didn't open my mouth. I used to just sit there or go and wash the dishes or something. But this time I started shouting back at him and that was it. He got angry and made a dive for me and started thumping me about.

At what point in the argument did he actually hit you?

When I answered him back, you know. He dived for me. No, I mean you couldn't really reason with him; he's too big headed, he's right. Even when he knows himself he's wrong, he won't admit it, you know.

Avoiding Violence

When and if a verbal exchange preceded the episode the women often attempted to alter the seemingly inevitable course of events by trying to reduce the potential for violence. Hepburn categorized various responses or postures that he argued are likely to reduce the possibility of violence.[14] The primary, and one would think potentially the most successful, technique is withdrawing from the situation. This opportunity is usually denied the women. Withdrawing from a potentially violent situation within the home is very difficult for a woman: there is no safe place to go in the home; children have to be attended to; and the husband might very well block her exit. A second alternative, according to Hepburn, is agreement with the accusations that the aggressor is making. Hepburn claimed that if a potential victim responds in either of these two ways, "the likelihood that the encounter will terminate in violence is reduced."[15] This may be true in certain situations, and is patently true if the individual escapes his or her potential attacker (at least temporarily), but there may be circumstances in which acceptance of the potential aggressor's definition of the situation will precipitate a violent reaction. Men described as "norm enforcers" by Toch actually see themselves as acting in a righteous and appropriate manner.[16] They are carrying out justice in their eyes. A woman who agrees, either truthfully or falsely, to her husband's accusations regarding her supposed infidelity or failure to meet his needs may actually guarantee a violent punishment. Gelles described long confrontations characterized by a husband's prolonged accusations as the "third degree." One of these sessions terminated in violence when the woman finally "admitted" to wrongdoing.

> He would come in and harp on a certain thing. And he would keep it up until finally you would admit to anything in the world to get him to shut up. He would keep it up for five hours and not let me sleep. I would say, "Yes! Yes! I did, are you glad?" . . . and then he would beat me.[17]

The women we spoke to described very similar all-night sessions that ended in violence when the perceived transgression was confessed.

Women attempt to avoid or divert the violence by other means: they try to reason with their husbands or they seek an alternative, nonviolent solution during the verbal confrontation. Some try to withdraw from the argument by not arguing. Other women take the opposite tack and attempt to point out injustices in their husband's claims or put their own point of view. On some occasions such efforts to avoid violence are successful.

> Well, if I thought I had time, you know, I'd sort of slowly back down, and sort of, you know, overcome the situation by changing the subject into something else. But other times, well, usually, I didn't, and I got it.

Regardless of the reaction from the woman she usually is unable to avoid or prevent a violent response. Almost 70% of the women told us that arguments with their husbands nearly always, or often, ended in an attack. The verbal confrontations were usually short, most lasting less than five minutes. Only a very few women on very infrequent occasions responded to their husband's verbal aggression by initiating violence.

VERBAL CONFRONTATIONS AND AUTHORITY

The specific issues over which couples argue are diverse, and throughout her married life a woman may be attacked after confrontations regarding almost anything. One woman wrote to Martin, author of *Battered Wives:*

> I have been slapped for saying something about politics, for having a different view of religion, for swearing, for crying, for wanting to have intercourse. I have been threatened, slapped, and beaten after stating bitterly that I didn't like what he was doing with another woman.[18]

This account illustrates that husbands believe that their wives cannot and should not make certain claims upon them. Claim making is not a two-sided process. Men who use violence consider it their right and privilege as men and as heads of households to make claims of their wives; if their demands are not met, as in the cases of the timing of meals or of responding to sexual advances, the woman may be punished. Conversely, the man does not believe that his wife can make such strong claims relating to his actions; he considers her claim making to be extraordinary and inappropriate and she might be silenced through the use of force.

Dennis, Henriques, and Slaughter captured this dual morality in their study of a Yorkshire community in the early fifties. The men were taught to think that women are incapable of commenting upon affairs that occur outside the home. The men felt that a husband's duty to his family extended only to the earning of the family income; any questioning of his autonomy of action was seen as unacceptable. Many men in this village saw as unreasonable their wife's requests that they talk to her more or spend less time with their male friends or with other women. Dennis, Henriques, and Slaughter recounted the story of a man who openly boasted to his wife and others of his extramarital conquests. He spent the bulk of his earnings on himself and thought his wife's complaints regarding this behavior were quite extraordinary.

> I bought her a new wireless, and then a television, and I hired a car for the holidays, and she still natters about what time I come in and where I've been, and can she have a extra shilling or two. There's no pleasing 'em.[19]

This view was held by most men in the village, some of whom backed it up with the use of force.

Toch found that violent men often view other people as objects to be exploited in their attempts to meet their own needs. They elevate the fulfillment of their personal desires to the status of a "natural law," operating on the premise that their own welfare is of primary and exclusive concern to others. In arguments and confrontations preceding their use of violence these men rarely note or admit to the discontent of the other person and to their concerns and needs, and this is especially true in relationships with women. Toch wrote: "In other words, there is a consistent tendency on his part to view women as objects of exploitation."[20]

Johnston interviewed a man called Adam who also found it hard to accept or consider his wife's views.[21] According to Adam's report about himself, he was a highly intelligent man who commanded his wife to work, keep house, pay the bills, and manage the money while he got on with the more important work for which he was "better suited." According to him, his wife had continually failed to meet his expectations and fulfill his wishes regarding the performance of the various tasks she was allotted. He demanded rigid adherence to his wishes and often attacked his wife when she failed to live up to his prescriptions by saying things that he defined as stupid or by smoking or by attempting to defy him. Adam exhibited very little regard for his wife's needs and wishes, they were irrelevant to the relationship, though, according to his own report, his rigid position caused repeated quarrels that ended in his using violence. If his wife behaved in a manner he thought inappropriate or attempted to redress what she saw as an injustice he, like the husbands we heard about, would use force to silence her.

This predisposition is not evident only in men who attack their wives. Many men in Western society learn to expect that their wishes and concerns come first, that because they are males and heads of households they have certain prerogatives and rights that supersede those of women— especially in the family where the rights of males over females are clearly defined from a very early age. The difference between violent men and other males is that the former are prepared to use physical means to enforce or reinforce their own views. When men do use force to chastise and punish their wives for failing to live up to their unilateral standards, they can be very violent indeed.

The Nature of the Violence and the Reactions of Women

Research conducted in the United States has indicated that men are likely to use diverse forms of violence against their wives. Eisenberg and Micklow found that men would push or shove their wives, slap and kick them, and in some cases attempt to choke or smother them.[22] Gelles's research revealed similar patterns. Men pushed, choked, punched, and kicked their wives.[23] The husbands of the women we interviewed also used various forms of physical force when they attacked their wives. The violence ranged from a single slap, usually experienced early in the marriage, to an attack involving punching, kicking, and choking; on occasion the men would use belts, bottles, or weapons. The most typical attack involved punches to the face and/or body and kicks (see Appendix B, Table 7). Like Eisenberg and Micklow we found that most men used several types of physical force when attacking their wives.

Gross categories such as slapping or punching fail to provide any real clues into the nature and severity of attacks since even a slap or a punch can result in serious injuries, such as a fractured jaw. In order to understand precisely what constitutes a physical attack we must turn to the detailed accounts of women subjected to these attacks.

The men usually employed various forms of violence but on occasion a man would use only one type of physical force as the following example illustrates.

> Well, he just started shouting and bawling and then he just called me names, you know, swearing at me. And he started hitting me, punching me. He kept punching my face all the time—it was my nose. And he wouldn't let me sit down or anything. He made me stand in the middle of the floor. He wouldn't let me go into bed and I was screaming and he just kept punching my face. He'd walk away, maybe go into the kitchenette, come back, and

have another punch at me. . . . All night. I wasn't to sit on the chair or the floor. I was to stand there. He fell asleep and I went into bed and he woke up in the morning and he asked me what had happened to my face because my nose was all swollen and bruised. I told him it was him, but he didn't say anything. Then that night he came back and thumped me again, and it was just the same routine.

This account illustrates that being punched can mean much more than one might envisage. The woman in this example experienced "only" bruising from numerous punches; another woman described her sensations after only one punch from her husband.

He punched me so hard that I thought my jaws were broken and every tooth in my mouth. I was convinced of it. All I could hear was grind, grind, grind, and I thought, "Oh Jesus, I haven't got any teeth." I could have sworn I had lost every tooth.

Many men use their feet in attacks on their wives. Commonly, the woman is pushed or punched to the floor and then severely kicked in the head and body.[24]

So he got into bed and I got up and he very calmly got up. He put his shoes on and his trousers and I got kicked from one end of the room to the other. It was so bad he actually broke his foot kicking me.

The dynamic aspects of violence to wives cannot be captured in a gross quantitative manner. Only in the first assault in a marriage, as discussed in Chapter 5, is the violence usually of a singular nature, such as one slap or punch. In the majority of incidents men use various forms of violence, as the following incidents reveal.

He punched me, he kicked me, he pulled me by the hair. My face hit a step. He had his bare feet, you know, with being in bed, and he just jumped up and he pulled on his trousers and he was kicking me. If he had his shoes on, God knows what kind of face I would have had. As it was I had a cracked cheek bone, two teeth knocked out, cracked ribs, broken nose, two beautiful black eyes—it wasn't even a black eye, it was my whole cheek was just purple from one eye to the other. And he had got me by the neck and, you know, he was trying, in fact, practically succeeded in strangling me. I was choking, I was actually at the blacking out stage. I was trying to pull his fingers away, with me trying to pull his fingers away, I scratched myself, you know, trying to get his fingers off. He hit me and I felt my head, you know, hitting the back of the lock of the door. I started to scream and I felt as if I'd been screaming for ages. When I came to he was pulling me up the stair by the hair. I mean, I think it was the pain of him pulling me up the stair by the hair that brought me round again. I can remember going up the stair on my hands and knees and the blood—I dinnae know where it was coming from—it was just dripping in front of my face and I was actually covered in blood. I just got to the kitchen door and he just walked straight to his bed. I just filled the sink with cold water, put a dish towel in it, and held it up to my face. I remember I went through to the living room and I fell asleep and I woke up in the morning with this matted dish towel and, God I couldn't move. There wasn't a bit of me that wasnae sore.

He tried to strangle me. He was sitting on me and he had his hand over my mouth and my nose and I couldn't breathe, you know. I was suffocating and when I came round I went to throw myself out of the window. I just didn't know anything. My mind just said "escape." I had marks all round my neck. I had two black eyes. I had severe marks to my face. I had bruises all down my legs. I got at him cos he spent all the money and of course he said it was my fault, so an argument broke out. We had three stone steps and he couldn't contain his temper and he exploded and he had one of these wire spring belts and he flew at me and pulled me by the hair down these stone steps. He hauled me out the back door and kicked me stupid with his great takkity boots and I didn't have a place on my body not hit. And then he had his belt and I was whipped over the shoulders everywhere, on my face, and everything, and this was to teach me not to argue with him.

As these examples illustrate, men who attack their wives often use extreme force and they do not restrain themselves because they are attacking a woman. As one confessed wife assaulter put it in a newspaper interview, "She was terrified of me. I would hit her as hard as I would any bloke."[25]

The Response of Women

Regardless of the severity of the attacks, women in Britain and the United States usually report that they seldom attempt to respond to violence with force. Often it is impossible to retaliate. The superior strength of men allows them to immobilize their wives' hands and/or feet or enables them to force the woman down to the floor or against a wall. As one woman told us, "I'd have loved to have been able to hit him back, but I just couldn't bring myself to do it. In fact, I was in situations that I couldn't hit back. In fact, the only thing I've done is bite his finger." In an interview with the American psychologist Palmer, a woman who was imprisoned for killing her husband after years of physical abuse discussed her inability to meet force with force: "One time he almost choked me to death. He was six foot-two, weighed a hundred and ninety pounds and there wasn't a thing I could do."[26]

The percentage of women in our study who attempted to hit back was about the same whether it was the first, worst, or last violent episode. When we asked about their typical response only a very small number (four women out of the entire group) said that they always tried to hit their husbands back. The majority said they never (33%) or seldom (42%) attempted to use force. The remaining 24% of the women attempted to use force on a few occasions. One woman described the only time she responded violently to her husband.

There was one time I hit him back. He started to hit me and I really sort of broke. I never used to hit him back when he hit me, but I sort of really cracked. He'd a good drink in him so that he wasn't very sober, and I just took him by the hair and I banged his face on the back of the chair and his glasses cut into his nose and his nose all bled. And I just screamed at him, and I'm shaking him by the hair, and I'm saying, "Are you going to hit me again?" And I just kept shouting, "Are you going to hit me again?" And, as I say, I shook him by the hair and I banged his face on the back of the chair and he was so drunk that he couldn't sort of help himself so he just sat down.

This is a very unusual reaction.

The majority of the women we interviewed responded to a violent attack by remaining physically passive. Women learn that it is futile to attempt to match the physical force of their husbands and try primarily to protect themselves during attacks. Two women summed up the experience of most of the women: "Well, I didn't try to hit him back. It just got worse if I did." "I just tried to defend myself, got my arms up to save myself." A woman who reported receiving only one black eye in all of the attacks she experienced during her married life indicated that this was because she learned to protect herself: "Just the one, and I never got a black eye again. It was always, I held my hand up to my face. That's the first thing I ever done as soon as he made a move, you know, automatically." Another common response was to scream or cry but this reaction often led to even greater violence. One woman described how she learned that it was always best to remain silent and passive.

> I found out the best way not to get him into a tirade would be not to cry out loud, do you know what I mean, not to cry out. I know it sounds silly, but if you can just think to yourself, "I'm going to get two or three and then he'll stop," that wasn't bad. He could just stop after two or three, but he wouldn't if you cried out or you protested.

Screaming and crying was likely to arouse the curiosity of outsiders, who usually did not intervene but who might learn that the public image of the husband as a decent, upstanding fellow was not the same as his private behavior.

Eisenberg and Micklow also found that only 30% of the women they studied usually attempted to defend themselves and even fewer tried to retaliate. The women they interviewed agreed that "the severity of the beating increased proportionately with their amount of resistance."[27] Not only do men who attack their wives not like their opinions and desires to be questioned or thwarted, they also do not like their wives to resist punishment. Women are supposed to accept physical abuse because their husbands feel that it is justified.

Physical Injuries

The physical consequences of violent events were often visible on the faces and limbs of the women we interviewed. It is difficult to appreciate the seriousness of the injuries received in a particular assault or from repeated attacks over a period of several years. The women reported that the usual assault resulted in bruising of the face, limbs, or body (see Appendix B, Table 8). The bruises ranged from minor discolorations of the skin to severe contusions requiring weeks to heal.

> The way it was described to me [by a doctor], my leg that time was like a raw piece of meat hanging up in a butcher's window. That bruise never left for about two months; two months it took for that bruise to go away. It bruised from there [top of the hip] down to there [the ankle]. I could hardly walk, and I had severe bruising down my left lung as well.

Bruising usually was coupled with other injuries such as cuts to the face or body, abrasions, torn hair, and fractures.

> Just mostly bruises and black eyes. Oh, sorry, I forgot, he knocked my top teeth out. That's how I've got falsers. There was one, two, three that he knocked out.

> My nose was bleeding and my lip was burst. I had a black eye. And the back of my head was all bruised and my legs—all over.

> Oh, I was knocked all about the mouth and bruised quite heavily over the face and my mouth and all up my arms and all—[he] pulled my hair. I wear a wig now because my hair, I don't know if you notice it, but my hair's very thin, it's well pulled out, and I've padding under it.

> Well, as I say, I had a black eye. I was bruised all over my chest, arms, and generally shocked, you know.

> Well, my lip was split open, I got four or five stitches in my mouth, and I'd two black eyes, and I had about two bruises on my legs.

These are common results of a violent attack but some injuries are more severe. Women are sometimes knocked unconscious.

> I mean, he had knocked me completely out. He knocked me a punch . . . two or three times he knocked me clean out.

But this did not necessarily mean that the attack ceased. One woman described the result of a particularly brutal attack during most of which she was unconscious.

> He grabbed me from the chair, dragged me into the sitting room, to the hall, pulled me halfway up the stairs, then pulled me back down and started to kick and stand on me. And that was in front of his own mum. I was knocked out with the first couple of blows he gave me. He was hammering into something that was just like a cushion on the floor. I had a broken rib, broken leg on the right side, two front teeth knocked out, burst chin—I've still got the scar—I had five stitches, and a broken arm on the right side.

The multiple injuries sustained by this woman were rather unusual. However, nearly 9% of the women reported receiving fractures or losing teeth at some time during their married life.

I was kicked and bruised and I had a sprained wrist and my head was—he had pulled out half the hair on my head—and my mouth was bleeding and I'd lost a tooth.

I had seven stitches for my lip and went to the hospital for a cracked rib and elbow.

The injuries often required medical attention and even hospitalization. Nearly 80% of the women reported going to a doctor at least once during their marriage for injuries resulting from attacks by their husbands; nearly 40% said that they sought medical attention on five separate occasions. Many women thought they required medical care but were prevented by their husbands from seeking such attention. Untreated injuries and vicious attacks often result in permanent disfigurement such as loss of hair, improperly healed bones, and severe scars from cuts, burns, and abrasions.

The doctor says if we had got him that night he would be put away that night. He would be put away for years because they couldn't set my jaw. I don't know if you can notice it, but I've no cheekbone—it was pushed in—I've no cheekbone on this side and the jawbone's out of line. I can't clench my teeth like other people because with me not going and getting it seen to, it healed up itself and it's healed the wrong way. I still have no nerve endings on this lip. He punched me right from that eye down to here in a triangle and I didn't feel a thing. It's actually numb. I have no nerve endings, you know. With the bones being broken the nerves have all been cut.

The women we interviewed, like the women studied by Eisenberg and Micklow, suffered serious woundings, innumerable bloodied noses, fractured teeth and bones, concussions, miscarriages and severe internal injuries that often resulted in permanent scars, disfigurement and sometimes persistent poor health.

Physical injuries are often coupled with serious emotional distress. Many women are chronically emotionally upset and/or depressed about the attacks and the prospects of the next one. For some women the emotional distress is so severe that medication and even hospitalization become necessary.

Just bang, bang, bang, and me heart used to be going fifty to the dozen. And I used to be shaking like a leaf [days after the attack]. But I hadn't to show him this, and I used to say to him, "I don't feel well." [He would say] "There's fuck all up with you, if you'd been through what I'd been through in this last year, you'd have been alright," and all this lot, you know, as if to say, "Look at the cover. There's nothing wrong with the cover. Don't bother looking at the inner tube."

I was always terrified. My nerves were getting the better of me in the finish, you know. I was getting so I used to shake through bloody fear. He knew this and I think he loved this.

Oh, I was really depressed, just sit and bubble for the least thing. If anybody said boo to me, I would bubble. I looked at myself and I said, I'm a grown woman, what am I sitting bubbling for. I must have cried a river now, all the years I've cried. I must have cried a river.

Presence of Others During an Altercation

Violent events like the ones described in the foregoing accounts usually occur in the home but this does not necessarily mean that they are not observed by others. Gelles concluded from his research in America that "violence in the home is a private affair with no bystanders."[28] This assertion is not borne out by our research nor, oddly enough, by Gelles's own evidence.[29] We found that 59% of the first violent incidents did occur without anyone observing them, but over 75% of the women reported that the last attack was observed by at least one other person, usually their children. Over the course of a violent marriage there was an increase in the probability that others would be present during an assault. This pattern is not surprising: young married couples are usually childless or have only infant children, who are not thought of as observers, but as the children grow older, it is very difficult for them to avoid witnessing attacks. A majority of women (59%) reported that the children usually were present during an assault, and it was not unusual for some children almost always to observe attacks on the mother.

The reactions of the children were varied. Many of the younger children were frightened and unable to comprehend what was occurring— "They just sat quiet,"—but some young children comprehended and reacted: "Donna used to get hysterical. The wee soul, she'd only be about six and one-half, and she would say, 'Come on, dad, you're going to be good and you're not going to fight with mum tonight. Please, dad, you promised.' " As the children grow older, they occasionally attempt to intervene either physically or verbally.[30] Three women described the attempts of their children to stop an attack.

> My son kicked him, told him to leave me alone.

> My son, he tried to keep out of his way. He was trying to protect me, but I said, "Look, John, leave it, just leave it."

> Rosalyn came running out of the back kitchen, where she'd gone to get out of his way. . . . She kicked him violently in the shins with her shoes.

The last incident occurred after the woman had divorced her husband and he was in her home visiting their children. The daughters in this particular family often had attempted to intervene in attacks on their mother, and although their father never attacked them, their efforts to assist their mother sometimes increased the ferocity of the attack.

> Rosalyn and Cathy, when they were little, used to go into their little bedroom and stay there. Cathy, as she got older, would come out and give

cheek, and in a way they made the situation worse sometimes because they made him angry. But as they got older, really older and big girls, he didn't get a chance.

Beatings are sometimes witnessed by friends or relatives, who, like the children, react in various ways. The woman's friends or relations are much more likely to intervene than the husband's friends or relatives: "My friends intervened but his friends never. They just sat there." The following account demonstrates both the intervention of friends, as well as the issue of domestic work as a source of arguments.

> He's hit me in front of his friends. One night we were out—it was our wedding anniversary—and I was really angry that night. I think it was our fourth or fifth wedding anniversary and he says he was going to take me out, you know, he was going to take me for a night out. . . . But then he says to me, "You're not going." Because his friend wasn't going with his wife, I wasn't to go. So I sat down and I told him that it was my wedding anniversary and not Bruce's [his friend]. And he says he was going out with Bruce. So he went out and he came back about half an hour after that and he said he'd changed his mind. Susan [Bruce's wife] would go. Bruce was taking his wife so I was to hurry up and get ready. So I'd been all ready so we went out.
>
> It ended up we were on a pub crawl. We went from place to place, you know. By this time it was after eight—it was too late to really go anywhere to eat, to get in. So we went home and his friend says to me, "Can I go into the kitchen and make some tea and toast?" I says, "Make yourself at home." Joe [her husband] was in the toilet or something, and he came back in. He says, "Where's Bruce?" I says, "He's making tea and toast." "You make the tea and toast," he said. I says, "Bruce says he'll do it." He says, "You make it. It's your house, you make it." So I went out to the kitchenette and I says to Bruce, "I'll make the tea and toast," and Bruce says, "No, it's alright, I'll do it. You go and sit down." And he came in and he says, "You'll make the toast." Well, he started bawling and shouting and he came over and he punched me in front of them, and Susan and Bruce were there, you know. So I was mad. I mean he's hit me—I don't mind so much when I'm by myself but I hate him doing it in front of his friends and that. But I had witnesses, but right enough it was usually his side he did it in front of when he knew they wouldn't go witness for me.

And whenever he's hit you in front of people, what have they usually done?

> Well, actually his friend, he sort of said, you know, "Come on, get a hold of yourself." This sort of thing. They didn't really tell him off. They didn't want to quarrel with him, too, but they sort of said, "Get a grip on yourself." You know, "Leave her alone" and that. Mostly when I was pregnant, you know. They'd pull him back, but they never actually fought with him because of it. They told him to calm down.

And how do you think these outsiders felt about you, seeing you getting battered?

I think they were just more embarrassed than anything else that they happened to be there at the time.

And do you think they felt sorry for you and reckoned—did they want to get involved?

I don't think they wanted to get involved at all. I mean most of his friends anyway was doing the same things to their wives. I mean Bruce used to give his wife knockings as well.

As described in the above account, the usual response of friends and relatives is simply to do nothing or to tell the husband to stop. Very rarely do friends or relatives attempt physically to intervene in the violence.

We had an argument and he grabbed me by the throat, up against the wall. He had my arm twisted behind my back and he had his arm right up there [across her throat] and I was going blue in the face. His mate was just sitting there, quite the thing, "Take it easy, John, don't get your temper out." He was sitting there and there was me choking. He never got up and helped me. He just sat there and said, "Cool it, John, just keep calm."

He didn't try and pull him off you?

No, he just sat there quite calmly. I think he was quite amused about it all.

Pleas from outsiders seem to make very little difference: "They used to tell him to stop but he didn't take any notice." Outsiders may actually touch off or aggravate an assault. If a woman were to question her husband's actions or his supposed rightful authority over her in front of friends or relations, he might consider this a double affront. Not only had she questioned his authority, but she had rebuked him in front of others, a double humiliation. In describing the first violent attack one woman told us about this type of confrontation. Her husband had invited another couple to visit them, but instead of coming directly home from work to help entertain the guests he stopped at a friend's home. When he arrived home with his friend, his wife protested about his late arrival—both in front of his friend and within hearing distance of the visiting couple. He responded by telling her to "mind her own business, I do what I like." When she complained that he was inconsiderate, he punched her against the wall and knocked her unconscious. This happened "simply because I chastised him and there was somebody there in the sitting room."

Though outsiders do at times inhibit a violent attack, the presence of an audience prior to or during such an episode may help escalate the assault. This depends upon the man involved, the nature of the verbal exchange with his wife, and the orientation of the outsiders to violent behavior.[31] The presence of others during a verbal altercation is most likely to precipitate violence if the potential aggressor perceives the observers as supportive of his actions or if, as in the example cited above, he feels humiliated in their eyes.

After the Violent Event

REACTION

After an assault, the typical reaction of both the man and the woman is to remain in the home. Almost all of the women (90%) reported that usually they remained in the house and were unable to do anything immediately after an attack.

> I didn't do anything about it. After he hit me I just cried and tried to keep quiet, hoping he would calm down.

> I just used to sit and cry because I know for a fact that if you start hitting back then you'll get more hitting back, you see. So I just sort of sat back and took it all.

In contrast, the majority of women interviewed by Eisenberg and Micklow reported leaving the home after a violent attack. A considerable proportion of the women we interviewed (20%) also indicated that their husbands forcibly kept them from going out. A few women, like those interviewed by Eisenberg and Micklow, discussed extreme restraints upon their mobility: "Before he went to work in the morning he would nail the windows shut, and padlock the doors from the inside."[32] Husbands might physically prevent their wives from leaving the house even to seek help or medical assistance, but usually women were restrained by verbal threats of retaliation.

Women sometimes responded to a violent attack by attempting to placate their husbands: "I used to ask him if he wanted something to eat. Or I wouldn't say anything, you know, sort of try and get him to cool down more or less."

Immediately after an attack husbands tended to do nothing, to ignore the act, or to behave as if nothing had happened. Almost 80% of the men usually acted in this manner.

> He just sat and read and that. He didn't talk. We didn't talk to one another.

> He went to sleep. Mind you, he was tired [from beating her]. I've no doubt that he was physically worn out. He was exhausted.

> He didn't feel anything. Most peculiar, [he] just starts talking to you, you know, as long as you're doing as you are told.

The second most common response of the husband following the attack was to go to a pub or just out to cool off. According to a woman who wrote to Martin, her husband "left the house and remained away for days" after a violent attack.[33] We found, however that when men leave the house they are much more likely to remain away for only a few hours.

Feelings about the Violence

The feelings and emotions expressed by the women we interviewed were complex. Women usually felt very upset after a violent episode, and these feelings persisted for several days and sometimes weeks afterward: "I was very upset about it. I mean, I had never seen anything like this happening. I'd never experienced violence in a home. I was pretty upset about it. . . . I was crying all the time." This account aptly describes the typical reaction of over 65% of the women. Women also felt shocked, frightened, ashamed, bitter, and angry after an assault: "Oh, I was frightened, you know, I was terrified, miserable. I was always sitting on an edge waiting for him to get to sleep." Emotions such as these were reported by women in American studies, too. For example, one woman told Eisenberg and Micklow, "When he hit me, of course I was afraid. Anybody would be if somebody larger than you decided to take out their anger on you. I really couldn't do a thing about it. I felt as if I was completely helpless in that situation."[34]

A woman often feels angry after a violent event because her husband ignores her feelings and concerns, because he reacts to her protestations with violence, because a special event such as Christmas or a child's birthday has been spoiled, or because he has shamed her by attacking her in front of friends or relatives. In our study intense anger was most likely after the worst assault since it was typically both humiliating and severe. One woman described how she felt after an assault that seemed particularly unjust and that had spoiled Christmas for the family.

> Oh, I was so angry after that time. I was angry at his sister cos I thought she'd caused it—cos I knew it always seemed to be his family that he was terribly loyal to and I thought somehow his sister's present had caused me to get this good hiding—and it didn't seem fair.

Men may also feel angry after a violent episode, but unlike the women their anger is a continuation of the feelings that gave rise to the verbal confrontation and not a response to the attack. However, men usually act, or at least appear to act, blasé after attacking their wives and express little or no remorse. The husbands of the women we spoke to very rarely apologized or showed contrition immediately following an assault. An atypical reaction came from a man interviewed by Kamisher: "I always felt guilty and ashamed. I would swear I wouldn't do it again and I meant it."[35] If there was any expression of remorse or contrition it usually occurred early in the marriage and after the first violent incident: "Well, at the beginning he used to apologize, but at the latter end he never ever apologized." Over 35% of the men apologized after the first attack, whereas only 14% did so after the worst attack. The bulk of the men typically acted as if nothing had happened. Whether it was the first, worst, or last assault, they very rarely expressed any remorse or regret, and if they did apologize it was usually after a few days or weeks. Only a small percentage (8%) of the husbands almost always expressed remorse immediately following the violent event; 22% usually expressed regret after a few days.

> Well, it was a few hours, a good twelve hours anyway, and he said, "Sorry." And I says, "Sorry." And then we made it up that night.

> No, he very seldom says he's sorry after he did it. Maybe about a week or so later.

On a few occasions men showed their contrition by doing something for their wives such as helping with the dishes. One woman described how her husband used this technique several weeks after a violent attack.

> Oh, he was sorry. He tried to make it up, you know. He would help me do things in the house that week, which he never did. And when it came up for New Year he was saying, "Oh, wait and I'll clean this. I'll do that." I think that was his way of trying to say he was sorry.

However, whether it was the first, worst, or last violent attack, expressions of regret or contrition, apologies or helpful behavior were not typical of the men. Instead, they rarely or never expressed remorse or contrition regarding their violent actions.

> No, he didn't apologize. He never said he was sorry. I used to say to him sometimes, "Do you not feel sorry about it," and he'd say, "No, I'd never say I was sorry because if I was I wouldn't do it in the first place." He always said that.

> I never recall him having any remorse whatever, never recall him ever coming to see me and saying, well honey, put his arm around me and say I'm sorry.

Not only did most husbands fail to apologize or show regret after a violent attack, they often continued to argue with, or to act aggressively toward, their wives, demanding that she do something for him, threatening to bring in a third party who he thought would take his side and condemn his wife, or threatening to put her out of the house.

> I just sat there and said nowt, but he kept harping on and harping on, harping on.

> Oh, I've seen it after he'd maybe stopped the hitting—the actual hitting would maybe go on for ten minutes or something—but then he would sit

and go on for hours. And you're sitting there in a cold sweat waiting on whatever else is going to happen. I couldn't talk. My mouth was shut. I would just sit and he'd maybe make me do things, you know, break something and say, "Right, sweep that up."

Men also attempt to rationalize their violent behavior by denying responsibility for the assault or by arguing that their wife's actions or inactions provoked them.

He'd always just deny it or say it hadn't happened or say it had been an accident. Even to this day he'll argue, "I never hit you when you were pregnant. That's a lie. That's the last thing in the world I'd do." He still insists he's not a violent man. He'll say, "That's one thing I hate is a man that hits a woman."

I said, "Why do you keep on beating me? Why do you?" "Well," he says, "you keep on asking for money." I says, "Well, I need it. You're supposed to keep us. We cannae live on air."

Oh, he used to pace the floor an awful lot, and he used to shout that he had hit me about the fact that you made me do it sort of thing.

He would always make out it was my fault. If I hadn't said this or if I hadnae done that, it would never have happened. He always claimed that I provoked him. It was always I provoked him.

I says, "What's gone wrong? What's happening to our marriage." And he says, "You should know." Of course it was me. I was to blame [for his violence]. I didn't know what or why, and I'm still puzzled what I've done.

Although most men were not drunk when they attacked their wives (30% of the men in our police sample [Appendix C] were described as intoxicated and 25% of the women described their husbands as often drunk at the time of an incident), some of the men who had been drinking denied that they had hit their wives or maintained that they were not responsible for the beating because they were intoxicated.

He always says that he never hit me, but I know that he knows because sometimes he says things about it.

He would say, "Look, this isn't me. It's the drink that is making me act this way."

Men who have only had a small amount to drink and could in no way be considered drunk also use alcohol as an excuse. Women, too, may use their husband's drinking (of even minimal amounts) as a means of making sense of the violent behavior and of placing blame upon something 'outside' the marital relationship.[36]

Thus, men deny responsibility for their violent acts by asserting that their wife's arguing or perceived inappropriate behavior led them to behave in a violent manner.[37] Toch told of a man who felt that the woman he had been living with for many years had no right to object to his pronouncement that he was leaving her. He told the researchers that after an argument relating to his imminent departure the woman he lived with "was nagging—you know how a woman keeps nagging and nagging—and I asked, I said, 'What's wrong with you girl?' I said, 'I'm telling you, I'm leaving tomorrow.' "[38] According to this man, the woman's continued nagging provided a clear justification for murder. He neutralized or rationalized her murder as a justifiable response to a woman who complained about him breaking off a relationship that had lasted for a number of years. He was surprised that she should behave in such a manner and felt that he was within his rights to react toward her in a violent way. According to his perception of the situation, he could not be held responsible for his action: it was the woman's own fault she was killed.

Accusations and claims of this nature, which place the blame upon the victim, may lead a woman to express shame or guilt regarding the violent event. In our study this was especially the case after the first attack since it was seen as a blemish on the marriage. An American schoolteacher told Search, "I felt bitterly ashamed the first time my husband hit me."[39] One of the women we interviewed told us that after the first assault she "was ashamed, I didn't want anybody to know. I was hoping the neighbors hadn't heard." Women often feel that if only they would try harder, keep the house cleaner, or cook better, then maybe their husbands would not beat them. As one woman told Leghorn, one of the founders of a refuge for battered women in Boston:

> I actually thought if I only learned to cook better or keep a cleaner house everything would be okay. . . . It took me [five years] to get over the shame and embarrassment of being beaten. I figured there had to be something wrong with me.[40]

Some women even apologize to their husbands for supposedly provoking the violence.

> Well, when I went back it was more me saying to him, "Okay, I'm prepared to forget all about it." It was always that way, you know. I'd always kind of say it was my fault.

Violent incidents are very rarely discussed by husbands and wives. Usually no explicit effort is made to effect a reconciliation and reconstitute the relationship or to explore and resolve the conflicts that keep surfacing. Couples usually just drift back together again.

> I just went about my business normally. It was just a case of talking and no more, like, "What are you wanting for breakfast? What are you wanting for your tea?" And he wouldn't say what he wanted, "Just anything will do." It was just talking and answering and no more.

> Well, I just sort of tried to get things back to normal again. . . . I was still frightened in case he would try and do it again, you know. He just didn't bother. He just went back to normal again, waiting for the next time.

Despite this pattern of letting things ride, women do make it very clear to their husbands that they are upset and dissatisfied with the pattern of violence and with the marriage. It is erroneous to assume because the couple does not talk about the violence that women accept it.

Location in Time and Space

Time and space also define the violent episode. For example, there is the amount of time a verbal altercation or physical assault actually lasts, as well as the time of day and the day of the week when it occurs. Time is also important in terms of changes in the frequency and severity of violence and in the marital relationship itself as weeks, months, or years of beatings go by. Moreover, we can look at the location of such events. Do they occur in public or in private settings? Inside or outside the home? In what rooms within the home?

A majority of the women experienced at least two attacks a week. Twenty-five percent said that the violence usually lasted from 45 minutes to over 5 hours; the other 75% reported that the physical attack lasted 30 minutes or less. Of the latter group, 22% told us that the violence usually lasted less than 5 minutes, another 25% estimated that the attacks lasted between 6 and 15 minutes, and another quarter (27%) said that it usually lasted about 30 minutes. Any particular physical attack might last only a few minutes or several hours, as one woman indicated.

> These carry-ons could last from eleven o'clock at night until about two and three in the morning, depending on when he got to sleep. It lasted the whole time he was awake. He could be sleeping in half an hour, but it would maybe take him four hours.

This account refers not only to the actual physical attack but also to the verbal confrontation before and after. Some men typically harangued their wives for several hours after the attack and/or continued the physical violence in a somewhat diminished manner.

> Oh, it was over, the actual battering, it was over in minutes, you know. But it was this harassing and having a bit punch at my head, while he was hauling on my hair, and this could last for a couple of hours . . . while his hand was around my throat. And he just sat and told me all what I was from the year I was born. The same old thing every week, every week.

The violence usually occurred during the evening hours, when married couples come together. Though women did report being assaulted during the day, this was unusual: only 4% of the women indicated that the violent incidents typically occurred between the hours of 9:00 A.M. and 5:00 P.M. The violence was most likely to occur between the hours of 10:00 P.M. and 12:00 A.M.; the second most frequently reported period was between 12:00

and 5:00 A.M. A large number of women (37%) reported that the violence could occur at any time during the day and that there was no usual time at which it was most likely.

We would expect this type of temporal pattern to emerge. Men come home from work for their evening meal between five and seven. At this time arguments and confrontations can arise over the wife's performance of domestic duties relating to meal preparation or over other matters. In Britain it is also not unusual for men to be away from the home between approximately 7:00 and 11:00 P.M. drinking at the pub. Many women reported that when the husband returned home after being in that predominately male setting he expected her immediately to meet his every need. Demands for the performance of various wifely duties, sexual and/or domestic, might be refused, with the result that the husband becomes violent.

Over 80% of the women reported that attacks usually occurred on Friday and Saturday night. None of the women mentioned Sunday as the usual day of an assault, and almost 44% said that a violent attack might occur on any day of the week. The typical sequence of events preceding a violent episode is most probable on weekends, when couples are together for longer periods of time. It may be, as other researchers have suggested, that weekends are periods of greater stress because of more sustained contact between husband and wife. They may confront each other with the long-standing problems that plague the relationship, and this results in an angry response from either husband or wife or both, which ends with the man's violence. It should not be assumed, however, that the husband and wife spend long periods of time in the home together. Rather, the husband may spend time in the home, go to the pub or out with male friends, and return to continue an argument or an assault. The interaction is sporadic and possibly extended over a lengthy period of time, and this type of pattern is likely to be more intense and of a longer duration on weekends.

Temporal patterns similar to the ones we discovered consistently have emerged from research conducted on violence both in the United States and in Britain. Wolfgang found in his 1958 study that homicides usually occurred at night or early in the morning; 80% of the murders he studied in Philadelphia took place between 8:00 P.M. and 2:00 A.M.[41] Curtis also concluded after an extensive survey of the patterns of criminal violence in several cities in the United States that violent assaults were more likely to take place at night on the weekends.[42] Gelles's interviews revealed that violent events were most likely to occur between 5:00 and 11:30 P.M.; over 69% of the individuals he interviewed indicated that the violence was most likely on the weekend.[43] Pittman and Handy's perusal of St. Louis police reports revealed that Saturday, Friday, and Sunday (in that order) were the most usual days for violence; McClintock's analysis of London police records revealed remarkably similar patterns.[44]

In our research the overwhelming majority of assaults, regardless of the time of day or day of the week, occurred in the home. Fifty percent of the women reported that the violent episode typically happened in the living room or hallways of their own home. Only 4% of the women said it usually happened in the bedroom; 3% reported the kitchen as the usual location of an attack. However, 29 of the women (27%) said that there was no particular room in which the violence tended to occur.

Wolfgang found that family disputes and arguments leading to homicides were most likely to occur at the end of the day and in kitchens and bedrooms. Pokornoy's study of homicides in the family revealed a similar pattern. He reported that 33% of the homicides occurred in the bedroom, 12% in the living room, and 5.7% in the kitchen.[45] Gelles found the kitchen to be the most usual setting for assaults, and he argued that this is because the kitchen is the center of family activity, especially at the end of the day.[46]

We prefer a more parsimonious explanation of the location of violence within the home since there appears to be no explicit and direct relationship between the subject of an argument and its setting. Kitchens, bedrooms, and living rooms are merely locations where husbands and wives make some contact, usually during the evening hours. We do not think that the location of these events has any great significance since the violence is likely to occur in any room of the house[47] and might very likely occur in all of the rooms during any particular violent incident.

> I'd get dragged from bedroom to living room, and when he scorched my
> back he dragged me in my nightdress on my back, and he burnt all my spine,
> and I couldn't sit, you know. I couldn't sit against the chair or anything, but
> I just said [to the doctor] that I'd fallen and bruised my back outside.

The most important point arising from our interviews and analysis of police records and from other investigations is that most violent attacks on wives take place in the confines of the home.[48]

In summary, the violent episode most often is preceded by a short verbal confrontation, although some prefatory arguments may be intermittent and last several hours. The altercations relate primarily to the husband's expectations regarding his wife's domestic work, his possessiveness and sexual jealousy, and allocation of the family's resources. The verbal confrontation may be initiated by either the husband or the wife, but it is usually initiated by the husband. When a husband attacks his wife he is either chastising her for challenging his authority or for failing to live up to his expectations or attempting to discourage future unacceptable behavior. Men use diverse and often severe forms of physical force. The usual method of attack is slapping, punching, and kicking, which results in bruises, lacerations, and fractures, some of which require medical treatment and even hospitalization. Men commonly fail to react to the consequences of their violent actions—ignoring the violence and acting as if nothing had happened. Although some men eventually may apologize they very rarely do so immediately following an attack. The majority do not express any contrition whatsoever and often deflect the blame for their violent actions onto their wives. Women, on the other hand, do not ignore the violence but they must remain in the home, often detained by the husband or because they have few places to go. Generally, women feel shattered, frightened, ashamed, and angry. Emotions of this nature may continue for days or weeks after the attack.

CHAPTER 7

THE VIOLENT MARRIAGE

VIOLENCE USUALLY ENTERS A MARRIAGE EARLY and in a relatively innocuous form, but over time it changes and so does the marital relationship itself. At first, the violence seems to be transient and the problems leading to the confrontations appear soluble. The man is remorseful, and the woman has hope that things will change for the better. The woman's belief that her husband will stop beating her is usually sustained for a very long time (and, no doubt, a few men do stop) and motivates her to try to change herself, her husband, and their relationship. But if the issues over which the couple argues are not or cannot be solved, or if the solutions, when they are achieved, do not end the beatings, then the woman begins to lose hope and the relationship suffers. The man becomes less concerned, less remorseful, and less willing to change while the woman's affection for him and estimation of her own worth begin to deteriorate. As the physical abuse becomes more frequent and severe it eventually dominates the relationship. This is especially true for the woman both because she is the victim of the abuse and because her life is more closely bound up in marriage. Her activities, identity, and worth are defined by marriage and her contacts with outside sources of support are more limited.

Changes in the nature of the violence and in the attitudes and responses to it were noted by many women we interviewed.

> Well, when I was first married, he never hit me at all. He was a good husband. . . . And he gradually changed . . . and then as the years went on he started becoming more violent.

> Violence then wasnae the same as it is now, you know. It's kind of grown over the years. . . . Well, he started throwing things at me first . . . then he'd punch me and then it got round to . . .

> [Eventually] I had it more or less all the time, you see. He battered me stupid.

In the beginning:

> He was ashamed. He just couldn't get over it . . . he practically was in tears every time he came up, face in his hands, pleading for forgiveness.

> Oh, he was remorseful that time because I did get a box of chocolates. . . . He didn't give them to me. He left them lying on the washing machine.

He kept on saying it was an accident. Oh, he helped with the work; he cooked the dinners that week. But it only lasted no more than a week.

Later on, these responses almost completely disappeared (except in some cases in which the woman actually left and the husband expressed sorrow in the process of convincing her to return) and were replaced by indifference, self-justification, and shifting of blame.

> His wickedness came out in him and I used to say to him . . . , "You're not actually like this so why are you like this now?" Cos he could be nice, he could be marvelous, and I used to say, "Think of the past, when we were happy." But . . .

> He'd say, you made me hit you, you know. And I didn't realize what I was doing to make him hit me, but he did say it.

> I used to say to him, "Do you remember that day you gave me the black eye?" . . . He'd say, "You deserved it." He still maintains to this day that I deserved it.

A Woman's Worth

Since a married woman's social and individual worth rests largely upon her ability to be a good wife and mother and since being a good wife includes, among other things, providing proper services for her husband (just as being a good mother involves providing proper services for her children), then her sense of self-worth depends in large part on how the recipients of her services, that is, her husband and children, evaluate her performance. When a man beats his wife (either for doing something he thinks is wrong or for refusing to do something he wishes her to do—or simply because he feels like it), he is making an explicit and powerful statement about his belief in her inability to be a good wife and to provide what he believes to be proper services. When he then blames her for the beating, this becomes an even more powerful statement of her worthlessness. When statements of blame are repeated often enough, the woman, who initially felt that she was unjustly treated, begins to have doubts.

> I don't know. I kept on thinking he was changing, you know, change for the better. . . . He's bound to change. Then I used to think it's my blame and I used to lie awake at night wondering if it is my blame. You know, I used to blame myself all the time.

Women do not, however, accept the evaluations of their husbands without struggling to establish their own position and to prove that the husband is neither justified in the claims he makes upon her or in the punishments he dispenses.

> I was concerned. I didn't do anything to deserve it. I mean, I never went out. I never went out of the house, you know. I never looked at anybody.

The batterings weren't caused through me although he always blamed me.

Over time, the increasing frequency and severity of the violence and the man's hardening position result in the woman's diminishing estimation of herself and of her husband and a loss of affection for him. She also has a growing sense of fear and isolation and a general feeling of hopelessness. These changes, of course, affect, and are affected by, the nonviolent aspects of the entire relationship. The apportionment of blame and the disputes about who is at fault are most closely tied to the nonviolent aspects of the relationship, including the nature of marital authority and responsibility, the separateness of the couple's lives, and the way in which daily issues are resolved.

Marital Authority, Responsibility, and Moral Obligations

As the marriage continues, the social lives of the man and woman move apart. He spends more time engaged in his own work and social activities, they engage in fewer activities together, and she is increasingly tied to the household. The birth of children brings increased domestic work, and since the responsibility for child care and domestic work usually falls almost exclusively upon the woman, she must remain in the home most of the time or make arrangements for someone else to be there when she is absent. The woman's wage work and social life are arranged around and to a great extent restricted by the notion that domestic work is basically her responsibility and the belief that it is a 'moral' obligation to be present in the home in the event that her husband or children need her services and simply because this is where a 'good' wife and mother is supposed to be. In this respect, Dahl and Snare have drawn an analogy between the contemporary position of Norwegian wives and the traditional role of Norwegian housemen. The houseman was expected to subsume his identity in his master's and to be available to provide service at all times. Thus he had only a very limited life apart from his master; his time was monopolized by the latter. All of this was done under the name of loyalty and was perceived as a moral obligation, which greatly limited the houseman's ability to protest, to exert any influence on his master, or to bring about changes even in the most unjust of arrangements or punishments.[1]

Husbands and fathers, unlike wives and mothers, are not viewed as morally responsible for domestic work or child care even when the woman is partially or fully supporting the family. Because of this notion, a man may help with housework and child care, but he is always free to withdraw from what is, after all, perceived to be the woman's responsibility. Men are viewed as the representatives of the family in the world of work and they move back and forth from the private, relatively isolated world of the family to the public world of work. Accordingly, men have much greater physical opportunity and 'moral' freedom to spend their leisure time outside the home. Although it may be desirable, for the sake of domestic tranquility, that a man receive his wife's at least tacit approval of his absences from home, he rarely needs also to arrange for child care or to complete domestic tasks before going out. Both husband and wife know that if there is a strong disagreement about whether or not he goes out, ultimately he has freedom of action because of his position of authority in the household and his lack of moral obligation to domestic responsibilities. He may return to an angered or sullen woman, but, unlike her husband, the woman has little leverage—moral, physical, or authoritative—over her spouse's activities. Usually, however, if there is a disagreement about the wife's activities, she must either accede to her husband's wishes or risk moral degradation, physical coercion, and/or punishment of various types.

It is in this more symbolic, all embracing, sense of a moral obligation to the domestic sphere that the woman becomes increasingly isolated from the world outside the family and under the control of her husband. She becomes subject to his ideals about what a good wife and mother should be, to his evaluations of her behavior and, thus, to his attempts to enforce this 'moral' order in their daily activities.

Negotiating Daily Life

The daily lives of husbands and wives are made up largely of mundane activities that center around such things as food, clothes, money, sex, child care, and recreation. All of these have a myriad of facets and involve the making of numerous decisions such as what will be done, how much each person will contribute, and how much responsibility each will have. Consider food, for example: what will be purchased? how much money will be spent? who will do the shopping? the cooking? the washing up? at what time will meals be served? will the family eat together or separately? will they eat at the table or in front of the television? Although making the necessary decisions and allocating the various resources involved in each sphere of daily life often becomes habitual and, thus, may go unnoticed or seem unproblematic, it is, in fact, a complex process that requires negotiation by the couple.

This process of negotiating day-to-day issues is usually conducted in the home and is thought of as a private matter that needs little or no intervention from outsiders. It is not, however, conducted apart from the wider social context and without influence from it. In fact, the husband's traditional position as wage earner, representative of the family in the outside world, and head of household, coupled with the wife's primary obligations to him, the children, and the household, are reflected in the way in which these daily activities are negotiated and performed. It is the husband who has greater access to and control over almost all of the family's personal and material resources, including money, time, and mobility; yet the woman must negotiate for these resources in order to go about her daily life. In this process of negotiating issues are raised that become immediate sources of contention or serve as challenges to the husband's authority and thus lead to his use of physical force.

We asked the women to discuss an array of common domestic activities including food purchase and preparation, care and discipline of children, and family recreation. These issues were considered in terms of the couple's ideals about who they thought *should* make decisions and who should have responsibility for carrying out the task. We also examined who in practice actually *did* make the decisions and take the responsibility and finally, who had the ultimate *authority* in the event of a difference of opinion. Out of this set of questions some striking and consistent patterns emerged that clearly illustrated a difference in conceptions of authority and responsibility between spouses. The preponderant belief among the women was that husbands and wives should ideally make decisions jointly; the men were overwhelmingly in support of separate spheres of decision-making and responsibility for each person. In practice, decision-making and responsibilities were segregated and their allocation was almost a mirror image of the husbands' ideals. The most striking finding, however, was that even in the areas in which the man believed that his wife should make decisions and take responsibility, she did so only as long as there was no disagreement about her decisions or actions. When there was disagreement, the husband's wishes prevailed and he had the final say on every question except those related to the children's clothing and nondisciplinary matters concerning them. This pattern can be illustrated by considering a few problems that arise daily over money, time, and mobility.

The allocation of money for various purposes including food, clothes, household expenses, and entertainment is an issue that the woman often must negotiate with her husband. Yet, this is a resource that she may feel belongs to the entire family and merits joint decisions and responsibility. The husband may feel money is primarily his own resource over which he should have final control even if he does not actually take direct responsibility for seeing that the bills are paid.

And how the housekeeping money was spent, who decided on that?

Well, him mostly. He would tell me what I had to do and what I had to pay and things like that.

And who do you think should have decided?

I think it's a joint thing because it's a house and that, you know.

And who did he think?

Him, because he always demanded that it was his money. He's a man like this, everything was his, not mine, not yours, not ours, but always his.

I mean, if it was problems like the electricity bills, I had to pay them even though I didn't have the money. He expected me to pay them and things like that. But when it came to decisions, really, if I tried to talk to him I just couldn't get through to him. He wasn't interested in the day-to-day running of the house or anything like that. . . . I kept telling him but he still expected me to pay the rent and he was taking the money off me, you know, and he'd say to me, "Well, it's your fault." I'd say, "Well, you take the money and don't give me any."

When a woman continues to negotiate with her husband about the use of money after he has made up his mind or persists in criticizing his use or misuse of their funds, she may find that he views this as an unacceptable challenge to his authority and stops the negotiation by force.

Bill came in from the pub and I had got on to him then. I would get on to him and tell him that, you know, he'd spent our money and all this. And next morning I'd go on about it and [say] I need money because there was nothing. And, of course, he said it was all my fault. So, of course, an argument broke out. . . . He couldnae contain his temper—this was the biggest thing—and he exploded and . . . he flew at me, you know. The argument got too bad that he couldn't take it. He hated anybody continually arguing against him. Then he pulled me by the hair doon these stone steps . . . and he hauled me out the back door and kicked me. Oh, he kicked me stupid.

The amount of free or personal time available to or allowed each partner and the way in which each spends such time is also subject to negotiations that are colored by ideals about the appropriate spheres for husbands and wives and by the hierarchy of marital authority. The woman's time is ideally given to her husband, children, and household work and this automatically restricts her mobility. And, if he so wishes, the husband has the authority to attempt to enforce this commitment, with the result that the woman has virtually no time of her own or freedom of movement.

We were two miles from the village. He allowed me half an hour to go up to the village and half an hour to walk back and ten minutes to get what I needed in the shops. That was what I was allowed, an hour and ten minutes. If I wasnae back inside that hour and ten minutes I got met at the door saying where the f——ing hell have you been. . . . I used to marvel at women that could go down shopping, you know, and their friends say, "Oh, come in for a cup of coffee." And they spend half an hour chatting and having a cup of coffee and then come home. But I couldnae do that.

In this case the restriction upon the woman's time and mobility was rather extreme. Much more common were limits on the time the woman might spend away from home engaged in any kind of social activity. Her supposed total commitment to the children was often used as the rationale here.

He's right old-fashioned. I mean, he really is. He's right old-fashioned. I say to him, "You forget times is changing, you know." He puts me in mind of 'em, Hitler. That's who he did put me in mind of. . . . He's the boss. A woman shouldn't do nothing as far as he's concerned. A woman's just here to have wains, and even having the wains is nothing to him. . . . He's got right, right old-fashioned ideas. Even the women round about me, they say, "Can Jane no have a night out?" "No, no, she's got to watch the wains," And I'll say, "Well, I'll get someone to do it." "No, there'll be naebody in here watching my wains, only you. You watch the wains. That's what you're here for." That's his attitude.

The husband's authority over the daily activities of the household is sufficiently strong that even in areas in which he takes little or no active role, such as domestic work or child care, he may nevertheless determine how and when such work will be done.

He didn't want the responsibility of the kids, but at the same time he wanted to think that he had more authority than what I had.

He expected the place—I mean, my house was clean but it did get untidy, you know. With four kids, you cannae expect anything else. But it was always, you know, the one day's dirt. . . . I would do the house, you know, and then the kids would go in the room and spill all the toys out and clothes out and dress up and then it was my fault because this was filth. It was only toys and things like that but it was dirt to him, you know. It was just normal untidiness but to him, he lived in a pig sty.

Did he do anything for you?

No, eh, no, no. He wasn't the type. A woman's place was in the home and it was her job to get on with it, you know.

Well, he maintained that he was a good husband because he went out and worked for us, but he never wanted to clean, tidy, wash, bathe the children, you know, do the dishes, cleaning up, nothing.

The type and amount of contact with members of the opposite sex and possessiveness are other areas that are differentially negotiated by husbands and wives and in which differing amounts of authority are used to attempt to insure compliance with various constraints on even the most innocuous activities. The most stringent limits were placed upon women almost as a matter of course and rarely in response to any flirtations or infidelity. Women were kept in the house, not allowed to go out with their friends, and closely scrutinized even when they were out with their husbands in mixed company. Sometimes cordial contacts with male relatives or old friends were restricted and even punished.

Did he ever hit you in public?

Oh, aye, he did once. Aye, slapped my face at a party. [I said], "What was that for? why did I get that one?" Oh, I was talking to somebody. I was talking to a boy that I had known for years, I was brought up beside, but he hadnae known that. And I got belted in the jaw for talking to him. . . . It's terrible. I used to say, "How do you think I look, like Raquel Welch or something?" I mean, I was like an inflated bootlace. Naebody would have looked at me. I don't know where he got that idea.

How do you think these people felt about you being battered?

They felt bad. They felt really bad. . . . If I had deserved it I don't think they would have bothered much, but they knew it was just Alan. He picked a row, you know, for nothing. I probably laughed with somebody too much when we were going out for the night. I probably paid too much attention to what somebody was saying, and I probably was in the loo too long that he missed me, you know, thinking I was away somewhere else with another.

He was always—he even admitted to me he was jealous, you know. I mean, I couldn't go anywhere, speak to anyone. I mean, even if I spoke to anyone, even with his brothers, you know, he was jealous.

What about your jealousy of him?

Well, I've never really been jealous. I think I've been hoping he would meet somebody and go away and leave me, you know.

None of the women were allowed to express the same degree of jealousy or make such demands concerning their husbands' social contacts with members of the opposite sex. Even when he was engaged in a sexual infidelity or in some behavior that made the woman jealous, she often found that her attempts to prohibit this or openly to question his actions were viewed as an inappropriate challenge to his authority. One woman recounted what happened one afternoon when she went for a stroll with their baby and later stopped to pick her husband up from the pub only to discover that he had gone walking with another woman.

All his friends, they were standing having a blether [talk] outside. I says, "Where's Vic?" He looked at me and he says, "Do you want to know?" I says, "Aye, I'm waiting up there for him." I says, "I've got the wee one, Jamie." He says, "He's away with some lassie. I don't know who she is and she's got a wee one in a pram." So, I didnae know what to think at first. I says, "I'll take a walk round and see if I can see him." By this time I was in a state of anger, you know, at the thought—he's away taking a walk with another girl and I'm waiting on him. So, I got up to boiling point, you know, I did. I saw him walking down the bottom of the street with the pram, saw him turn along with this other girl . . . . it sort of gave me a jolt.
So, I says to him, "I've been down here waiting on you coming out of this pub for you to go for a walk with me and your child. So, you're away with this other woman and her child. If that's the way you act you can take your ring along with the two of youse." I really was dreading. She was standing in the street [saying], "Oh, there's nothing like that in it." I says, "Look, I'm not saying there is anything like that in it, but I'm waiting on him

to go with me and his own kid and he's away with you and yours." . . . I think they must have got a fright, you know, for God's sake, but I was a bag of nettles, you know. So, I just went up the stair and he came after me and he was shouting, "You wait." . . . I was all gone because I knew I had done wrong. I did, I realized that I was in the wrong, but waiting all that time . . . me standing there waiting on him and he's away with somebody else . . . and what was it he says to me? We started arguing anyway about it and he says, "Don't you dare accuse me." But I hadn't accused him of anything. I said, "I didn't accuse you of anything." . . . Anyway it developed into an argument, you know. He said I'd accused him of, you know, but it wasn't exactly that. But it was a point, he should have come up to his own house and not for a walk with another woman and her kid.

This husband rejected his wife's right to be angry with him and she felt guilty about questioning his behavior. He became so annoyed that she should challenge him that he beat her up.

Most women had no social life with their own female friends (except for visiting female relatives) and yet they still had difficulty persuading their husbands that they should go out together. The following case illustrates the very real differences in the amount of time and mobility allowed each partner.

Did you argue about him going out?

No, not really, because, as I said he used to go out on his own to the pub, like, you know, after we got married and I had the children. I didn't really mind it so much because, as I said, he worked all week and I thought he deserved it, you know, if he wanted to go fishing. But just like any other normal woman at times I would say to him I wish to God he would take us away with him. Because you got fed up, fed up stuck in the house or going up to your mother's all the time. Same with the kids, you know. Right enough, when I got to that stage, I'd say, "I'll need to get a night out. I'll have to get out for a wee while." Well, he would take me out cos he knew I needed it.

It should be emphasized that women are taught to believe in the husband's authority to limit their activities; thus, they do not ask for total freedom nor are they desirous of escaping or neglecting their family obligations or even of denying the husband's authority.

Thus, the wife must negotiate with her husband not only over her own time and mobility but also over his time and mobility. This is, of course, a very different process. Because some of a man's time is promised to work and the rest is not morally owed to the family, the woman must negotiate with him to spend time with her and the children. Since his obligation to them is not viewed as total, his absences, unless excessive, do not have the same moral overtones. This and the difference of authority render her unable to impose her wishes upon him even when she believes that he is not spending enough time with the family or that he is engaging in social activities of which she does not approve.

The wife's objections to his going out or her requests or demands that he stay at home are likely to be defined by the husband as unimportant, or inappropriate, or threatening to his authority. The outcome of such disputes was less likely to be his submission, as it was in the case of most women we interviewed, than refusal to comply or denial of the wife's right to question the husband's authority. If she persisted in her demands or tried to get back at or punish the husband he accused her of nagging.

> It was more or less he got on at me for nagging him for being out every night and no coming in till three o'clock in the morning. And if I was in my bed or if I had been sitting up waiting on him, the first thing he used to say to me is, "What's for eating?" Sometimes he used to go to the pub straight from his work and I had his meal ready for him. Well, it was ruined, and naturally I had to put it in the bucket, you know: after a certain length of time it was all dried up. That was the main thing that annoyed me, him coming in at two or three in the morning, saying what's for eating. I'd say, "Your tea, but it's lying in the bloody bucket. Go and get it out and eat it." You know. And if I didnae go and make something for him then, you know, it started an argument.

> In the beginning it was okay. I thought, "Well . . . I am nagging too much. Maybe I shouldn't nag at him. He's entitled to go for a drink if he likes. I just don't understand why he goes so often. . . . Well, I'll just have the tea ready and I'll be in a good mood by the time he gets in."

> I just thought . . . I must be nagging too much or something. I'm probably just a nagger. He said I was always nagging. "You're always moaning."

Nagging—continued discussion once the husband has made up his mind—represents in the eyes of the husband an illegitimate challenge to his authority and his right to make the ultimate decision. Thus, nagging is one of the behaviors identified by the man as provoking his violent responses: "He felt that was just a way, sort of shutting me up, you know. A belt, you know, he says it's the only way that worked with me."

Provocation

The idea that nagging provokes or causes the violence is not merely a justification provided by the man for his behavior, it is very much a part of our cultural beliefs and is also used by researchers and representatives of social agencies to explain wife beating or to justify their own actions or inactions. Let us consider some of the statements about provocation that have been made by researchers and representatives of agencies working with battered women. Storr in his book *Human Aggression* wrote quite emphatically:

If it is not safe to let oneself be dominated, it is not possible to be fully feminine. . . . The nagging, aggressive woman is often unconsciously demanding that which she most fears. By irritating a man, making *unreasonably demands* and criticizing, she is really trying to evoke a dominant response by attacking him for his lack of virility. Her aggression is fulfilling a double purpose, both protecting against male dominance and, at the same time, demanding it. It is also true that, if one is feeling aggressive, it is reassuring to provoke this in someone else, for it makes one less guilty [emphasis added].[2]

In Marsden and Owen's study of 19 middle-class battered women in England they raised the question of provocation in a less certain and more perplexed manner.

There were few patterns among these 19 relationships: violence was not clearly associated with poverty, or always transmitted from generation to generation, or all-pervading. The large unexplained element in violence, and the Jekyll and Hyde quality of the women's descriptions, still leaves open the question of how far these women were insensitive and unaware of behaving in a way which exacerbated conflict in the relationship.[3]

They concluded:

None of the women felt they should tolerate the violence and only two felt that it might be at all justified. Were they insensitive to some aspects of their own behavior which may have irritated their husbands, or provoked them beyond measure? Several admitted there was some justice in their husbands' charges that they were untidy, irresponsible or immature. . . . However these admissions by no means justified the degree of violence experienced.[4]

The phrase "justified the degree of violence experienced" is very telling, indeed, since it implies a certain acceptance of violence. It also shows a failure to understand the nature of the marital relationship. To imply that a certain degree of violence is appropriate when a woman admits to untidiness, irresponsibility, or immaturity is a clear indication of the errors of a superficial analysis.

Gelles also concluded that physical violence is an acceptable response to various forms of nonviolent behavior. He stated that "while there were some families where the victim precipitated the violence by being violent, the majority of incidents of physical violence were *caused* by the victim's verbal behavior" [emphasis added].[5] One section of his book was devoted to extending his analysis "by theorizing how the victim's actions lead to the response of the offender. It is proposed that certain verbal assaults made by the victim, if directed at vulnerable aspects of the offender's self-concept, are likely to produce violent reactions."[6] This analysis included a subsection entitled "Nag, Nag, Nag," which begins, "When one thinks of victim-precipitated family violence, one often conjures up the image of the nagging wife who finally drives her husband to 'belt her in the mouth.' . . . There is a grain of truth in this image."[7] Included in Gelles's list of provocative behaviors were "verbal attacks" that consist of nagging—the "liberated woman" who "may attack her husband's 'male chauvinist' attitude towards her"—and "verbal abuse provoked by the partner's drinking or sexual deficiencies."[8] He cited two examples of such verbal provocation: in one case a woman was called a Polack and in another a man maintained that he was called a bastard.[9] One of the major weaknesses of Gelles's discussion of such behavior was that he did not separate his own analysis of the causes of violence either from what is stereotypically called provocative behavior or from the couple's excuses and feelings of guilt about what happened in the short period immediately preceding the blows. He examined provocation with only a fleeting glance at a complex and ongoing behavior, which he did not place in the wider context of the institution of marriage, the couple's history, or even the long-term buildup to the particular assault.

Even if one agrees that verbal behavior somehow merits physical retaliation (which we do not), a wider analysis would nevertheless make it difficult to know if the verbal provocation was itself provoked. It seems absurd and even unjust to maintain along with Gelles that a woman instigates violence through "verbal abuse provoked by the partner's drinking or sexual deficiencies" or by his male chauvinism. If her provocation is itself provoked, then who or what actually provokes the assault? Gelles claimed that violence is most likely to produce violence, but his egalitarian terminology about which partner ultimately is the victim belies reality.[10]

The types of behavior that have been defined as provocative either by researchers or by husbands are diverse and contradictory, ranging from aggression and nagging,[11] to submission,[12] through dominance and "psychological disfigurement," or emasculation (i.e., failure to be submissive),[13] and on to insinuating language or gestures.[14] Being too talkative or too quiet, too sexual or not sexual enough, too frugal or too extravagant, too often pregnant or not frequently enough all seem to be provocations.[15] The only pattern discernible in these lists is that the behavior, whatever it might be, represents some form of failure or refusal on the part of the woman to comply with or support her husband's wishes and authority.

The idea of provocation, or victim-precipitation, as it is sometimes called in the social sciences, is both naive and insidious; it represents an acceptance of the use of physical violence. It is naive because it represents a failure to see the marital relationship within which the wife must negotiate with her husband in order to conduct her daily life and to see that she must do so from a greatly disadvantaged position. It is insidious because what is really being said is that the woman has no real right to negotiate with her husband about how their money is spent, the time he spends away from home, the amount of assistance he gives at home, and her freedom to go to work or dispose of her own time. It also assumes that she has little or no right to engage in any behavior, no matter how innocuous, of which her husband approves and that she should not challenge his decisions even if they are unjust or unreasonable. If the woman goes beyond these limits, she is said to be provoking her husband and this supposedly explains or justifies the violence she experiences. The idea of provocation is a very powerful tool used in justifying the husband's dominance and control and in removing moral indignation about his resort to force in securing, maintaining, and punishing challenges to his authority.

The belief in female provocation is socialized into everyone, and it is expressed, albeit ambivalently, even by those women who are repressed by it. When the women were asked whether they thought there were circumstances in which a man has the right to hit his wife, 69% replied with an emphatic no. The others replied in terms of the stereotype that women may deserve to be hit if they neglect the children, are sleeping around, or fail in various ways to take care of their husbands. Those who supported the idea that under such conditions a man may hit his wife were quick to add that this meant only to slap her and did not include beating her.

Women have been so exposed to claims that they have few rights of their own, that they should not go very far in challenging a husband's behavior, and that they should look to themselves for the causes of problems that they are uncertain about how to evaluate what is happening to them. They vacillate between seeing almost anything they might say or do that their husband does not like as illegitimate and deserving of some mild, usually nonphysical, punishment and asserting that they do have some rights and that their own behavior is legitimate and does not deserve punishment.

> He came in about eleven o'clock in the morning and he had a smell of drink on him then, and I asked him where he had been and he said, "Oh, staying with a friend," and I started to shout. You know, it was me that actually started it. He says, "This has gone on long enough. It'll have to stop." And I says, "I know where you've been." And he just turned round on me then. . . .

> *Did you argue?*

> Not for long, he just lashed.

Another woman stated that although she could no longer remain silent about the way she was being treated, she still felt she had no real right to speak and thus "brought it on herself" when she did so: "I wouldn't hide it any more. I used to just . . . you know, just say things. I mean I dae bring it on myself half the time, but I just don't see why I should let him get away with it." All women, however, see the injustices done to them and deny that they deserved to be hit or punished simply because their behavior was not totally submissive.

> He maintained he was in the right: I deserved that black eye. So, therefore, to me, he wasn't ashamed of it. I felt about the size of twopence. I felt terribly embarrassed at this black eye and what was inside me. But I went out with that black eye. [I thought], "I'm no going to hide this, I'm definitely not, cos I didn't deserve it." I don't think I did even although I argued. I believed that he was mature enough to understand me, you know, my feelings inside.

Another woman, commenting on her behavior and her husband's estimation of it, illustrated a widespread idea that if a woman believes she has a few rights she has become independent, equal, or even dominant.

> I don't think I'm a stupid person, you know. I think I've got a brain. It's just I don't get a chance to use it, you know, I'm no saying I'm dead intelligent. I would like if I could have had a better education, which I didn't have, but I believe I've got some rights as a woman but I'm not, I mean, I wouldn't go, you know, join the women's lib, burn my bra, and all this. I believe that I'm entitled to my own opinion, you know, and things like that, but Paul thinks that I'm 100% women's lib and this caused arguments as well.

For a woman simply to live her daily life she is always in a position in which almost anything she does may be deemed a violation of her wifely duties or a challenge to her husband's authority and thus defined as the cause of the violence she continues to experience.

Continued Violence and Changes in the Woman's Life

Most women go through long periods in which they heed their husbands' evaluations of the relationship (although often with considerable reluctance and a feeling of injustice) and they shoulder most of the blame for what happens. They seek to change the behavior the husband has singled out as the cause of trouble. They comply with the husband's wishes in a spirit of hope.

> Like he doesn't like black men, so you don't like black men. He doesn't like Catholics, so you don't like Catholics. And if there's a television program on that has a colored person in it, it's switched off. . . . I was trying to find some way to solve the problem and the best way was that I agree with him.

It is only when these efforts fail to stop the violence that the woman ceases to view the beatings as a passing phase and, with great reluctance and horror, begins to view her husband as a violent man and their relationship as a violent one. It is at this point that she really begins to change and fear becomes an integral part of daily life.

Did this particular fight make any difference in the way you felt about each other?

Well, previous to that, you know me, I was quite happy and relaxed in a sort of every way, you know. I could accept, you know, the ups and downs, but when that happened to me that was my life starting all over again. And I found I got tensed up again a lot easier, you know. The least wee thing I was getting feared. I didnae like to talk about it really cos I was too scared.

I was frightened and I didn't want to cause arguments and I was trying to do things to please him so as it wouldn't start him off again.

He always terrified me. Each time he made me more scared. I just sat like a mouse, just sat quietly.

For a few women we interviewed, this fear eventually extended to almost all men.

[I have] a fear of men. I cannae have a man go near me, you know. Even when I first came here [the refuge] and Paul [a Women's Aid worker] was here, I had a fear of him. It's ridiculous because he's so nice and he's tried to be so kind to me. But I couldn't even start thinking about going out with another man, you know. As a friend I'd like to just sit and talk, just to talk. Just sit and talk and it's marvelous and he's so different, you know, to other men. . . . I've experienced no proper man. I'd never marry again. No, he's put me off marriage for life.

Along with this change in the woman's view about the permanence of the violence and her growing fear of her husband comes a reluctant loss of affection for him.

I'd begun to not like him. I began to not like him then, really. I don't mean not love him, but not like him.

I started feeling a wee bit less for him. I started feeling a wee bit insecure because I didnae know how long it was going to last, how many times I was going to get it.
But when he done that, I think that really, from then on I was sort of lost in a way because I didnae think that he would ever have hit me like that. . . . But when he done it to me I—What made him do this to me?

This loss of affection is often followed by a feeling of hate and an outraged sense of injustice.

I didnae really hate him at first but as it got on and on and on I started to hate him. [At first I was] more angry and upset and then it turned to hate.

That was the time when I was very angry inside myself because I knew then it was never going to get better. And I knew then that he didn't really, you know, love me. It was when he showed me in front of the girls [during an assault he degraded her by lifting her nightgown and exposing her naked body to their two young daughters] and loads and loads of other times when he'd shown me up. But there was the time when he shouted and called me names in front of a strange couple in a pub. Really, I began to hate him.

You know, they just cannae come to grips with the situation and change it. They can't do it. But at the same time I think you get to the stage you just couldnae care less if they never made it, you know, because you hate them that much for what they're doing to you.

Feelings of fear, hate, or rage are usually most intense just after a beating but they cannot be sustained at a high level for very long, and between incidents the woman tries to cope simply by trying to ignore the problem of violence.

I just used to forgive and forget. . . . I tried to forget the past, but it was just all brought up again. I'd just push it back again, and you know, just live for tomorrow and hope tomorrow would bring happiness.

Eventually, it becomes very difficult to forget. Because the woman knows that the violence will probably happen again, she remains in a state of constant apprehension and depression. She becomes nervous and on guard as she tries to avoid the next incident and wonders whether she will ever be free from fear and pain.

My nerves in my stomach used to just turn . . . waiting to see if he was going to continue or if it was forgotten.

The only problem always was how am I ever going to get out of this, you know. How long will I have to put up with it? Oh, God's truth, I used to say if I won money you wouldnae see me for dust. I couldn't sit at peace. The house was—you could have ate dinner off the floor. Cos I mean my nerves made me. I couldn't sit doon. I was forever up cleaning and when I couldnae see dirty I found something to do. You know, I even washed the paint work round the windaes every week. Just nerves.

Well, the point was, we were going on and on in the same road, but there was nothing between the two of us. I mean, we were just together for the fact we were married and it was convenient. That was all there was to it. And I wasnae happy. I mean, I've had a great life since I've left—no enjoying myself—but the peace of mind and body and everything. I mean, I was six stone [84 pounds] when I left; now I'm nearly nine [126 pounds]. I thought I would never put on weight. I mean, you know, I wasnae eating. I never ate in the house. It was only cups of coffee I lived on. Life wasnae worth living, and I used to sit and say to myself when Mary leaves school, I'll leave then cos she'll be old enough to understand. I mean, I had it all planned when I was going to leave him.

Once this level of desperation and negative feelings has been reached, the relationship deteriorates still further. The man often makes more frequent threats to throw the woman out of the house and this adds to her feelings of insecurity and vulnerability. His expressions of affection become more infrequent and sometimes cease altogether and she reaches a state of emotional numbness.

> I began to, oh, I began to feel that he was just walking all over me because he knew I had nowhere else to go and he was just taking advantage of me and really walking all over me. You know, he used to say to me—well, the house was in his name—and he used to say to me, "If you don't like what goes on in this house you can f—— off any time."

> Yes [my feelings] had changed. I mean, I just lost all feelings for him. I mean, how can you live with a person that treated you like that? One minute they say they love you and next minute they're belting you and not even allowing you to sleep in bed and making you sleep on kitchen floors and putting you out at night in the cold and things like that. It's impossible. It changes you.

> I didn't have any feelings for him now. They just wouldn't come. I couldn't even, you know, I couldn't even try and kid on that they were there. I wasn't bad to him or anything, and I didn't refuse him sex or anything like that, but at the same time he sensed in me that my heart wasnae there and, as I said, it was still the same thing, you know, where you were getting hit and punched and what have you.

> Well, instead of waiting for him to come home every weekend I used to dread the fact that he was coming home every weekend. My happiest day was Monday because he was going away.

Obviously, the couple's sex life is affected. Usually they continue to have intercourse although reluctantly and less frequently, and it is without joy for either partner.

> I mean, since I went back, it was alright for a week and after that it was really murder, you know. . . . I'm just . . . no interested in him now. I've lost interest and he knows this, you know, and I've no been, you know, kindly towards him, you know, even in our sex life. I just don't like him touching me anymore, and I think this is why he got so angry. He blames himself as well. But I can't get through to him, I mean, he blames me. He says it's me. . . . I didn't refuse him—I was too scared to refuse him—more or less because I mean it's no the first time I've been kicked out of bed or pulled out of bed and things like this, you know.

> It was usually always a Sunday. He wanted you to stay in bed all day on Sunday, and he used to say, "You'll wait an awful long time before I ask you." And I got in the end, I didn't even . . . want him to touch me.

Each successive violent episode leaves the woman with less hope, less self-esteem, and more fear. The positive aspects of the relationship become weaker and the man becomes accustomed to hitting his wife and inured to the sight of her pain. By and large the husband ceases to see himself as engaging in anything wrong or unjust. The woman's struggle to change the pattern of violence through adaptations in her own behavior is almost invariably ineffective because she is engaged in an impossible and false struggle: the problem of wife beating is primarily the husband's problem. When women's efforts fail, as they must, their isolation from outside sources of support or assistance leave them with an overwhelming sense of hopelessness.

> I wouldn't like to go back on the depression I felt before we split up. . . . I used to walk round the town center and . . . wonder if I smashed a window in Safeway would they lift [arrest] me and would Tom care? You know, would it be enough to shock him, to make him care sort of thing. And then I'd say, "I'll lift one of the wains out of a pram." But no, I know what I'd have felt if somebody had lifted my wain out of the pram. But it was just something to draw attention. . . . [When you get to that point] you just walk about. I used to walk up to the town center and stand in the middle of that big square part in the middle of it and wait to meet someone to have a cup of coffee. It really was that empty. You felt nobody cared. There was nobody. I used to just wander round, my mind a blank. . . . I used to say to myself, "Walk into Safeway and pinch a bag of messages and let them catch me. They'll take me to the police station and somebody will come and talk to me." You realized it was stupid. I mean, I had enough. I still wasnae that far that I realized it was only going to cause myself trouble, my mother trouble, and everybody else trouble. And I says no. Then I used to say, "That swine, he wouldn't bother his shirt anyway."

The isolation is lessened somewhat for those women who have jobs or who have greater opportunities to maintain contacts with friends even if they do not confide in them about their problems.

> As I said, with being, you know, when you're working, you sort of say to yourself, "Well, I have to go to my work," which I believe was a good thing for me because it helped me to get out and, sort of, it helped me to keep it away from my mind. I believe if I hadn't been working I would have been in a hospital, you know. Because being out and meeting other people and, you know, talking to them, it did make things that bit easier for me.

It is at this low point that many women entirely cease to struggle to improve the relationship. They cease to argue and to defend themselves from even the most blatantly false accusations or unjust treatments in the hope that they will avoid an escalation of violence. Either they turn inward and attempt to build a protective shell around their emotions that will allow them to cope with the continuing violence or they consider that their only escape is suicide or murder.

> In all the time that we was married, this last three years I'm talking about, in all the time that he hit me, bounced me, bounced me from one wall to another wall, he could never make cry. But as I sit here talking to you, I can cry.

> He phoned up his sister and says, "I've just battered and raped Jane." And he actually told his sister that. And his sister was really sick—and I mean I don't really get on all that well with his sister,—but she said to me she more

or less pitied me. One day I bought a knife, I actually bought a knife, and I was going to stick it in him cos I wanted to see him dead. I did. I hated him. I began to hate him that much. . . . But, he didn't know about this knife. I even had it underneath my pillow, just in case he come near me. But I was—I was going to kill him. I had it in my mind I was going to kill him.

And I used to plan. Well, not plan things, but I used to, in bed at night, I used to think . . . of ways of doing it. But at the same time, deep down in my heart, I didn't really. But it used to give me great satisfaction to know that I could do it, to cover him under a pillow. Many times . . . I've seen him and I've thought, "I could so easily press that on him." And then I used to think, "My God, they'll know it's suffocation, and they'll arrest me, and I'll get sent to prison . . . and if I get seven years they'll take the children off me." I used to think of all things like this. They never came to anything. I mean, I just couldn't, I couldn't do it to him, but I used to like thinking about it.

If I had stayed I would have put a knife in his back because the children were really, well, I'll say nervous. . . . I thought that if I had stuck it six years I could stick it twelve years. But really, at the end it was really bad. I would have either ended up putting a knife in his back or else taking an overdose. And if I would have done that I would have took the kids with me.

Obviously, not all women reach this point, but we were struck by the number of women who revealed such strong feelings of desperation. Still, all battered women do become desperate because there appears to be no solution to their problem and no means of escape from it. At this point, many women begin to overcome a lifetime of training to respect the husband's authority, comply with his wishes, and accept his decisions and judgments: they begin to fight back. They overcome the fear of punishment for defiance and they begin to question the reasonableness of his demands, deny his justifications for chastisement, and reject his claims of provocation. Some women even begin to hit back.

I'm more defiant now that I ever was, you know. Earlier I'd jump up and do what he told me to do, but not now.

He kneed me actually, right in me front, you know. And we were outside the dispensary in Manchester and I just turned round and I says, "You mental bastard." I says, "You're at it again. You're always hitting me. It don't make no difference where you are." Mind you, as I say, this is all in this last six months, when I don't know where I got the courage from, but somebody's given me the courage from somewhere. Maybe I've just taken enough and I couldn't take no more that I just had to answer him back. Normally, before this, I wouldn't have said a word. I would have just taken it and just cowered down to all this.

About three days before—no, maybe five or six days before—I left, he picked a knife up. You know, you get a set of three knives—you know, the big one—and he come with this. He says, "You bastard. I'll stick it." So I just stood there. Don't ask me where I got the courage from, I don't know. I says, "Well, why the fucking hell don't you stick the bastard and have done with it?" Because at that time I just couldn't take no more. I just wasn't bothered. If he had stuck it and he'd killed me, I'd have been glad, you know. And maybe that's self-pity, I don't know what you call it. I just put me hands on me hips and I says, "Fucking stick it just there, just put it there," I says, "Put the bleeding knife there. . . . If you don't," I says, "put the fucking thing down and stop talking about it."

CHAPTER 8

STAYING, LEAVING, AND RETURNING

IF THINGS ARE SO BAD, then why does the woman not leave? The twin questions of why women stay in or why they fail to leave violent relationships to a large extent miss the point: they are based upon the assumption that a woman engages in either one behavior or the other. Most women engage in both behaviors. Some women leave quite frequently but do so with varying intentions about the permanency of that act. Certainly, a few women never leave the house even for several hours, but most women have at some time left, sometimes with every intention of returning and sometimes intending to make a permanent break. Some of the women in this latter category succeed in terminating the relationship; others fail and return home. Thus, what needs to be considered is the part that temporary leaving plays in the relationship, as well as the personal and material factors associated with a woman's decision to leave permanently and her ability to implement such a decision.

Of the women we interviewed, 88% (96 women) did at some time leave after an assault. Of those 96 women 20% left only once, 47% left from two to five times, and 33% left more frequently. Almost half of these 96 women, 48%, spent less than one week away from home on such occasions—often just staying a weekend with relatives. Another 7% stayed away from one to two weeks; 20% from two weeks to one month; 17% from one to six months; and 8% stayed away more than six months. The time away from the marital home usually was spent with parents (44%), other relatives (25%), and friends (18%), and sometimes wandering the streets, in a rented flat, or in the care of neighbors, a social worker, etc. (13%). On many more occasions, women left the house for periods of less than one day; this time typically was spent just wandering the streets or talking to a relative or friend. The pattern of staying, leaving, and returning reflect the complex pushes and pulls of the numerous personal, social, and material factors that motivate the battered woman. The pattern of leaving and returning and the reasons for doing so change over time as the woman's perceptions of her position change and as the couple's relationship deteriorates.

Leaving Temporarily

As has been noted already, the woman initially believes that the violence will not continue and that her husband will reform.[1] At this point she may go to her parents' house for a few hours or a few days in order to emphasize her objections to such treatment and to try to hasten what she believes will be the process of reform by letting her husband see what it would be like without her presence, her affection, her domestic work, and, in many cases, her financial support or contributions. The intention is not to leave the relationship permanently but to try to gain some form of redress and to change the relationship by removing the violence from it. At this very early stage the sequence of events is almost always the same: the woman's husband goes after her, apologizes for hitting her, acknowledges the error of his ways, promises that it will never happen again, reaffirms his affection for her, and pleads with her to come home.

> *Why did you go back?*
>
> Oh, because he gave me so many promises that it was unbelievable.
>
> Well, he kept coming up to my mother's and at first I thought maybe it taught him a lesson.
>
> Because I was sure there was something in me that could make the marriage work. I was quite positive about that.

Initially, the woman almost always is forgiving (though sometimes not for several days) and she goes home in the belief that her husband will change.

> I wanted to try and make a go of it and find the things that were going wrong. It might have been just a period he was going through, you know. I mean you cannae just walk out at the first thing. For all I knew it might have been something out of the blue that happened and whether it was going to go on again or not. I tried to make it work, but it didnae.
>
> Angus contacted me and he said he wanted me to go back, he would never lift his hands again, it wouldn't happen again. So I went back. I was only back for about a fortnight when the same thing occurred again. So I left again. And I came [to the refuge].

This pattern may be repeated several times before the woman gives up her belief in his promises of reform.

> I've left him and I've been back but it was against my grain. I didnae want to go back again because I knew for certain that he had no intentions of changing and he didnae want to change, but he . . . kept coming up to pester me at my mother's and kept talking to my dad and keeps telling my dad how much he loves me.
>
> The last time he begged and pleaded with me to go back home and he said he loved me and he didn't want me to get a divorce and all this. And even if I

did divorce him he'd still come up and see me and all this, you know, and he'd want me to marry him again and all this. So I went back to him, but I wasn't sure myself. I mean, I told him before I went back that I wasn't sure of my feelings. I didn't think, I certainly didn't feel, about him the way I did when I married him, you know. I told him that I just didn't feel the same way about it and he was quite willing to make a go of it and he said he would try and get my love back and all this, but things got worse. I just hate him all the more now.

Later, the woman may leave for a temporary respite from the beatings and go back home without any hope of change. She returns because she believes that it is right to keep the marriage together and because others encourage her to keep it together. Often, however, she returns because she has no alternatives that would allow her to leave permanently and set up a new life.

Leaving Permanently

Several researchers have commented upon the numerous personal, social, and material reasons why women fail to make a permanent break from a violent relationship. Truninger interviewed 30 women from California who had been beaten by husbands or cohabitants and offered several explanations for why the relationships were not terminated by divorce (although this, she maintained, was one of the few effective solutions):[2] a negative self-image creating doubts about the ability to be successful on one's own; "romantic delusions concerning married life," which fostered a belief that the husband would reform and/or "that marriage must be preserved at all costs for the sake of their families";[3] difficulties of financial support; low prospects for employment; lack of child care facilities; and the "extensive psychological pressures" to which "society subjects divorcees."[4] Carlson's study of women in a refuge in Michigan noted that the reasons for not leaving permanently included a devastatingly low self-concept, isolation, and fear of living independently.[5] Roy, in studying 150 American women who had contacted Abused Women's Aid in Crisis, isolated two main factors—hope for reform and no place to go—although fear of reprisals, children, economic dependence, fear of loneliness, and stigma of divorce were also mentioned in decreasing order of importance.[6] Levinger,[7] O'Brien,[8] and Gelles[9] all noted that a woman is more likely to leave when the violence is severe or frequent. Gelles also found that women who had experience with violence as children were less likely to leave or to seek intervention, as were those who were more "entrapped" in marriage because of lack of educational or occupational resources. He also cited external pressures from various social agencies as another factor influencing a woman's actions. Added to this list of factors deterring a woman from leaving a violent relationship permanently are two others that are much more tenuous: the woman's supposed acceptance of violence as normal,[10] as well as the woman's supposed masochistic tendencies.[11] In the following discussion, we will examine many of these personal, social, and material factors as they affect a woman's decision to terminate a violent relationship and her attempts to implement that decision.

Women who do consider the possibility of leaving the relationship permanently usually do so, at least initially, with very mixed personal feelings about themselves and their husbands. It is not easy to decide to leave a man who may not be "all bad" and to give up a marriage that may have many positive features. When women were asked to evaluate their marriages apart from the violence, their ambivalence was evident.

> Well, I've always had strong feelings for him and I know that he has for me. . . . I'm willing to make another go of it but for the last time.
>
> They used to tell me to get rid of him, but when you feel something for somebody it's difficult.
>
> As far as he was concerned, I was perfect and if anybody said a wrong thing about me, you know, he would argue that black and white that I was perfect. We had perfect kids. It's unbelievable. That's why it took so long to demolish all the feelings I had.
>
> When I saw him, I used to start feeling sorry for him and I went back to him. I used to be that determined that I wasn't going back and he'd talk me into it.

Leaving permanently means giving up the status of a wife and taking on the still somewhat stigmatized status of a divorcee and learning to live alone and independently. In our society the status of wife is deemed to be so necessary to a woman's identity that she may have considerable difficulty thinking of herself in any other way; thus, she will not readily give up that status. Moreover, a woman who has been dominated, controlled, and frightened for years has lost a great deal of self-confidence and self-esteem. The prospect of living on her own may be frightening.

Why do you think you stayed with him as long as you did?

> Fear, I think. Fear of going, fear of staying.

The experience of women who have gone to refuges that emphasize self-help illustrates how ungrounded this fear really is and how quickly and remarkably women become independent especially in a supportive climate in which they are encouraged to take control of their lives by making decisions and taking actions that affect their daily lives as well as their future.

In order for a woman to leave her husband permanently she must overcome not only personal fears, the loss of status, and ambivalent feelings about her husband but also the deeply ingrained ideas that marriages should be held together at almost any cost, that the split up of a marriage is mostly the fault of the woman, and that a broken home is worse for children than a whole, though violent, one. These cultural notions are urged upon her by friends, relatives, and representatives of social agencies.

One of the central concerns raised about the split up of a marriage is that of the consequences for children. Their material and emotional welfare takes on a primary importance both in the woman's decision about leaving and in the various forms of advice, pressure and/or assistance given by others. Children are also central to many of the financial and material problems the woman will face in trying to implement her decision to set up a new life.

Children

The most common reasons given by women for leaving their husbands, or staying with them, or returning to them are related to children. Women stay for the "sake of the children"—in the belief that children must live with their father, come from a good, stable home, and not be stigmatized by coming from a broken home. They also stay in order not to disrupt the children's schooling or friendships.

> I thought they should have a daddy, you know, so I always went back.

> I would have liked my marriage to work for my kids' sake. I don't like the idea of them growing up and just with me, you know. I mean, you hear of kids in trouble and they say, "Oh, well, their mother and father's divorced." "She's a widow." Things like that, you know. And it worries me really.

Women also stay in a violent relationship because of the practical difficulties of leaving with children in tow. Since the responsibility for the physical care of children usually rests almost exclusively with the woman and since she will almost never consider leaving without taking them with her, they will present a very great strain upon her limited or nonexistent income or upon the facilities of those who take them in.

> I used to leave and go to my mother's but that wasn't an answer either because he kept coming up. . . . And you get to the stage, you say, "Well, where can I go? There's nowhere else." And, let's face it, when you've got four children, you really need a home of your own. When you go and stay with somebody, it doesn't matter who it is, it's alright for a wee while but not forever.

Women do, however, also leave for the sake of their children, especially if the physical abuse that they have long endured begins to spill over onto the children. Women will rarely tolerate it if the children are also being beaten or treated badly. She will make this limit perfectly clear and if it is crossed, which is not often, she will either pull out all stops in order to reestablish it or leave and take the children with her.

He never ever marked the kids. I mean, if he ever would have done that . . . I would have been, I'd have been through him.

After a particularly violent assault upon this woman, the violence did spill over onto their daughter and the woman responded with great fury and a determination to leave.

> He hit my daughter. As I said, I was lying in bed. I could hear the kids up and him. And he had asked Jane to put on a boiled egg for him and then he'd asked her to to something else and all she said to him was "Och, I cannae do two things at the one time." And he started battering her. I mean, I jumped, you know, and I ran in and I got a hold of him. I says, "Don't you dare." I says, "You leave her. You've done enough damage when you do it to me. You're not going to do it to her." I said, "That's enough." So this time I said somebody will need to help me because I think I'd eventually either've killed him—I think I'd have done something to him or myself if I couldn't have, you know, managed it with him, if I couldn't have got rid of him. I'd have to have done. I mean, it was really desperation.

Another woman had a terrifying experience when her two young daughters went missing at two o'clock in the morning. Earlier in the evening her husband had backed her up against the fireplace and was beating her when their son came to his mother's defense and, for the first time in his life, hit his father. The two younger girls heard this and could take no more, so they left their beds, crawled out the window, and went to hide.

> I said to [my son] Alexander, the lassies arenae in bed. Well, even he, big laddie that he was, he was crying, you know, they're all that close. . . . I says, "Oh, where are they?" So I went outside and I shouted on them and I was going mad, you know. It wasn't the fact that I'd had a belting—that didn't bother me. It was the fact that the lassies were oot in the dark and they were scared stiff. I couldnae find them, and I knew they'd taken blankets off the bed because the blankets were gone, and I went out with a torch [flashlight]. And here, underneath the hoose, we had a kind of cellar where the kids had a playroom, where they put their big toys, bicycles and things, and I happened to look in there and there they were sound asleep on the floor, with their blankets, underneath the hoose.
>
> My husband knew if he ever did anything to the kids I would kill him. I would have killed him, and this was the nearest thing I could think of. How could he do this to the wains, you know? Lying there, they were like a pair of orphans lying on the stair, sleeping right enough. So on my way up I gets the axe and Alexander's getting the lassies up the stair, you see, lifting their blankets. So I ran up to the shed and I got the axe and I went in and I was standing like this. I would have, I mean, that would have been him. I would be in prison today if it hadn't been for Alexander, because I was standing there and he took the axe off me. He said, "That'll no solve anything, mum."

So that was that?

Aye, and we had a cup of tea. I mean, I was glad next day. Well, when I'd come to my senses, you know, I was. I would never have done it. No, I would have. I would have made sure the kids wouldnae suffer. I mean, I wouldnae let them take that from him. I could take that, you know, I could take it, but I wouldn't let him do that to the kids.

Incidents such as these usually were isolated ones and the men who systematically and brutally assaulted their wives did not typically treat their children in a similar fashion. For example, in our analysis of 933 police and court cases of assaults on wives, we found that only 13% (125) involved any form of physical violence directed at a second person. A closer look at these 125 cases revealed that half of them (62 cases) involved the couple's children; the remainder, other relatives (33 cases), acquaintances (17), police (9), boyfriend (2), wife (1), and a stranger (1).[12] Most of the incidents occurred either when a child intervened on the mother's behalf or when he or she became the unintended target of a blow directed at the mother.[13] In a very few cases the woman was assaulted as she intervened on behalf of a child who was being assaulted by his or her father. Our interviews also revealed that the great majority of violent husbands did not treat their children brutally or beat them. This is not to say that they did not hit their children (42% almost never hit their children and another 23% hit them no more than three times a year), but most of the children were hit infrequently by their fathers. They usually were slapped or given punishments not intended to do them any injury or severely to intimidate them. In about 3% of the cases one of the children was singled out and subjected to severe forms of physical violence either for coming to the mother's defense or for failing to meet the father's very high expectations. About 20% of the men did at one time or another hit or punch one of the children, usually the eldest, very hard, but most of the men were in fact quite concerned about their children's welfare and did not mistreat them even though the women complained that their husbands did not take a sufficiently active part in rearing the children.

> He's never threatened the kids right enough. Although he might hate me, he really . . . loves the kids.
>
> I mean, that's one thing about him. If he comes in and I say, "John's no well. He's in his bed," he says, "get a doctor," you know, or "Take him to the doctor and make an appointment." Things like that. . . . He worries about the kids.

In many families the children were protected not only from the violence itself but also from the knowledge that it was happening. Often they were put out to play before their mother was hit or the beating occurred when they were asleep and at least in theory out of earshot. Nevertheless, concealment is very difficult, if not impossible, to keep up. In this sense, the child's primary role in the violence is that of witness to it.

The children's role as witnesses was quite varied and had numerous effects both upon the violence itself and upon them. For example, their presence often resulted in the limitation or cessation of the assault.

When the kids were there and upset it died down pretty quick, but when it's just the two of us it could go on and on and on.

He was still angry enough to fight with me and I think if the kids weren't there he would have went further. It was only the kids that stopped him, you know. And my son, he came up the stair, and then the kids were talking about it. Patrick was telling Christopher that his daddy was going to throw me out the window and Patrick was walking behind me saying, "Was my daddy going to throw you out the window?" and all this, you know.

It got to the stage where he wouldn't hit me in front of them. As soon as he knew Cathy was in, he seen her coming, or he seen Paul, he'd let me go.

In some families, however, the children were called in to witness their mother's punishment as an additional degradation to her.

Oh yes, they've seen me be hit. He used to delight in lifting them up out their beds so that they could watch.

And this was 2 A.M. and he sat on the chair and sat and told me everything he thought about me and he dragged the full three kids out their beds and made them all sit. He lined them right up against the couch and told them all what I was. He says to them, "Now you see her, she's a whore." And he'd say to Chris, "See her, she's a cow." And the bairn was only months old, and he'd say to him, "See her, she's nae good. She's dirt. That's what women are. They're all dirt. There's your daddy been out working all day and there's nae tea ready for him. See how rotten she is to your daddy." And all the bairns were dragged out of their beds for nae reason at all.

Even though her children often were the only witnesses a woman had to use in a court of law, most women we interviewed were very reluctant to subject children to this and therefore failed to take legal action.

The police came down to me with this citation and it was for my two wee girls as well. They were getting brought up in court as witness against their father. Well, I didnae want that because I've never been in a court. I didnae want it. So I wrote my husband a letter telling him this and would he change his plea to guilty cos he plead not guilty. And he wrote back saying no, he wouldn't change it and he sent a pass out. He wanted to see me. So I went up to the jail, but he was awful bitter.

When we asked women what effect the violence against them had had upon the children and might have in their futures, the women always reported different responses for each child. Some children either were too young to know what was happening or were carefully kept from finding out. Others were aware of the violence but seemed to be able to cope with it without too much difficulty; some became nervous, clinging, wet the bed, were prone to hysterics at the first indication of an altercation, or grew very resentful toward their father.

What about in the future? Do you think, well, how do you think it'll affect them then?

I don't know about Mary. I mean, she is very, very strong indeed at the moment, and she's the type that can stick up for herself. It might affect her, you know, as far as her relationship with men later on. I'm quite sure it will because she's no going to take anything like this from them. Susan is kind of young to think that. She's kind of young for me to say it'll affect her in any way later on in life, but I don't think so cos she's very even natured.

My kids don't want to go back. My son, who's only seven, he's not really had a very good life. He's seen an awful lot of this and he's even that nervous. He is a nervous boy, you know. He gets awfully upset and he says to me the other night, "Don't go back. Don't even talk to my daddy." I says, "I'm not going back to him." He says, "But don't even go to see him because you know what he's like. He'll talk you into it and you'll end up going back." He says, "Just get married to someone else and get us a new daddy." He says, "Just stay away and get married and we'll have a new daddy and just forget about him."

Well, my daughter always stood in front of him. She came between us and she'd say to him, "Leave her alone. Stop hitting her," you know, these sort of things. Well, my daughter I believe is really upset inside, you know. She pretends that she's, you know, quite able to take it. . . . I don't believe she is inside. Because she has seen most of it, you know, going back. Ian hasn't, and the younger ones haven't, but Joan was the one. She saved me on quite a number of times. She really did.

LEARNING VIOLENCE

One of the common questions and concerns about the children and whether to remain in the home or take them out of it focuses on the extent to which they will learn to be violent by living in a violent home and by witnessing their father beat their mother. Most of the research on learning supports the contention that children are more likely to use physical force when it is used against them and when they observe it being used by people with whom they identify as an effective means of achieving some desired goal. Though we do not deny that direct observation is one means by which children may learn to accept violence, to identify which family members are the most "acceptable" targets, and to know which circumstances might be considered "appropriate" for the use of violence, it would be erroneous to leap to the conclusion that all children who witness assaults on their mother or other forms of violence between family members are necessarily the seed pods of the next generation of violent families. This assumption, however, has been confidently made by many people, some of whom are supported in their belief only by folk wisdom, others by limited personal impressions, and a few by incomplete or highly inadequate research data.

Since this view on learning violence and its intergenerational transmission has wide-ranging and serious implications both for the children concerned and for those who deal with the problem of wife-beating, it deserves thorough analysis and study before it is either accepted to rejected. Let us make a few observations and point out some issues that we believe should be considered in a more thorough examination of the possible intergenerational transmission of violence. First, it should be clear by now that the use of various types and degrees of physical force between all family members is far more prevalent than was once thought. Thus, many more children than previously suspected come from homes in which at least some physical force has been used. Second, there is considerable variation in the frequency and severity of the force used, and research findings are likely to be misleading if they do not provide specific and detailed information on the nature and extent of violence observed or experienced by the child. Third, a child who does observe the use of physical force in the family of orientation may learn many other things rather than simply mimic the violence or identify with being a victim of it. Children may learn to accept, admire, emulate, or expect such behavior, but they may also be repulsed by it and reject its use. It would be naive in the extreme to assume that a child is such a simple creature that he or she learns only one thing from what he or she observes, and that is to emulate the observed behavior in a robot fashion.

Learning theorists propose numerous models of how children learn at various stages in their social, emotional, and cognitive development. Those who have analyzed the processes of *human* learning note that even when we are explicitly trying to teach a person something we may unintentionally teach many other lessons, which sometimes contradict the one purposely being taught. Another very important point made by researchers in human learning is that human beings continue to learn all their lives, and as important as childhood experiences may be, the learning process is not arrested at the childhood stage. These considerations should enter into any assessment of the legacy of violence.

Children who observe their father beating their mother (or experience such beating themselves or observe other forms of violence) are observing not merely the effective use of physical force in order to achieve certain goals but also the pain and suffering such treatment brings to the victim, as well as to other people involved. So while their father may be giving the children a model to emulate, their mother may be going to great lengths to teach them that such behavior is wrong and that they should treat their future wives better or expect better treatment from their future husbands. Children are usually very idealistic and have a relatively well developed sense of justice, and it is certainly equally likely that they view physical violence as evil and to be avoided rather than as beneficial and to be emulated.

Do you think it will affect them when they grow up?

I hope not. But with Johnny . . . it's amazing what that kid says to me. [He'll say], "See, when I get married I'm never going to hit my wife. I'm going to work all the time and earn money for her and I'm going to help her in the house." I mean, he's only seven, and he said this before he was seven. He's saying to me, "Im going to let her go out to the bingo if she wants . . . and I'm not going to hit her and I'm going to wash the dishes for her," and things like this. . . . I'm hoping it will make him a bit wiser when he is older, you know, when he gets married. I hope he'll remember the bad bits and try not to do that to his family.

It's as if they understand what I'm going through and they're trying to help me. I mean, the other day we were sitting in the kitchenette and we'd just finished our dinner and Davey lifted the plates and went and washed them. He was standing at the sink, my wee boy, and he stood there and he came over and he said, "I've washed the dishes for you." I mean, see, it was my birthday and he wouldn't let me wash the dishes. He washed the dishes up all day long because he hadn't any money to buy me anything, so he washes the dishes for me. He's really marvelous. They're all good, really.

And what about the boys? How do you think it's affected them now that they're grown? Their engagement and their treatment of girls?

It's had the opposite effect on the boys. It's had the effect I'd hoped for. I used to say to them, "I've had to spend my time telling you this," that this wasn't the right thing for men to do, that they hadn't to treat a woman like that. They should treat a woman the way they'd like their own sisters to be treated, you know. . . . So it did work, whether it was that or whether in their own inside they say to themselves, "Well, I'm no going to be like that. I've seen how my mother suffers. I'll no do that to any woman." I've tried to tell them, so I think it's worked. They're hard working, safe, look after their money. They're just normal blokes. They never have any trouble. They wouldnae hurt anybody. I mean, they're very hale and hearty boys, and they're well brought up. So I've won, you know, I feel a great—I've a great satisfaction in knowing that all the time I did spend trying to teach them the things that their father should have taught them, I've won in the end.

We can see that children within the same family are differentially exposed to or aware of the violence directed at their mother and that they respond in distinct ways to this experience. Therefore, it is wrong to assume that all children of wife beaters, or any of them, for that matter, will learn to accept or imitate the violent behavior they see and will grow up violent themselves or victims of violence. In fact, when we asked women about violence among their own adult brothers and sisters, as well as among those of their husband, a very striking pattern of nonviolence emerged. Of all the couples' siblings only 12% were in any way violent either to their wives or children or to others. If they had been exposed to and learned violence in their home, then one must ask why 88% of their brothers and sisters did not also learn the same lesson.

This finding emphasizes one of the major problems with studies on the cycle of violence thesis. Most have taken a sample of people known either to be violent in some way or to be the victims of violence and have looked into their backgrounds for any evidence of violence in the family of orientation. Little attention has been paid to the siblings of the individuals studied and little effort has been made to specify what a violent background is. We see at least two very serious flaws in such research. First, we can say that almost everyone comes from a violent household if our definition of violence is sufficiently vague. The confirmation of the thesis is made simple, although it is relatively meaningless. To discover that a murderer was sometimes slapped by his mother or father may superficially confirm the cycle of violence theory, but such confirmation is suspect indeed. Second, confirmation of this thesis would also seem to require knowledge about whether or not the siblings of the violent person, who may or may not have come from a violent background, are themselves violent. If we discover that a man who beats his wife comes from a home in which his father beat his mother but that his three brothers do not beat their wives, then we have one case that appears to confirm the cycle of violence thesis and three that refute it. In short, conclusions about the long-term effects upon children of observing or experiencing violence in the home will be incomplete and suspect until we have conducted much more sophisticated and highly specific studies of violent individuals—from both violent and nonviolent backgrounds—and their siblings, as well as of nonviolent individuals—from both violent and nonviolent backgrounds— and their siblings.

Though concern about the children of battered women is very important, it should not be the only or even the central concern. There is great danger that this will happen. It is not uncommon to hear both social service representatives and abused wives claim that they are concerned only about these children. Surely, it is not possible to care about, or do very much for, the children of battered women without caring about and doing something for their mothers, who usually are the sole victims of the violence. To a great extent the overriding concern for the children of women who are being beaten reflects the idea that in the hierarchy of worth among family members, women are the least important or are not important at all. Quite often, the problems of women assume importance only when they affect family members of greater worth—children and husbands. This devaluation of her problems is often so extreme that the battered woman feels she has little or no right to leave the marriage in order to free herself from harm or to seek help for herself, and this idea tends to be reinforced by outsiders and even imposed upon her. But even women who accept this view in general, as would be expected after a lifetime of learning, may eventually be forced to reject it.

> I think a good wife is somebody that sees to her husband and family, not necessarily in that order, but completely, the whole family, giving and taking. She must have some—I mean, it's alright being a good wife and

mother—but she must have some time to herself for to be herself and no be just something for the family.

I'd asked the doctor several times, "I'll need to get away. I can't stick it staying there." It was pure mental torture. And he says, "You'll just have to stick it for the sake of the wee ones, you know." And at that stage I thought, "My God, all anybody can ever say to me is, 'the wee ones, the wee ones,' " What about me?

Surely this hierarchy of worth is damaging to everyone and should be eliminated from all social policies that operate to entrap a woman in a violent marriage "for the sake of the children."

Alternatives to the Violent Marriage

The pattern of staying, leaving, and returning is not related just to personal concerns, say, the children's happiness, but also to structural or material factors such as financial support, accommodation, and child care. In order for a woman to get out of the house even if it is only to escape the violence temporarily, she must have some money and a place to stay. In order for her to leave permanently, she must have sufficient funds to support herself and her children and be able to find suitable accommodation. Involved in this are a whole host of material problems which are sometimes insurmountable and over which the woman may have little or no control.

Despite the fact that a substantial proportion of women are now the sole wage earners in their families and an even larger proportion of couples jointly support their families, many women are either completely or substantially dependent upon their husbands for financial support. The concept of the dependent wife does, of course, continue to permeate most of our social institutions and results in many arrangements that limit the battered woman's opportunities to become financially independent and thus able to establish a reasonable life, or any life at all, apart from her violent husband.

Because women are still to some extent expected to be partially or totally dependent upon their husbands for financial support they are much less likely to have been trained either at home or at school to take on financial independence or to see wage work as anything other than a part-time or temporary activity.[14] Much of the organization of wage work is also based upon this principle and many businesses either exclude women or include them in dead-end and low paying jobs. Women tend to be channeled into positions in which they serve men (secretaries) or nurture others (playschool attendants, nurses, teachers). Most women, like most men, work in factories and service industries and it is well documented that women have poorer prospects of getting such jobs initially, that they are more likely to be hired into jobs that are low paying, and that they are paid less for the same work men do. Also, they are likely to be the first to be laid off.[15] The Finer report thoroughly documented the dire circumstances of single-parent families (usually headed by women) in Great Britain, illustrating how difficulties in the areas of housing, finance, and child care, among others, are in part the result of the legal and economic structures, which actively discriminate against women in general and female heads of households in particular.[16] Perhaps one of the most abbreviated statements on the financially dependent status of the British wife is contained in the income tax form, which states that a married woman should treat her income as though it belonged to her husband and all contact with the tax office, even on matters that concern her alone, should be made by her husband. Martin documented the economic dependence of the battered woman in America,[17] and her findings are similar to others in the more general area of women's employment.[18]

Closely related to problems of finance are problems of child care and child support for a woman who does work. Day care facilities are very limited, and an underpaid woman is likely to spend a considerable portion of her income on child care. Martin noted that although there were 36 million working women in America and one household in eight was headed by a woman in 1974, there were only about 1 million licensed day care places available for the more than 6 million children under six who had working mothers. She also noted the low wages usually earned by women and the problems that divorced women have in getting money for child support from their husbands.[19]

For many women the first financial hurdle is getting enough money to get out of the house. Pizzey recounted the story of a woman who got on a bus without a penny in her pocket to pay the fare,[20] and Eisenberg and Micklow described the predicament of a woman who spent a long time saving $1.70 with which to escape.[21] Martin told a story of a woman who found it almost impossible to get hold of just $5.00,[22] and there were numerous similar cases in our own research. If a woman runs from the house in her nightgown and bedroom slippers without any money in her pockets or spends her last pennies on bus fare, she is in no position even to consider trying to find shelter that is not both temporary and free. She may walk the streets (if she was fortunate enough to be properly clothed when she fled) or she may spend the night with a relative or friend, but in most cases, she must soon return home because she can afford to do nothing else.

> Sometimes he just threw me out and I had to walk the streets until it was morning and he went out.

> My friend loaned me the money for bus fares to get away, but I didn't know where I could go.

> I had to go back, I mean, where can you stay with three children?

Even if a woman plans her escape well in advance, the difficulties of obtaining and paying for accommodation are still very great. Without sufficient money or at least a subsistence level of income, the woman has no alternative except various forms of social security or welfare, and it is debatable whether they are a real alternative. It is only with the opening of refuges that short-term accommodations—in much greater demand than supply—have become available. For women who have escaped to a refuge, finding another place to live becomes a major preoccupation and a prerequisite for a new, violence-free life.

> *Probably quite a lot of people would wonder why you stayed with him as long as you did. Why did you?*
>
> Well, as I said before, you leave them and you go and stay with somebody. Even if it's your parents, you've got small children and they've got their family, so therefore it does tell. A strain shows on everybody concerned. You go to the welfare for help and you get told you can't get help. There's nobody can help you.
>
> You can't get a house of your own. The only way that any battered wife, or a person in my position, could help themselves is if they had money. That's the only way and that's one thing that very few of us have.
>
> Even if you do get a house, I mean, let's face it, you just get the bare essentials. You don't get anything. If you would like to take your kids out or go with your kids anywhere, you would need to sit down and work out a right tight budget because everything's that expensive.

Britain has far greater provisions for public housing than does the United States, but even there this hurdle is fraught with difficulties, delays, and barriers, and is sometimes made impossible or so intolerable that the woman leaves the refuge and goes back to the violent home in despair.

But why do the women and children have to leave the home? Why does the victim have to flee to the streets while the offender remains by the fireside? Unjust as it may seem, this situation reflects the traditional position that the house belongs to the male head of household. Although, to some extent this has been rectified by law,[23] it is still very difficult for the woman who has been beaten to remain in the family home while the husband is forced to leave.

> See, this time, I'd rather we had a discussion. Well, I realize my marriage is finished because any feelings I had for him, they're dead. I couldn't feel anything for him again because he's done that much hurt to me that I don't know if I'll ever get over it. I don't suppose I will. I don't think I'll ever feel deeply for anyone again, you know. That's that . . . If a man could leave and maybe go into lodgings or buy a flat on his own and give the wife the home . . . it would be a lot easier for everybody concerned, but this is a thing that you cannae do with these men. It's you and the kids to get out, you know, and they don't give a damn what happens either.

Alternative housing in the private sector is, of course, even less available to most women than public housing. Getting and keeping a job that pays enough to support a family and meet child care costs is very difficult. It is almost impossible for a woman to survive on her own at anything other than a subsistence level, if at that. The woman who leaves her husband may also lose many of her belongings and, of course, the home she has built up over the years. Equally important, however, is the potential increase in isolation. One worker from a refuge summarized the problems of women who move to another house and find themselves without their old friends and neighborhood baby sitters. She was told by a woman who recently had been rehoused that things were very hard and that they would get worse as winter set in. By this she meant that as the world became cold and dark and getting outside became more difficult for her and the children, her loneliness and isolation would increase. Also, Christmas was coming—at a time when families should be together loneliness is harder to bear. With all of these difficulties, it is no wonder that many women never leave a violent relationship or that they go back numerous times before they even consider, much less attempt, a final break. Surmounting all of these obstacles and making a final break is truly a leviathan task, and even the most determined fail numerous times before succeeding. Yet many people believe that a woman gets only one chance to leave; if she fails, she does not deserve another. Rather than being seen as a necessary part of the process of leaving a marriage and a reflection of the difficulties of doing so, leaving a marriage and then returning is usually viewed as a sign of capriciousness or lack of sincerity, resolve, or determination on the woman's part.

If we reconsider the question of why the battered woman does not leave and never go back, we can see that both the question and its answer eliminate the moral indignation that should be aroused by wife beating. The question is a simple one: leave or stay. The answer is thought to be equally simple. But the answer is also thought to measure the "true" extent of the violence and the direness of the woman's predicament. If the woman leaves, then things must have been as bad as she claimed and she must be sincere in her desire to be free from violence. If she stays, then things must not be that bad, or she must not really mind the beatings as much as she says she does, or she must accept the violence as a normal part of life.[24] Indeed, some would argue that if the woman does not leave a violent husband, then she must somehow be drawn to the excitement or danger of the situation or see her husband's behavior as a sign of his masculinity or believe it indicates love for her. It is maintained that the woman cannot prevent herself from engaging in behavior that is likely to result in her own abuse or that she actually likes being hit.[25] The ideas of masochism, pathology, or acceptance of violence certainly have caught the public imagination and are a part of the mythology about battered women despite findings to the contrary.[26]

To accept the masochistic explanation of why a woman does not leave a violent relationship is very comforting. It removes the moral outrage over the wife's victimization and it means that outsiders can quietly ignore the problem without feeling guilty. If the woman is "used to violence," "doesn't mind it," or even "seeks it," then why should people go out of their way to help her or lose any sleep over the fact that they have done nothing or have failed to respond to her requests for help. We have spoken with hundreds of battered women from Britain, the Continent, and North America and we can say unequivocally that not one of them liked being beaten or found it exciting. None of their actions were aimed at eliciting a violent response. It is essential to reemphasize the points made in the discussion about provocation and to consider whether it is normal and acceptable for a woman to argue about an unreasonable demand, or any demand made of her, or to complain about an unjustice, or any treatment she has received, or to negotiate for money for food or rent, or to make a request for herself. Should such behavior be seen as abnormal, unacceptable, and thus directly or indirectly calculated to push the husband to a violent response? If we view such behaviors as provocative instruments of masochistic desires, then we deny the woman even the most meager rights of independence and individuality and make her husband the sole arbiter of her acts. If we define as masochistic the woman who cannot find a job or provide another home for herself and her children or resolve her mixed feelings about remaining married, then once again we make the error of blaming the woman for being beaten. In so doing we not only fail to grasp the nature of the problem; we also commit a grave injustice.

Chapter 9

Relatives, Friends, and Neighbors

Introduction to Chapters 9–11

The violence and humiliation that many women experience at the hands of their husbands are both persistent and extreme, and yet many women are virtually trapped in such relationships. The decision to leave is a complex and difficult one, and there is little hope for change in the man's behavior or little support for the woman except through effective outside intervention; and this is largely unavailable. Thus, the woman feels that she is trapped in a relationship in which she is brutalized and humiliated and there are few people or agencies who are willing or able to help.

Given this situation, it is not surprising that some battered women consider killing their husbands. A few even make mock plans or daydream about how it might be done, but rarely are such daydreams taken seriously and only the most minute fraction of women who are beaten by their husbands actually take this fatal step. All but a few of the most frightened or desperate are deterred by the horror of the idea of actually killing anyone, much less a loved one; by the certain knowledge that such an act will bring further public humiliation; and by the fear that the various social agencies that heretofore may have been unresponsive to her pleas for help will act quickly to remove the children and prosecute her.

Despite the eventual treatment of such cases in the courts, social work departments, prisons or mental hospitals, the actions taken by relatives, friends or the representatives of these agencies are simply too late. In some cases the violence never was reported to outsiders and they could not have been expected to know of it. The woman's silence reflects the cultural ideal of the inviolable nature of the family.

The recent case in England of a 35-year-old mother of five who shot her wealthy husband illustrates how the climate of secrecy, and the resulting lack of intervention, can contribute to continued violence and result in tragedy. The jury was told of the "high life of the young landowner—who had his own plane, several expensive cars, including a Rolls-Royce, racehorses and the other woman." They were told also of the 17 years of "domination and ill-treatment," threats of murder, and "regular beatings" he inflicted upon his wife, who "waited on his every need." The woman testified that on the night of the killing her husband had hit her and that while she lay on the bedroom floor at the side of the bed on which he was sleeping off a heavy bout of drinking, she feared that he would wake up and beat her. She recounted the events.

> He rolled over. His hand touched my hair and then he gripped it. I was terrified. He released his grip and I crept downstairs quickly and quietly telephoned the police for help. I thought I would have to protect myself and I got one of his guns. I loaded the gun and went back upstairs. I stood beside the bed and he started to move. . . . I thought he was coming for me. I fired the gun. . . . The gun was held low. I just wanted to stop him getting me, and I fired the gun at the bed . . . nowhere in particular. I went downstairs and shortly afterwards the police came. I did not try to tell any lies. I told them things I had never told people before.[1]

The woman testified that her husband had threatened repeatedly to kill her and that she always had thought that it would be she who would be "killed in the end." Despite that, she stated that she did not want to kill her husband but acted out of great fear based on years of experienced brutality. Their 17-year-old daughter testified: "My father was always hitting my mother and making her life a misery. Sometimes she was covered in bruises." Defense counsel stated that "the only person who bore any responsibility both morally and legally was the dead man himself." And the father of the dead man, who described his daughter-in-law as a "girl in a million," said he thought that if either party had confided in him the murder would have been prevented. The woman was found not guilty.[2]

Speaking of similar cases in America, one judge remarked:

> I see a lot of wives killing husbands after many years of beatings. Usually they will reach for a gun after many years of putting up with violence. The gun will be there and they'll reach for it and then the husband will be dead.[3]

Mercy, leniency, and support often come from many sources for the murderess who has long been a victim of her husband's brutality.

> Just about everybody in the courtroom wept for joy, and tears rolled down even the judge's cheeks as he ordered Sandra Smith, a 38-year-old battered wife, freed in the slaying of her husband. "I've never gotten so emotional," said Queens [New York] Supreme Court Justice George Balbach as he put Mrs. Smith, mother of three, on probation for five years on a manslaughter charge.
>
> Mrs. Smith was recovering from surgery when her husband John, 39, beat her for the last time. . . . She pleaded guilty to stabbing her husband with a kitchen knife at the height of the beating.
>
> The District Attorney told the judge that he saw no purpose in sending her to prison and noted that she had three children to care for, and one of them was emotionally disturbed. The judge had received numerous supportive letters from relatives, neighbors, clergymen, school officials and community leaders. Even the dead man's mother and sister had petitioned the

court to be lenient . . . supporting her story of frequent beatings over a long period of time. When she heard she was to go free, she collapsed in sobs, saying repeatedly, "Thank you, thank you for your mercy." Then relatives began weeping too, and finally even the judge and courtroom attendants were wet-eyed. "I've never seen anything like it," said the prosecutor. "I've never seen an entire courtroom in tears."[4]

In these two cases, as in many others the fact that the women had been victimized for so many years may have been a major factor in the lenient verdicts, but it is equally if not more likely that the woman would have been further victimized either by receiving prison sentences or by being committed to mental institutions or by herself becoming the homicide victim. Commander Bannon of the Detroit Police Department agreed that the killing of a spouse is usually preceded by a long history of violence directed at the wife, but it is not always possible to predict who will be the perpetrator and who was the victim. The woman "often becomes a homicide statistic," but it may also be the husband[5] "because in the final resolution of the conflict situation, it is frequently the former victim of all those assaults who resolves the problem *society has ignored* [emphasis added] and kills her tormentor.[6] This is especially true in America because of the easy availability of firearms.

To repeat, a battered woman who kills her husband may receive widespread support and sympathy—most probably if there is a history of particularly brutal attacks, documented by outsiders, and if she has an impeccable character. As in these cases, the woman may also be supported by numerous individuals and representatives of social agencies who claim that the homicide might have been prevented if only they had known. In almost all cases, however, somebody does know. Secrecy and underreporting are serious problems in all cases of violence between family members, and we will return to this question later, but with respect to homicide, total secrecy is very unusual. At least one formal agency usually has been made aware of grave problems between the couple and often there have been numerous reports of the violence being directed at the woman.[7] So it is often not a complete surprise to these individuals and agencies when one of the spouses is killed.

Only an extraordinarily few cases of wife beating end in murder: what happens to cases that do not go that far? In Chapters 9–11 we will consider the interaction between battered women and those from whom they seek help and examine the broader implications of the responses they receive. First, we will focus upon contacts made with relatives, friends, and neighbors; then we will examine contacts made with formal agencies such as doctors, psychiatrists, social workers, police, and courts.

We will discuss how frequently women turn to each of these sources after an assault, the nature of the assistance they seek, and the responses they receive. We will also consider how particular responses either support or reject the violent behavior of the particular man concerned and how actions, attitudes, policies, and practices either support or reject the patriarchal ideologies and structural arrangements that form the underpinnings of wife beating. It is imperative that we consider the response of third parties not just in terms of the particular violent incident that has been reported to them but also in terms of the implications of their beliefs and actions for the woman—her isolation, subordination, and dependence. The responses and their implications will tell us most about the current position of battered women, assist us in understanding the implications of such behavior, and provide direction for the future. Given this distinction between the immediate response of a third party to a specific violent act and the ideals and beliefs which are embodied in that response, it is important to recognize that the ideas and actions of individuals and agencies may reject wifebeating, yet at the same time actively uphold numerous conditions which contribute to, justify and support this violence.

Nonreporting

It would be erroneous to discuss the patterns of help seeking without first stating most emphatically that most assaults go unreported. Although very few women maintain complete silence throughout the years that they are beaten, most of them report only an infinitesimally small number of the assaults they experience. For example, the 109 women we interviewed reported a total of approximately 32,000 assaults during their marriages; yet only 517 of these assaults, less than 2%, were reported to the police. Underreporting to all other sources, including relatives, friends, neighbors, ministers, doctors, and social workers, was also very high. A large percentage of women never made a single contact with a minister (76%), neighbor (57%), or friend (51%) regarding the violence. Although most women did make at least one contact with relatives, social workers, doctors, and police, the number of times they approached each of them was still small in proportion to the number of beatings they received. This sense of isolation and general reluctance to report is generally acknowledged and appears repeatedly in British, American, Dutch, French, and Australian research.

Although there is a general tendency not to report violent incidents, the patterns of nonreporting are very complex and change throughout the relationship. Women do not report the violent treatment they are receiving because of factors that center on themselves, their husbands, and the agencies themselves. First, the woman's belief that the violence will cease makes outside help seem unnecessary, and her internalization of ideals of privacy and respectability, along with her sense of shame and guilt, operate to deter reporting. Second, the man's conceptions of privacy, respectability, shame, and guilt deter him from seeking help for himself and he in turn prevents his wife from revealing the violence to others. Finally, the woman's decision to approach others for help is affected by her initial perception of the ability and willingness of various individuals or agencies to give help and, later, by her experiences with outside assistance.

Most women do not tell anyone when their husbands first begin to slap, shove, and hit them, and in our sample over half also remained silent when the beatings became more systematic and severe. This initial silence is related to the fact that at this point most battered women do not consider themselves to have a real or continuing problem and confidently conclude that no assistance is needed.

> I didn't know anything about battered wives and things like that, and I didn't really consider myself as a battered wife then. It was only once he had battered me a few times, and it was only once he'd really battered me, you know. I didn't think I was bad enough to leave home and things like that.

The judgment that no assistance is needed, an evaluation that seems so reasonable after the first assault, when there is no history of violence and when the woman has every reason to believe that it will never happen again, is rarely made after subsequent assaults. Over time the woman's silence ceases to be dictated by her idea that help is not needed. Rather, it is increasingly pressed upon her by her husband's actions and her own ideas of privacy, respectability, shame, and guilt. The stigma attached to excessive violence between family members results in a great reluctance on the part of all family members to seek any assistance from outside sources. The problem remains secret and unsharable.

In the beginning the women are often participants in this conspiracy of silence. The majority of women interviewed did not confide in anyone after the first assault they received (see Appendix B, Table 9) and spoke of the facade of harmony that surrounded their relationships. Some women even managed to maintain the image of the husband as a "great fellow" or of themselves as a "perfect couple" right up to the moment that the relationship broke up. In the words of one woman, "None of them knew until the last battering I got. They thought we were the perfect couple."

It is very common for a woman to worry about the family's reputation even while she is being beaten.

> He came across and whack right on my arm, and I said, "What was that for?" The next thing, this big glass ashtray was hurled against my arm and hit against the door and made holes. I was screaming and I was worrying about the neighbors.

> I had fear of what the neighbors might think about. You know, what would they say? I used to worry what they would say.

A woman Gelles interviewed expressed the same sentiments.

> I didn't want any of the neighbors to know that he was behaving the way he was. I didn't want anyone around when Ralph was behaving that way

. . . that's why I didn't have any neighbors. I didn't even call the police because I was afraid they'd put it in the paper.[8]

Another woman we interviewed described how she used her husband's desire for a good public image as a means of gaining a temporary respite from his violence.

The thing that was strongest in my mind was how to get out of the room. I used to think to myself if there was a pause in the proceedings I would fly. I got fast at flying out of a room. Most of the time I'd go and hang the washing out. He wouldn't come out because he wouldn't make a scene outside the house, wouldn't let anyone hear him shouting. When I got out of the house, I was alright.

This initial sense of shame, self-blame, failure, and stigma, which is felt by almost all battered women, has been noted by most researchers in this area.[9] It derives from our cultural ideals about the nature of a good marriage and about the woman's responsibility for insuring that the marital relationship is successful. This feeling results in the woman's confusion about how much she is to blame for the violence, her indecision about what to do, her reluctance to seek assistance, and her fear that outsiders will find out. Her silence is also upheld by the belief that what goes on inside a marriage is strictly the business of the couple.

Oh, I had plenty of friends and neighbors, but I just didn't want anybody involved. A family row was a family row. Even as sordid as ours. It was still a row.

The abusive husband may also feel guilty or ashamed and strive to protect his image and keep the violence a family matter. He may do so by beating his wife only when the two of them are behind closed doors and out of the public eye and then by threatening violence if she tells an outsider or seeks help. He may also physically restrain her from using the telephone or from leaving the house in order to seek assistance. When asked why she did not go to the police for help, one woman replied, in a typical fashion, "You think twice about it, cos if I brought police to the door, my life wouldn't have been worth living at all." This fear was attested to in many of the police and court cases we examined. In these records, there were frequent notations made by the police concerning long histories of unreported assaults upon the wife. In many instances, a report to the police brought threats from the husband: "I'll fucking kill my fucking wife"; "I'll get her for this." Another police case reads, "The accused became very agitated and said that he should have done her in years ago because she was a 'grass.' "

As time goes by and the beatings reoccur, fewer and fewer women maintain a complete silence although most continue to feel fear and shame and the overwhelming desire to cope on their own with as little outside intervention as possible. For some it is at the point of desperation—when assaults are most frequent and severe, when they can take no more, and when the sense of isolation and helplessness is highest—that the woman breaks the barriers of secrecy and shame and seeks outside assistance. For others, contact is made when the woman feels most capable of taking the risk of a retaliatory assault and of coping with the bureaucratic maze of helping agencies and the mixture of positive and negative responses both to her as a person and to her predicament.

Most battered women endure a great deal and draw heavily upon themselves in their attempts to cope without involving others. Yet, fear of further injuries and emotional strain drive women to seek occasional protection, solace, or escape. A pattern of infrequent and sporadic contact with individuals and agencies develops, and this pattern, like the pattern of nonreporting, is complex and changing. Once a woman does seek outside assistance, of whatever form, her subsequent decisions to seek further help depend in part on the responses of those she approaches.

In describing and seeking an understanding of this process of help seeking, we will begin where the woman usually begins: the informal circle of relatives and friends. We will see whom women contact, what forms of emotional and material assistance they seek, and what responses they receive as they try to cope with or solve what is basically seen as *their* problem. Neighbors are included in the category of informal third parties but, as will be seen in the discussion, the woman is not very likely to define them as approachable or to seek their assistance.

Help from Relatives, Friends, and "Good" Neighbors

When women first reveal to an outsider that they are being beaten, they usually approach those whom they judge to be closest to them personally and/or those whom they judge most likely to give some help or consolation without making their private problem any more public than necessary. Less than half of the 109 women we interviewed made any contact with a third party after the first assault. These 52 women made a total of 113 contacts, of which 61% were with individuals such as relatives (33%), friends (18%), and neighbors (10%) and 39% were with representatives of more formal agencies (doctors 18%, police 11%, social workers 5%, clergy 3%, others 1%). This pattern of contacts changed as the violence continued. With subsequent assaults, there was an increase in the number of women who sought some form of assistance from a third party and there was also an increase in the total number of contacts they made with formal agents like doctors, police, and social workers (see Appendix B, Table 9).

There is very little systematic information available about help seeking among battered women. Other sources, however, do not vary widely in terms of the general categories of third parties contacted and the types of help sought.[10] In some research, there is an overrepresentation of a single group like lawyers or social workers. This finding no doubt reflects to some extent the social class of the women studied and, more important, the time period being studied. In separations, divorces, or court cases involving battered women there would naturally be many contacts with lawyers, police, and social workers.

Our detailed findings and the findings of Pahl's research in England show a clear preference for contacting relatives, especially parents, and to a much lesser extent friends and "good" neighbors.[11] In our study, the most typical pattern of contact throughout the marriage for those women who sought help consisted of relatively frequent contacts with parents and other relatives, avoidance of neighbors (sympathetic neighbors were soon redefined as friends), and either avoidance of friends or the development of strong bonds and frequent contacts with them. Parents were usually the first to be told and they were approached much more frequently and consistently than anyone else (see Appendix B, Table 9).

The woman feels that she has a legitimate access to her parents and other relatives and thus believes that they are more likely and willing to give help and comfort. Yet, the very act of approaching someone outside her marriage, even her own parents, is nevertheless viewed by the woman, and often by her parents, as a violation of the sanctity of the marriage and a negative reflection upon her adequacy as a wife, specifically her ability to maintain a harmonious relationship with her husband. Thus, the initial approach, even to her own parents, is fraught with reticence and ambivalence.

> I didn't actually want [my mother] to do anything. I didn't want her to know. In a way I did, in a way I didn't, you know, because I mean she says, "Oh, what happened to your eye?" I said, "Oh, I had an accident." She said, "What happened?" I says, "I fell down the stairs and I bumped my face." She says, "He hit you." I says, "No, he didnae." She says, "Don't you try to kid me on. He done that, didn't he?" And she kept on, and I said, "Aye, he did." She says, "Right, get down to your father." So I goes down to my father and I think she must have phoned him before I got down because my father was standing at the top of the stairs. He says, "What happened to you?" And I told him and my father was going to go over, but as I say, they're not the type. I believe if my father had gone over then he would have went for him, but I didnae want my dad to do that either. "Just leave it, I know what I've done now, and I'll just have to bide my time."

In Miller's study of battered women in England, he also noted that the woman's approaches to her parents and friends were hesitant. She wondered about their willingness or ability to provide emotional support, temporary shelter, or financial assistance and about the possibility that they might question her own adequacy or make her the target of unhelpful interference or gossip.[12]

Requests and Responses

In general, the women may approach third parties in search of physical protection, emotional support, advice, medical treatment, referral to a formal agency, peace, security, or refuge, but requests for a sympathetic listener and for accommodation outnumber all others by about three to one. Initially, the woman simply wants someone to talk to and hopes that this person will give her moral support in dealing with the fact that violence has entered the relationship and in coping with it. These requests continue throughout the relationship although later, especially after the worst and last assaults, they decrease somewhat as women increasingly seek temporary or permanent accommodation.[13]

Let us consider the nature of the response of relatives, friends, and friendly neighbors to these two main requests and examine some of the implications of their responses. The requests for a sympathetic listener were made consistently throughout the relationship. Having someone to talk to is exceedingly important to a woman. She does not, however, always expect that the person approached will be willing to listen and she is extremely grateful when someone does. Having someone to talk to usually is seen by both parties as very important to the woman, but it is implicitly agreed to be something of a useless exercise as far as the cessation of the violence is concerned.

> I've told quite a lot of my friends about it, you know. They were sympathetic but there was nothing they could do really, you know. They couldn't do anything.

> I had to go to them because I couldn't stand the beating up again. I had to go and I had a good cry in one of the neighbor's houses and she gave me a nice cup of tea. . . . She just said that she's sorry about it. She said, "You seemed so happy, the two of you." I says, "I don't know what's happening at all, but he blames me and it's really his blame and he's gone off the rails like this, but he doesn't drink or smoke or go out with women."

Relatives, friends, and friendly neighbors (usually females) were almost all willing to lend a sympathetic ear, even throughout most of the night on some occasions.

> Then when he fell asleep I went to my girlfriend's, which is just over the road, and she made me coffee and I sat there until about three or four in the morning, just talking about it, telling her what had happened, and generally wanting sympathy.

Did she offer you any advice?

Aye, leave him, leave him. Everybody offered me that advice.

But sympathetic listening did not usually lead to any active involvement.

One of the neighbors was very helpful inasmuch as she listened to what I had to say. But she didn't want to become involved in doing anything, you know. There was nothing she could do.

Requests for temporary accommodation, which initially were made almost exclusively to the woman's parents, met with a more mixed response. Parents usually gave shelter to their daughter.

The cruelty on that day made me more determined. I went down to my mother's that very night with my suitcase and Andrew [her son] and I pleaded with her to let me come back. You know, I really did. I was on my hands and knees pleading. I said, "Mum, I don't want to go home. I've no hope left." But I couldn't describe what had happened. I felt the dirty party. I didn't understand if my mum would understand the strain I'd been under or anything, and I pleaded and pleaded and pleaded with her to keep me there.

This woman remained at her mother's house for several days until she, like many others, felt that she could no longer impose upon her parents and that she had no alternative but to return to her husband.

In their study of women seeking divorce because of brutality, Elston, Fuller, and Murch noted that 13 of the 23 women had severe problems in finding accommodation for themselves and their children and they also noted the feeling of intrusion that women had when staying with relatives. A typical case involved a woman who was forced to leave home because of her husband's continued violence. The woman described the period immediately after the separation, when she and her sons lived with her brother during the week and with her parents at the weekends.

I was out on my ear and I felt I was intruding on everyone, because I lived with my brother and felt I was intruding in on his life and then I went to my mother and felt I was intruding on her life. She had to give up her bedroom and I took her bed. I felt I was in everyone's way all the time, you know. I used to take the children out, rain or snow or whatever, just to be out of everyone's way. . . . I wasn't sorry that the marriage had broken down (her husband had been so violent that she had landed up in hospital a number of times). I was ashamed it had broken down I suppose. I didn't want nobody to know. All I wanted was to be left on my own and be quiet and lead my own life. I lost two stone in weight [28 pounds] the two years I was living up there.[14]

Parents who gave shelter felt that the assistance was temporary and that their daughter would not remain long. Sometimes, although not very often, parents refused to provide even temporary accommodations. One woman said, "I wanted away. I wanted through. I went to my mum's and begged her to keep me and she wouldn't." Some parents refused not because they were unwilling but because their own houses were over-crowded or their finances were strained. A very small number of parents refused because of an indifference brought about through their own histories of violence.

> My father couldn't do very much because he's been a guilty party all his days. As long as I've known him, he [has] said, "You make your bed. You lie in it." In other words, "Your mother's put up with it, so why shouldn't you?" My mother was obviously very upset.

For most parents, however, the decision not to take their daughter in or to do so only temporarily rested on their beliefs about the nature of the marital relationship. Thus, even concerned parents felt that what goes on between husband and wife is the couple's own business and that they had no right to intervene even at their daughter's request.[15]

> I had a shock with my mother, as I'd always imagined that we were fairly close. She seemed as if, when she knew there was something wrong with the marriage, she didn't want to know, she was frightened because she thought she was going to be involved in it.[16]

There nevertheless is a contradiction between rejecting the violence and accepting the ideals about privacy and the sanctity of marriage, which allow it to continue. Acting upon these beliefs results in the continued isolation of the battered woman. If belief in the sanctity and autonomy of the family is so strong that even parents desert their daughters, albeit reluc-tantly, it is easy to imagine why friends and neighbors rarely intervene or assist.

Of course, relatives, friends, and friendly neighbors do sometimes help the women in numerous ways—caring for the children, taking her to the doctor, social worker, lawyer, or police, or helping her escape to a refuge.

> *Did you contact any of your friends after this particular assault?*
>
> No, I didn't really have any after I was married. I wasn't allowed to have friends. I mean, I've got a friend now. She lives down the stair from me. She knows I'm here [Women's Aid refuge]. She helped me to get away, and she's the only real friend I've had since I got married. And, he doesn't like her. He can't stand her. And the first time he met her he said, "I don't like her." He was giving excuses for it which weren't true. It was just the fact that I had somebody to talk to and he doesn't like this.

Sometimes, though rarely, friends or relatives may try to help by confron-ting the abusive husband in an attempt to convince him to stop beating his wife or by threatening to give him a bit of his own medicine.

> There was a slight argument at my mother's because my father . . . had pulled him [up] for hitting me at Christmas time and he didnae like it. We

went to my mother's for New Year and had a couple of drinks; then my father approached him about what did he give me a black eye at Christmas Eve for. He denied it, so dad got really angry. My father said, "Don't sit there and deny you never. We saw her. I saw her. What are you denying it for?" Then my brother jumped in. He said, "If you ever touch my sister again, you've had it. I'll definitely, I'll touch you, and I'll leave you marked the same as you leave her."

The neighbors were very sympathetic. In fact, two or three of the boys that live in the village had a word with him one night and he put them out. I mean, they were actually sitting and drinking and blethering [talking], you know, in our house, and I had had a black eye the week before, and one of them said, "It's time you drew yourself together, Alan. It's not right with Janie going out with a black eye." And, he just put them out, and told them not to come back.

The woman across the road came across cos she had heard the fighting during the night. She came across at seven o'clock in the morning to talk to him cos she was going away to her work and she came over to see if I was alright. She asked him what was wrong with us last night. She'd heard him come in and she says, "I hear you shouting and swearing and the bairns all greetin.' " And she said, "You near had the neighborhood up. The next time I'm going to phone the police for you because this is getting ridiculous." He says to her, "I never done nothing. It's her—she never had my tea ready." She says, "You dinnae expect your tea at two o'clock in the morning cos that's what time the car drew up outside the door." He says, 'She'll have my tea ready when I go into this house, not when she feels like it. Going to her bed and all this. She doesnae work. I work. She should be up for me." And she says to him, "What did you hit her for? Look at the state she's in!" He says, "I never touched her. That's all lies. She fell down the stairs." There weren't stairs in the house. I had a flat. I mean, there weren't any stairs or anything like that, and Alice says to him, "But Paul, she couldn't have."

This discussion continued. The husband persisted in his denial that he had hit his wife; he continued to claim that she had fallen down the nonexistent stairs. Finally, the man informed the neighbor that this was none of her business, threw her out, and told her never to come back.

Direct intervention in the form of a counterassault upon the husband, although a very rare response from relatives, friends, or neighbors, sometimes had a startling effect upon the man, who was not used to being the victim.

I just lay in bed. By this time people had heard me screaming and the boy next door, he was in the army, he came. He only struck [my husband] once but that was enough to get him out of the house. He was really scared then because nobody had defended me before. I'd always tried to fight back myself.

I ran round to my friend and my husband came after me. He knew where I would go. Oh, he came in and my friend tackled him. She hit him, actually, and she said, "My God, Tom, what have you done this for? Look at the state of Mary's face." It did look bad then, but once it was cleaned up it wasn't so bad. And I remember his reply to her was "Oh, Marion, I don't know. I don't know what's coming over me." . . . He says, "I really love Mary and the kids, and I didn't mean for this to happen."

In this case, the husband's response after the first assault upon his wife was not to attempt to deny or justify his actions or to assign her the blame but to express a deep-felt and sincere regret and to reaffirm his affection for his wife and children and his commitment to them. It is at this moment that the husband would appear to be most receptive to efforts to help sort out his problems and change his behavior, but the first assault usually occurs either without being reported to an outsider or, if reported, without the issue's being taken up with the husband. Instead, he is avoided in hope that he will somehow change by himself or that the couple will work out the problem together.

The fact that some people do actively try to help the woman is an indication that many forms of help and intervention are possible and that the woman can be supported. It cannot be stressed too strongly, however, that such actions are exceptional. Usually the problem is seen by outsiders as none of their business and as something that probably cannot be solved except through divorce.

Outsiders will rarely intervene in an attempt to change the husband's behavior, and thus the woman is left either to free herself from the violence by leaving the relationship or to remain within the relationship and attempt to cope with what is defined as *her* problem. This assessment of wife beating is clearly reflected in the advice given by relatives, friends, and neighbors. Though advice usually was not given, when it was, it rarely included suggestions about possible changes in the husband's behavior or in the relationship but concentrated almost solely upon leaving and divorce or upon the mechanisms of coping and/or techniques for self-protection:

I used to talk to his mother about it. I'd have bruises and she'd say, "Has he been striking you?" I'd say, "Yes," and she'd say, "Well, clear off now and make a new start or you stay together." Cos his mother understood all about what it was like to be struck.

My mother told me to divorce him because he would never change.

[My friend] advised me to leave. She advised me to, you know, leave, and I went back to see her actually about four or five months after I was away and she couldn't believe it was me. I had changed that much.

In half of the cases in our study and in Elston, Fuller, and Murch's, parents advised daughters to leave a violent marriage.[17] However, everyone recognizes that this is a very difficult decision to make and an even more difficult one to execute, so advice was also given on what the woman could do within the relationship to protect or avenge herself.

[His mother] said to lift the next plate and throw it at him.

Did you?

No.

Why not?

I'm not that type of person. I'm not a violent person. I'm a very peace-loving person. I'll go out of my way to avoid trouble at all costs. I hate trouble, just move out of the way, go anywhere as long as I can avoid trouble.

Following such advice may prove disastrous unless the man is very drunk or in some other way incapacitated or the woman can take him by surprise and land a blow and escape before he has a chance to retaliate, or the woman can use some implement or weapon effectively in order to compensate for his greater strength and size without having it taken from her and turned against her. If the woman succeeds in protecting herself, subduing her husband, or retaliating on occasion, she may so surprise him that he stops hitting her entirely (our impression is that this result is very unlikely). For most women, however, such efforts only intensify the beatings as the husband seeks to reassert his authority.

Hopelessness or resignation is also often expressed in the advice to learn to accept the beatings because there is little else that can be done unless or until the woman can leave and support herself and her children.

Mrs. Johnson advised me to sit down and have a cup of tea and think about it, and I said, "Oh, I just couldn't take any more of this." She says, "Well, he works hard." I said, "But working hard isn't good enough, and I don't get the money he's working for."

In summary, when battered women do reveal their private troubles to friends, relatives, or neighbors they usually seek emotional support from a sympathetic listener and material assistance in the form of a temporary refuge. The responses to these requests usually are sympathetic. Most of those approached are willing to listen to the woman and many will give a few hours' or overnight refuge and some help with the children and sometimes even a loan of money. However, most of the reponses are limited to advice on how the woman can cope with the violence rather than on how to change or leave the relationship. Much of the emotional and material assistance offered battered women reflects various beliefs about the privacy of the home, the inviolability of marriage and the family and the hierarchical relationship between husbands and wives. It also reflects the realities imposed by the structural embodiment of these beliefs: the economic dependence of women in marriage, the woman's responsibility for children, and the lack of alternative housing. Thus, the advice and assistance, though usually sympathetic and helpful, rarely questions the husband's authority and control over his wife and seldom poses a challenge to the continuation of the violent relationship. Although the woman wants a cessation of the violence or, if that is not possible, some reasonable means of escaping it, the net result of the ideals about marriage and the responsibilities of a wife coupled with difficulties of change or escape, that she is left to cope with the violence.

Neighbors

It was not a mistake that the previous discussion included only those neighbors defined as good or friendly: most neighbors are not thought of as sympathetic. Despite the fact that neighbors are most likely to see or overhear the beatings and are thus most able to intervene or call for outside assistance, they often do nothing even when approached directly for help. Neighbors tend to be socially distant. It is possible that because of their proximity, neighbors feel a need to avoid becoming involved in something that might take up a great deal of time and place them in a socially uncomfortable of not physically dangerous position. Conversely, the reputations of both the woman and her husband are subjects of neighborhood gossip, and the woman may try to protect the couple's image by remaining silent though she is well aware that her cries have been ringing throughout the neighborhood. For these reasons, and possibly many others, neighbors are defined by the women as negative, unsupportive, and distant, and they usually behave in such a manner.

> We got a new house but we were only about a week in there and I got the hiding of my life. I ran out the house and the blood was all pouring down my face and I'm screaming for a neighbor to come out: "Somebody come out and help me." And not a soul opened their door. I was in my pajamas, and he came out on the landing and he grabbed me by the pajamas and this just ripped open and I had nothing under it and he's calling me everything at the top of his voice and I'm shouting, screaming, "Somebody come out. Somebody come out and stop him. He's going to kill me." And not a soul came out, and he dragged me back into the house, and he kicked into me again, and then he left me lying. I was just sitting huddled in a chair. I was frightened even to go and clean away the blood off myself. . . . I wanted to run for the police but I was only in my pajamas and they were all ripped and I had nothing else on. And I didn't want to run out in the street like a maniac with nothing on, so I sat huddled in a chair, oh, shaking like a leaf, no even greeting. I was even past the greeting. I was just sitting shaking and I couldn't even think of nothing . . . and then it started again. . . . Hours and hours it would go on for.

Even in cases in which neighbors see an assault or assuredly hear the woman's cries for assistance, they are unlikely even to call the police.

Well, you know, he's given me that black eye. The woman whose landing it happened on—I was down a couple of times and she came out. She had an Alsatian and she grabbed her Alsatian and went back into the house. So, I believe that there's very few people who want to get involved when a couple have an argument or any violence.

In the police cases we studied, only 7% of the contacts with them were made by neighbors. The motivation behind the neighbor's call to the police sometimes was to save the woman from further assault, but often the greater concern was to maintain the tranquility of the neighborhood or to prevent the loss of a good night's sleep, as the following police report illustrates.

The husband awoke about 5 A.M. and began shouting, bawling and swearing that his wife had stolen his cigarette lighter. The son [11] was awakened by the noise, and he entered the bedroom just as the husband grabbed hold of his wife's hair and pulled her from the bed to the floor. The wife and son left the house and ran to the police who had already been called by an unknown neighbour. When the police arrived, the husband became very aggressive and shouted, "What the fuck dae youse want?" At that point someone in an apartment up the stair was heard to shout, "For God's sake, shut that man up!"

Neighbors usually do nothing about the assaults they hear or see, and such assaults may embarrass them.

And was there any reaction from the people in the pub when you walked in with your black eye?

Yes. There was a lot of people turned to offer me a drink or to speak to me. They just turned away again immediately because they knew I was very upset. And the following day I met two or three people in the village and they said, "Well, we would have spoken to you last night but," you know, they realized there was something wrong and just didn't want to know me.

Everyone is embarrassed. No one knows quite what to do. Do you ignore the assault or the evidence of it or do you acknowledge it and try to help? Most neighbors avoid this dilemma by contriving not to know what is going on.

Another very important factor in the response of neighbors is the concern for respectability. It is deemed unacceptable for couples to violate the image of marital peace and harmony, at least in a public way. Often such transgressions viewed as a stain upon the character of all couples within earshot, who might also be thought to behave in a similar manner, or as a threat to the reputation of the neighborhood. So, a social distance is maintained from the couple. This is managed through neighborhood gossip.

In fact, it used to be really embarrassing because after we'd had a fight I wouldnae go outside the door for about a week cos I knew they were all standing talking about me, saying, "Did you hear her last night?" . . . I mean, they used to come to the windows and that, but naebody came across to help me. I was screaming for help when he was hitting me and naebody came to help.

Sometimes neighborhood indifference and gossip turn into abuse of the battered woman and her children. An article in the *Guardian*[18] recounted the story of a 28-year-old former primary schoolteacher, with three young daughters, who became a social outcast and was abused by her middle-income neighbors because of the disturbance created when her 32-year-old husband beat her up.

> . . . openly vicious behavior from her town-house neighbors was the cause of months of extra, unnecessary suffering. Dog shit was lined up along the dividing wire mesh back-garden fence so that her girls might dabble their exploring fingers in it: abusive language was shouted over the front fence and the threat to "black the other eye for you". A newspaper cutting was cellotaped to Jane's dustbin: with the headlines "Husbands of Battered Wives Should go to Prison".[19]

Although in this case there was one neighbor who was sympathetic she did not wish to get involved. The other neighbors were openly hostile and their behavior toward the woman alternated between ignoring her even when they stood a few feet apart hanging clothes on the line and making snide remarks like "My husband looks after me." They even refused to cooperate with her lawyer when asked to give evidence in her divorce case. Neighborhood children did not invite her three daughters to play, and the adults often shouted at them that they were making too much noise and threatened to blacken their mother's other eye if she did not take them indoors. The turning point came when the husband saw the newspaper cutting taped on the dustbin.

> He quietly tore the paper off its plyboard backing, folded and put it into his wallet . . . since then, he has never hit her. 'It was as if he suddenly realized that people outside his own four walls knew about him, and he was ashamed at last into facing up to his—our—problem . . . the treatment he needed was shock—those awful neighbors "cured" him!'[20]

Neighbors often justify their inaction on the ground that they might be assaulted, and those who do help often do so with this fear in mind.

> I hear her screaming . . . it sounds like he's throwing her against the wall. I don't want to go over or call the police on him because he might just come over and beat me up. That's why we haven't become good friends. I just don't want to be part of that at all.[21]

This fear is rarely justified, but it certainly seems legitimate to be frightened of a man who has proved to everyone in earshot that he is both willing and able to subdue at least one person by force. The police and court records we analyzed showed that only 13% (125) of the cases of wife assault involved assault upon a second person. These victims included strangers (1) other (3), police (9), friends or neighbors (17), adult relatives (33), and the couple's children (62). In the rare case in which a second person was assaulted, it was usually a child who had intervened on behalf of the mother,[22] and the attack generally consisted of a single blow. Two examples from the police records illustrate both the fear of outsiders who come to a woman's aid and the difference in the attacks upon the two people.

> The man had assaulted his wife earlier in the evening, and later an argument developed which culminated in him shouting, bawling and swearing and wrecking the household ornaments. A neighbour, who was in the house for a social call at the time, tried to calm the husband down and received a black eye for his trouble.

> He cursed and swore at her, punched her face and body, knocked her to the floor, kicked her head, body and hands. She shouted to the male lodger to assist her but he ran from the house and has not returned. She went to the police station and then to the hospital where she was treated for lacerations to the back of her head and given four stitches in the hand before she was allowed to go home.

The fear that the violent man will turn with the same ferocity upon an outsider as upon his wife is usually not justified. It is nonetheless a very real fear and may impede even the police, who sometimes abandon the woman and avoid the man because they are afraid of what he might do to them.[23] The task is left to children.

CHAPTER 10

THE HELPING PROFESSIONS

As THE VIOLENT EPISODES INCREASE in frequency and severity, injuries become worse, silence becomes more difficult and dangerous to maintain, and more and different types of help are needed, the intimate and informal sources of assistance are augmented by the more formal social agencies. The caring agencies, including doctors, social workers, and psychiatrists, and the legal agencies, including police, courts, and lawyers, are approached for the particular form of assistance they are expected to provide. These agencies offer a wide variety of services that are directly related to the violence and are most desperately needed during or immediately after an assault. The police may stop the man from beating his wife, remove him from the household, or arrest him. The social worker may provide counseling for the husband or the wife or both and may help find accommodation for a woman and children who have fled from the house. The doctor may treat the physical injuries and provide drugs for the emotional ones.

Because the services provided by these agencies are so necessary to battered women, it is important that we examine what actually happens when women approach them for help. This means not merely considering an agency's official policies or statutes but also examining the actual practices that they employ. Taken as a unity these policies and practices tell us a great deal about the specific treatment of women who are currently suffering from violent assaults and about the status of the problem. The policies and practices employed in dealing with any individual case of battering have implications both for the cessation or continuation of violence in that particular relationship and for the more general acceptance or rejection of wife beating. These implications are not always clear and they are often contradictory. For example, an agency may condemn wife beating, and yet at the same time actively support the type of marital relationship that encourages it. An agency may support the dominant position of husbands and the conditions that contribute to the isolation, subordination, and dependence of wives, thereby acknowledging the husband's right to control his wife and making it physically and morally difficult for a woman to seek outside help when her husband uses physical force against her. The support of this type of marital relationship is not necessarily a result of malevolent motivations on the part of social agencies or their representatives, but is

179

often due to a failure to see the implications of these contradictory acts. However, it is also possible for the policies of an agency to overtly reject any form of wife beating, and yet, for the particular practitioner involved to ignore, excuse or justify it when they have a case before them.

When we begin to examine these policies and practices defenses are put up, temperatures rise, and tempers flare. It is easy to consider the failings of the social agencies of another country or of a different time period in a dispassionate manner; time or distance makes the issues seem more clearcut and the criticisms less threatening. Yet, it is just such a close analysis that must be undertaken if the work of helping agencies is to provide the greatest possible benefit to battered women and not indirectly to work against them. What is needed is a clear, honest, appraisal of the positions which are actually taken when a battered woman comes for help, and this cannot stop at the statute books or at the level of official policies but must also consider the face to face treatment which a woman receives. The failings which do exist should not be defensively viewed as immutable flaws which must be defended, covered up or disguised but rather as areas in need of immediate and positive change. It is with this consideration in mind that we have undertaken the analysis of the helping professions and the legal agencies.

The Medical Profession

Reluctance to Seek Help

Most people who receive injuries such as large cuts on the head or face, massive or multiple bruises, broken teeth, burns, or the loss of large quantities of hair usually seek medical treatment.[1]—*unless* the unjury has been deliberately inflicted by a family member. When the victim is the wife of the offender, she may not seek medical care for her injuries because she is ashamed of being beaten, afraid of retaliation, or prohibited from leaving the house or telephoning for help. For a host of reasons, the woman may try to hide her injuries by not going to the doctor or, if that cannot be avoided, she may fabricate an explanation for them.

Of course, not all beatings result in injuries that require medical attention, but many of them do. Yet, of the women we interviewed only 3% of all the beatings they received throughout their married lives were ever reported to a doctor, and 20% of the women never made a single visit for any of the injuries they received from beatings. One woman revealed:

> That first night I thought he'd broken my nose. I really did. . . . I was in a hell of a mess, but I was just too scared [to go to the doctor]. I thought it would only make him do something worse to me. I don't know how often I needed [medical attention]. I never went.

Most of the women (80%) did, however, go to the doctor on at least a few occasions, especially after the worst assault (53%) and the last assault (43%) (see Appendix B, Table 9). When visits to the doctor were made usually they were made against the husband's explicit prohibition or were allowed by him only after the woman had given assurances that the source of the injury would not be revealed to any medical staff. This meant that the time spent in the doctor's office or the emergency room often was very tense and that the woman sometimes had to lie about the cause of her injuries in order to protect herself from further attack.

> I was always afraid in case the doctor would say something to [my husband] and that would make it worse for me. He'd be that mad about it.
> I was at the doctor quite frequently, but I never ever told him why or what.
>
> I wouldn't go to him for [the black eyes or bruising]. Well, my husband wouldn't allow me to go to him with all I had.

And you never told him why you miscarried?

> No, but the doctor in the Royal Maternity had asked me. In the five miscarriages I ended up in hospital. The doctor in the hospital had asked me if it was through beating from my husband, and I had said no, which was the wrong thing to do. I'm not saying he believed me, but I had to say no.

Although it is unlikely that doctors with any knowledge of forensic medicine would fail to be curious about the nature of such injuries and question or guess their cause, a consipiracy of silence often exists between doctor and patient. The doctor's failure to question the woman about the injuries or his willingness to accept a clear fabrication concerning the cause of the injury results in a mutual denial of the violence leading to it.[2] In such cases, treatment often consists of bandaging wounds from an "unknown source" and administering drugs so that the woman can cope with a problem known to both doctor and patient but mentioned by neither.

> Well, as I said, later on, when it did get worse, sometimes I used to say to myself, "I'll tell the doctor, maybe he can help." But I was always scared in case he would say something to David, you know, and David would really be angry about that and it would make it worse for myself.

And could you have said anything to your doctor? Would you have wanted him to know?

> Well, I felt as if he knew. I mean, there was times when I went to the doctor when I wasn't well and he'd ask me questions. I mean, when I was first expecting Bill and Andrew, I wasn't happy and I was sort of going downhill . . . and I had the impression that he knew what was happening, but I wouldn't admit to it. I was ashamed of the fact that I was a battered wife.
>
> He just asked what had happened and I just says that I had fell and I was still feeling awfully sore and things like that. . . . He gave me an internal and I

had a germ in my urine and he just treated me for it. He says, "I don't believe your story." I just couldn't explain it to anybody. I didn't tell anybody. It was just really terrible, the thought of my husband raping me. I mean, if he wanted sex I always gave him sex. You see, there was no need for rape. I didn't know why he did it.

In both of these cases, the doctors at least suspected the cause of the injuries but they were either unwilling or unable to pursue the matter in a way that would overcome the woman's fears and anxieties and, thus, her reticence. For the woman there are several countervailing forces affecting her decision to confide in the doctor: her fear and shame dictate silence, whereas the need for physical care and emotional support urges her to speak. Accordingly, the woman may only hint at her problems and hope that an insightful and concerned doctor or nurse will then pursue the subject.

In one case cited by Byrne and Long in their detailed study of two thousand doctor-patient consultations, the woman had confused the doctor completely about what was wrong. She made what seemed to be totally unrelated and irrelevant comments about not liking a new house and moving back to her old one and several halfhearted, bungling requests, first for contraceptives for herself and then for a friend, and finally asked to be represcribed a tranquilizer she had been given a week earlier. The doctor later confessed to complete confusion and admitted that he had prescribed some antidepressants, skirted around the fact that she had been in the week before, and tried to get her out of the office. When it looked as though she was going to be sent away without having fulfilled the purpose of her visit, the woman then almost offhandedly revealed her injury.

D: Oh, yes. Of course. Let's see. Ah, yes. You should have come in last week, shouldn't you. Mmm. There you are then. Take that off to the chemist.
P: Can I show you this?
D: Good God! Where did you get that?
P: He done it last night. When I walked out.
D: How long has it been bleeding?
P: Since last night.
D: Right. Let's get it cleaned up.
P: You'll not tell the cops, will you?
D: Tell the police? Why?
P: Well, I thought you had to every time you see something like this.
D: For severe cuts and lacerations. Well, no.
P: Oh, that's good. He hit me with a sheet of glass.
D: A sheet of glass?
P: Aye, he threw it as I were leaving.
D: Now, look, you are going to have to get this properly stitched. I think I had better send you up to the hospital. I'll get someone to run you up now and I'll phone them.[3]

Such incidents are referred to by doctors as the "by they way syndrome." The patient's "by the way" comments usually occur near the end of the consultation and typically signal to the doctor that the most important reason for the visit is about to be revealed. Doctors may dread such comments because they introduce issues that usually are complex and sensitive, involving a mixture of physical, social, and emotional problems.[4]

THE PATIENT'S OFFERS AND THE DOCTOR'S RESPONSES

Just as a mixture of forces determines whether the woman will confide in the doctor so the doctor for a number of reasons is uncertain about whether he wants to be told and what he should do if he is told. A woman who tells her doctor that she is being beaten is likely to be met with a whole array of responses: she may get treatment for her physical wounds, drugs to help her cope with her emotional injuries, and, sometimes, a sympathetic ear or some advice. Most often the doctor, who usually knows or suspects the problem, tries to avoid the subject and thus he denies the woman the opportunity to reveal the cause of her injuries and to discuss her troubled marriage.

Very little detailed and comprehensive research has been conducted on the delivery of medical services to the battered woman. It is generally agreed, however, that battered women seek medical care for only a very small proportion of the injuries that require such care. Despite this high rate of underuse, it is nevertheless the doctor who is usually the first professional to be approached for help or confided in.[5] The doctor may be the first person to be turned to simply because some injuries cannot be left untreated. In our own study we found that 75% of the women who went to the doctor received treatment for their physical injuries alone, although most of them either told the doctor about the cause of their injuries or suspected that he knew.[6] Only 25% of the women who went to a doctor ever discussed the beatings with him and on such occasions he usually was noncommittal and just listened. Although advice was sometimes given, referrals were seldom made.

A physician interviewed by Eisenberg and Micklow discussed his reasons for not probing into a suspected case of battering.

> Interviewer: Would you accept a patient's explanation that she had fallen down the steps or had run into a door, if the evidence clearly contradicted such a story?
> Dr: If a woman comes in with bruises—how did you get those bruises, what happened—I fell down the stairs, we accept her reason for her injuries. Upon examination, however, I may feel that she didn't sustain these bruises by falling down the stairs. Somebody may have hit her. But I do not ask her or delve any further with it. Accept the patient's theory. . . . We don't have the time or the inclination to go into sociological background as for the

reason of the assault. . . . It's a personal problem between a man and wife and if she doesn't want to prefer charges, that's her privilege and her right and her business to do as she pleases. As far as I'm concerned, personally, I don't care if she prefers charges or not. She was the one that was beaten, not I, and if she doesn't want her husband arrested or put into jail that's her privilege. [7]

Eisenberg and Micklow maintained that there are four reasons for this noninvolvement: the doctor's nonjudgmental approach; the lack of facilities and financing necessary to provide additional care such as overnight accommodation; the fear that reporting the incident to the police might result in the patient's going elsewhere or losing confidence in the doctor; and the lack of any official recordkeeping procedure, which, "inhibits an ability to identify . . . the repeatedly assaulted wife." They concluded that this nondisclosure further assures that "some assaults will never come to the attention of the legal system."[8]

In general, the reasons for this noninvolvement center on the nature of the medical profession itself, the individual doctor's daily experiences and conceptions about how medicine should be practiced, as well as the doctor's personal beliefs about marriage and the family and about wife beating.

THE ORIENTATION OF THE MEDICAL PROFESSION AND DAILY DEMANDS OF THE JOB

In Balint's well-known study of doctor-patient relations, he noted that one of the serious problems facing doctors is the fact that they are trained to deal almost exclusively with physical or organic illnesses and to see this as their sole task. He noted that because of this training doctors feel inadequate when they are called upon to "enquire into the intimate details of the relationship between husband and wife, or into any other 'psychological' problem." He further maintained that "medical training does not offer the future doctor sufficient experience in this skill, though it is a necessary skill in dealing with at least a quarter of his patients, if not more. It is his everyday practice that compels him to learn this skill at his own cost and peril—and at that of his patients."[9] Balint also found that in order to see the doctor, the patient has to get past the nurses or receptionists, who serve as the doctor's gatekeepers, by playing a game in which she presents only her most severe organic ailments and avoids all other complaints even though they might be germane. Once the patient is allowed in to see the doctor for the specified organic ailment, it is difficult or impossible for her to bring up other problems without the explicit consent or request of the doctor.[10] To some extent, this constraint is necessary and understandable because a few patients consider the doctor to be akin to a sage, priest, or wise old woman of the village and ask advice on matters completely outside the medical sphere. For example, in Byrne and Long's intensive study of what happens during the 2–13 minutes a patient usually spends with the doctor, they found that a few patients actually asked the doctor's advice about when or where to spend their holidays, what household appliance to buy, or how to respond to their child's cohabitation.[11]

For the most part, however, researchers have found that patients visit the doctor only when they do have a physical complaint, but many of these complaints involve problems that are also social and emotional. In the consultations that Byrne and Long studied, they found innumerable accounts of patients who came to the doctor for pains, nerves, depression, anxiety, flu, or birth control pills who were equally if not more concerned about family problems such as sexual inadequacy, unwanted pregnancy, infidelity, or violence.[12] In such cases, it is debatable to what extent the problem is medical, legal, social, economic, or psychological. Battered women present the doctor with just such dilemmas. They have a problem that is clearly both physical and social, and to complicate their cases even more, they have a problem that belongs to them as well as to someone else, their husbands. Many doctors attempt to meet the challenge that such cases pose and to provide diverse forms of care, others avoid involvement.

Though doctors disagree about organic versus whole person medicine, the fact remains that many of their patients present them with ailments and injuries that do require multifaceted diagnosis and treatment, and doctors sometimes feel put upon by patients[13] and try to protect themselves from their patients' emotional problems.[14] In order to do this, each doctor develops a personal style of consultation, which includes numerous techniques to manage patients and thus to cut off, redirect, or avoid discussions about the emotional and social problems related to patients' physical ailments.[15] Byrne and Long referred to these as doctor-centered consultations—as distinct from patient-centered ones—and noted that about 77% of the two thousand consultations they studied were of this type.[16] They also noted that individual doctors were relatively consistent in the style they used with their patients[17] and that doctor-centered consultations often resulted in inadequate or incorrect diagnosis and treatment, which sometimes continued for years before the doctor took the time either to let the patient speak or to listen to what he or she was saying and thus gain insight into what was really wrong.[18]

Byrne and Long attributed the doctor-centered approach to the busy practice, in which the doctor saw one patient approximately every five minutes, to the doctor's distinct preference to treat the first symptoms offered by the patient, and, most important, to the way the doctor prevented any expression of feeling during consultations.[19] The doctors themselves saw this as a basic problem of the medical profession, but felt that they had to protect themselves against the equivalent of the medical profession's "Catch 22: You cannot afford to spend too much time looking for deep-seated problems in patients because too many patients keep coming back all the time for more treatment."[20] Given this general orientation of the medical profession and the daily demands of the job,[21] then, it is unlikely that the doctor will be either willing or able to deal effectively with the battered woman who comes for care. These conditions mean that the doctor will almost automatically be predisposed to simply treat the injury, accept superficial explanations and stifle or ignore all others and send the woman back to the man who inflicted the injury.

THE PERSONAL ORIENTATION OF THE DOCTOR

The actions of the individual doctor are not, however, completely a reflection of the ideology of the profession or of the constraints associated with the way it is now practiced, but are also related to his or her personal ideas about the family and marriage and the use of violence within it. The doctor who maintained that "women are funny creatures"[22] may believe that this particular category of patient is not always worthy of being taken too seriously. Some doctors also believe that violence is a normal part of the family life of certain people and this attitude lessens the likelihood that they will respond sympathetically to the battered woman. This view was expressed by two doctors who gave evidence to the Parliamentary Select Committee on Violence in Marriage.

> I think there are occasions in certain levels of society in which the woman is prepared to take a fairly regular black eye and looks upon it as a kind of evidence of virility in her husband.[23]

> I think we have also got to recognize in many of these families there is a sadomasochistic sort of polarization.[24]

Other doctors believe emphatically that what goes on between husband and wife is strictly their own affair and that they should in no way intervene even at the request of the woman who is being brutalized.[25]

> You must understand, wife beating, fights between man and wife are purely personal things between two people. It does not involve anyone else. It does not involve you or me or society in general. What two people do in their home is their business. If they want to beat each other up they have the right to do so if they wish. There is nothing you and I can do about it.[26]

The flaw in this argument, of course, is that such cases rarely involve two people who "want to beat each other up" but rather two people one of whom is systematically beating up the other.

Not all doctors, of course, take such negative and unsupportive views. Many abhor the idea of wife beating, and the wounds they see on the faces and bodies of their patients make them even more committed to this position. Yet because doctors do hold a wide range of often contradictory beliefs about wife beating and the factors associated with it, their treatment of such cases varies considerably. Although most doctors just stitch and patch, some allow, or even encourage, the woman to discuss the beating. An example from one of the cases studied by Byrne and Long illustrates how such a doctor can proceed when the patient tentatively presents a problem that is not strictly organic in nature.

> D: Come in. What can I do for you?
> P: Well, I have got flu, doctor. I have got all pains in my arms.
> D: When did you start to feel not so well?
> P: The week-end. It started Saturday afternoon, shivering with cold. . . . I came mostly about my head, it is paining me a lot. My husband . . . with a shoe, it cut me there, I couldn't comb my hair or touch my hair.
> D: Oh, dear, when was this?
> P: Saturday night.
> D: How come?
> P: He came home drunk as usual. He has hit me in the past but not for a long while . . . causing trouble . . . people next door banging on the walls and it is getting on my nerves.
> D: Does he drink much during the week?
> P: Not so much during the week, but at week-ends, Saturday and Sunday.
> D: Does he drink beer or spirits?
> P: . . . It is a young couple next door . . . disturbing them . . . banging on the walls and this is affecting my nerves.
> D: Does he drink at all during the week?
> P: Well, maybe once or twice.
> D: Does he get drunk then?
> P: Not bad.[27]

In this case the doctor responded to the woman's problem in a patient-centered manner by pursuing a relevant line of questioning. One might, however, question his exclusive focus on the husband's drinking.

The Doctor's Advice

Most women are extremely grateful when the doctor allows them to talk, even if they receive no advice or assistance. Being given the chance to speak provides the woman with at least a modicum of much needed moral and emotional support.

In our study whether it was the first, worst, or last assault, only one-third to one-half of the doctors who were informed about the beating actually gave the woman any advice. When advice was given, it was almost always the same: "Leave him."

And did the doctor know how you'd got the injuries?

Oh, yes.

Did he offer you any help or advice?

Yes. Leave him. Get the hell out of it.

And would you say that the doctor was generally quite helpful?

To me he was.

Did he give you any advice?

I think at one stage he did advise me that I've got to accept that the marriage is over and make a decision to go.

And what did you usually want the doctor to do? Calm you down or just talk to you?

Well, I used to talk to the doctor. It helped me to talk to someone. And the advice I got was to get away from it, but that wasn't so easy. And he tried to give me pills to help keep me calm and let me get to sleep.

And she just says, "Well, I don't like to see anybody splitting up but your health is going down. I'd advise you to have a separation and see a lawyer and social worker."

The advice to leave indicates to the woman that the doctor is supportive of her and feels that she is being wronged. This knowledge is crucial and to some extent it alone provides emotional support. The advice itself, however, must be viewed in the harsher light of reality. As one woman put it, "He advised me to leave him for good, but as I said, 'Where can I go with five kids?' I never knew about the refuge [for battered women]."

THE DOCTOR'S EXCEPTIONAL ACTIONS

Some women gave accounts of a few instances in which a doctor clearly went well beyond just allowing her to talk or giving her advice and took direct steps to try to change the husband's behavior. One doctor unequivocally rejected the idea that a man has any right to hit his wife.

Well, I don't know. I don't. The doctor turned round and told Edward that a woman can never do enough wrong for a man to hit her, and I agree with that.

Another went out of his way to talk to an abusive husband and convince him to stop the beatings.

So you went to the doctor this time just to tell him what happened?

Aye, I always went to him and he came over. He seen my eyes and I had a great big bruise on the side of my leg and my breast was all bruised and he says to me, "Someday he's going to really do you an injury and he's got to be told to make him try to realize this. Someday he's going to punch you and it's going to be worse. I'm not going to let that happen." So he came over to my house.

The doctor did?

Uh-huh, the next day. I told him. I said, "The doctor's coming to see you."
And he was mad, raging cos he was coming over. But I wasn't caring and the
next morning the doctor did come and he was in his bed and he says, "Well,
get him up out of his bed." Well, I went up to the bedroom. I says, "That's
the doctor." Oh, he was raging, calling me all the b's and c's under the sun.
He never met my husband before so I took him into the sitting room and introduced him. Then, the doctor asked me to leave the sitting room and he
would talk to him. So I don't really know what they said but the doctor
says, "I'd like to see you tomorrow again." So I went to the surgery and he
said, "Well, I listened to him," he says, "but as far as I'm concerned it was a
lot of lies he told me."

And did he give you any advice?

He advised me to leave him for good.

In another case, which was also atypical, the doctor tried to lighten the
burden on the woman by advising her not to have the baby she was expec-
ting.

The only person I ever used to talk to about it was the doctor. I went to the
doctor, yes, I did go to the doctor about it and he said to me—he used to
give me tablets and he once saw my wrist when he pushed my hand through
a glass door and he gave me stitches for my wrist—"I can't advise you," he
said, "there's only one thing I can advise you to do, and I doubt if you'd take
it. I can't give you a recipe"—what is it—"a prescription for a happy marriage." That was the only thing he said. As much as to say, "You won't do
what I more or less tell you to do." He never said, "Leave this man." I was
having a baby and he told me to get rid of it.

These examples of doctors who went out of their way to try to treat the
woman in a wholistic and positive manner and to deal with the numerous
problems associated with their injuries show what a doctor can do even
without benefit of established programs that would facilitate referrals or
provision of other forms of help. Other doctors take a completely negative
and destructive approach.

I never ever got medical attention. I used to go round to the doctor's quite
often because I couldn't sleep at night and my nerves were bothering me and
I wasnae eating. He just said, "I just can't help you while you're living with
him." He says, "If he leaves you or you leave him, come back and then
maybe I'll be able to help you."

This ultimatum is an extraordinary prerequisite to care.

The harsh treatment some doctors give to battered women is based
upon the dangerous and insidious idea that if the woman cannot surmount
all of the emotional, social, and financial difficulties associated with leaving her husband, then she does not really mind being beaten or actually
wants or likes it.

> The doctor just put me on. He just told me to get away. He asked me if I like getting beaten up, you know, and I says no. And he says, "Well, there must be something wrong with you," he says, "because nobody would stand that much pain."

A similar attitude was expressed by one of the doctors interviewed by Eisenberg and Micklow.

> There was a certain masochism to a woman who gets beaten up more than once, that you can't deny. That I can't deny. If I go back to the same place and I get beaten up more than once, then there is something in me that is making me do that. I don't have to get the shit beat out of me, do I? I mean you don't have to have very much intelligence to know that you can leave.[28]

The simplicity of this attitude and the apparent lack of insight into the difficulties and complexities involved in leaving a marriage are quite extraordinary. Even more extraordinary, however, is the fact that such insensitivity to suffering could be expressed by someone dedicated to caring for people and relieving their pain. The conclusion that those who return to the scene of a violent attack are merely asking to be attacked again is debatable even in a general sense. It might be necessary, for example for a person who has been mugged on the way to work to continue to use that route in order to get to work. But to equate the ability to find an alternative route to work or to stay away from a deserted street with the ability to find another place to live or to stay away from one's own home is ludicrous.

Such negative evaluations of the woman lessen or eliminate the doctor's moral indignation over brutality and thus reduce his sense of urgency, his desire to be supportive, and his willingness to make referrals or to take other action available to him. And unsympathetic treatment may discourage the woman from seeking medical care except in extreme cases of injury or depression.[29] It also contributes to her sense of shame and self-blame and to her growing feeling of helplessness and isolation[30] and may inadvertently strengthen the husband's sense of justification and blamelessness.

It must be reemphasized, however, that many doctors are neither neutral nor negative in such cases but that when they allow, or even encourage, the battered woman to reveal the cause of her physical injuries or emotional distress, they have taken on something for which they are not trained, about which they probably know very little, and for which they have, at this moment, few remedies[31] other than to advise her to leave the relationship or to prescribe drugs to help her cope.

PRESCRIBING TRANQUILIZERS AND ANTIDEPRESSANTS

Research into the prescribing of psychotropic drugs (hypnotics, tranquilizers, antidepressants, and stimulants) has indicated that in the past few decades both doctors and the population at large increasingly have come to regard them as a panacea and there has been a marked upsurge in their use.[32] In one study of general practitioners in England, Parrish found that 12.6% of a sample of 13,259 cases were given such drugs during a one-year period. He found a sharp increase in such prescriptions for 18–25 year olds and then a steady increase up to the age of 50 and another rise after 65.[33] Over half of the drugs were tranquilizers[34] prescribed for a period of less than one month[35] and for symptoms such as anxiety, stress reactions, nervousness, insomnia, depression, or tension headaches, which rarely were psychotic in nature or associated with a persistent physical disorder.[36] Parrish concluded that the fact that three out of five patients were treated on a single occasion or for short periods indicated a treatment of *symptoms* rather than *disease*.[37] Psychotropic drug therapy is being used in the *management* of patients, especially those with anxiety or depression,[38] and in such cases "it is easier for the practitioner to give a prescription than to give advice."[39] Parrish also found that women were twice as likely as men to receive such treatment,[40] and the same pattern has been found by many others.[41]

Indeed, Elston, Fuller, and Murch's study of battered women seeking divorce found that 16 of the 17 women who went to the doctor were given drugs.[42] In our own study, we did not specifically ask women whether they had been given drugs, but 40% of the 87 women who went to the doctor spontaneously mentioned that they had received drugs. We suspect that this figure would have been higher had we specifically asked for such information, and impressionistic material from others working with battered women, as well as the general pattern of drug use, would seem to lend support to this conjecture.

Elston, Fuller, and Murch noted that among their respondents, the women were divided almost evenly about whether they thought the doctor had been helpful.[43] To a great extent this finding would seem to be related to the woman's willingness or desire to take psychotropic drugs. Diverse attitudes toward the use of drugs certainly were evident among the women we interviewed. Some of the women felt that drugs were used by the doctor as an alternative to dealing with the real problem. In the words of one woman, "He just listens to me, you know, and gives me Valium." Other women requested that the doctor give them drugs and felt that they could not really cope without them.

> I went to him. He gave me pills for my nerves. I went to him and I explained to him. I mean, I was awfully depressed. . . . This was a couple of weeks ago. I was awfully run down. I wasn't well and I had bother with my blood and I had to go for iron pills and I told him that I'd been separated from David and I'd put in for a divorce and I'd gone back but it wasn't easy and I needed something for my nerves. And he gave me nerve pills.

Most women start off not wishing to take drugs and may even reject them when first offered by the doctor only to find that they eventually reach a point at which drugs seem necessary.

The first time I had to go up [to the doctor] he gave me help and said, "Do you want tablets?" I said, "No." "Do you feel strong enough to cope?" I said, "Yes." This time I had to take tablets for my nerves because the doctor had to quiet me down for the sake of the kids. I hadn't eaten for five days, and you know, he sat and made me eat a bowl of soup. My doctor was marvelous.

Drug therapy soon becomes a pattern and the doctor repeatedly gives the woman prescriptions to help her get through periods of crisis. Although one might expect that great caution would be exercised in prescribing medication that must be regarded as dependence forming, the findings of many researchers have suggested otherwise:[44] the longer the patient is treated with such drugs, the easier it is to obtain a repeat prescription. According to Parrish, the patient thus becomes dependent upon both the doctor and the drugs.[45] Elston, Fuller, and Murch questioned the wisdom of giving drugs that induce "drowsiness and ataxis, giddiness and loss of control of voluntary movements" at a time when a woman is trying to make an extremely difficult decision. They also questioned the appropriateness of treating the woman instead of the man: "These women are being treated for anxiety and other reactions to their husbands' behaviour, thus one could say they are being treated for their husbands' behaviour.[46] Though not denying the benefits to those who actually suffer from severe anxiety, agitation, or schizophrenia, Parrish asked whether it is rational for the medical profession to drug large numbers of people in order to suppress symptoms for which only a few really need medication.[47] By increasing the use of such drugs, doctors "are blanketing their patient's emotional reactions to an excessive degree and they must ask themselves whether it is right for them to produce a pharmacological leucotomy on contemporary society?"[48]

It could be argued that given the few alternatives open to the battered woman—the lack of agencies or resources available for care or referral, the general unwillingness or inability to deal with the violent man, the social and emotional pressures on the woman to remain in the marriage—coupled with the doctor's lack of training in whole person medicine and the low priority given to such cases, the sympathetic doctor also feels helpless and powerless. Since he thinks there is really nothing he can do for the woman, he may give her drugs in an attempt to give her a bit of relief and perhaps increase her ability to bear the anxiety of waiting for another beating or to cope with the fear and pain she feels when her husband attacks her. The alternative, beating without drugging, seems more cruel and yet to some extent the very drugging that may give the woman a false sense of coping may also contribute to her difficulties in seeking a change in the relationship or escaping from it. Furthermore, it has been noted that one of the sad, and very ironic, side effects of some psychotropic drugs is sudden and unexplained outbursts of violence.

Psychiatry and Psychoanalytic Theory

There has been a sufficiently large number of scholarly and journalistic critiques of psychiatry and psychoanalytic theory in the last few years and that area's negative stance concerning women and women's problems have been so thoroughly exposed[49] that any further critique would seem like cruel and unusual punishment. That is, of course, if it were not for the continued popular appeal of many psychoanalytic and psychiatric myths within the helping professions and the eagerness with which the public, government officials, and social practitioners accept them uncritically as the explanations of wife beating. Despite rather widespread agreement among researchers in the field of family violence, including many psychiatrists, that men who beat their wives, like parents who beat their children, cannot usually be characterized as emotionally disturbed,[50] the popular explanation is that people who commit such acts, and sometimes even their victims, are by definition mentally ill, inadequate, deprived, or in some way incomplete. Hence, no explanation beyond these personal inadequacies need be sought. Underlying this belief in individual pathology is the implicit assumption that the legal, political, cultural, family, and economic institutions in our society contribute little or nothing to the violence. Because this belief is seductive and comforting and has been widely adopted within the culture, it should not be surprising that psychiatrists and psychoanalysts are turned to as the mandarins of marital violence. Therefore, let us briefly consider the psychoanalytic principles most germane to their analysis of wife beating, examine how they have been used in several studies, and consider their implications both for the treatment of the individual and for long-term solutions to the problem.

The key areas in a psychiatric analysis of wife beating include the conceptions of normal relationships between men and women, the nature of the parent-child relationship, the importance of early childhood learning, and, finally, the emphasis placed upon individual illness and therapy. The general focus of psychoanalytic theory is upon identifying and treating individuals who fail to act in what might loosely be defined as a socially approved or normal fashion. The causes of personality disorders and mental illnesses are seen as integrally related to the unsuccessful inculcation of a constellation of attitudes and behaviors appropriate to one's sex and to the unhappy nature or poor quality of parent-child relationships and the form and content of early childhood learning.

The psychoanalytic ideology concerning the normal, or healthy, relationship between males and females is extremely patriarchal. That is, the male, if he is to have a healthy masculine identity, must be dominant and independent. The healthy female, on the other hand, is to take on such feminine characteristics as dependence, subordination to masculine authority, nurturance, service to others, and identification through them.[51]

Deviations from these patterns of male dominance and female subordination are seen as abnormal and the cause of friction or conflict as each person struggles to establish or to regain what is seen as his or her appropriate sex role.

Parent-child relationships, and early childhood learning are believed to be related to this struggle in two ways: first, children are taught the appropriate masculine or feminine behaviors, which they will take into adult life, through parental example and instruction; second, this early training is thought to form the basic personality, which will then shape the individual's relationships with his or her own children and thereby be transmitted to the next generation. If this training is somehow inadequate or flawed, the adult personality will be, too; such individuals need therapy, treatment, or some strong outside influence to correct the ill effects of improper early learning. In this sense a personality disorder, like a cold, is catching. But, unlike a cold, it is caught in one generation and not transmitted until the next. Since women are viewed as the primary caretakers of children, they are obviously seen by proponents of this view as playing a very important role in insuring the psychic health of their own children.

Saul put this position quite clearly in his article "Personal and Social Psychopathology and the Primary Prevention of Violence."[52] He maintained that the parent-child relationship, especially up to the age of six, conditions the child permanently: "Children reared with love and respect mature adequately and become loving, responsible, and productive spouses, parents and citizens. Those reared in such a way that they hate their parents will also hate other persons for life."[53] Saul argued that this "displaced irrational parricidal rage against psychopathogenic parents or substitutes" is the source of disturbed interpersonal relationships; it is this kind of individual who "is the primary cause of violence in the world today."[54] Thus, "regardless of the form of social and economic organization" all violence (including crime, cruelty, and war) is basically a problem within the individual which arises from a single source, "emotional patterns of hate and hostility which are generated, shaped and conditioned within children by parents."[55]

Saul proposed in general terms that we eliminate neurotic, hostile patterns of child rearing and replace them with parental love and understanding—certainly an admirable proposal and one with which no one would disagree. He then put forward six specific suggestions that clearly indicated that it is the mother's behavior he had in mind.[56] Given the emphasis this perspective places upon the mother-child relationship and the mother's responsibility for child care, it is not difficult to see how the mother becomes defined as the cause of the child's rage, which is later transferred to child abuse, rape, war, or wife beating. According to this theory, the woman, first as mother and then as wife, becomes the primary cause of all violence, even that which is directed at her. In case this sounds too harsh, let us consider the way in which battered women have been studied and treated by those using this perspective. The conclusions of Schultz,[57] Snell, Rosenwald, and Robey,[58] and Gayford[59] showed a remarkable similarity in their adherence to this ideology, despite obvious weaknesses in the evidence presented to support their premises.

Schultz analyzed the cases of four working-class blacks from the southern United States, all of whom had a history of wife beating and who were on parole for attempting to murder their wives. In his attempt to find the "common dynamic core" underlying the assaults, he began with the statement that "the victims in spouse assaults can always be assumed to have played a crucial role in the offense, and may have directly or indirectly brought about or precipitated their own victimization."[60] With this assumption in mind, he presented a single case study of the early childhood and first and second marriages of a 47-year-old man who stabbed his wife four times in the chest during an argument about an alleged "other man." Schultz concluded that the general childhood pattern in these four cases "was characterized by a domineering, rejecting mother relationship." The child responded to this maternal authority in a passive, submissive way in order to avoid further rejection and punishment. Consequently, these men failed to learn patterns of aggression management and became submissive, passive individuals who were dependent upon the mother and later the wife: "The husbands tended to parentify their wives and appeared foredoomed to take a submissive role toward them, as they did toward their mother."[61] When this dependence is frustrated, for instance, when the man fears that his wife may leave him, he attacks the frustrating object, his wife. Schultz judged the "three surviving wives . . . to be very masculine, outspoken, domineering women who had much in common with their husbands' mother" and who "tended to exploit and profit from their husbands' passiveness and dependency."[62] At one point he actually referred to the relationship as "the husband-*wife* (victim-*offender*) relationship"[63] and the tenor of the article certainly would support the contention that despite the murder of one woman and long histories in which women seemed to get the worst of a violent relationship, Schultz regarded the women as the offenders. Two points stand out very clearly in the work of Schultz. First, the blame is squarely placed upon the woman in the violent scenario—the "domineering, rejecting mother" and the "masculine, outspoken, domineering" wife. Second, the tone of the argument reflects the authoritarian and condescending attitude taken toward the client; the therapist-client relationship is suspiciously similar to the mother-child and wife-husband relationships Schultz condemned.

Another very interesting twist on the theme of female accountability for the violence that is perpetrated upon them appeared in an early work by Snell, Rosenwald, and Robey entitled "The Wifebeater's Wife."[64] They studied twelve cases of women from a middle-class Massachusetts suburb who, after long histories of being beaten, had charged their husbands with assault and battery. Although the researchers routinely interviewed both husband and wife, who had been referred to them by the court for psychiatric evaluation, they concluded that the women were more willing to talk to psychiatrists whereas the men usually were resistent and denied that "problems existed in their marriage which required outside help."[65] Interviewing the wives began as an expedient but the authors soon moved into "direct interest in exploring the wives' roles in the marital strife."[66]

All of the marriages had histories of violent assaults upon the wife, and the focus of the study was how and when the woman made the decision to redefine the violent offense as one requiring judicial notice. The most common answer given by the women as to why they had sought outside help involved the children. Particular attention was paid to cases in which an adolescent son intervened on his mother's behalf and attempted physically to restrain his father. The author cited the case of a 44-year-old mother of six who had for 20 years been in a marriage marked by recurrent attacks upon her, especially when her husband was drunk.

> On the night of the fight which brought the husband to court, the son [19] for the first time stepped between his arguing parents and physically restrained his father. At this point the wife called the police. She said later that the sight of her boy hitting his father was terrifying to her and she acted in panic. She later felt a strong sense of guilt and swore she would never again turn her husband in.[67]

The analysis of this case concentrated upon the personality characteristics of the couple. The husband was described as fond of his mother, a good worker, and a heavy drinker who was shy, aloof, and passive when sober but sexually aggressive when drunk. The wife was described as a small, intelligent, efficient, hard-working, aggressive woman who had assumed responsibility for handling money, paying bills, and disciplining children. The sex life of the couple was described as unsatisfactory to them both. The man complained about his wife's coldness but admitted his inability to initiate sex when sober. The woman complained about her husband's "very aggressive sexual demands when drunk" and stated a firm decision "never to have relations with a drunken man."[68]

Since during the initial meetings the husband was hostile to outside intervention, whereas the woman was seen as intelligent, concerned about her marriage, and genuinely motivated to get help, he was not treated. She entered therapy, which lasted two years. It is not surprising, of course, that the woman was more desirous of outside help since it was she who was being beaten up. The twist in the conclusions of the research illustrates what can happen when a woman submits herself to this helping process. Concerning the sexual impasse, the authors unabashedly stated that the woman's "firm decision to 'never have relations with a drunken (and aggressive) man' seemed to effectively preclude any mutually satisfactory sexual meeting ground."[69] Surely it would have been better to work on his inability to have sex when sober and in a non-aggressive manner, than to place fault with her for her unwillingness to have sex with a drunk and aggressive man. The authors saw this case as typical in many ways, with the "passive, indecisive, sexually inadequate husband" defined as an "ineffective man," whereas the wife was defined as an aggressive, masculine, frigid, masochistic woman who had a "need to control the marital relation," which "served to meet [the husband's] strong dependent needs."[70] The evaluation of the woman as masculine and aggressive seemed to be based upon her ability to keep the household running against great odds. One cannot help but wonder what their evaluation would have been had she failed to care for the household, husband, and children. There appears to be no evaluation of the woman that would not have been negative. The relationship was seen to be in a state of equilibrium in which periodic violence served to "release him momentarily from his anxiety about his ineffectiveness as a man" while apparently giving her "masochistic gratification and helping probably to deal with the guilt arising from the intense hostility expressed in her controlling, castrating behavior."[71] This arrangement "worked well enough for *both* partners [emphasis added]" until the oldest son intervened and "destroyed the working of this delicately balanced system and this necessitated outside intervention. . . . The wife calls for outside help to change a situation which *she* has fostered but which now appears out of her control [emphasis added]."[72] The authors maintained that through therapy the wife "gained insight into the meanings of her behavior," learned to see how she might be at fault, was able to let her oldest son leave home, and was less likely to allow the second son to intervene and thus disrupt the delicate balance between husband and wife in which he *had to* beat her up periodically.[73] By some magical mental twists and contortions come these extraordinary conclusions. Interviewing the wife of the wife assaulter may have started out as an expedient but it ended with the problem being made hers.

Scheff discussed the process of blaming the victim in psychiatric analysis in terms of what he called negotiation of responsibility. He analyzed psychiatric interviews and legal plea bargaining and maintained that the assessment of the responsibility for an act always includes negotiation between client and practitioner.[74] Scheff quoted the English psychiatrist Balint, who referred to this process as one of "offers and responses." The patients "offer or propose various illnesses, and they have to go on offering new illnessess until between the doctor and patient an agreement can be reached resulting in the acceptance of both of them of one of the illnesses as justified."[75] Practitioners have an advantage in this process because of their greater power and authority, and Balint observed "that the negotiation process leads physicians to influence the outcome of medical examinations independently of the patient's condition . . . the physician induces the patient to have the kind of illness that the physician thinks is proper."[76] He labeled this the "apostolic function." The particular case chosen by Scheff to illustrate this process is particularly apropos since the woman went to a psychiatrist because she was being ill-treated by her husband. The psychiatrist's response to the woman's initial complaint about her husband's behavior (i.e., an external source of trouble) was to ignore or fail to respond to her remarks, appearing bored and impatient and reminding her frequently that "she has come to a psychiatrist" (i.e., "subtle requests for analysis of her own contributions to her difficulties").[77] The woman eventually mentioned something that stimulated his interest, a single sexual infidelity that had happened years earlier but about which she still felt guilty. At this point he gave obvious signs of interest: there was a flurry of questions and attempts to probe further. The psychiatrist had identified the problem he was going to treat: it was not the husband's present ill-treatment of the woman, but her guilt about a past infidelity.

More recent psychiatric papers have not abandoned the general pattern of placing responsibility for wife beating upon the wife. Of particular note in the research of Gayford, a consultant psychiatrist who gathered information by closed questionnaires administered to 148 women at the Chiswick's refuge in London.[78] There were numerous serious flaws in this research including the discarding of one-third of the questionnaires for some undisclosed reason,[79] the way in which the questionnaires were administered,[80] and some of the questions asked. Gayford offered a typology of "Ten Types of Battered Wives": Downtrodden Dorothy, Well-meaning Wendy, Tortured Tina, Laura the Long-suffering One, Fanny the Flirt, Go-Go-Gloria, Violent Violet, Alcoholic Anna, Neurotic Nora, and Pseudo-battered Sally.[81] In a critique of the methodological and conceptual flaws in this research, Wilson remarked, "The vulgarity of this way of writing about what is a serious and tragic problem for men, women and their children needs no comment."[82] She noted that Gayford's analysis once again "throws the problem back onto the woman" and implies that the root of the problem lies in the "shortcomings of their personality." Wilson challenged psychiatry's "class and sex based assumptions about the proper place of women," and asked why Gayford did not discuss "Naughty Norman," "Vicious Victor," or "Drunken Derek."[83]

In Faulk's study of 23 men who severely assaulted their wives and were on remand for charges ranging from malicious wounding to murder, he developed a scheme of five types of men who commit such offenses.[84] The stable, affectionate group (four men) consisted of those men who had affectionate relationships with their wives but were violent during an episode of mental disturbance or depression. Three other types appeared to Faulk to be "at fault": "violent and bullying" (one man who was generally violent), "dependent and suspicious" (four men who were extremely jealous), and "dominating husband" (five men who "would brook no insubordination" or "threat to their position of power"). The largest category, however, contained nine men described as "dependent, passive husbands"—men who tried to "please and pacify" a "querulous and demanding wife," who was attacked only after committing some "precipitating act" or "after a period of behaving in a 'trying' manner."[85] Faulk did not specify the behavior of either partner or place it in the overall context of the violent episode or the ongoing relationship, so it is impossible to know what he regarded as "pleasing and pacifying" or "trying and precipitating." One cannot help but note that the category in which women were blamed constituted his largest category and also to wonder whether such evaluations were made in accordance with the psychoanalytic framework previously outlined. It is also noteworthy that in this analysis of abusive men the focus was at least partially upon the woman's precipitating behavior or upon the relationship, whereas the analysis of battered women tends to center almost exclusively upon the *woman's* behavior and contribution to the violence.

The idea that women cause the violence is not just common to psychiatry but has permeated Western culture. Such a view was put in an article by Dotson Radar, a psychiatrist, entitled, "The Sexual Nature of Violence" which was published in the Opinion Page of the *New York Times*.[86] It became the subject of refutation by Letty Cottin Pogrebin. Rader asserts that "dominant mothers (and female teachers) are figures of repressive, defeating authority who emasculate the young male."[87] He maintains that since violence is rooted in the "psychological disfigurement" of emasculation, women cause brutality and "reinforce men's impulses toward aggression". Young males, not women, "experience the greatest inability to cope with contemporary life" and since women rear them, it is they who must bear the responsibility.[88] Pogrebin refers to this later challenge as the 'prize of creative backlash'.[89]

To sum up, the psychoanalytic idea that violence is a manifestation of individual pathology created by an imbalance in male dominance and female submission and developed through inadequate mothering implies that women (first as mothers, then as wives) are the primary source of violence, including that which is directed at them. Although such ideas have never been adequately supported and have been severely criticized and challenged, the theory has a great deal of appeal in a patriarchal society; it is very popular, especially with the media, and underlies much of the training in the helping professions.

Social Work and Counseling

Women who seek help from social work agencies or other helping professionals directly involved with marriage problems (e.g., marriage counselors and ministers) usually have sought advice or assistance from other individuals or organizations first. Mayer and Timms, in their study of clients' evaluations of the services offered by a family welfare association, discovered that people generally exhausted all other avenues of assistance prior to contacting a helping organization.[90] This finding appears in a number of other studies of the social services.[91] In a similar vein, the women we interviewed told us that if they had been able to share their problem with anyone they would most likely have spoken to a friend or relative, occasionally a doctor, prior to seeking assistance from an official helping agency. Relatives, friends, or doctors sometimes advised the women to seek such assistance but usually the woman decided on her own to do so—in most cases because others were unwilling or unable to help and/or because the violence became unbearable.

> I just knew I had to get help or else. I didnae know where to turn or who to go to and I just knew that when I went there that I had to tell him [social worker]. I had to tell somebody.

The majority of the women rarely or never sought assistance from the helping professions and some of them offered explicit reasons for this. Battered women, like most other members of the public, have only a vague knowledge of the nature of the services and assistance available from the helping professions and consequently do not consider the social services as a source of possible help.[92]

Have you been to the social worker for help?

> No, I thought they were for naughty boys and pregnant girls and things like that. . . . I thought I would get the answer that "Well, really Mrs. Jones. I mean, what do you expect us to do? If you will insist on staying with him there's not much we can do."

Some women also have very definite views about the propriety of using the helping services and considered them inappropriate as sources of help: "No, I don't believe in them [social workers]. I don't think that it's right that you contact people off the cuff, so to speak, just when you need help." A more common reason for not seeking help is fear of an unsympathetic response or of condemnation.[93]

> I was terrified . . . cos I was always scared they'd say because of the kind of environment the wee one's being brought up in, we'll just take him into [a foster home]. You know, I was prepared to stick it out rather than get him put in a home.

(This concern is not confined to battered women. Mansfield and Smith interviewed a woman who needed help with her financial affairs but would not seek assistance from the local social work department because she was afraid her children would be removed from the home.[94] Occasionally, social workers do take such action, but it is certainly not routine.)[95]

THE ORIENTATION OF THE HELPING AGENCY

The social services in welfare states lack sufficient resources and money, personnel, and so forth, must be allocated to problems considered the most important and to clients deemed the most desperate and deserving. As such, social service departments may attempt to conserve resources by arguing that certain problems do not require their help because no problem actually exists, that the problem is not very serious, or that it affects only a small number of people. In Britain, social services departments at one time argued that wife beating was neither widespread nor generally severe; thus, more services and resources were not needed.[96] Though this position has been modified somewhat, resources are still scarce, and battered women may be treated with indifference by social work departments and marriage guidance agencies.

When a battered woman approaches a social agency she may be distraught, confused, and frightened of retaliation from her husband. Also, she may be unsure of the sort of help that might be forthcoming but she is very sure about the nature of her problem: her husband is beating her and she wants him to stop. She wants help in achieving this end. Social workers or counselors often have alternative conceptions about the nature of what they term the woman's presenting problem and of her needs. Numerous research reports have revealed a considerable disparity between the client's view of his or her problem and the helper's conception of the same problem.[97] The battered woman and the caseworker thus must negotiate a definition of the 'real' problem. At the outset the negotiation is a one-sided affair since it is based on a professional belief that the client's viewpoint is distorted and inaccurate and upon a differential in status and authority, which makes the social worker's interpretation of the woman's predicament the correct one, what Becker called the "credibility hierarchy."[98] Caseworkers undertake to distinguish between the woman's perceived and real problems and needs—real needs and problems being those decided upon by the social worker. A family caseworker in Massachusetts argued that though physical abuse is a common complaint among wives seeking help "caseworkers rarely pick abusiveness as the focus of intervention; rather they tend to ignore this symptom."[99] This failure or unwillingness to consider the violence as the important problem has several sources.

The social background and the training of helping professionals often lead to a detachment from the everyday lives of their clients.[100] This detachment may lead them to think that the woman is exaggerating the severity and frequency of the violence. As a battered woman interviewed in another study put it:

> [Social workers] read nice books, psychiatrist's books, they go to nice lectures . . . but they want to go into some pubs and meet some of these people who've been dragged up—because it's all very well when you put feelings of violence in nice words and you cotton wool it.[101]

The social backgrounds and sentimentalities of caseworkers may also make it difficult or impossible even to consider such distasteful possibilities as violence, or their training may have convinced them that violence is merely a symptom of some other, 'more serious' problem.[102] Whatever the specific reason(s) for failing to identify the problem as one of violence, the caseworker who does so is likely to ignore or dismiss the woman's complaints about the violence.

The diagnostic skills of professional helpers have been traditionally derived from Freudian psychoanalytic theory. The psychoanalytic perspective is not the only one adopted in casework but because it reinforces conventional wisdom about the relationships between men and women, it has great appeal.[103] According to Nichols, caseworkers often uphold a position that "supports a belief that the wife encourages, provokes or even enjoys abusive treatment."[104] Beliefs of this nature, coupled with professional ideals of "affective neutrality," obviously reduce a caseworker's willingness to accept the battered woman's complaints and decrease the probability of her receiving assistance.

The masochistic view of wife beating may also be combined with an inaccurate view of the *social* nature of violent marriages. A number of professional helpers discussed the supposed acceptability of the violence before the Parliamentary Select Committee on Marital Violence.

> *A family caseworker:* "There are a certain number of women who would accept an amount of ill-treatment. . . . Some women seem to accept this as part of the price of marriage."
>
> *A Catholic Marriage Advisor:* "It would appear that in some groups of people violence is a normal part of character of life and that their tolerance towards it may be high."
>
> *A principal social worker:* "There has been a history of [violence] though within that history the family . . . may exist quite happily in that situation . . . it is accepted as part of [the marriage] that there should be occasional assaults."[105]

Beliefs such as these reflect an inaccurate conception of the acceptability of the violence by the woman. They confuse acceptability of the violence with the woman's inability to do anything about it or to escape from it. Such views reveal either a considerable insensitivity to, or an ignorance of, the *woman's* evaluation of her marriage, the violence, and her predicament. The ill-conceived belief that the woman considers the violence to be normal or acceptable may lead the worker to treat the case in an unproductive manner that is not oriented toward either eliminating the violence or helping the woman escape from it. The result of these beliefs and inaction is that the woman's position remains unchanged, which confirms the caseworker's belief that the woman considers the violence to be normal or acceptable and does not truly want it to end—surely a self-fulfilling prophecy. Battered women *do not* accept the violence; rather, they endure it because they have few or no alternatives and because social agencies offer them little, if any, assistance.

Not all professional helpers adopt this negative view and some caseworkers are sympathetic and supportive: "I'd sit and cry all day on the phone to him . . . he [the social worker] says, 'Just go ahead.' He just used to listen to me through the tears and sobs." This approach results in some temporary feelings of relief that may aid the woman in coping with her problem, but it usually does very little to end it. At present few, if any, provisions are made either for trying to change the man's behavior or for helping the woman to escape, and without more efficient means of intervention from the helping professions, the woman's life continues basically as it was prior to contact with them. The battered woman continues to be assaulted and to have no place to go.

THE SOCIAL WORKER'S RESPONSE

The responses and assistance the women we interviewed received from professional helpers, especially social workers, reflected the lack of agency resources, especially housing, their beliefs about the nature of the violence and the women's real problem, and their broader, well-entrenched views on family life. Social workers and marriage counselors exist to reinforce and protect the nuclear family against dissolution, and this goal is often achieved at a very high cost to some family members. Various government reports relating to the organization and intentions of social work agencies in Britain have reaffirmed the aim of protecting and reinforcing family unity. The Beveridge report, the cornerstone of the British welfare state, and the Seebohm report, which formed the foundation of the recent reorganization of social work in England and Wales, expressed similar beliefs about the natural aspects of motherhood and the primary importance of maintaining the complete family.[106]

> The attitude of the housewife to gainful employment outside of the home is not and should not be the same as that of the single woman. She has other duties.
>   . . . In the next thirty years housewives as mothers have vital work to do in ensuring the adequate continuance of the British Race and British ideals in the world.[107]

More recent policies reflect the belief that the family is the source of, and the cure for, a vast and impressive array of social problems.[108] Ideologies of this nature are reinforced by experts on child rearing such as Bowlby[109] and are reflected in the official policies and practices of social service departments in Britain and America. They identify the healthy and normal family as one with two parents (male and female) and children. The structure of the family unit seems to count more than its actual substance and quality, as helping professionals generally make clear to battered women.

> They always wanted you to go back with your man, but they just don't have the responsibility.

> The only reaction I got out of them was "Well, we think it's really up to you to try and make a go of your marriage." It was always just a case of "We feel it's up to you to make a go of it."

> Yeah, he did give me advice. He said, "How about sort of trying to accept things for what they were?"

> They said I had to stay. I had went to the doctor and I spoke to Mrs. Westerton, the welfare, and I said, "I just can't stay." And they said, "You just have to stay, you know, for the sake of the wee ones."

> I was with her [the social worker] for about a year. She was very nice, but I felt she couldn't help me. I had my child fostered at one time to get away from [the violence], but it's all I think she bothered about was the child, you know. That was my opinion.

Lack of assistance to the battered wife sometimes reflects the very real problems the caseworker has in obtaining accommodation for the woman and her children. But they also reflect a deeply held set of beliefs that the family should be kept together for the sake of children.[110] Yet, if a child's mother is being assaulted, how beneficial can the family setting be? Nevertheless, helping professionals continue to argue that an intact family is healthier than a broken one regardless of the quality of the relationships within it.[111]

Helping professionals do act quickly to assist women or recommend that the family be broken up when the children are perceived to be in danger of receiving treatment that is the same as or even less severe than, that received by their mother.[112]

> Well, that time he used the weapon. She said if he used a weapon get out because the bairns could be injured as well.

Women were sometimes placed in intolerable dilemmas regarding their responsibilities for their children. Professional helpers, who are concerned primarily about the welfare of children, may inform a woman who has left her husband and is residing in inadequate accommodation that she must find appropriate accommodation for her children or they will be taken from her. Some women must then return to their husbands in order to prevent this.

> The social worker told me that they could only give me to the end of the week and if I hadn't found accommodation for myself and the wee one by the end of the week they would take him off me and put him into a home. I thought, well, rather than get him taken off me I'd go back. So I went back to him and that was that, right up until now.

The responses of the professional helpers not only reflect the ideals of the priority of children but also illustrate a philosophy which emphasizes the maintenance of the traditional position of men and women as husbands and wives.[113] Most helping professionals did not make these beliefs explicit, but on occasion, as in the following incident, the appropriate authority relations in the family were explicitly evident in the advice to the couple.

Well, he spoke to both of us and he sat down for about an hour and he spoke about our financial situation and how having a child affected a marriage and things like that. Then he would bring in the vows of marriage—"to love, honor, and obey until death do us part." And I argued on the point of obeying because I feel, I felt at that time, to obey, it's alright in certain principles but you cannae obey all your life. I mean, if I asked him to stop gambling he wouldnae obey me, but I have to obey all his rules. The minister wouldnae talk about that fact.

When the professional responds to a battered woman by threatening to take away her children or by tacitly reaffirming the husband's right to control his wife, she is likely to stop seeking such help.

I had been to the social worker a few times before and explained about different things and they sort of wanted us to stay together. And I says to myself, I'm going to the social worker and I'm no really getting the help I would like. I would like to get away from him all together. I think that's how I stopped going to them, you know, to tell them different things because I felt I wasnae really getting anywhere.

The caseworker's explicit rejection of the woman's account of the relationship or of the severity of the violence might even exacerbate her problems.[114] Women who are already isolated and lacking in self-esteem after years of being told by their husbands that they are inadequate as wives and mothers need supportive and sympathetic responses. If a response of this nature is not forthcoming or if the response and evaluation of her predicament are equivocal, the low self-esteem and sense of isolation experienced by the woman may be aggravated.

I thought they [social workers] should have known better than me and this is when the guilt complex actually started in my marriage. Where I felt everybody was up against me even socially, you know. As far as they were concerned, I was inadequate, he was alright, he could do what he liked to me, and everybody excused the fact—what he done to me. And from that time on the strain was getting worse on me and I never knew that I should have seeked advice, mentally and physically. But I couldnae, you see, because I was too embarrassed. Because I thought, "Well, if the social worker's saying that, well, the doctor's going to say the very same thing, isn't he?" I mean, he's not going to help me much either because he's no there to see it happening and I found that nine times out of ten the doctors didn't have time for you to talk things over.

Another factor that enters into a woman's decision to terminate her relationship with a helping professional is the inability or unwillingness of the professional to contact and deal with her husband. This may be in part because the husband refuses to cooperate. The husbands of women we interviewed usually were not interested in obtaining help because they did not believe that they were at fault or that they needed help and, of course, they were not the targets of the violence.

> I knew he wouldn't entertain the idea of going up to see them [marriage guidance] because he always maintained he doesn't need anybody to sort out his problems.

> Aye, I went to marriage guidance and that, but . . . that was really a washout because he wouldnae entertain them. I mean, they need the two sides of the story for to try and get at the root of the problem.

On the rare occasions when abusive husbands were contacted by a social worker, minister, or marriage counselor the meetings were abrupt and the men usually denied that they were violent and/or claimed that their wives had provoked them.

> Well the only advice [the social worker] could give me was, to speak to Ian, which she did try to do once, but Ian used to walk out.

> A husband: . . . yes, it's true I slapped her around a little, but she was following me from room to room yelling and I finally exploded.[115]

Women are ambivalent about such meetings since they fear that if an outsider confronts her husband the probability of violence may actually be increased rather than decreased. By seeking help the woman has 'defied' her husband and may have embarrassed him, thereby "challenging" him and becoming subject to punishment.

> *What happened when she [the social worker] spoke to him?*

> He just walked out. And he slapped me across the face for bringing a social worker into it.

> So [a minister] come up and he asked a lot of questions to him and me, and he just says that your wife's very depressed and she's come to me for advice but it just went in that ear and out the other because when the minister went out I was beaten again, you see. But it's not worth it—I mean, talking to people—it's no worth me bringing anybody in to help John because he just ignores them. He says, "Yes, yes, I'll do that," but as soon as they go out that's what happens.

Finally, if the husband is aware that his wife has sought help and has received an unsupportive or ineffective response, this may increase his sense of justification and reinforce his belief that he can act with impunity because he now knows that his option for assistance has been virtually closed to her.

CHAPTER 11

THE POLICE AND JUDICIAL RESPONSE

IF A MAN ATTACKS HIS WIFE within the confines of the home he is, without a doubt, committing a crime as specified in the various statutes of Great Britain and North America.[1] Depending upon the seriousness of the attack and the nature of the available evidence, the man is subject to charges ranging from simple or common assault, assault and battery, to serious assault or attempted murder. However, arrest and judicial processing are ususual in cases of assault on women within the home. Police officers and judicial officials are apt to see the offense either as unimportant and not worthy of attention or as a civil and social problem that requires the services of another agency and to use their discretionary powers to avoid arrest and prosecution.

Police Discretion and Violent Offenses

Considerable discretion is employed by the police in making arrests. Research has indicated that in general the decision to arrest is neither solely nor even primarily based on the nature of the illegal behavior but rather upon the police officer's assessment of the circumstances surrounding the commission of the crime and the characteristics of both offender and victim.[2] This discretionary process is a necessary and beneficial aspect of police work,[3] but when it results in a pattern of overenforcement in the case of certain racial and ethnic groups[4] or underenforcement, as in the case of violence against wives, it subverts the course of justice. Systematic underenforcement in cases involving violence may also endanger life.

Research relating to the use of discretion among police officers has revealed that officers are *very unlikely* to make an arrest when the offender has used violence against his wife. In other violent situations, officers typically arrest the attacker regardless of the characteristics of the victim and offender or the circumstances surrounding the crime.[5] Field and Field's survey of police and court dispositions in Washington D.C. during 1967 revealed that of all the assault cases involving strangers or unrelated people, 75% resulted in arrest and court adjudication, whereas only 16% of all cases involving assaults in the family ended in arrest and trial. Moreover, all of the assaults against spouses were charged as misdemeanors and not felonies.[6] Black's comprehensive study of police responses in Washington D.C., Boston, and Chicago revealed similar patterns and he concluded that "the probability of arrest is highest when the citizen adversaries have the most distant social relations to one another, i.e., when they are strangers."[7] In Black's study arrests were about half as likely when family members were involved in illegal behavior as when strangers were involved in the same behavior.

Police are actually more likely to arrest individuals involved in non-violent acts outside the home than they are to arrest husbands for violent offenses committed within the home. Blum's study of police discretion revealed an arrest rate of 80% on minor charges such as public drunkenness, suspicious behavior, and verbal abuse of police; the arrest rate for physical disputes involving family members was only 8%.[8] Field and Field concluded after their extensive study of police and judicial responses to women assaulted by their husbands in Washington D.C. that, "The poles of enforcement are the rigorous prosecution of the person accused of assaulting a stranger and the nonprosecution of the one who assaults a marital partner."[9]

The source of this pattern of differential police response is the common law, which at one time allowed men to beat their wives, and a series of judicial decisions made in the latter half of the nineteenth century and the first quarter of the twentieth.[10] The common law principle of coverture, which views husband and wife as a single entity, made it very difficult for a woman to bring her husband to court for an offense committed against her since the courts viewed such an action as illogical and impossible: an individual cannot offend against himself.[11] By the beginning of the twentieth century courts had rejected a rigid application of the principle of coverture and had ruled that the use of extreme force by a husband against his wife was illegal; yet, doctrines still existed that explicitly acknowledged the rights of a husband to regulate his household and to restrict his wife's movements and visitors. Eventually, *explicit* principles relating to the absolute rights of husbands were no longer recognized in law in Britain. Nevertheless, magistrates and judges continued to be reluctant to intervene in matrimonial disputes. The sanctity of the home and the ideal of family privacy[12] were powerful counters to legislative acts and court decisions that were meant to give married women greater rights and protections. The primary outcome of this legal and judicial effort was the constriction of the husband's rights and the setting of limits on the physical force he might use. At the same time, emphasis was placed on civil, rather than criminal remedies to domestic cases.

This legacy is reflected in contemporary criminal and civil statutes and in the practices of the police and courts. New Mexico laws on domestic violence specify "wilful and wanton assaults" and Maryland laws require "brutal assault."[13] Until the 1950s, in Texas, Utah, and New Mexico husbands were granted special immunity from prosecution if they were to find their wives in an adulterous situation and commit homicide. The New Mexico statute specifically stated that "any person [husband] who kills another who is in the act of having carnal knowledge of such person's legal wife shall be deemed justifiable."[14] This same right was not granted to wives. Indeed, a Texas court ruled that a wife did not have the same immunity from prosecution. The spirit of such laws is still evident in police and judicial policies and practices throughout Britain and the United States. Bannon succinctly summarized the cultural beliefs that reflect this spirit in his address to the American Bar Association Convention in 1975:

> We [males] are socialized into the conscious perceptions of masculine-feminine roles. In our society this process translates into dominance-submission terms. The man is the boss, the owner the female subordinate. . . . Taken together without views on the sanctity of the home the above factors guarantee that police will be less than enthusiastic in becoming involved in family disputes.[15]

Police Policies and Practices

POLICIES AND TRAINING

In both Britain and the United States a considerable proportion of all requests for assistance received by the police concern problems occurring in the family.[16] Parnas concluded that the Chicago police received more calls concerning family conflicts than they did calls concerning murder, aggravated assault and battery, and all other serious crimes combined.[17] The evidence is clear: the police spend a great deal of time and resources on problems relating to family conflicts and a considerable proportion of these cases involve assaults on women. Yet, very little time and attention is devoted to domestic disputes in police training programs. In Michigan, for example, the law requires that police officers receive 240 hours of training, yet only 3–5 hours are spent dealing with problems in the family setting.[18] The training emphasizes that the officer should, if at all possible, avoid taking any action.[19] Police departments teach their recruits directly and indirectly that a man who attacks his wife is not committing a real crime unless he exceeds the limits tacitly set by the department. These limits usually relate to the severity of injuries and/or the use of a weapon.

A memorandum from the London Metropolitan Police Department submitted to the Parliamentary Committee on Marital Violence expounded the policy of nonintervention in domestic disputes with intervention reserved for cases involving severe injury.

> Whereas it is a general principle of police practice not to intervene in a situation which existed or had existed between husband and wife in the course of

which the wife had suffered some personal attack, any assault upon a wife by her husband which amounted to physical injury of a serious nature is a criminal offense which it is the duty of the police to followup and prosecute.[20]

The training manual issued by the International Association of Police Chiefs proposed various types of responses to domestic disputes, all of them oriented toward avoiding arrests.

> For the most part these disputes are personal matters requiring no direct police action. Once inside the home, the officer's sole role is to preserve the peace. . . . In dealing with family disputes the power of arrest should be exercised as a last resort. The officer should never create a police problem when there is only a family problem existing.[21]

A Detroit police manual also made similar recommendations.

> When a police officer is called to a private home having family difficulties, he should recognize the sanctity of the home and endeavor diplomatically to quell the disturbance and create peace without making an arrest.[22]

Labeling the violent incident a "family dispute" or "family problem" obscures the fact, as established in numerous research efforts and explicitly recognized by police authorities, that these episodes usually involve violence directed at women by their husbands.[23] This policy toward domestic assaults is justified by the police in both the United States and Great Britain on several grounds: women will not pursue the charge of assault against their husbands; women have civil remedies available to them; and these disputes are social problems rather than criminal ones. The argument that violence toward wives is a social problem is well founded, but in this case it merely rationalizes inaction since a myriad of other illegal behaviors that are generated by social factors (riots, for example) elicit swift and aggressive police action.

The assumption that the problem is not a police problem is further rationalized by the belief that other agencies exist to deal with it. A Wayne County (Michigan) circuit court judge summed up this view.

> The law enforcement agencies say well, that's just a domestic problem and you should see your lawyer and handle it in civil court. A domestic call is not serious in their view. They view other calls as more serious.[24]

Police departments assume that domestic problems should and will be dealt with by other social agencies and that women will obtain relief and assistance from the legal and social service professions. However, social service agencies often take the position that wife beating is a police problem; therefore, they offer very little guidance or assistance to battered women. In 1973 there were over 150 court connected agencies in the United States dealing with marriage problems "but almost everyone of these exclude[d] from its jurisdiction problems of marital violence.[25] A chief constable from north Wales told the Parliamentary Committee that the general practice in police forces was to advise the woman attacked by her husband "to take further advice from one of the statutory agencies or by consulting a solicitor."[26] The assumption that a woman can seek such advice is little comfort to her when she is being continually attacked by her husband. It is often difficult for a woman to leave her home and/or find a lawyer because of her child care responsibilities, her husband's threats of retaliation, or various other reasons. Likewise, she may not be able to afford the services of an attorney or the attorney may be unwilling to help her in filing for divorce or separation.[27] The consequence of all this neutral posturing, euphemistic language, and unfounded supposition regarding the avenues available to battered women, is that women are left to seek help from an agency that does not wish to help them. The police alone provide 24-hour service to individuals in distress, but given their training and policies, it is likely that they will provide little or no assistance to a woman being assaulted by her husband.

DEPARTMENTAL PRACTICES

Police inaction in domestic disputes is evident in the telephone screening procedures that are widely used in urban police departments throughout the United States. Police departments establish a priority list to be used in evaluating which calls should receive attention: the highest priority problems are responded to immediately. Incidents considered less important are responded to more slowly and some are ignored. In keeping with this practice, justified by limited resources and personnel, the first telephone calls to be screened out are calls regarding domestic disturbances.[28] This practice was started in Detroit during the mid-1960s, and LaFave found that when demands on the Detroit police were particularly heavy, the police dispatchers "screen out those family disturbances in which there does not appear to be any threats of *excessive violence* [emphasis added]."[29] In the same city, the general orders relating to "Telephone Requests for Police Service" state that "family trouble is basically a civil matter."[30] A woman who telephoned the Syracuse Police Department complaining about her boyfriend's threats to beat her up was told, "Call us again when he does."[31]

A woman may increase the probability that an officer will be sent to her aid if she can convince the dispatcher that her husband is using a weapon: "A near breathless woman beaten by her husband dialed 911 to ask police assistance. "Does he have a weapon?" the operator asked. She answered he did not. "Then I am sorry we won't be able to help you," the operator said."[32] A woman who had experienced numerous assaults from her husband told Eisenberg and Micklow how she was effectively and brutally screened out by the police dispatcher: "Yesterday my husband came and knifed my car, ripped the tyres, slashed the roof, grabbed me and told me next time I was going to get it like the car. . . . After he left I called the police. I was put on hold . . . they didn't even ask me my name."[33] In this case an assault had not been committed (though some statutes define threatening behavior as an assault), but certainly a crime had occurred and acting on official policy the police telephone operator ignored it. This woman's experience parallels the experiences of untold numbers of women who call the police for assistance. Practices such as these are brutal reminders of battered women who seek assistance that their problems are considered less important to the police than malicious mischief, public drunkenness, and traffic offenses.

INDIVIDUAL RESPONSES

The orientation of the police is such that if and when an officer is sent to the scene of a domestic assault, his inclination to arrest the husband is very slight indeed. Blum's study of police responses to various crisis situations revealed that police officers very rarely entered a house with an initial plan to arrest. In only 6 out of 165 incidents involving police calls to homes were police officers predisposed to make an arrest.[34] It is, however, erroneous to assume that individual officers' responses to violence in the home are totally dictated by police training and departmental policy. A police officer entering a house where an assault is in progress or recently has ended makes a number of evaluations of the situation. Research has shown that his ultimate decision regarding arrest is based on his assessment of the circumstances relating to the incident and includes at least the following factors: the severity of the violence, the nature of the evidence, the social processes preceding the violence, the behavior and attitudes of the attacker, and the behavior and attitudes of the victim.[35] Some police authorities explicitly recognize these factors. The Association of Chief Police Officers of England, Wales, and Northern Ireland specified the following criteria as relevant to assaults on wives:

> (i) the seriousness of the assault; (ii) the availability of witnesses; (iii) the character of the alleged assailant; (iv) age, informity, etc., of the complainant; (v) previous domestic history; (vi) the wishes of the complainant; and (vii) if prosecution ensued against the wishes of the complainant, would the domestic situation be adversely affected.[36]

A police officer's assessment of these factors is affected not only by his training and socialization as a policeman but also by his individual beliefs about the appropriate relationship between men and women and husbands and wives. Given the legacy of patriarchal control and the contemporary view that men are the wielders of rightful authority within the home, police officers are likely to identify with the husband.[37] If the husband is able to convince the police officer(s) that in using force to chastise his wife, he was behaving simply as befits a head of household then the probability of arrest is reduced. The husband's claims may be further substantiated by enumerating his wife's supposed offenses against his authority. 'Scolding,' 'nagging,' and failing to keep the house clean or to manage the household budget represent only a few of the 'failures' to live up to the appropriate duties of a good wife and mother, failures and offenses that the police may accept as 'provocation' for the assault.[38] A consideration of these factors may lead the officers to minimize the husband's culpability and maximize the wife's, and thus accept the use of a certain amount of violence against her. As Bannon has argued, "There appears to be some acceptance of the idea that a little corporal punishment to the recalcitrant wife is not all that deviant."[39] The failure to arrest is in many ways an indirect support for the husband's attacks.

The set of beliefs and ideals regarding the duties of wives and the right of husbands to use force against them is somewhat contradicted by another constellation of beliefs that emphasizes the rejection of violence and especially condemns its use against women. Accordingly, the officer may not make an arrest but may indirectly condemn the violence, for example, by threatening arrest.

One of the women we interviewed described the way the police refused to arrest her husband after he attempted to suffocate her: "The next thing she [her mother] did was to get my dad up and he got the police, but they came up and said it was just mother-in-law trouble and that was it." This was not an ususual response. Many of the women we spoke to said that though the police were sometimes courteous, they usually were unwilling to arrest the husband even at the woman's request.

Did you find the police quite helpful whenever you did have them in the house?

Oh, no. They just gave him a ticking off—said it was a family tiff, sort of thing. They just dispelled it. . . . And I used to say, "Can you not help me," you know, "come and check and see if I'm alright at nights and that?" But they never bothered.

A few officers were openly hostile toward the woman for making a complaint and "wasting their time." For example, one woman had contacted the police a total of four times throughout her married life. Each time she asked them to arrest her husband and each time they refused.

Even once they told me—they gave me a telling off for phoning the police. It was a sergeant that came, it was. I went for them and they came up, you know, and he just walks in and he says, "What's the trouble?" I says, "He's been battering me and that. He's assaulted me." [Police officer], "What do you want me to do?" I says, "I don't know what you can do. Surely you can do something." Then the police officer says, "Look, you can't come phoning us every time your husband decides to hit you." I says, "That means I have to sit here and let him knock hell out of me anytime he feels like it." He says, "You don't have to live here." "Well, where can I go?" "That's your problem," he says, "not mine." So I asked him, "Are you married?" "Yes," he says. "Well, do you hit your wife?" He says, "That's none of your business." I says, "You probably do. That's why you've no sympathy for me."

Such outward expressions of hostility from the police were rather unusual. According to the women we interviewed, the typical response was refusing to arrest and treating the assault as a private and/or civil matter. This pattern was also reported by many women who testified before the Parliamentary Select Committee and by women interviewed in studies in the United States.[40]

Although officers usually enter a house with a predisposition to avoid an arrest, they may consider it necessary or appropriate to arrest the abusive husband on certain occasions. The particular factors likely to lead to arrest are often not related to the seriousness of the offense, but to requirements necessary for a successful prosecution, the officer's perception of the circumstances leading up to the assault as well as his evaluation of the 'justness' and of the moral characters of the victim and the assailant. In our reading of nearly a thousand cases of wife assault that were processed by the police, it was clear that neither the seriousness of the assault nor the extent of injury was decisive in the decision to arrest. For example, one of the cases we examined described a rather minor assault; the husband had kicked his wife's leg causing a slight bruise. This offense would usually have been treated as unworthy of police action. In this case the husband was charged with assault and detained. It was noted in the police report that in three days' time, the woman was to enter the hospital in order to undergo heart surgery. The officers obviously felt sympathetic toward a woman in this position and thought that she did not deserve to be kicked by her husband.

The behavior and attitude of both victim and attacker also affect the probability of arrest. Thus, the husband who attacks his wife can nearly guarantee arrest if he continues to cause a nuisance by behaving in a belligerent manner when the police arrive.[41] As these court cases from our own research illustrate, this is especially true if he verbally abuses the police.[42]

> The police were called to a house where the wife alleges wife assault. The police refuse to charge because of lack of evidence but they do warn the husband of possible arrest. The husband becomes belligerent and shouts at the police to get out. As the police begin to leave the husband follows them into the common close and begins to bawl, shout and swear at them. He was warned but took no notice so he was charged with breach of the peace and detained.

On Monday at 11:45 P.M. the police were called by a woman who alleges her husband assaulted her in the common stairs in the building. Since the husband had left the police did not pursue the case. They were called back later to the same location regarding a disturbance. When they arrived they observed the husband kicking the door of the woman's flat. He was shouting, bawling, swearing, "You fucking bastard, I'll be fucked if you'll keep me out." As the police approach he warns them, "Don't you cunts lay a hand on me." He was arrested and detained for breach of the peace.

He also increases the probability of arrest if he creates enough of a disturbance that outsiders such as neighbors are aroused and demand that the police take action.

The police received a call about a man who had been causing a disturbance which had kept his wife, children and elderly parents awake most of the night. When the police arrived they found that the man had "also assaulted his wife," but the police stated that "as there were no witnesses, no charges could be preferred." The police then warned the man and he appeared to take heed. But as the police were leaving, he began to shout, bawl and swear at the police and at his family. By this time several neighbors had appeared at the windows and demanded to know what action the police were going to take as this behavior had been going on all night. At that point, the police arrested and detained the man for breach of the peace.

American and British police departments traditionally have followed unofficial "stitch" rules whereby assaults requiring medical treatment, especially woundings, automatically result in police action.[43] In such cases, the police are likely to arrest both because they are required to give the woman assistance due to the severity of her injuries and because another agency, usually a hospital, is involved.

The police just took one look at me and said, "Oh, you'll have to get treatment," and they took me to the hospital. They left me in the hospital getting about four stitches in my leg, and they got my eyes sorted as well. The police went back and my husband said to them that it was a lot of rubbish. He never touched me. But they said, "Oh, no. We've had to take your wife to hospital so this time you're definitely getting done [arrested]." So they lifted him and came back up and collected me.

In some instances the reluctance to arrest may be justified by the rules of evidence. It is important, however, to consider the possibility that the police employ different criteria regarding the rules of evidence in cases involving assaults on wives and in those involving strangers.[44]

When a man is arrested for assaulting his wife the officers are implicitly supporting the wife by removing the husband from the home,[45] but officers can support the woman even when they do not arrest the man. According to the women we interviewed a common sympathetic response from the police came in the form of advice regarding the violence and the marital relationship.

They [the police] just said to me, "get the place cleaned up, get into bed, and forget about it, but don't take it again. You just watch what you're doing—don't let him lift his hand'like that."

They advised me to leave him, to try and get a separation or try and get a house in my own name and that.

This sort of advice may seem unimportant in the context of the overall pattern of indifference, yet it is important because the battered woman experiences such a degree of isolation that she often has not shared her problem with anyone. A police officer who openly condemns the husband's behavior may be the only person who has ever supported the woman. Sometimes officers go much further. If a woman is reluctant to file a charge against her husband because she thinks that it will do very little good or that it might exacerbate the situation, police officers may urge her to file charges. This response is especially likely if the police have been called to the house on several occasions in the past and are sympathetic toward the woman's situation. One woman who lived in a small village described this type of reaction.

Well, the neighbors had phoned the police and when they came I wouldn't charge him. That's when we lived in the village and that particular night he had a knife and the next door neighbor had come over and they sent for the police. Of course, the policeman there was the local policeman, which everybody knew. He said, "For God's sake, Margaret, charge him." They'd been waiting. See, they knew what he was like. . . . In a small village everybody knows everybody else and they knew what I was taking from Keith.

Police officers may also go so far as to provide tangible assistance to the woman. The police in the following example gave considerable help even though they did not charge the husband with assault.

So the officer says, "What are you going to do?" I says, "I dinnae kin. Well, just take me up to his Uncle Arthur's. He'll keep me for the night." Even his Uncle Arthur told the police about Dennis: "See he's mental. He's going to kill her." So I stayed with Uncle Arthur that night and the police came back in the morning and picked me up again, really nice, and they took me to a social worker.

This type of response is rare but it is very important to the women who are the recipients of such assistance. It represents the public service nature of police work, a role that is rather reluctantly accepted by the police, who prefer to emphasize the crime control and detection aspects of their work.

It has been argued that police officers should be given greater and more intensive training in dealing with domestic violence. Training programs relating to assaults in the home and family disturbances would emphasize the mediation and peacekeeping aspects of police work.[46] In some respects this is a laudable and worthwhile proposal, but it also has certain inherent dangers that should not be ignored. Programs and proposals that emphasize the social work role of police officers in dealing with assaults against women should not override the law enforcement function. The sanction of arrest, though admittedly clumsy and brutal, does demonstrate the social disapproval of various behaviors in society.[47] To withhold that sanction, as in many cases of assaults on wives, and to apply only unofficial sanctions or none at all demonstrate to the husband that his behavior is not illegal and thus is not truly inappropriate. The sanction of arrest, even the threat of arrest, indicates to the husband that his behavior will not be tolerated and it may deter him from continuing his assaults. For example, one of the women we interviewed told us how her husband ceased to use violence against her after he was merely warned by the police. This was the only time the police had been called in and the husband was exceedingly embarrassed because he had a reputation in the neighborhood as a "very nice guy." On this occasion, an argument, which usually resulted in a beating or choking, had begun with a slap; before it could continue the wife escaped from the house and fled to the police station. Two officers accompanied her back to the house, where they interviewed her and her husband.

> When they went in he was as nice as ninepence, and he made out that I was daft. I seen him, standing going, "She's a wee bit daft." And I'm shouting, "He slapped me. He slapped me and if I hadnae run out of the house he would have done more." The policeman said, "Is there any marks on you?" I said, "I don't know, but he slapped my face." The policeman said, "I don't see any marks, hen. Are you sure you've no just had an argument and you've exaggerated matters a wee bit and just ran out thinking you'd frighten your man by bringing the police back?" And he's [her husband] sitting there smiling away and I'm dreading for the police leaving. The policeman said to him, "Well, she's come around to us." Cos I'm shouting to the police, "Don't go out this house. He'll kill me, he'll kill me." And the police says, "Well, your wife's been around and put in a complaint, so if anything does happen to her we'll know what it has been. I cannae do anything to you—maybe you did hit her, maybe you didnae hit her—but she hasn't any marks to prove that you hit her, so she's got nothing to charge you with." . . . The police told him they would be hanging around that area and if they heard any screams they would be up in a flash.

The response of this police officer might not have been completely sympathetic toward the woman but it nonetheless had a considerable effect on the husband. He vowed that the police would never come to the door again and he stopped using physical violence against his wife.[48]

The Judicial Response

The judicial response to violence against wives generally reflects the same pattern of indifference, official inaction, and occasional unofficial reaction exhibited by police departments. Very often police departments use the judicial system as a means of appeasing the woman or discouraging her from pursuing complaints against her husband. Rather than arrest the husband when this action is clearly warranted, police officers will tell the woman that her problems are really personal and/or civil and not criminal but that if she wishes to press criminal charges she can go to the district attorney's office (magistrate's court in England) and attempt to file a complaint.[49] The woman must appear before the magistrate or public prosecutor the following morning and request that criminal proceedings be brought against her husband.

In England, Wales, and the United States battered women often are required to pursue their complaints directly with the courts because the police refuse to take action. Police officers very often utilize this technique to divert the woman from pursuing an assault charge, what Field and Field call "cooling off" the situation and testing the woman's resolve to pursue the complaint.[50] Such refusal is less likely in other types of cases, and it certainly does test the strength and resolve of the woman to go to court, often with her bruises from the previous night, her children, and her very real fear that she may be attacked again when she returns home. When she arrives at the prosecutor's office she is most likely frightened and anxious. The response of court officials probably does little to allay her fears and reduce her anxieties. On the contrary, as Field and Field and Eisenberg and Micklow discovered, attempting to file a complaint may prove to be a tedious and time-consuming process, which again tests the woman's resolve. And signing a complaint does not necessarily mean that the prosecutor will automatically issue an arrest warrant. Understandably, women tend not to take this drastic and important step to seek help unless they have exhausted all other sources of help (e.g., doctors and social workers).[51]

Prosecutors, like police officers, often view the problem of wife beating as primarily a civil and personal matter requiring neither arrest nor judicial response. Accordingly, the court official tries to assess whether the victim is 'worthy' and whether she is sincere about following up the arrest complaint.[52] A woman must demonstrate that she did not 'deserve' to be attacked and that in the face of all her difficulties she will pursue the complaint against her husband. Very often the sincerity and resolve of a woman is judged by her willingness to institute divorce proceedings against her husband.[53] The woman may also be required to secure various forms of evidence in order to reinforce her case in the eyes of the investigating officer and/or prosecutor. She may be required in police districts that do not have a police doctor to go to a private physician and obtain her own evidence of injury.

If the woman can convince the court officials that she is a worthy victim and is sincere in her complaint, they may issue a warrant for the husband's arrest. The decision to charge the husband is, however, quite an unlikely outcome of the negotiation between the woman and the court. In 1966 over seventy-five hundred women appeared at the district attorney's office in Washington D.C. seeking to file complaints against their husbands. Only 200, that is, 2.7%, succeeded.[54]

The fact that a husband is charged with assault does not mean that he will actually come to court. The woman may, as is her right, decide to drop the charges: she may feel that a reconciliation has been reached between her and her husband, she may feel that criminal prosecution may do little good, or she may be forced to drop the charges because of threats from her husband. Alternatively, the prosecutor may through judicial review decide to drop the charges or he may persuade the woman to withdraw the charges in order to reduce the burden on the court or to help effect a reconciliation between husband and wife.

In some U.S. jurisdictions court officials may not file an official charge but instead pursue quasi-judicial remedies to demonstrate to the husband that his behavior is unacceptable. Public prosecutors in Washington D.C. conduct informal hearings, threaten arrest, write out mock divorces, and produce official looking complaints for "failure to do right," all in an attempt to deter the offender while avoiding arrest.[55] Prosecutors believe (perhaps hope) that by conducting these mock judicial proceedings the man will be deterred from subsequent attacks on his wife and the woman will be satisfied because justice appears to have been done. The refusal to charge and the process of appeasing the woman and threatening the husband through quasi-judicial action mean that the man is not charged, the case load is kept down, and the woman receives neither "justice nor peace."[56]

Generally, husbands who are charged are charged with a less serious offense, such as common assault or disturbing the peace, rather than with assault and battery. Disposition of such cases may also reflect the judge's view that wife beating is not truly criminal behavior and that the man's attacks may be somewhat justified by his wife's provocations. This attitude is epitomized in the beliefs of the American judge: "These [assaults] are not unilateral, by all means. A lot of the assaults are provoked by the wife, a lot of them come out of a tense situation in which the parties are living."[57] A conception of the genesis of the violence as primarily, or somewhat, justified reduces the potential moral indignation of the judiciary and obviously encourages leniency toward the man who assaults his wife.

Field and Field found that the most common sanction used in Washington D.C. was the peace bond. This was also a common sanction in Detroit in 1972: well over four thousand women attempted to lodge complaints in that year and over eighteen hundred cases were resolved through the issuance of peace bonds.[58] Peace bonds are primarily a civil action though they sometimes include the threat of penal or financial sanction; for instance, California law specifies a surety of up to $5,000.[59] Like Lord Lee, who during the reign of Charles II was bound by the court to give a security against future attacks on his wife, whom he had imprisoned to the detriment of her health, men are today bound to keep the peace. Peace bonds may be applied against offenders other than abusive husbands, but they seem to be used primarily in cases of domestic violence. Recourse to peace bonds, which were instituted in the fourteenth century, demonstrates the courts' view of violence against wives as a civil and not a criminal matter.[60] Peace bonds have no specific statutory basis and are more properly seen as a civil rather than a criminal action. Judges and legal observers disagree regarding the effectiveness of peace bonds: some think they can be a deterrent against assaults; others consider them unenforceable and maintain that they rarely discourage wife beating.

When judges do apply a criminal sanction it is likely to be very light indeed. Fines, probations, deferred and suspended sentences, and admonishments seem to be the principal sanctions in Britain and America.[61] In Glasgow during 1974, the majority of men who assaulted their wives were punished by being either admonished by the magistrate (24.6%) or forced to pay a small fine (58%). Another small percentage (3.4%) were placed on probation; only 12% were imprisoned.[62] These statistics refer to all types of assaults on wives, ranging from the very serious to the minor. Men who are sent to prison probably have long histories of attacks against their wives, but the particular attack that lands them in jail may not be the most serious one.[63]

Women who meet with inaction or indifference from the courts may eventually seek redress through civil action. Until 1976, it was necessary in Britain for a woman to file for divorce before the courts would entertain an application for an injunction or interdict against her husband. If the injunction was granted it usually enjoined the husband to leave the home and to desist from attacking or molesting his wife. Observers and lawyers on both sides of the Atlantic have commented on the ineffectiveness of injunctions. The Parliamentary Select Committee on Marital Violence observed that injunctions were very often "not worth the paper they were written on" because they are virtually unenforceable. If the husband disobeys the injunction by attacking or harassing his wife he violates the court order and is in contempt of court. Yet, it is essentially impossible to obtain police action, especially at night, when it is most needed, since the police require a guarantee from the court that such an injunction has been granted before they will act to enforce it and this guarantee can be obtained only during office hours. It seems that it is very rare for the police to enforce an injunction and even rarer for them to arrest a husband for disobeying the injunction. An American attorney observed:

I've never run into a contempt [charge] of a violation of a restraining order during the five years that I have been practicing. I've never once seen a husband put in jail. Never once. . . . It's not really an effective remedy because judges won't do anything.[64]

In 1976–1977 a new form of injunction was introduced in England that allows women to apply for a nonmolestation order without first filing for divorce. It also added the possibility of a criminal sanction for breaking the injunction. This is certainly an important outcome of the deliberations of the Parliamentary Select Committee, but given the history of judicial and law enforcement inaction, the attitudes of police as expressed to the Select Committee, and the knowledge of women regarding their rights in this respect, the nonmolestation order is not likely to be widely used or aggressively enforced.[65] Police officials in Scotland and England have pointed out that injunctions are very seldom applied for: "Very few women in my experience in Glasgow who are assaulted . . . have the knowledge of how to go about getting an interdict, and it is certainly not common in Glasgow for this action to be taken."[66]

The judicial response to assaults on wives reaffirms the husband's view that his behavior is not truly illegal and the imposition of minor sanctions further reinforces police officers' views that wife beating is not a serious crime. Even sympathetic police officers may be deterred from making arrests when they observe the manner in which the courts treat assaults against wives and the attitudes of court officials to women and their problems. Judges, it seems, may have little time for the complaints of women. As one judge told an English jury, "It is well known that women in particular, and small boys are liable to be untruthful and invent stories."[67]

Courts and police argued, too, that prosecution and arrest may jeopardize the marriage.

"Vigorous action by the police in many instances might blow the whole situation up."[68]

It is important for a whole host of reasons, to maintain the unity of spouses. Precipitate action by the Police could aggravate the position to such an extent as to create a worse situation than the one they are summoned to deal with.[69]

In other words, the family should be held together at all costs.

Finally, the court personnel and police maintain that a woman will not pursue a charge against her husband and testify in court. Note, however, that in a large number of cases of wife assault husbands, like other accused individuals, plead guilty in courts, 90% in our police sample, which in Britain usually means the morning after the arrest.[70] Thus, in most cases women are not required to give evidence and since the court will most likely only admonish the husband or impose a peace bond or a nominal fine, it is also difficult to understand the concern about the impact of police action on the family.[71]

It seems that in order to decrease the probability of dropping a charge a swift response is the best one, as a police superintendent from Manchester argued before the Select Committee on Marital Violence.

> Over the last twelve months in the force I belong to 193 husbands have been charged with wife assault. Of these 160 were committed within the matrimonial home. . . . I feel the way in my force is the best way, arrest, in custody and before the court the next morning.[72]

In our research only 6% of the assault charges were dropped by the women before the final adjudication—in all instances *after considerable postponement of court proceedings*. Such delays place the complainant in an uncomfortable and unpleasant, if not dangerous, position. It may be true that some women will not pursue charges against their husbands, though it has not been adequately demonstrated that battered women are any more likely to drop charges or fail to appear than other plaintiffs, but reliance on this supposition as a rationale for inaction betrays insensitivity to the predicament of abused wives. One woman told us how her husband threatened her for charging him and for not dropping the charges after continual court delays.

> Well he kept telling me I better write in and drop the f-ing charges, or I'd be sorry for it and what he'd do to me if I didnae. And did I think he was going to do time for a 'B' like me, and all this. And at the finish up I dropped the charges.

The indifference of the legal system may increase the isolation experienced by a woman and discourage her from seeking further help; eventually, she may stop calling the police.[73] If the violence continues, she may become a murder victim. Research on homicides has revealed that most murders are preceded by a long period of attacks that are known to the authorities.[74] According to Field and Field, there is a select group of attorneys in a large American city who belong to the "club."[75] One enters this group through an accident of ommission.

> The common bond among the members of the Club is that they had, to a man, refused as prosecutors to issue warrants against someone alleged to present a clear, immediate danger to the victim, shortly after which the victim was murdered by the alleged offender.[76]

In a way the entire community belongs to such a club and is responsible for the continued assaults on women and in some cases their deaths: the friends and neighbors who ignore or excuse the violence, the physician who does not go beyond the mending of bones and the stitching of wounds, the social worker who defines wife beating as a failure of communication, and the police and court officials who refuse to intervene. The violence is meted out by one man but the responsibility for that violence goes far beyond him.

CHAPTER 12

REFUGES AND OTHER ALTERNATIVES

THE INDIFFERENCE AND EVEN ANTAGONISM that has too often character-ized institutional responses to women assaulted by their husbands was dramatically challenged and altered during the early 1970s. A new social movement emerged that would not only directly and unequivocally assist battered women but would also, through its policies, procedures, and ac-tions, directly and indirectly challenge patriarchal ideals and practices. In 1972 a group of feminists established a women's center in Chiswick, a borough of London, where women could come to discuss their problems and find mutual support.[1] The idea of establishing a women's center was not unique to this group of women. Women's centers had been established in other countries and in Britain by feminist groups interested in creating a focal point for mutual support, discussion, and political action. What was unique about this particular house was that its primary concern eventually became the assistance of women who had been assaulted by their husbands. Aided by the sympathetic, though often sensationalist, media Chiswick Women's Aid thrust the plight of battered women into the public arena, and the problems of battered women began to be taken up by other feminist groups throughout Britain. These groups began to struggle to gain resources and to establish local refuges along the lines of the first refuge at Chiswick.

The women who began to work on wife abuse were primarily feminists and members of women's liberation groups who were unencumbered by professional beliefs and theories, nor committed to maintenance of patriar-chal family arrangements. They were not concerned about therapy, treat-ment, or apportioning blame. Rather, they acted pragmatically to assist women by providing them with a reasonably secure refuge from their husbands. It soon became clear that these diverse local groups could benefit from a national network of information and assistance and a coordinated effort to publicize and highlight the problems of battered women. This led to the establishment of the National Women's Aid Federation (NWAF), which developed throughout 1974-1975.[2] Over 25 Women's Aid groups from all over Britain were represented at the first national meeting held in London in spring, 1974. By the time of the second meeting in 1975, 82 groups had been established, 25 with refuges. A number of issues were raised at the second conference that resulted in a break between Chiswick Women's Aid and the majority of the other Women's Aid groups. The contentious issues leading to the split involved profound differences in philosophy, organizing principles, leadership styles, and the definition of the problem of battered women. The meeting was stormy, with the majority arguing for a National Federation of Women's Aid groups which would function as a reference point for information, receive resources, and be a platform for efforts to work for polictical change. The federation was to be broadly based, have egalitarian and diffuse forms of work and organization, and uphold the autonomy of local groups. The general philosopy was to be guided by the principles of the women's movement and violence against wives viewed accordingly. Chiswick and a few other groups declined to accept all of these principles and consequently withdrew from the organization.[3] Today, the NWAF has a membership of over 100 local Women's Aid support groups in England and Wales operating 150 refuges; the Scottish Women's Aid Federation (SWAF), that grew out of the NWAF, is operating 20 refuges and has more than 30 support groups.[4]

The Women's Aid movement was a unique response to battered women. It was the first organization with the distinct purpose of assisting battered women by providing them with support and temporary accommodation. As Marcovitch, a member of Acton Women's Aid, wrote about the beginning of Women's Aid: "Our unifying concern was for a group of women whose urgent needs had been hitherto ignored by the Welfare State; and we held the belief that women in our society are undervalued in many respects, and battering is an extreme example of this."[5] Members of the federations were, and are, trying to put the principles of the women's movement into practice on a day-to-day basis by working with women on their own terms and relative to their own needs and by attempting to work and deal with each other in an open, critical, but always supportive manner. As Jo Sutton, the first national coordinator of the NWAF, put it, "Most women saw themselves as members of a nonhierarchic support group—to support not only battered women but each other. They were women working with women for women."[6]

The principles of the women's movement are reflected both in the operation of the federations themselves and in the setting up and running of refuges. In the words of Sutton, "The principles are directly derived from the Women's Liberation Movement, 'democratic and cooperative.' "[7] These general principles are translated into the aims of the NWAF:

1. To provide temporary refuge, on request, for women and their children who have suffered mental or physical harassment.
2. To encourage the women to determine their own futures and to help them achieve them, whether this involves returning home or starting a new life elsewhere.

3. To recognize and care for the emotional and educational needs of the children involved.
4. To offer support and advice and help to any woman who asks for it, whether or not she is a resident, and also to offer support and after-care to any woman and child who has left the refuge.
5. To educate and inform the public, the media, the police, the courts, social services, and other authorities, with respect to the battering of women, mindful of the fact that this is a result of the general position of women in our society.[8]

Living and Working in a Refuge

The refuges are run in accordance with these general principles and aims and are as informal and democratic as possible. Refuges provide, first and foremost a sanctuary for a woman and her children, but they also provide women with the opportunity to consider and discuss their alternatives with other women in the same predicament. There are no experts, professionals, paraprofessionals, or wardens in the refuges to direct, cajole or otherwise interfere in the lives of the women. The emphasis is on self-determination, which will allow a woman to regain her self-confidence and begin to manage her own life. Self-help, group discussions, mutual support, and self-determination are stressed. Women, however, are not left to manage on their own. On the contrary, the other women living in the refuge and the members of the Women's Aid support group offer empathy, support, and advice, but only when a woman requests such help. No one is required to talk to a counselor, advisor, or professional helper; the emphasis is on aided self-determination. When a woman first enters a refuge she often needs medical, legal, and social services. If she feels she requires some assistance in dealing with the various representatives of social and legal agencies, a member of the support group or another woman living in the refuge will accompany her. The women living in the refuge organize and run the day-to-day affairs of the house in conjunction with members of the support group. Decisions about the general operation of the refuge, such as domestic work, child care, and the introduction of new women into the refuge, are made on a collective basis, usually at a weekly meeting attended by the women and members of the support group.

Through the process of living in a refuge and beginning to assume more responsibility for their own lives and taking part in the running of a refuge, most women quickly regain the self-confidence and self-esteem they may have lost and at times even surprise themselves. Of course, it takes considerable courage and determination for a woman to make the decision to leave home and then to consider the very real problems of living on her own and to cope with the complicated and often formidable welfare state. And living in a refuge is not easy. As one NWAF publication put it, "It's no picnic." When a woman first comes to a refuge she is often euphoric as a result of having achieved liberation from years of violence and oppression, but she may soon be plagued with guilt and depression—guilt because of leaving her husband and placing her children in a potentially stressful situation and depression because she must confront extraordinary problems in her furture. In many cases she faces the daunting prospect of living on her own and subsisting on meager social security payments (welfare) or working at a poorly paid and demoralizing job. Worries and problems of this nature are often compounded by continual threats and at times actual attacks from her husband. Men have traced their wives to the refuge and a few have attacked their wives and/or damaged the refuge. (A woman in Glasgow was even shot at through the refuge door). Communal living, though crucial to provide mutual support and to aid in problem solving, also has its disadvantages. The lack of privacy and comfort, often increased by moderate to extreme overcrowding, can lead to irritation, friction, and considerable additional stress and strain. Yet, even the problems and potential unpleasantness facing women living in a dilapidated and overcrowded refuge are minor compared to the situation they have fled.

The members of the Women's Aid group try to support women in dealing with the problems of living in a refuge and in making decisions about their future, but they always try to avoid transferring a sense of dependency from the husband to themselves or anyone else. If a woman decides to remain in a refuge for two days or two months (there is no limit on the length of stay), it is up to her. If she wishes to seek separation or divorce or go back to her husband, it is her decision. Although members of the support groups are concerned and fearful and perhaps disappointed when a woman decides to return to a violent husband, they support her in her decision and attempt to avoid being judgmental. This principle of avoiding dependency and encouraging self-determination is stressed in all of the various types of assistance offered by members of the support group. Some centers now run play groups and child centered activities but the workers are always careful not to assume responsibility for the children.

Problems of communication do arise between members of the support groups and women living in refuges, but this problem is recognized and discussed on an individual basis and at the weekly meetings. The members of a support group engage in numerous activities ranging from talking with the women as they work through various decisions and helping them in their initial dealings with social agencies to fund raising and wallpapering. When working within the refuge women attempt to be sympathetic listeners who "accept the women as they are and simply [do] what is required without judgment."[9] One member of Edinburgh Women's Aid indicated that the most important part of the job "is just being there each day, available for women to talk to and being supportive and understanding of the needs of each individual woman."[10]

WOMEN'S AID AND OTHER AGENCIES

The Women's Aid refuges provide a unique form of assistance unencumbered by the bureaucratic rules, policies, and practices of traditional helping institutions. This new form of assistance was not easily established.[11] Women's Aid initially had to struggle against apathy and at times outright antagonism, which reflected patriarchal ideologies, support for male dominance within the home, and noninterference in the family. In each city or town, resources and a house to be used as a refuge were not automatically and willingly provided by local government. Each local group had to "prove" that the area needed a refuge. Often, those demanding such proof requested that the local group present statistical evidence of need, evidence that was generally not available or not accessible. This demand continued to be made long after wife beating began to receive national and international recognition as an important social problem about which something should be done. The opposition to assisting battered women was usually not blatantly expressed, though on occasion it did take such a form, as in the case of two Scottish Conservative politicians, Evelyn Scott-Walker, a local councillor, and Nicholas Fairbairn, M.P., who rejected both the need for refuges for battered women and the aims of Women's Aid.

> They're just a group of amateur do-gooders without any professionally qualified help. And I think they are playing with fire if they attempt to interfere between a husband and wife in this way. . . . Anyway, some of these women might well deserve the batterings they get from their husbands.[12]

> We have heard a lot recently about battered wives which is not something new, and we have also heard a lot from pressure groups demanding that the Government set up centres for these wives, but I do not think this is right. I know there are battered wives in Britain, but why should the Government get involved in a family squabble as the Courts are quite capable of dealing with violent husbands? Surely they could go to a neighbour or a relative for some time and think things over rather than run to the State to look after them.[13]

Since the major efforts of the NWAF are oriented to establishing refuges for battered women and assisting them in finding accommodations after leaving refuges, local groups usually dealt with the local council and housing department officials (not noted for their forward looking and sympathetic views on social problems). Not all local housing authorities were unsympathetic to the aims and requirements of Women's Aid, but many were antagonistic toward the objectives, philosophy, and policies of the movement and the manner in which the group proposed to operate the refuge when and if it was allowed to rent a house to be used as a refuge. The negotiations over resources and housing were protracted and sometimes acrimonious; many housing officials refused or avoided meeting with local Aid groups. Even though many groups were backed by the press, it usually took at least a year to establish a refuge and for some groups it was over three years from the point of initial organization and lobbying until the refuge opened.[14] In some instances a local Women's Aid group would engage in an open squat in order to secure a refuge from a reluctant local authority and to bring the need for a refuge to the public's attention.

When a support group was offered or secured a refuge it was usually a dilapidated structure slated for demolition and located in an area distinguished by its lack of amenities (e.g., shops and playgrounds). Accordingly, the workers needed funds for furnishings, kitchen equipment, and repairs. The sources of these funds were and still are diverse, but most groups began and continue with donations and contributions; a few eventually gained partial government support.

Local groups now report that some housing departments are beginning to be more sympathetic toward the problems of battered women and as such are likely to aid in the establishment of refuges and in the rehousing of women. If this is the case it will be an important reversal of patterns of indifference and antagonism shown by certain housing authorities. For example, some authorities refused to rehouse women because they did not consider them homeless if their violent husbands were willing to take them back even if the women did not wish to return. Although there have been major improvements in the housing area the goal of the federations is to establish a refuge in every town or provide a place in a refuge for every ten thousand individuals in the population, a goal endorsed by the Parliamentary Committee on Marital Violence, has not been achieved. Additionally, the prospects of rehousing women who wish to establish separate residences are still very bleak in some localities.

Local Women's Aid groups have attempted to create links with social service departments in order to facilitate the provision of various forms of assistance to battered women. It is our impression that considerable cooperation has been achieved in some cities and Women's Aid groups have worked out amicable arrangements with quite a few local social work departments.[15] This cooperation, where it exists, has not been easily achieved. Social workers often have been skeptical of the aims and philosophy of the NWAF and SWAF and at times have found it difficult to deal with nonhierarchical organizations and to work with refuges that lack wardens or some type of professional or expert direction. As the English Northwest Region of Women's Aid pointed out, "Social workers may and do find refuges a threatening or confusing situation—no hierarchy, no formal rules, no experts and no officials. They must deal directly with the women themselves."[16] This difficulty is gradually being overcome and professionally trained social workers are finding it easier to deal with refuges. This possibility has been greatly increased by the fact that the federations have provided placements for trainee social workers in refuges and count among their members many women who have been, or are now, social workers.

Beyond Refuges

The necessary negotiations with local and national officials also have had an important impact on members of the federations, who have in the spirit of the women's movement recognized and developed their own skills and abilities. Women in support groups have acquired organizational and negotiating skills and "learned a lot, fast, about the various legal proceedings, about the rules governing housing, and the ways to protest over their being withheld."[17] Members of Women's Aid groups have realized that the practical problems of battered women go far beyond the confines of refuges. They have become aware of these problems because they confront them every day, and they realize that in order to transcend the temporary solution of a refuge the policies and practices of various agencies and the beliefs about battered women must change.

One of the major tasks now performed by the National Women's Aid Federation and the Scottish Women's Aid Federation is educating the public about the problems of battered women and the relationship between assaults on wives and the position of all women in society. This campaign was initially waged through the mass media, and while the federations continue to participate in, and even produce, television and radio programs, they are now also producing literature of their own. The literature is oriented to the presentation of an alternative and competing perspective on battered women.[18] It aims to inform battered women of their rights and of alternatives, educate the general public, and provide information to social agencies dealing with the problem. The NWAF and the SWAF have produced pamphlets on the social, legal, and housing problems of battered women and the routes a woman might follow to overcome these problems and obtain help, for example:

Half the Sky and Still No Roof
Battered Women Need Refuges
And Still You've Done Nothing
Battered Women in Scotland: Your Rights and Where to Go for Help
Battered Women: How to Use the Law
Women, You Don't Have to Put up with Being Battered

Battered Women: How to Survive
Battered Women: Refuges and Women's Aid[19]
Information on Setting Up and Running a Refuge

The federations have also put out information sheets directed at social agencies:

Information for Doctors
Information for Police
Information for Social Workers
Battered Women Demand Control over Their Own Lives
Unhelpful Myths and Stereotypes about Battered Women
Battered Women: Changes in the Housing Law
National Women's Aid Federation: How We Work[20]

The federations likewise have produced an educational kit to be used in schools to increase schoolchildren's awareness of the problems of battered women and of the issues regarding the position of women in the family and society. The federations are continually seeking to argue and express their perspective in national and local forums, organize national conferences, and give talks and send out information to local groups. These efforts both educate the public and help to keep the issue before politicians and the public.

An additional by-product of the movement has been the discovery of the innumerable problems facing a battered woman once she leaves the refuge and sets up a house on her own. When a woman moves out of a refuge she leaves a situation characterized by support and mutual aid and moves to a setting in which she may be isolated and lonely. This problem was recognized very early by members of support groups and a number of groups have launched programs to alleviate the sense of isolation and sometimes despair and depression experienced by women. Some groups have organized second stage housing, encouraged the rehousing of several women in the same area, and advised women who want to share a house. A number of support groups have tried to maintain contacts with women by appointing, when funds are available, backup workers who visit women once they leave a refuge. These paid workers were usually involved initially as volunteers in the support group. A few groups have started newsletters featuring contributions from women who have lived in, or are working in, refuges. Edinburgh's Women's Aid calls its newsletter *Broken Rib*, and it includes letters from women who have left the refuge and up-to-date information regarding Women's Aid. These attempts to overcome problems of isolation involve considerable time and resources, which are always stretched, and social service departments have been enlisted in the effort to provide this important backup service.

Despite all of the efforts and successes of the federations, the continued support of the community and the government and the freedom to pursue their aims remain uncertain and problematic. The NWAF and SWAF are now supported by the central government, which provides resources for national coordinators and the running of English and Scottish information offices. However, the grant under which these funds are furnished must be renegotiated every year. This means that the organization can lose its funding and that the aims of the federation are subject to frequent scrutiny and possible subversion. It is impossible to operate the national organization, run local support groups, and keep up refuges without outside resources, yet this very arrangement means continual negotiation with various funding bodies that may constrain the group's activities and their political principles. The federations are aware of this potential and struggle to maintain their position and ideals while negotiating for the public funds they need and rightly deserve.

The movement has had enormous successes. It has raised public awareness about the problem of battered women, assisted and provided refuges for thousands of women and their children, and engaged the sympathetic support of the media. Women's Aid has been instrumental in the establishment of a Parliamentary Select Committee on Marital Violence and has lobbied for legislation pertaining to violence against wives. The Domestic Violence and Matrimonial Proceedings Act was passed in 1976 in England and Wales (but not Scotland) and a clause was inserted in the Homeless Persons Act of 1977–1978 that explicitly makes battered women a priority group for housing. The clause in the Homeless Persons Act is very important because many local housing authorities have refused to identify battered women as homeless if their husbands agree to accept them back.

The new Domestic Violence Act expands the powers of existing court injunctions. This act is meant to provide greater protection to a woman from assault by her husband and it gives temporary rights to the matrimonial home to the woman and her children while separation, divorce, or reconciliation is being considered. The new act also allows magistrates to attach powers of arrest if a man breaks an injunction by attempting to enter the house and molest his wife. Magistrates, however, are reluctant to attach the power of arrest to these injunctions. Since the enforcement of the new act, only about 25% of the injunctions have included the power of arrest.[21] This law has numerous inherent problems. For example, the woman may return to the home but the husband then knows where she is and can easily attack her. The effectiveness of this new form of injunction has yet to be assessed; the NWAF is now undertaking such an assessment by monitoring court cases. Although considering this type of legislation crucial in the present context the federations are fully aware that a solution to the problem of violence against wives involves much more radical changes in the institutions and ideologies of the entire society.

The efforts and activities of the British Women's Aid movement has brought the plight of battered women to the attention of other groups throughout the world. These groups often have taken their example from the British movement and have begun to establish and run refuges in their own countries. Refuges now exist in Holland, West Germany, Switzerland, Norway, Belgium, Canada, France, Australia, New Zealand, and the United States.[22] Not all of these refuges are operated by feminist groups espousing the principle of self-determination, but many of them are.

The activities and groups in North America appear to be especially diverse, with some groups recognizing the relationship between the oppression of all women and their specific subjugation through force, whereas others are approaching the problem as a purely personal one demanding therapeutic and psychiatric counseling. Feminists established two of the first refuges explicitly for battered women in the United States, Transition House in Boston and Women's Advocates in St. Paul. They offer 24-hour information and referral services, temporary shelter, support, and advocacy in family law, public assistance, and tenancy rights.[23] Other groups offer only advice, or operate a referral system, or provide extremely short-term accommodation (e.g., overnight). Some groups operate democratically and subscribe to the principles of supported self-help and self-determination; others, such as that in Orange County, California, have rightly structured programs relying heavily upon professional decision-makers.

> The Women's Transitional Living Center [in Orange County] is a counseling-centered "program" with mandatory counseling provided by staff and consultants.[24]
>
> Counseling, both group and individual, is mandatory for those residing at the center. This includes an initial interview with the consulting psychiatrist. . . . Women are involved in either individual or group counseling sessions five days a week.[25]

In general, all efforts to assist battered women are noteworthy and at least help alleviate their immediate problem, but we consider those programs that make counseling or therapy mandatory to be particularly unfortunate. If groups consider professional help to be appropriate, it should be made available on a voluntary basis and not be a precondition for receiving assistance.

We have serious doubts about the need for therapeutic helpers in refuges. We think refuges should be places where, in the words of the French group SOS Femmes, women will have an opportunity to "take charge of themselves."[26] There is a greater possibility of achieving this goal in refuges that operate along the lines of the British Women's Aid refuges. An important difference between federated refuges (NWAF and SWAF) and the few other groups attempting to help battered women in Britain is that the groups in the federations support self-help and self-determination whereas most of the others emphasize therapy in preference to self-determination. Groups not belonging to the federations also commonly fail to see the connections between assaults on women and the oppression of all women, as Women's Aid workers writing in *Spare Rib* have pointed out: "They [groups outside the NWAF and SWAF] don't see battering as a Women's Liberation issue, nor do they recognize its relationship to the general oppression of women."[27]

The first Dutch group, Blijf van m'n Lijf (Stay Away from My Body), which obtained a refuge in Amsterdam in 1975, also sees the problem as firmly related to the oppression of all women and explicitly rejects the helping professionals' individualized approach to battered women.[28] Members of the Dutch group, many of whom work in the helping professions, had observed on a firsthand basis the way in which the social services ignore violence against women and fail to provide meaningful help. One member of the group wrote about the manner in which the Dutch social services deal with the problem:

> Abuse of women, as such, thus is never discussed: it is a complaint that is first 'translated' and then unfolds as a 'relational' problem, 'Marital difficulties,' 'communication disturbance.' The 'solution' is thus readily seen as the 'rebuilding' of the 'relationship' in the sense of bringing the relationship together.[29]

The principles of Blijf van m'n Lijf are roughly the same as those of the SWAF and NWAF: there is no limit on admissions or lengths of stay, visitors (especially men) are usually not allowed, the residents decide and control what goes on in the house, there are weekly meetings, and only women are served by the organization.

The international interest that has been raised in the problem of battered women has resulted in the creation of hundreds of groups in several countries that have either established or are seeking to establish refuges. Many of the groups in the United States have joined together to form a National Coalition Against Domestic Violence (NCADV) that held its first annual conference in autumn 1979. National and international communication and information networks have been set up. The Americans have been particularly productive in this work, beginning in 1976 with Warrior's comprehensive directory of American and international refuges, publications, and sources of funding. Other American sources include: Aegis-Magazine on Ending Violence Against Women; National Technical Assistance Center on Family violence; and Response to Violence and Sexual Abuse in the Family. An International Bulletin published by ISIS collectives provides an information and communication service for the women's movement, and includes information on refuges and battered women. And the first international meeting of groups working on the problem of battered women was held in Amsterdam in April 1978.

The Future

The road ahead is littered with obstacles and contradictions regarding the means of assisting women who are systematically assaulted by their husbands. This book has provided documentation of the legacy of violence against women in the family and its relationship to wider social, economic, and political institutions and processes. The legacy of patriarchal domination and rightful authority maintained through force is still evident in the phenomenon of assaults on wives and in the responses and ideologies of various institutions in society. It would be an overstatement to argue that nothing has changed during this century in the practices and beliefs of institutions. However, though laws no longer provide explicit support for violence against wives, the inaction, indifference, and contradictory policies and procedures of social institutions continue to reflect the ideal of the subordinate position of women in the family and of the right of men to dominate and control their wives by various means including force. The general content of these reactions is best described as indifferent or ambivalent rejection of the violence and unintentional, though at times intentional, acceptance of the circumstances that surround the violence and the relationships that promote and maintain such violence.

This book has demonstrated the nature of institutional responses to violence against wives, documenting their ineffectiveness and at times their aggravation of the violent situation. At one time legal and religious institutions openly supported the marital hierarchy and the subjugation of women through force. Today, such support is usually no longer explicit, but ambivalent institutional responses do little to reduce the incidence of such attacks and implicitly support the abusive husband by failing to question the patriarchal nature of the marital relationship. In order to reduce the incidence of wife assault and provide relief for battered women, members of communities and the agents of community organization must unequivocally reject both violence as a means of problemsolving and control and the hierarchical, patriarchal family order.

Women's Aid Federations are organizations that condemns the violence of men against women, locates the problem, as we do, within the general oppression of women within society, and provides meaningful and tangible assistance and sympathetic support to women attacked by their husbands. This is the sort of response that is calculated to help solve the problems of battered women. What is also needed is an equally practical and supportive response from the agencies dealing with violence in families—the social services, the police, the courts, and the medical profession. Specifying the changes these institutions must make is difficult. At present, indecision, indifference, and antagonism constitute the usual institutional responses to violence against wives. Yet, we have observed and reported on more helpful and sympathetic responses from physicians who advise women to leave their husbands and attempt to convince abusive husbands that violent behavior is inappropriate and from police officers who go out of their way to assist battered women. What we see in these exceptional actions are the possibilities of responses that are more helpful and effective than are typical reactions. The exceptional should be allowed, encouraged and expanded and become the rule, easily arrived at and facilitated rather than occurring against all odds. In order to make the exceptional response the usual response there must be considerable change in the training, policies, and practices of the institutions that deal with family violence.

The reversal of prevailing patterns will require a continual struggle against patriarchal, and thus negative, practices and against the ideologies that support them. If social workers and other members of helping professions are to provide assistance to battered women, they must cast off their ideological blinders and begin to view marital relationships in an alternative manner. They must analyze and scrutinize their own actions when dealing with families and recognize the manner in which they may, and often do, lend support to oppressive situations within the family. They must begin to perceive families as relationships of power involving, at times, the use of systematic force against women to achieve their subordination and chastisement. Adopting this perspective will take them beyond the usual efforts to seek blame or cause in the victim's behavior and will lead to a form of response closer to that of the advocate than to the physician's.

Armed with the patriarchal ideologies of experts, members of helping professions may continue to focus on the behavior and attitudes of the woman, seeking to explain (justify) the violence relative to the woman's actions. Or, in a more sympathetic vein, they may help her to cope with the violence but fail to seek or to effect a change either in the husband's behavior and patriarchal beliefs or in the marital hierarchy. To think that the best possible response to the problems of battered women is to provide psychological counseling results in a narrow and shortsighted focus. If the reactions of outsiders tend to increase the woman's self-blame by requiring her to ask questions like "What was my role in eliciting his anger? Have I baited him, criticized him, or been extremely demanding? Can I avoid triggering anger?"[30] or if helping professionals encourage the woman to change her own behavior supposedly to discourage further violence from her husband—"In a family where children are a source of anger, it is wise not to complain to the husband about them . . . if she desires the marriage to continue it makes for a more tolerable marriage to be sexually compliant"[31]—then women are better off without such 'help'.

If individuals who are contacted by battered women will reject these misguided and muddled views of the problem, they may be able to offer genuine assistance. A clearer and more straightforward view of wife beating means that helping professionals will be able unequivocally to condemn the violence, reject the authority of husbands over wives, and, most important, attempt to change the marriage power relationship as they seek nonviolent resolutions to the couple's problems. This type of reaction may not meet with approval from some social workers and marriage counselors who are often taught to see themselves as 'objective' and 'neutral' in encounters with husbands and wives. In fact this false sense of neutrality and the failure to reject the violence means that the reaction is not neutral but is biased and indirectly bolsters the man's position and his use of violence.

Changes are also needed in other areas. The courts and the police have been identified in Britain and the United States as especially ineffectual in dealing with the problems of battered women.[32] Inaction and failure to treat the problem as a serious threat to the lives of countless women cannot continue. Laws must be changed to provide greater protection for women, and the judicial system must become willing to apply sanctions and demonstrate to men that their abusive behavior is inappropriate and unacceptable. At present, police officers are unlikely to arrest a man who assaults his wife or to provide sympathetic help or useful advice to a woman who finds herself in an assaultive relationship. On the whole, the police response to the problem is best described as indifferent; they take action primarily in cases of serious injury or death, attempting only to keep the peace in other cases. Police officers leave the home with little or no effect on the pattern of violence.

What is needed is a change in police practices and policies at various levels. As Bannon argued, there needs to be a thorough change in the thinking of police administrators, who should "cease viewing domestic violence as beyond the pale of the criminal justice system."[33] Such a change in the conception of violence against wives should lead the police to take an active role in this area and to end telephone screening of domestic complaints. Though we recognize that the job of the police officer will always be a clearly delimited one, they are nevertheless very important in identifying the problem and providing an initial reaction to violent episodes. This reaction should be twofold. First, the police should enforce the law and, when appropriate, arrest a husband who has assaulted his wife, demonstrating to him, his wife, and the community that this form of behavior is illegal and unacceptable. The second form of reaction would involve a well-developed and publicized backup system, coordinating the efforts of medical, legal, and social workers, to which the police could refer a battered woman (or where she might go on her own) for legal, medical, and financial advice and support.

Some of the these changes have already begun. In 1976, a coalition of New York lawyers brought a class action lawsuit on behalf of twelve battered wives against the New York City Police Department, claiming that they had acted without legal authority in making a distinction between wives and other victims of violence and failing to provide for their protection.[34] One of the plaintiffs, Carmen Bruno, stated that her estranged husband still had his hands around her neck when the police arrived, but that they refused to arrest him. In the case of *Bruno* v. *Codd*, the plaintiffs sought a court declaration that it was a violation of New York law for police to fail to aid and protect battered wives; an end to police discrimination against battered wives by beginning to treat family violence the same as violence between strangers; an order that the police arrest when there is probable cause for the officer to believe that the husband has been violent; a cessation of police comments supportive of men who assault their wives; the enforcement of injunctions; and a requirement that police help the woman obtain medical care when needed.[35] Fields, one of the attorneys bringing the action, maintained that "*Bruno* v. *Codd* is the first comprehensive attack on the failure of the criminal justice system to provide protection and medical aid to battered wives."[36]

The New York Supreme Court agreed with the plaintiffs and declared:

> For too long, Anglo-American law treated a man's physical abuse of his wife as different from any other assault, and indeed as an acceptable practice. If the allegations of the instant complaint—buttressed by hundreds of pages of affidavits—are true, only the written law has changed; in reality, wife beating is still condoned, if not approved, by some of those charged with protecting its victims. . . . the police owe a duty of protection to battered wives, in the same manner they owe it to any citizen injured by another's assault. . . .[37]

In June 1978, the plaintiffs and the Police Department defendants agreed to a consent decree, "setting forth significant changes in police procedures in New York City."[38] Other state laws protecting battered women have now been passed or are under consideration.[39] In Canada, a few cities are now operating, in collaboration with police departments, 24-hour services for victims of violence in the home that offer such assistance.[40] Regardless of the particular police reaction, what is required is a response that represents a condemnation of wife beating on the part of the law enforcement community. More vigorous police and judicial action is of crucial importance in a whole network of responses from other sources.

The offense should not be decriminalized nor should it necessarily result in imprisonment. There have been various proposals in the United States and Britain for the creation of family courts (some states do operate such courts) that would divert cases of wife assault, and what are seen as other lesser family problems, away from the overburdened criminal courts. Proponents argue that family courts would save money and would provide counseling for families, not offered by criminal courts. Nevertheless, such courts have been ineffective in dealing with violence to wives.[41] By reliance on family courts or mandatory counseling the liberal state is able to reduce the criminal court case load while presenting itself as benevolent and concerned. The reason the state is willing to offer such alternatives in cases of violence against wives is that it is an offense not viewed as urgent in the first place.

We are very skeptical of programs oriented to treatment and reconciliation. Concepts such as treatment and therapy are powerful but often vacuous metaphors that promise changes in human behavior yet often deliver very little. The medical model of disease also has unfortunate connotations when applied to problems such as violence against women. It deflects the focus from the historically established authority relationships between men and women to personal explanations. Certainly, women who are continually attacked by their husbands are suffering on a personal level, and we must provide immediate solutions to their problems such as refuges. The danger lies in focusing on the supposed personal pathologies of the men or, even more insidiously, of the women. Members of the helping and legal professions must rethink their views on violence against wives. They must stop denying the seriousness of the offense, blaming the victim, and/or seeking causes in the man's supposed mental aberrations. They should seek to enter into the assaultive relationship with a view to aiding the husband in realizing that he does not have the right to subordinate and chastise his wife. Helping professionals must realize that the primary issue is the husband's conception of his rightful authority. (The very fact that the battered woman is seeking help should refute the masochism and acceptability of violence arguments.) The attempt to change the husband's conception of rightful control will not be easy since, as this book illustrates, most abusive men do not think that their actions are unjust and in need of change. Some men, especially those who have not been married very long, will feel repentant about their use of violence and may seriously desire to change; these feelings provide a useful starting point for working with the family, as does a woman's stay in a refuge. When a woman leaves her husband she may be taking one of the most positive steps she has taken in her entire married life as she directly or indirectly indicates to her husband that she has had enough and asserts her independence. This action may shock the husband and might, just might, lead him to question his own behavior and beliefs. When the woman returns, if she wishes to return, she often enters on new terms; the husband may be somewhat apprehensive that his wife will leave again and he may feel more of a need to constrain his own behavior. Because he now realizes that his wife can leave again or seek support, both moral and at times material, from other women who live or work in the refuge. This is also a very good time to work on the man's conception of authority and dominance.

For those of us concerned about the state's intervention in the lives of private citizens we would argue that the intervention and assistance is not being forced upon the family. What is being done is that the complaints and concerns of the *woman* are being taken seriously. She is asking for help and the social agency is responding to *her* request, though the husband may not, and probably will not, desire or seek help and may wish to prohibit his wife from doing so. The contradiction between wishing to assist battered women and considering the state's intervention in the lives of people to be less than desirable is not resolvable. Since community controls are no longer operative or effective, if they ever were, the alternative is assistance by an agency.

All of these actions may ultimately be irrelevant. Court action may not deter a husband from assaulting his wife and professional helpers may not be successful in gaining the cooperation of the husband and eliminating the violence. In these cases, and when the woman desires it, the alternative is divorce. We recommend divorce as a most suitable solution for such women rather than see it as an unfortunate alternative. Some women who seek help and/or leave their husbands will wish to file for divorce, others may not, and the pursuit of a divorce should not be a prerequisite for receiving assistance or refuge. We have found in our research that a divorce or legal separation is not lightly entered into by women who are assaulted by their husbands. All of the factors that operate to prevent her from leaving the relationship, such as the moral order, her primary or sole identity as a wife, economic problems, and her husband's threatened or actual constraints, likewise prevent her from permanently breaking off the relationship through divorce. As did Truninger in California, we found that British women enter into divorce proceedings only after careful and prolonged consideration: "She makes her decision when she can neither believe her husband's promises of no more violence nor forgive the past episodes of violence."[42] We should not make the assumption that because divorce is a more widely used remedy for present day marriage problems women easily enter into such a decision. Each woman must reach her own decision, often in isolation and without support from her friends or relations.

Me, no, I never thought about divorce even when I went to see the solicitor finally. I went to see a solicitor in August, and I walked in off the street, and funnily enough if somebody had said to me, "Don't be silly. Go home and get his tea [dinner]," I'd have gone home and got his tea. And the secretary said, "Yes, there is someone who is free to see you." I got this particular solicitor, a Mr. Adams, and I went in. He said, "Good afternoon." Got to discussing things. I said, "I wanted to ask you a few questions." He said, "What is it? Is it about being married?" And I said, "Yes, I was wondering about separation." And he said, "Well, tell me a few things." And in the end he said, "I don't think you want a separation, Mrs. Jamieson. I think you need a divorce." And that's really his exact words. And even then it was a bit of a—I thought, a divorce? I walked, I thought, "Me divorce? I don't get divorced. I don't get divorced." You know what I mean? Nobody in our family's ever been divorced, nobody in his family's ever been divorced, and it seemed a very—sort of a—big step. It isn't now. It isn't now at all, you know, but then it did.

Divorce should be made easier and cheaper, and members of the legal profession should be supportive of battered women who seek divorces. Marjory Fields, a New York lawyer working with the Brooklyn Legal Services Corporation, has represented thousands of battered women, offering them support and enlightened legal aid.[43] She pointed out that her office is often the first "unreservedly [to] disapprove of the husband's violence"[44] and that she and her co-workers still have a difficult time convincing judges with patriarchal attitudes that women do not deserve to be beaten and that they do deserve a divorce. Fields noted that women must present a certain demeanor in court. In order to qualify for patriarchal justice and mercy she must appear to be the soft-spoken, feminine, and helpless woman who does not deserve violence because "if she appears to be strong and self sufficient, the judge will not believe that she lived with her husband's assaults, or did not provoke the attacks."[45]

After a woman obtains a divorce or a legal separation or merely leaves a refuge to begin life on her own, numerous obstacles emerge, both problems that plague women who are escaping assaultive husbands—for example, the husband may continue to harass or assault the woman—and problems that plague women who are trying to manage single parent families. At this time social agencies can offer practical assistance by helping women locate a single parent family association for support (or start one if necessary) and begin to develop inexpensive or free child care facilities and by informing women of their rightful entitlements and seeing that they receive them.[46] Adequate provisions for children's day care do not exist at present,[47] forcing many women who might like to work to subsist on meager social security and child care benefits. When women do go out to work they usually fill the most poorly paid and menial service jobs and thus they are often better off remaining at home receiving child care and welfare benefits. Research on women in the economy and the work place consistently has demonstrated their disadvantaged and underpaid position. It is extremely difficult for women to live on their own and cope with their children and the lack of resources. This situation often drives women back to their husbands.

The efforts of groups working on the problem of assaults on women in the home and proposed changes in the ideologies and practices of various agencies will aid women who find themselves in relationships characterized by violence and who eventually decide to live on their own. If we wish to do something about the social processes and cultural ideals that generate patriarchal and violent relationships we need to work toward fundamental changes in society.

We have explored the processes and types of relationships that lead to women becoming the appropriate victims of violence: the socialization of men and women into rigid gender-specific behaviors that include male dominance and aggression and female subordination and obedience; and the patriarchal and moral hierarchy within the family. A form of marital relationship that has been, and still is, revered in Western society and supported by other social institutions. However, this form of family relationship is neither absolute nor inevitable, and most women are continually struggling against their specific oppression at the hands of their husbands. The hierarchical structure and moral order makes this struggle an extremely difficult, and even immoral one in the view of outsiders and, at times, the women themselves. Of course, nonpatriarchal intimate relationships do exist. A small minority of couples might even be termed egalitarian. The task is to make this type of relationship the predominant one, but this goal will not be achieved easily.

The way to begin to dramatically reduce the number of marriages likely to become violent is to work on the subordination, isolation, and devalued status of women in society and to change the hierarchical family that characterizes Western society. Are the authorities in the West prepared to go as far as the Soviets did in their experiments in social change carried out in Central Asia during the mid-1920s? In order to destroy the tribal patriarchy and the ideology that supported it they sought first to destroy the old family order. The vanguard of this effort was to be those members of the society who had been the "most consistently 'humiliated [and] exploited,' . . . 'segregated, secluded, and constrained,' who were, in effect, 'the lowest of the low,' 'the most enslaved of the enslaved': its women."[48] The pillars of religious, family and cultural institutions were to be toppled by Moslem women, who became "surrogate proletariat." The undermining of traditional male authority and the improvement of the position of women were to be achieved by giving women unprecedented political and bureaucratic power while other reforms attacked "female dependence, segregation, and seclusion" in public and private life. This campaign initially had extraordinary results: "In relatively urbanized locales . . . some women (especially maltreated wives . . .) showed themselves willing to exercise their rights and challenge the traditional status quo through massive, public and dramatic violation of traditional taboos."[49] Throughout 1926 organizers reported "divorce waves" and "demands for equitable division of property," and women organized and "surged through the streets unveiled, chanting challenges to the old order." In the context of a traditional peasant, patriarchal, and Moslem society such acts were truly revolutionary. Gradually, however, the old religious and hierarchical order began to fight back by evading the new laws giving women equal rights. Hostility and violence were directed at women. This attack was both symbolic and physical. For example, men who "allowed" their wives and daughters to be unveiled in public were excommunicated and women who showed signs of emancipation were "shamed, raped and killed." There ensued "a wave of terror" against those women and families that had participated in the emancipation movement and the attack on the old order. Traditions such as wife beating, which had been forbidden, were reinstated: "If a local policeman saw a woman being beaten by her husband (at home or in the street, and no matter how savagely), he took good care, as traditions called for, not to intervene."[50] The failures and partial successes such as those which became apparent in Central Asia may have been partially responsible for Trotsky's conclusion that the achievement of political and industrial equality between men and women is comparatively simple, but to "achieve the actual equality of man and woman within the family is an infinitely more arduous problem."[51]

This goal will not be reached solely through bureaucratic and legal maneuvering; yet, Western societies focus almost exclusively upon the introduction of amelioratory legislation. Proposals for bringing about changes in the status of women in the United States and Britain typically have centered on laws relating to the equal opportunities of women within the work force. Some reformers think that if women were to achieve equal employment with men that this would automatically improve their position in society and the family. In general, legislation has made some contributions to the change in the position of women in society; however, it has not effected significant changes in the relationships between men and women, as is evident in societies that do have a large percentage of the women in the work force earning nearly equal pay to that of men. It is erroneous to assume that if women enter the work force in large enough numbers their relative position and power will automatically improve in other institutions. As long as they continue to enter wage work in subordinate positions and as long as the patriarchal family continues to exist, the far-reaching changes that are needed in the family will not begin to occur. To improve the overall status of women in society depends on integrating the social, political, and economic lives of men and women. The work place needs to be more firmly associated with the home and the home needs to be interrelated with the work place. There should be a greater integration of the lives of men and women and of the legal, medical, and social institutions. The split between the family and society should be overcome. Only in this way can women leave behind their subordinate status as wives and mothers. Yet, is this likely within an economic structure that benefits from a patriarchal family system in which domestic work is devalued and women are isolated and relegated actually and symbolically to the role of reproducers of labor? Violence against wives is firmly embedded in this legacy.

The struggle against wife beating must be oriented both to the immediate needs of women now suffering from violence and to more fundamental changes in the position of women. We now stand at a point where we may either work toward removing the very roots of wife beating by eliminating patriarchal domination or we may work only toward limited reforms which, while providing vital assistance to women currently being beaten, will do little about the problem itself. We must take up the challenge and address the issue in its fullest form, otherwise we will commit the errors of the past. The problem lies in the domination of women. The answer lies in the struggle against it.

APPENDIX A: GLOSSARY

SCOTTISH COLLOQUIALISMS AND IDIOMS USED IN THE QUOTED INTERVIEWS

awfie	:	awful
bairn	:	child
beetled off	:	went away angry
close	:	entrance to tenement building
cos	:	because
daein'; dae	:	doing; do
doon	:	down
greetin'	:	sobbing
hoose	:	house
lift him	:	arrest him
lobby	:	hall
man	:	husband
messages	:	groceries
nae	:	not, combining form with verbs (cannae, wasnae, dinnae)
naebody	:	nobody
no	:	not
nowt	:	naught
oot	:	out
roarin'	:	crying loudly
takkity boots	:	heavy working boots with steel capped soles and/or heels
wains	:	children
windaes	:	windows
youse	:	you all

Appendix B: Tables

List of Tables

TABLE 1. How Frequently the Couple Went Out Together throughout Their Relationship

FREQUENCY	BEFORE MARRIAGE		FIRST YEAR MARRIAGE		LATER MARRIAGE	
	N	%	N	%	N	%
6–7 times per week	33	30	3	3	0	0
1–5 times per week	69	63	52	48	21	19
1–2 times per month	1	1	18	16	16	15
1–6 times per year	2	2	21	19	47	43
Never	4	4	15	14	25	23
Total	109	100%	109	100%	109	100%

TABLE 2.   How Frequently the Man Went Out with His Own Friends throughout the Relationship

	BEFORE MARRIAGE		FIRST YEAR MARRIAGE		LATER MARRIAGE	
FREQUENCY	N	%	N	%	N	%
6–7 times per week	14	13	18	17	42	39
1–5 times per week	39	36	59	54	47	43
1–2 times per month	8	7	6	5	0	0
1–6 times per year	3	3	4	4	1	1
Never	45	41	22	20	19	17
Total	109	100%	109	100%	109	100%

TABLE 3.   How Frequently the Woman Went Out with Her Own Friends throughout the Relationship

	BEFORE MARRIAGE		FIRST YEAR MARRIAGE		LATER MARRIAGE	
FREQUENCY	N	%	N	%	N	%
6–7 times per week	0	0	0	0	0	0
1–5 times per week	30	28	14	13	4	4
1–2 times per month	6	5	3	3	1	1
1–6 times per year	7	6	11	10	12	11
Never	66	61	81	74	92	84
Total	109	100%	109	100%	109	100%

TABLE 4.   Types of Assault Occurring Between Family Members

	N	%
Wife assault	791	75.8
Husband assault	12	1.1
Child assault	112	10.7
Parent assault	73	7.0
Sibling assault	50	4.8
Mutual assault	6	0.6
Total	1044	100.0

TABLE 5. Percentage of All Offenses Involving Violence Dealt with by Selected Police Departments in Edinburgh and Glasgow in 1974*

	N	%		Total
Wife Assault	759	(25.1)		
Alleged Wife Assault†	32	(1.1)		Family
Husband Assault	12	(0.4)		Violence
Child Assault	112	(3.7)		34.5%
Parent Assault	73	(2.4)		N = 1,044
Sibling Assault	50	(1.6)		
Mutual Assault	6	(0.2)		
Male–Male	1,169	(38.7)		
Male–Female	295	(9.8)		Nonfamily
Male–Police	288	(9.5)		Violence
Female–Female	142	(4.7)		65.5%
Female–Male	53	(1.8)		N = 1,976
Female–Police	29	(1.0)		

% 0 5 10 15 20 25 30 35 40

Total Number = 3,020

* This includes the reports for all of Edinburgh and one district of Glasgow that were subsequently prepared for and/or dealt with by the courts.
† The term alleged is used by police and courts, but from our reading of the cases there appears to be no significant differences between alleged wife assaults and wife assaults. Hereafter they will be combined.

TABLE 6. Sources of Conflict Leading to Violent Episodes

	VIOLENT EPISODE							
SOURCES OF CONFLICT	*First*		*Worst*		*Last*		*Typical*	
	N	%	N	%	N	%	N	%
Sexual jealousy	31	31	28	30	21	22	48	45
Expectations about domestic work	37	37	32	34	31	32	17	16
Money	7	7	12	13	11	11	18	17
Status problems	3	3	3	3	6	6	3	3
Sexual refusal	6	6	1	1	2	2	2	2
Wife's attempts to leave	5	5	7	7	15	15	0	0
Relatives and friends	3	3	1	1	2	2	4	4
Husband's drinking behavior	1	1	1	1	2	2	7	6
Children	5	5	6	6	6	6	4	4
Other	2	2	4	4	2	2	3	3
Total	100	100	95	100	98	100	106	100

TABLE 7. Types of Physical Force Used During Violent Episodes*

| | Violent Episode | | | | | | | |
| | First | | Worst | | Last | | Typical | |
Physical Force	N	%	N	%	N	%	N	%
Slap or push/pull into non-injurious object	73	29	48	12	68	21	78	15
Punch face and/or body	85	34	126	33	102	31	226	45
Push/pull into injurious object	27	11	67	17	48	15	19	4
Kick, knee, or butt	39	16	82	21	60	18	140	28
Attempt to drown, smother, or strangle	9	4	20	5	18	5	9	2
Hit with object/weapon	13	5	24	6	17	5	26	5
Other (bite, stand on, rape)	3	1	12	3	18	5	8	1
Total	249	100%	389	100%	331	100%	506	100%

* We recorded up to five *different types* of physical force in any single violent episode. These figures reflect only the *different types* of physical force used and not the number of times each type was used.

TABLE 8. Types of Injuries Resulting from the First, Worst, and Last Violent Episode*

| | Violent Episode | | | | | |
| | First | | Worst | | Last | |
Injuries	N	%	N	%	N	%
Bruises to face and/or body	101	74	182	64	148	70
Abrasions	0	0	2	1	3	1
Burns	0	0	4	1	5	3
Cuts	18	13	48	17	27	13
Hair torn out	5	3	13	5	10	5
Fractured bones or broken teeth	6	5	11	4	9	4
Internal injuries, miscarriages	4	3	8	3	2	1
Knocked unconscious	2	1	14	5	7	3
Total	136	100%	282	100%	211	100%

* We recorded up to five *different types* of physical injuries in any single violent episode. These figures reflect only the *different types* of injuries, and not the number of times a particular type of injury was received.

TABLE 9. Third Parties Contacted by Women after Violent Episodes

	VIOLENT EPISODE					
THIRD PARTY	*First*		*Worst*		*Last*	
	N	%	N	%	N	%
Parent, other relative	37	33	47	19	42	11
Friend	20	18	20	8	33	9
Neighbor	13	11	24	10	23	6
Doctor	21	13	53	22	43	12
Minister	3	3	5	2	3	1
Social Worker	6	5	35	14	63	17
Police	12	11	35	14	47	13
Women's Aid	—	—	14	6	93	25
Other	1	1	13	5	24	6
Total Contacts	113	100%	245	100%	371	100%
Number of Women Making Contacts	52		88		105	

APPENDIX C: THE STUDY

AN IMPORTANT ASPECT of our research has been the consideration of the problem of violence directed at wives in specific families. This effort included an assessment of violent marriages over time and an examination of the violence relative to the overall marital relationship. We looked also at the impact of the extended family and various social agencies such as the police and courts upon the marital relationship and the maintenance of violence, focusing upon how institutional policies and beliefs and the hierarchical nature of the family indirectly support the right of husbands to attack their wives in certain circumstances. The results of this research demonstrated the relationship between the patriarchal legacy and the subjugation and control of women in contemporary society.

The elucidation of the problem of wife beating requires the use of diverse research strategies that extend the interview-survey methods usually employed by social scientists. Social scientists tend to employ a very narrow conception of theory validation: theory testing is generally conceived of as the employment of narrowly circumscribed procedures that are meant to test discrete, often abstract hypotheses. This narrow view of theorizing and theory testing derives from the logical positivist tradition and is unlikely to produce useful evidence that explains, rather than merely describes, the phenomenon of wife beating. The history of science reveals that the proof of an argument may demand very different procedures from mere scientific hypothesis testing. Feyerabend's account of Galileo's proof of the Copernican thesis indicated that Galileo employed various devices for assessing evidence and convincing his audience of the truth of his claims.[1] Recent work in the philosophy and history of science has revealed the folly of a narrow conception of scientific activity.[2] Social scientists need to conceptualize evidence and research in a wider sense than is commonly done. To that end we have used structured interviews, impressionistic accounts, our background knowledge, police and court records, statements of public officials, newspaper accounts, and the results of other researchers in substantiating our theoretical claims.[3]

This is the general method Weber proposed to use in his study of industrial workers in Germany in 1911.[4] The outline brief he prepared for this unfinished study clearly illustrates his concern to explore the history of

250

the economic, social, and cultural factors relating to factory production before proceeding with a contemporary survey of German factory workers.[5] In his brief he relied on reports, documents, and often diverse research materials in an attempt to set his proposed study in the wider sociohistorical context. He ended his brief by stating that "only all these investigations combined could furnish a picture of the cultural significance of the [factory] process."[6] Weber also emphasized the importance of the actor's perspective and feelings in the understanding of human behavior. However, he stressed, though sociologists often forget, that attitudes and values can be understood only through a careful consideration of the history of the institutions and culture in which they occur. This is the procedure we employed in Chapters 3 and 4.

In this appendix we consider the major techniques we used in our exploration of violence against wives in contemporary society. Two methods were rather traditional: in-depth structured interviewing and the analysis of police and court records. The following sections will focus on these two techniques. First, however, we will briefly describe our own development during the research.

The Development of the Study

We think that it is crucial to discuss how we as researchers arrived at the theoretical position we argue for in this work. Those engaged in abstract research deem it important to exclude the investigator from the report of his or her findings but we prefer to make our relationship to the research explicit and agree with Cicourel, who argued that we must include the researcher's activities as an object of study.[7]

We did not set out with a research problem related to abstract issues in sociology; from the beginning the research was firmly embedded in concrete social issues. The problem of wife beating became apparent to us, as it did to other members of the British public, during 1973, when women's groups throughout the country became very concerned about battered women and the news media began to explore the problem. We wondered whether we might do some research to elucidate the problem and suggest possible 'solutions.' This concern was an outgrowth of our more general and long-standing interest in the status and problems of women. Since we hoped to carry out a study on a fairly broad scale we attempted to gain research funds. Obtaining such funds required a statement of our general theoretical position, a statement that reflected our backgrounds in the logical positivist tradition and thus emphasized abstract theorizing and data collection. At the time we proposed to use a context specific technique for gathering data but we gave little credence to the necessity of a general methodology that stresses the importance of history and the wider social context. We were interested in the history of wife beating, but at the time (1973) it was merely an aside and played no prominent role in our proposal. The substance of our argument was that violence between husbands and wives is the result of subcultural factors that come into play most clearly in deviant interacting couples. We emphasized the importance of the subordination of women in the family and the wider society but we did not comprehend its extraordinary significance until we engaged in a pilot study involving the reading of historical accounts, discussions with people dealing with the problem, and discussions with battered women.

The Pilot Study

The pilot study was designed both to aid in the development of an interview schedule for a more extensive study of wife beating and to allow for the discovery of factors not included in our initial conception of the problem. In order to avoid intellectual rigidity we did not begin with an extensive interview schedule or questionnaire; instead, we engaged in a dynamic process of learning about the problem in its concrete form, thinking and reading about it, and returning again to its concrete form.[8] The concreteness of the problem impressed itself upon us through discussions with people who had firsthand knowledge about wife beating—battered women—and with those working with families characterized by violence.

We attempted to examine the information we gathered in terms of its own importance, to compare it with existing ideas and research, and to deal with the many contradictions, disparities, and commonalities in order to understand the violence. This moving from the literature to the concrete problem and back again should not be construed as an attempt to develop what Glaser and Strauss termed grounded theory, theory that emerges from research begun without any preconceptions.[9] As we argued in Chapter 2, we think it is impossible to investigate phenomena without some preconceptions. What we were attempting to do was check our initial conceptions against concrete information, reformulate these ideas when necessary, and then return to the problem to check the reformulated ideas.

We developed a list of orienting questions that were used to elicit the opinions and impressions of women who had been assaulted by their husbands and of individuals who had worked with violent families. At a later stage in the pilot study we began to use an interview guide[10] to aid our exploration of the processes relating to the development and maintenance of violence directed at women in the home. This guide had an open-ended format and focused on questions that we thought would be useful in elucidating the problem. We explored areas such as socialization into the use of violence, status differentials between husbands and wives, role expectations and conflicts, childhood experiences with violence, and the use of alcohol.[11] These general areas were pursued during interviews with women who had been systematically assaulted by their husbands and during discussions with social workers, members of the Royal Scottish Society for the Prevention of Cruelty to Children,[12] police officers, and organizers of refuges for battered women.

Eventually we used a standardized interview guide to conduct interviews with 28 women who resided in houses of refuge for battered women in Edinburgh and Glasgow. During this early, exploratory stage of our research, we interviewed together and used a tape recorder. We initially thought, and the pilot study confirmed this view, that two people could elicit greater recall from respondents. Two people can probe further than one since many issues are raised during an interview, but asking questions and recording responses means that one may not have the presence of mind, or time, to ask for clarification of particular issues that arise spontaneously. Interviewing together was a very useful technique during the development of the pilot study for discovering areas of importance that might not have emerged if we had employed more restricted and conventional techniques.

No attempt was made during the pilot study to exclude topics that were "nonsociological" or to ignore factors that were not a part of our original conception. In fact, it became necessary to discard our ideas on the subculture of violence, to reformulate our ideas about the role of alcohol, to add a historical analysis of the family and of violence against wives, to stress the status of women in society, the family, and marriage, and to examine more closely the role of other social institutions in the complex system that supports or discourages wife beating. None of our original ideas went through the initial process untouched.

The Interviews

The interviews conducted during the pilot study also led to several important conclusions regarding techniques appropriate to the more complete and extended study we eventually conducted. We had decided prior to the pilot study that paper and pencil questionnaires that employ closed response categories were totally inappropriate for this type of research problem. The pilot study interviews confirmed this view. We rejected self-administered questionnaires that appear to be standardized and systematic but in reality are standardized only relative to the investigator's perspective and so constrict respondents' alternatives as totally to misrepresent their impressions. Paper and pencil techniques also use a language, or a conception of the problem, that is believed to be universally understood and assume a general acquaintance with forms and questionnaires, which may not in fact be found in the population at large.[13] We think it is important to allow people to place their experiences, subjective assessments, and recall in contexts that have relevance to them, and a face-to-face, in-depth interview is the best method for achieving this goal. An interview is also a much more realistic technique since, if properly constituted, it more closely approximates a conversation and allows women to share their feelings with an empathetic interviewer rather than be subjected to questions that may seem harsh, artificial, unclear, or irrelevant.[14]

The interview schedule that emerged after several revisions emphasized the open-ended nature of interviewing but exposed the respondent to what Galtung called "systematic stimuli."[15] That is, we used standardized questions but we did not limit respondents' answers by providing fixed categories of response. We developed a systematic schedule of questions relating to the theoretical and pragmatic concerns of the study but allowed interviewers to clarify or change the order of some questions, if appropriate, and to pursue interesting areas. This open-ended technique increases the probability of the interviewer's understanding "the context of the answers, perceptions or motivations"[16] of respondents. It puts people at ease, allowing them to speak freely and at some length about sensitive topics, and provides detailed information. Interviewers are able to probe and seek clarification within the individual's frame of reference, yet it is also possible to explore topics not discussed voluntarily or spontaneously by the respondents.[17]

The final interview schedule sought to develop an understanding of the violence in the context of the wider marital relationship. We began by exploring the backgrounds of the husbands and wives, attempting to learn about their own family backgrounds: where they grew up, their schooling, and their experiences with violence as children. This discussion logically led to a series of questions regarding the couple's premarital, or courting, relationship: how they met, how courtship altered their lives (if at all), and why they got married. We then looked at the nature of their relationship during the first and subsequent years of marriage. This led to the specific and systematic exploration of the emergence and continuation of violent episodes and their impact on the ongoing relationship.

In exploring the violence we decided to ask detailed questions about violent events rather than focus on abstract issues. We asked the women to tell us what happened in the first, worst, and last act of physical violence they had experienced. We began the discussion of each of these episodes with a general question such as "Can you tell me about the first time your husband hit you?" which allowed women to describe the events in their own words. We then asked specific questions regarding the violent event. Each of these discrete episodes, the first, worst, and last, was discussed in terms of when it occurred, the circumstances preceding the violence, the physical nature of the attack, its location, the presence of others during the attack, the extent and severity of injuries, and the immediate responses and feelings of the husband and wife. When women were allowed to talk about these incidents in their own words, as well as to answer our more specific questions, they gave very detailed accounts of even those incidents that had occurred many years earlier. They provided us with thorough descriptions of the development of violent episodes and enabled us to achieve an understanding of the structure and dynamics of the assaults and to make comparisons between them.

The following extracts illustrate the interviewing technique and reveal some of the substance of our exploration of the first episode of violence.[18]

You've already told me what led up to the attack: there was an argument and he accused you of going out.

He accused me of going out with another man.

At what point in the argument did he actually hit you?

When I said to him, I said that the girl down the stairs was going into hospital to visit her husband, and she asked me to run her in the car because it was an awful difficult place to get to—you had to get two buses. By going by car it was straightforward so I said I would run her into hospital. Well, we left at eight o'clock, and she got into the hospital and she stayed with him till about quarter to ten. And we came out and she said, "Well, you know, I'll buy some petrol." And I said, "No, it's okay." She said, "Well, I'll take you for a drink then." So she was a bit shaken up and I thought a drink will do her the world of good, you know. It's not like Brenda to want to go for a drink, so we went over to the pub and she had a couple of drinks and she sort of started talking to me about having Tony and saying she wasn't getting on well with him. I think she really just wanted somebody to chat to and somebody she thought would understand. She sort of compared her marriage to mine because on the surface mine looked a very happy marriage. And, you know, I didn't have the heart to tell her it wasn't as happy as she thought it was. She was only someone looking from the outside in and seeing everything all rosy.

I came back and when I started getting the better of him—saying, "Well, go down and ask Brenda, why dont' you?"—I mean, he knew she wasn't the sort of person that would ever have anything to do with another man, because though her and her husband didn't get on well, she thought the world of him and would do absolutely anything for him. She's the perfect wife and mother, and he knew that. I said, "Why don't you go down and ask Brenda? She's just now in. You know she is. She came back in the car with me." And he said no. He says, "I'm not going down to have anybody else involved in our arguments." He hit me when he knew that I had somebody that could corroborate my story and he knew that he wasn't going to get his own way.

How long was this after you actually started to argue?

About half an hour.

Did you try and reason with him?

Well, I did, but it didn't work.

This woman spontaneously provided a detailed account of the violence and it was necessary to ask only for elaboration and clarification of a few points. Other women did not volunteer sufficient information and we had to ask all of the questions in the schedule, such as in the following example.

Can you remember what actually led up to the first time he hit you then? I mean, as you say, it was . . .

It's only now that I remember back. It's just that we used to sit and quarrel and he'd end up going for me. I don't know. I used to feel he was very jealous and I couldn't wear makeup or anything if I got all dressed up and that. That's how the arguments used to start. I hadn't even sort of gone out, but I'd maybe feel like doing myself up. He'd start hitting me, you know.

And can you remember what happened that first time? How he hit you? Was it just a punch?

He just punched me under the chin actually. I seen stars.

Was it just the once the first time?

Uh-huh.

Did you hit him back?

I was too astounded. I'd never been hit before, so I was just standing there for the short time that I had to take it.

And can you recall what time of day this was?

It was always, nearly always, nighttime.

And did it happen in your house?

Well, at the time, yes, it was a house.

Can you recall, was it the living room, or the kitchen, or the bedroom?

It was in the living room.

And was it just the two of you or were the kids there?

No, there was people in the house at the time.

There were other people there? Were they relatives or friends?

No, just friends.

And what did they do when he hit you?

They all started edging up, quite honestly, cos the girls started screaming, a couple of girls that were in, and the men that were his pals stood. They were used to seeing things like that.

They didn't try and pull him off you?

They used to tell him to stop, but he didn't take any notice. I don't think they really bothered.

And were you hurt at all after that? I mean, apart from the shock?

Well, I couldn't believe in that he just hit me, you know. I didn't feel the same towards him after that.

This interview had a very different character from that of the first one. It was necessary to ask each of the systematic questions in order to collect comparable information so that we could quantify all our data and treat them in a systematic manner.

In the interviews we also asked about what usually happened during a violent episode. This allowed us to overcome the possibility that the first, worst, and last assaults might in some way be unusual and gave us an indication of how the violence changed over time. This approach enabled us to assess in considerable detail the nature of the violent events, their meanings for the participants, and their impact on the marital relationship.

At the end of the interview we explored issues relating to the nonviolent aspects of the relationship. We were attempting to uncover beliefs and values relating to marriage and violence; yet this general approach was always embedded in the reality of the woman's marriage. For example, we asked broad questions such as "What do you think a good husband should be like?" as well as, "Do you think your husband was a good husband?" allowing the woman to consider general issues in light of her own experiences. This is the only technique that will make such issues meaningful to people since human values and attitudes do not exist in a vacuum but are the products of our own diverse experiences in specific settings. As Kaplan argued in his consideration of values and research, "Value judgements can be generalized over a wide range of contexts, but they cannot be abstracted altogether from the concrete in terms of which both the value problem and its solution must be formulated."[19] Our approach yielded qualitative and quantitative information that enabled us to describe the typical structure of violent episodes while considering the dynamics of such events.

We eventually conducted 28 interviews in the pilot study and 109 in the major study, from which the evidence and interview material presented in this book were derived. The 109 interviews were conducted primarily by two research assistants, Catherine Cavanagh and Monica Wilson, during an 18-month period beginning in June 1975. The majority of the women interviewed (67) were residing in refuges for battered women in Edinburgh and Glasgow, another 26 were living in refuges in smaller cities or towns in Scotland, and the remainder (16) were interviewed at home after leaving a refuge. With the exception of the 16 women living at home, the women usually were interviewed a few days after their arrival in a refuge, and none of the women asked to participate refused. The women came from diverse backgrounds; though primarily from Scottish working-class families, some were from middle-income and/or English backgrounds. They ranged in age from late teens to early sixties with the majority between the ages of 21 and 30. The majority had two or three children and came from both rural and urban backgrounds. The background characteristics of the 109 women we interviewed were compared with those of the women in the 933 police and court cases we analyzed and they did not differ in any significant manner. Looking at our evidence and that of others working in this field, we think that the profiles of women who go to refuges and the circumstances surrounding the violence directed at them are not different from those of women who seek other avenues of escape or who are still trapped in violent marriages.

Conducting the interviews required continual contact with the women residing in the refuges. The research assistants were not mere interviewers but rather became permanent fixtures in the life and activities of the refuges. They spent considerable time in the refuges apart from the time engaged in interviewing and often were sympathetic listeners to women concerned about their present predicament and future prospects. The researchers were not strangers but people with histories that were learned by the newcomers to the refuges from those who were already residing in them for a period of time and who had been previously interviewed by ourselves or Cavanagh and Wilson. This continual contact with the refuges had the unintended but important consequence of developing considerable trust between the interviewers and the women, which in most cases meant good rapport during interviews.[20]

The interviews lasted from 2 to 12 hours, typically 2 1/2 hours, and all of them were tape recorded. The use of tape recorders allowed us to adopt a more conversational style of interviewing and concentrate on the discussion and the development of specific issues rather than on the recording of answers. This advantage became something of a disadvantage when we began to collate the responses since playing back the tapes and transcribing the answers was an exceedingly time-consuming, although worthwhile process.

Interviews of this nature, carried out with women who had decided to make their personal troubles public, are more likely to lead to an explanation and understanding of the processes involved in violent episodes and marriages than are research efforts that attempt to establish the distribution of violent events or families in the general population. Our intent was systematically to explore the factors related to violence against women and the best way of achieving this purpose was to conduct interviews with a group of women who had been subjected to assaults and who were willing to discuss their experiences. We purposely chose a sample of battered women who were willing to speak in considerable detail about what is for many people an unspeakable and unsharable problem.

It is impossible to choose a random sample of families characterized by violence since the universe from which to draw such a sample is impossible to specify. Researchers interested in assessing the distribution of violence in the general population have a well-defined universe of a whole country or a particular city from which to draw a random sample and can with certain limitations generalize their results to the universe from which they sampled.[21] This procedure was inappropriate and impossible given the type of research questions we were pursuing since the universe of all families characterized by violence is not knowable and cannot be specified (the minimum requirements for drawing a random sample). The fact that we did not have a statistically based random sample of all battered women does not mean that the results we obtained cannot be generalized; it merely means that generalization from this research cannot be based on inferential statistics.

The inability to interview the husbands of these women should be seen as unfortunate but not as devastating to the goals of the research. We explored several possibilities for interviewing abusive husbands (though not the husbands of the women we interviewed because this could have put the women at risk) but none of them proved satisfactory.[22] Other researchers have reported similar problems in interviewing husbands.[23] After conducting many interviews with battered wives we think that the women are capable of reporting accurately the circumstances surrounding violent episodes, their feelings and responses to these events, and the feelings and responses of their husbands. Toch observed that the men he interviewed who engaged in violence were capable of reflecting both upon their role in a violent event and upon the perspectives and feelings of the victim.[24]

We considered the reports of women relating to their husbands' acts and feelings as sound, especially since these relationships were of long duration. And one does not necessarily need to rely solely on accounts of feelings and attitudes when accounts of behavior, such as a husband's response to a violent episode, are often more revealing. It might be argued that the women presented a one-sided view of the violence, failing to note their own behaviors relating to violent episodes. However, the women we interviewed were willing to explore their own actions related to the violent episode and indeed we would have been surprised if they failed to do so given the widespread tendency to blame women in such situations.

The technical problems inherent in research on wife beating are evident in other studies of violence and especially of violence within the family. The major difficulty in this area arises from the methods of gathering information. Most studies of interpersonal violence have relied upon official police reports,[25] prison samples,[26] or purposively selected or convenient samples.[27] The few observational studies of violence that exist have tended to examine interpersonal violence that occurs in public.[28] The practical difficulties and ethical problems relating to research in the home preclude observational research in that setting, and we reject experimental studies[29] since artificial settings exclude any consideration of biographical background or the history of the marriage. Limitations of this nature leave researchers with a rather small set of research techniques, a not unusual state of affairs in the social sciences. This situation should not, however, result in despair or arguments in favor of only certain types of restricted research thought to lead to a perfect state of knowledge. Rather, we should continue to use those techniques available to us in a careful and reasoned manner.

Police and Court Records

In order to expand our base of knowledge we explored violence against women that was reported to the police and courts in two Scottish cities. We analyzed all of the arrest reports presented to courts for the entire city of Edinburgh and for one large police district in Glasgow during 1974.[30] We read all of the full reports (34,000) to determine whether any violence had actually occurred in the incident on record. This task was especially crucial since many violent episodes in the home were listed simply as breaches of the peace. Going beyond the official charge allowed us to learn a great deal about violence in the home and to make a much more accurate assessment of the comparative rates of violence in public and private places.

After identifying all cases involving attacks on wives we proceeded to glean as much information as possible from each record. The information included in the police and court records allowed us to determine various socio-demographic characteristics of the couple (e.g., age, occupation, and number of children), to learn about various structural factors relating to incidents of violence (e.g., time and place of the incident), to understand better the sequence of events preceding a violent episode and the nature of the episode, and to categorize the responses of wives and husbands to the violence. We were also able to learn a great deal about how police handle violent episodes. This information augmented the information from the interviews and allowed us to construct accounts of the role of the police in violent incidents.

There has been considerable discussion and debate regarding the use of official police statistics in social research. We do not wish to enter into this debate but do consider it necessary and important to make explicit our position on this question. The most assumptive and unreliable use of official police reports is the calculation of so-called absolute rates of crime or violence in various countries or cities and the comparison of such rates with those of other countries, cities, or time periods.[31] This common technique ignores or slights the arguments and evidence that indicate the potential biases of such calculations and comparisons.[32] We also consider attempts to explore or validate theories proposing relationships between structural factors such as class membership and criminal or violent behavior as dangerous and ill-conceived.[33] The differential treatment by the police and the courts of various types of offenders has been amply documented; differential "absolute rates" of criminal activity are just as likely to be an artifact of police response as they are to be a true reflection of behavioral differences between groups in society.[34] Accordingly, police reports must be used with care and for clearly delimited purposes.

In our research we did not attempt to make any statements about the absolute rates of violence against wives or to substantiate any theoretical claims requiring different rates of violence between individuals differentially distributed in the social structure. We did use the police reports to conduct a comparative analysis of crimes of violence that are reported to and dealt with by the police and to describe various aspects of these violent events. This exercise is important not only for sociological purposes but also for policy decisions. If research indicates that assaults against women in the home constitute a significant proportion of all violent offenses dealt with by the police then this finding should have considerable implications for police work and training.

We wrote this book to describe and to explain the phenomenon of wife beating in contemporary Western society. To achieve that end we used diverse sources and types of information. Verbatim accounts from battered women formed a crucial part of our analysis. It should be stressed that these accounts were included because they were representative of all of the accounts we heard and because they illustrated the most significant factors relating to the problem of wife abuse.

NOTES

Chapter 1 Violence against Wives:
A Case against the Patriarchy

1. Caroline Charlton, "The First Cow on Chiswick High Road," *Spare Rib* 24 (1972):24–25; Jo Sutton, "The Growth of the British Movement for Battered Women," *Victimology* 2 (3–4) (1977–1978):576–584.

2. There were similar women's centers in the United States that provided a community meeting place for women, and at least one group in Boston, spearheaded by Betsy Warrior and Lisa Leghorn, was aware of the problem of battered wives and working with it. At the time, however, the major concern of feminists in the United States was equal opportunity and rape rather than violence against wives. Thus, the work of this group was not associated exclusively with battered women and these concerns were less well known. To some extent this was because they did not set up a refuge specifically for battered women, nor did they receive the same publicity as Chiswick Women's Aid received in Britain. Lisa Leghorn and Betsy Warrior, *Houseworker's Handbook* (Somerville: New England Free Press, 1974):25–51. Betsy Warrior, *Wifebeating* (Somerville: New England Free Press, 1975).

3. Erin Pizzey, *Scream Quietly or the Neighbours Will Hear You* (Baltimore: Penguin, 1974):14–23. The terms "husband" and "wife" refer to the social relationship between men and women who live together and not to the legal status of that relationship.

4. Ruth Adler, Lea Harris, and Fran Wasoff, "Edinburgh Women's Aid: A Review of the First Year" (Available from Scottish Women's Aid, Ainslie House, 11 St. Colme Street, Edinburgh, Scotland; 1975); Glasgow Women's Aid, "Interval House: Report for the Year February 1974 to February 1975" Del Martin, *Battered Wives* (San Francisco: Glide, 1976):225–226; National Women's Aid Federation, *Battered Women Need Refuges: A Report from the National Women's Aid Federation* (London: Rye 1975); Sutton, 577–581; Women's Aid, "Battered Wives" (Available from Women's Aid, 2 Belmont Terrace, London, England; 1973).

5. Parliamentary Select Committee on Violence in Marriage, *First Special Report from the Select Committee on Violence in Marriage*, Vol. 1, Session 1974–1975 (London: HMSO, 1975).

6. *South Carolina Gazette*, 1764.

7. *South Carolina and American General Gazette*, 1776.

8. Quoted in Linda Grant DePauw and Conover Hunt, *Remember the Ladies: Women in America, 1750–1815* (New York: Viking, 1976):2.

9. Sir William Blackstone, *Commentaries on the Laws of England*, Vol. 1 (London, 1765); R. Emerson Dobash and Russell P. Dobash, "Wife Beating: Past and Present" (Paper presented to the First Meeting of the Anglo-French Exchange on Violence against Women, London, November 1975); Sue Eisenberg and Patricia Micklow, "The Assaulted Wife: Catch 22 Revisited (An Exploratory Legal Study of Wifebeating in Michigan)" (Mimeographed paper, University of Michigan Law School, 1974):4, published in revised form in *Women's Rights Law Reporter* 3, nos. 3–4 (1977):138–161. Eugene A. Hecker, *A Short History of Women's Rights: From the Days of Augustus to the Present Time* (New York: Putnam, 1910):125. Anthony Manchester, "The Legal History of Marital Violence in England and Wales, 1750–1976" (University of Birmingham Faculty of Law, 1976):4. Lady McLaren, *The Women's Charter of Rights and Liberties* (London: Grosvenor, 1909):16.

10. Frances Power Cobbe, "Wife Torture in England," *Contemporary Review*, April 1878:55–87; McLaren, 15–17, 70.

11. Parliamentary Papers, "Reports of Chief Constables for the Years 1870–74 Pertaining to the Law Relating to Brutal Assaults," in Reports to the Secretary of State for the Home Department of the State of the Law Relating to Brutal Assaults, Cmnd. 1138, 1875.

12. Hecker, 127.

13. McLaren, 15–17, 70.

14. Bertrand Russell, "Rights Husbands Had Once," *Sunday Referee*, December 15, 1935:12. Russell erroneously dated the event as 1888. For correct date of 1878 see Cobbe pp. 69–70.

15. *The Guardian*, May 8, 1976.

16. Cf. Pierre Van den Berghe, "Bringing Beasts Back In: Toward a Biosocial Theory of Aggression," *American Sociological Review*, 39 (December 1974): 777–778.

17. R. Emerson Dobash and Russell P. Dobash, "Wives: The 'Appropriate' Victims of Marital Violence," *Victimology* 2 (3–4) (1977–1978):426–442.

18. C. Wright Mills, *The Sociological Imagination* (Baltimore: Penguin, 1971):9–17, 148–150, 159–182.

19. Ibid., 14–20, 138, 156, 158.

Chapter 2   Wives as Victims: Evidence and Explanations

1. Hans Toch, *Violent Men: An Inquiry into the Psychology of Violence* (Chicago: Aldine, 1969):6.

2. James F. Short and Fred L. Strodtbeck, *Group Process and Gang Delinquency* (Chicago: University of Chicago Press, 1965).

3. Robert Faulkner, "On Respect and Retribution: Toward an Ethnography of Violence," *Sociological Symposium* 9 (Spring 1973):17–35.

4. The importance of considering the history of social settings and relationships between individuals acting in these settings is well illustrated in the case of Duke, described in Short and Strodtbeck, 187–189. Duke, an otherwise "cool" and nonaggressive gang leader, became quite violent upon his release from jail. This confinement resulted in his loss of status and leadership in the gang. Upon his return to the gang he attempted to reestablish his position by overconforming to the group norm of toughness in relation to other gangs. Without the knowledge of Duke's background, the norms of the group, and the meanings attached to contacts (individual and collective) with other gangs, we could not comprehend Duke's violent and aggressive acts.

5. We will treat these reports as relatively unproblematic in respect to their research techniques. This should not be taken as naiveté regarding the problems of using official statistics and research reports. On the contrary, we are very much aware of problems inherent in relying on official statistics but in this consideration we are interested only in discerning patterns and direction in violence between husbands and wives. These research reports come from extremely diverse sources, e.g., criminology and family sociology, and they are often difficult to compare directly because they use different categories, resulting in the inclusion of certain information in some reports and the exclusion of comparable information in others.

6. Arthur MacDonald, "Death Penalty and Homicide," *American Journal of Sociology*, 16 (1911):96.

7. Ibid.

8. Hans Von Hentig, *The Criminal and His Victim* (New Haven: Yale University Press, 1948):392.

9. Ibid.

10. Von Hentig's arguments regarding the reason for this high rate of homicide among female servants are interesting. He maintained that the usual pattern is sexual exploitation on the part of the head of the household resulting in pregnancy; the man then seeks to rid himself of the rather embarrassing or inconvenient pregnancy through murder—an argument that fits very well with our conception of violence as social control, the ultimate control being the ability to decide life and death.

11. Marvin E. Wolfgang, *Patterns in Criminal Homicide* (New York: Wiley, 1958):32.

12. Ibid., 50–67.

13. Ibid., 204.

14. Ibid., 213–214.

15. Ibid., 214.

16. Ibid., 217.

17. James Boudouris, "Homicide and the Family," *Journal of Marriage and the Family* 33 (4) (1971):671.

18. There is some debate about the differential rates of homicides between husbands and wives. Some investigators report or argue that men and women are about equally likely to commit homicide in the home and indeed in the category of homicides involving family members. Wolfgang reported about

similar numbers of men and women. This finding has certainly not been replicated in the British research on homicides. Yet, even if homicides are equally likely to be committed by husbands and wives we still need to consider the context and the relationships in which they occur. Going beyond the immediate statistics it becomes evident that the genesis of the two types of homicide is quite different. For example, a federal commission in the United States estimated that women who commit murder are motivated by self-defense 70% more often than men. Cited in Martin, 17.

19. Evelyn Gibson and S. Klein, *Murder, 1957 to 1968: A Home Office Statistical Division Report on Murder in England and Wales* (London: HMSO, 1969).

20. Ibid., 19.

21. Evelyn Gibson, *Homicide in England and Wales, 1967–1971*, Home Office Research Study no. 31 (London: HMSO, 1975); see especially pp. 18, 36, and table 13, p. 20.

22. Boudouris, 667.

23. Richard Moran, "Criminal Homicide: External Restraint and Subculture of Violence," *Criminology* 8 (4) (1971):357–374. This study reported that 88% of the homicides in Boston occurring between 1962 and 1966 were committed by males. Alex D. Pokorny, "Human Violence: A Comparison of Homicide, Aggravated Assault, Suicide, and Attempted Murder," *Journal of Criminal Law, Criminology, and Police Science* 56 (4) (1965):488–497.

24. Harwin L. Voss and John R. Hepburn, "Patterns in Criminal Homicide in Chicago," *Journal of Criminal Law, Criminology, and Police Science* 59 (4) (1968):499–508.

25. Ibid., 506.

26. F. H. McClintock, *Crimes of Violence* (New York: St. Martin's, 1963b).

27. Ibid., 249–251.

28. Board of Directors, Home Intervention Team Project, "Proposal for Home Intervention Team Service: Hamilton–Westworth Region" (Hamilton, Ontario, Canada, November 1976).

29. Philip H. Ennis, *Criminal Victimization in the United States: A Report of a National Survey*, National Opinion Research Center, University of Chicago (Washington D.C.: U.S. Government Printing Office, 1967).

30. This statistic was extrapolated from ibid., table 20, p. 38.

31. The validity of divorce petitions and allegations contained within them may be questioned, but we agree with other researchers who have accepted the validity of incidents reported in divorce petitions. See Robert Chester and Jane Streather, "Cruelty in English Divorce: Some Empirical Findings" *Journal of Marriage and the Family* 34 (4) (1972):706–710, 711.

32. John E. O'Brien, "Violence in Divorce Prone Families," *Journal of Marriage and the Family* 33 (4) (1971):695.

33. George Levinger, "Sources of Marital Dissatisfaction among Applicants for Divorce," *American Journal of Orthopsychiatry* 36 (5) (1966):805.

34. Chester and Streather, 709.

35. Ibid.

36. Robert Whitehurst, "Violence Potential in Extra-marital Sexual Responses," *Journal of Marriage and the Family* 33 (4) (1971):683–691.

37. Ibid., 687.

38. Elizabeth Elston, Jane Fuller, and Mervyn Murch, "Battered Wives: The Problems of Violence in Marriages as Experienced by a Group of Petitioners in Undefended Divorce Cases" (Department of Social Work, University of Bristol, 1976):10.

39. Richard J. Gelles, *The Violent Home: A Study of Physical Aggression between Husbands and Wives* (Beverly Hills: Sage, 1974).

40. Ibid., 50–51.

41. This point was noted in table 3, p. 53, but Gelles failed to recognize its significance. Also, his gross categorization and oversimplification of the violence—e.g., treating slapping and severe kicks in a mere quantitative manner—resulted in failure to consider the qualitative aspects of the use of physical force. We suggest that it is a grave error to fail to differentiate various forms of physical force and ignore their meanings to the actors in the social settings in which they occur.

42. We have not attempted to differentiate various forms of violence in this overview of research reports. This treatment may lead to the assumption that we consider these various acts as cumulative and intrinsically related. We make no such assumption, preferring to explore the meaning of murder, serious assaults, and pushing and shoving in their concrete circumstances.

43. See Suzanne K. Steinmetz, "The Battered Husband Syndrome," *Victimology* 2 (3–4) (1978):499–509, for an example of the use of cartoons to represent reality. In the same issue see E. Pleck, J. Pleck, M. Grossman, and P. Bart, "The Battered Data Syndrome; A Reply to Steinmetz," for a critique of this paper. See Mildred Daley Pagelow, "Violence Against Women in the Family" (Paper presented at the 9th World Congress of Sociology, Uppsala, Sweden, August 1978) for a critique of the statistical analysis of Straus.

44. Murray A. Straus, Richard J. Gelles, Suzanne K. Steinmetz, "Violence in the Family: An Assessment of Knowledge and Research Needs" (Paper presented to the American Association for the Advancement of Science Convention, Boston, February 1976):34.

45. Mary Lystad, "Violence at Home: A Review of the Literature," *American Journal of Orthopsychiatry* 45 (5) (1975):332.

46. Straus, Gelles, and Steinmetz, 2; M. Straus, "Wife Beating: How Common and Why," *Victimology* 2 (3–4) (1978):450.

47. William J. Goode, "Force and Violence in the Family," *Journal of Marriage and the Family* 33 (4) (1971):624–636.

48. Ibid., 624.

49. See Walter Buckley, *Sociology and Modern Systems Theory* (Englewood Cliffs: Prentice-Hall, 1967): chap. 6.

50. Goode, 626.

51. Ibid., 627.

52. Marvin E. Wolfgang and Franco Ferracuti, *The Subculture of Violence: Towards an Integrated Theory in Criminology* (London: Tavistock, 1967).

53. Raymond D. Gastil, "Homicide and a Regional Culture of Violence," *American Sociological Review* 36 (June 1971):412–427.

54. William A. Westley, *Violence and the Police: A Sociological Study of Law, Custom, and Morality* (Cambridge: MIT Press, 1970).

55. Sandra J. Ball-Rokeach, "Values and Violence: A Test of the Subculture of Violence Thesis," *American Sociological Review* 38 (December 1973):736–749.

56. Michael Clarke, "On the Concept 'Sub-Culture,' " *British Journal of Sociology* (January 1975):428–441.

57. Whitehurst, 683.

58. This conception of crime has been evident in the sociological literature at least since Sutherland's theory of differential association. Edwin Sutherland and Donald Cressey, *Principles of Criminology* (Philadelphia: Lippincott, 1966). The learning view of crime and deviance is a persistent aspect of theoretical work in this area. See Richard Cloward and Lloyd Ohlin, *Delinquency and Opportunity: A Theory of Delinquent Gangs* (New York: Free Press, 1960); Howard S. Becker, *Outsiders: Studies in the Sociology of Deviance* (New York: Free Press, 1963).

59. See A. Bandura, *Aggression: A Social Learning Analysis* (Englewood Cliffs: Prentice-Hall, 1973); Herbert Selg (ed.), *The Making of Human Aggression*, trans. Arnold Pomerans (London: Quartet, 1975).

60. Leroy G. Schultz, "The Wife Assaulter," *Journal of Social Therapy* 6 (2) (1960):103–112.

61. John E. Snell, Richard Rosenwald, and Ames Robey, "The Wifebeater's Wife: A Study of Family Interaction," *Archives of General Psychiatry* 11 (August 1964):107–112.

62. Schultz, 107.

63. Snell, Rosenwald, and Robey, 11.

64. Murray Straus, "A General Systems Theory Approach to a Theory of Violence between Family Members," *Social Science Information* 12 (3) (1973):105–125, and "Sexual Inequality, Cultural Norms, and Wife-Beating," *Victimology* 1 (3–4) (1976):54–76.

65. O'Brien, 695.

66. Straus (1973):110.

67. Charles Tilly, "Chaos and Violence in the Living City," in Paul Meadows and Ephraim Mizruchi (eds.), *Urbanism, Urbanization, and Change: Comparative Perspectives* (Reading: Addison-Wesley, 1966):379–394.

68. Ibid., 379.

69. Albert Cohen argued that the proponents of multifactor theories were very likely to commit the fallacy of evil causes evil. Albert Cohen and James F. Short, Jr., "Crime and Juvenile Delinquency," in Robert K. Merton and Robert Nisbet (eds.) *Contemporary Social Problems*, 3d ed. (New York: Harcourt, 1971):89–146.

70. Ibid., 116–118.

71. Straus, Gelles, and Steinmetz.

72. J. J. Gayford, "Wife Battering: A Preliminary Survey of 100 Cases," *British Medical Journal* 1 (January 1975b):194–197.

73. See Norwood Russell Hanson, *Patterns of Discovery* (New York: Cambridge University Press, 1972); Karl Popper, *Objective Knowledge: An Evolutionary Approach* (Oxford: Clarendon, 1972):341–361.

74. Gayford (1975b).

75. Herbert Feigel, "The 'Orthodox' View of Theories: Remarks in Defense as Well as Critique," in Michael Rudner and Stephen Winokur, *Minnesota Studies in the Philosophy of Science*, Vol. 4: *Analyses of Theories and Methods of Physics and Psychology* (Minneapolis: University of Minnesota Press, 1970):3–16; Carl C. Hempel, *Philosophy of Natural Sciences*, (Englewood Cliffs: Prentice-Hall, 1966); P. Achinstein and S. Barker (eds.) *The Legacy of Logical Positivism: Studies in the Philosophy of Science* (Baltimore: Johns Hopkins Press, 1969).

76. One of the most, if not the most, influential proponents of logical positivism in the social sciences was George Lundberg, whose introductory textbook set many a student of sociology off on the road to logical positivism.

77. Tom Bottomore (ed.), *Crisis and Contention in Sociology* (Beverly Hills: Sage, 1975); Alvin W. Gouldner, *The Coming Crisis of Western Sociology* (London: Heinemann, 1971).

78. See Buckley; Ruben Hill, "Modern Systems Theory and the Family: A Confrontation," *Social Science Information* 10 (5) (1971):7–26; Alfred Kuhn, *Unified Social Science: A System Based Introduction* (Homewood: Dorsey, 1975); Joseph H. Monane, *A Sociology of Human Systems* (New York: Appleton Century, 1967); Anatol Rappaport and William Horworth, "Thoughts on Organization Theory," *General Systems* 7 (1966):129–141; Straus (1973).

79. Straus (1973).

80. Ibid., 110.

81. Ibid., n. 3.

82. Max Weber, *The Methodology of the Social Sciences*, trans. and ed. Edward Shils and Henry A. Finch (New York: Free Press, 1949):67.

83. Ibid., 79.

84. Ibid., 76.

85. This point requires considerable qualification. Marx did not completely reject the process of developing generalized proposals, but his general laws were firmly embedded in the context of a specific society at a particular time, capitalist society in the nineteenth century. Of course, Weber did at times explicitly reject a Marxian analysis. However, this should not prevent us from seeking similarities between his work and that of Marx and from recognizing his contributions to methodology and to the understanding of capitalist societies. See Stuart Hall, "The Hinterland of Science: Ideology and the 'Sociology of Knowledge,' " *Working Papers in Cultural Studies* 10 (1977):9–32; Alfred Meyer, "Aufhebung: of Marxism," *Social Research* 43 (Summer 1976):199–219; Irving Zeitlan, *Ideology and the Development of Sociological Theory* (Englewood Cliffs: Prentice-Hall, 1968).

86. Karl Marx, *Capital*, Vol. 1: *A Critical Analysis of Capitalist Production* (London: Lawrence and Wishart; 1970b; first published 1867): sect. 1, and *A Con-*

tribution to the Critique of Political Economy, ed. Maurice Dobb (Moscow: Progress, 1970c), especially pp. 205–214.

87. See Paul Feyerabend, "Against Method: Outline of an Anarchistic Theory of Knowledge," in Michael Radner and Stephen Winokur (eds.), *Minnesota Studies in the Philosophy of Sciences*, Vol. 4: *Analyses of Theories and Methods of Physics and Psychology* (Minneapolis: University of Minnesota Press, 1970):17–130; Thomas Kuhn, *The Structure of Scientific Revolutions* (Chicago: University of Chicago Press, 1962); Imre Lakatos and Alan Musgrave (eds.), *Criticism and the Growth of Knowledge* (New York: Cambridge University Press, 1970).

88. The fetishes of statistics and measurement often dictate the problems that the researcher is interested in, with the available and approved methods of research determining the research problems to be explored. This has also resulted in a sociology of the individual and an emphasis on social psychology in North American sociology.

89. Ernest Becker, *The Structure of Evil* (New York: Free Press, 1968):x.

90. Karl Marx, *Capital*, Vol. 3: *Capitalist Production as a Whole* (London: Lawrence and Wishart, 1970a):797.

91. Georg Lukács, "What Is Orthodox Marxism?" in *History and Class Consciousness: Studies in Marxist Dialectics*, trans. Rodney Livingstone (London: Merlin, 1971):8.

92. See Arthur K. Davis, "Social Theory and Social Problems," *Philosophy and Phenomenological Research* 18 (December 1957):190–208.

93. Dick Ogles introduced us to the context specific approach during graduate work at Washington State University. Our articulation and use of this approach to social analysis relates primarily to its utility as a research method; whereas Ogles's conception of the approach was developed for comparative research and included "the context of all aspects of one's research" (personal communication, 1977)—a position we accept but do not develop in this book. See also William Wilson, Nicholas Sofios and Richard Ogles, "Formalization and Stages of Theoretical Development," *Pacific Sociological Review* (Fall 1964):74–80.

94. Eldon Wegner, "The Conception of Alienation: A Critique and Some Suggestions for a Context Specific Approach," *Pacific Sociological Review* 18 (2) (1975):172.

95. The study of alienation provides an excellent example of the use of abstracted measuring devices in the Srole scale of alienation; Wegner labeled the items included in the scale "clichés." Leo Srole, "Social Integration and Certain Corollaries: An Exploratory Study," *American Sociological Review* 21 (December 1956):709–716; see also Arnold Rose, "Alienation and Participation: A Comparison of Group Leaders and the Mass," *American Sociological Review* 27 (December 1962):834–838.

96. Wegnar, 189.

97. Short and Strodtbeck.

98. Ibid., 185.

99. Howard J. Parker, *View from the Boys* (London: David and Charles, 1974).

100. Ibid., 63.

101. Faulkner.

102. Ibid., 17.

103. Ibid., 20.

104. Ibid., 4.

105. Ibid., 18.

106. Aaron V. Cicourel, *Method and Measurement in Sociology* (New York: Free Press, 1964).

107. Ibid., 4.

108. Aaron V. Cicourel, *The Social Organization of Juvenile Justice* (New York: Wiley, 1968).

109. Aaron V. Cicourel, *Theory and Method in a Study of Argentine Fertility* (New York: Wiley-Interscience, 1974).

110. Cicourel (1974):84.

111. Cicourel (1968).

112. Cicourel (1974).

113. Toch.

114. Ibid., 18.

115. Cf. Murray A. Straus, "Wife Beating: How Common and Why?" *Victimology* 2 (3-4) (1978):443-458. This article discusses the author's attempts to develop various scales and measuring devices, such as the Conflict Resolution Techniques (CRT) scale for assessing the extent of violence in families.

116. Lukács, 34.

Chapter 3   The Legacy of the "Appropriate" Victim

1. G. M. Trevelyan, *History of England*, 3d ed. (London: Longmans, Green, 1966; first published 1926):260.

2. Kate Millett, *Sexual Politics* (London: Abacus, 1972):64; Sheila Rowbotham, *Hidden from History: Three Hundred Years of Women's Oppression and the Fight against It* (London: Pluto, 1973); Virginia Woolf, *A Room of One's Own*, 15th ed. (London: Hogarth, 1974; first published 1929):46-47.

3. Woolf, 66.

4. Whores, although not members of families, are not excluded from this singular conception since they were seen in terms of their inability to be "good" family members rather than in terms of some other criterion, such as their position as workers.

5. The current emphasis upon the history of women would seem to indicate that many historians simply failed to mention or to emphasize the achievements and exploits of women even when these acts came within the boundaries of what they saw as historically significant unless these acts fit the stereotype of women in the family. For example, it was more likely to be noted that Betsy Ross made the flag and that women followed the Revolutionary soldiers in order to prepare

their food, etc., than that many women also served as soldiers. See DePauw and Hunt, 89–94; Peter Laslett, *The World We Have Lost* (London: Methuen, 1973):20; Juliet Mitchell, *Woman's Estate* (Baltimore: Penguin, 1974):100–101.

6. Saint Augustine, book 22, quoted in John Knox, *The First Blast of the Trumpet Against the Monstrous Regiment of Women* (London: Southgate, 1558):20.

7. Julia O'Faolain and Lauro Martines (eds.), *Not in God's Image: Women in History* (Glasgow: Fontana/Collins, 1974):70–88.

8. For a discussion of the ancient Roman family see Panos D. Bardis, "Family Forms and Variations Historically Considered," in Harold T. Christensen (ed.), *Handbook of Marriage and the Family* (Chicago: Rand McNally, 1964): 433–440; Jerome Carcopino, *Daily Life in Ancient Rome* (New Haven: Yale University Press, 1940), especially chap. 4; James Donaldson, *Woman: Her Position and Influence in Ancient Greece and Rome and among the Early Christians* (London: Longmans, Green, 1907), especially book 2; Ludwig Friedlander, *Roman Life and Manners under the Early Empire* (New York: Dutton, 1908–1913), especially vol. 1, chap. 5; Willystine Goodsell, *A History of Marriage and the Family* (New York: MacMillan, 1939); Harold Johnston, *The Private Life of the Romans* (Glenview: Scott, Foresman, 1932); Gerald Leslie, *The Family in Social Context* (New York: Oxford University Press, 1967):170–176; Walton B. McDaniel, *Roman Private Life and Its Survivals* (Boston: Marshall Jones, 1924); Ovid, *The Art of Love*, trans. Rolfe Humphries, (Bloomington: Indiana University Press, 1957); Stuart Queen and Robert W. Habenstein, *The Family in Various Cultures*, 3d ed. (Philadelphia: Lippincott, 1967):159–180; H. L. Rogers and T. R. Harley, *Roman Home Life and Religion* (Oxford: Clarendon, 1923).

9. Hecker, 2; Leslie, 170–171; O'Faolain and Martines, 65–68; Queen and Habenstein, 166–168.

10. Queen and Habenstein, 166.

11. Ibid., 167.

12. Ibid.

13. Ibid., 168.

14. O'Faolain and Martines, 65.

15. Dionysius of Halicarnassus (25 B.C.), quoted in O'Faolain and Martines, 53; see also Arnold S. Nash, "Ancient Past and Living Present," in Howard Becker and Reuben Hill (eds.), *Family, Marriage, and Parenthood* (Boston: Heath, 1955):97.

16. O'Faolain and Martines, 53.

17. Manus, or holding someone in one's hand, was the power exercised by the head of the family over his wife and children. It took its origin in patriarchal Rome and had fallen into disuse by the second century A.D. O'Faolain and Martines, 58–59; see also Leslie, 171; Queen and Habenstein, 165–170.

18. Leslie, 172–173; O'Faolain and Martines, 164–165; Queen and Habenstein, 165–170.

19. O'Faolain and Martines, 60; Queen and Habenstein, 164–165.

20. Leslie, 171; Queen and Habenstein, 163–165.

21. Dio Cassius (c. A.D. 150–235), quoted in O'Faolain and Martines, 65.

22. Dionysius of Halicarnassus, quoted in O'Faolain and Martines, 53.

23. O'Faolain and Martines, 53, 63; see also Goodsell, 126; Hecker, 23.

24. Leslie, 173; O'Faolain and Martines, 55; Queen and Habenstein, 169. Divorce was discouraged during the early period—it was considered to be a family matter and was only later controlled by the state. There is some disagreement about the date of the first divorce on record. Donaldson, 116–117, suggested 300 B.C.; O'Faolain and Martines, 54, noted its mention in the Twelve Tables of 451 B.C.

25. Valerium Maximus, quoted in O'Faolain and Martines, 55–56.

26. Plutarch, quoted in O'Faolain and Martines, 55.

27. Hecker, 23; O'Faolain and Martines, 67.

28. Goodsell, 126; O'Faolain and Martines, 55; Queen and Habenstein, 170.

29. O'Faolain and Martines, 53–56, 67–69.

30. O'Faolain and Martines, 54; see also Queen and Habenstein, 169–171.

31. O'Faolain and Martines, 55.

32. Ibid., 63.

33. The Oppian Law of 195 B.C. specified that no woman could own more than an ounce of gold, wear colored clothing, or ride in a horse-drawn carriage except on certain feast days.

34. O'Faolain and Martines, 56–57.

35. Bardis, 437; Leslie, 173–176; O'Faolain and Martines, 63; Queen and Habenstein, 171–179.

36. Queen and Habenstein, 174.

37. O'Faolain and Martines, 72.

38. Ibid., 70–71.

39. Bardis, 441; Leslie, 176; Queen and Habenstein, 179, 181.

40. Hecker, 55; see also 237. For a discussion of the early Christian family see Alexander Roberts and James Donaldson, cited in Queen and Habenstein, 181–201; Bardis, 440–451; Donaldson, especially book III; Goodsell, especially Ch. V; Leslie, 176–185.

41. Corpus Iuris Canonici, quoted in O'Faolain and Martines, 143; see also Terry Davidson, "Wifebeating: A Recurring Phenomenon throughout History," in Maria Roy (ed.), Battered Women: A Psychosociological Study of Domestic Violence (New York: Van Nostrand Reinhold, 1977):11.

42. Genesis 2:18.

43. Note that it is assumed that God is a man. Genesis 2:22–23.

44. Genesis 3:12.

45. Genesis 3:14.

46. Genesis 3:16.

47. Genesis 3:17.

48. See also Ephesians 5:28–29.

49. I Timothy 2:13; I Corinthians 11:8.

50. I Corinthians 11:9.

51. I Corinthians 11:3; see also Ephesians 5:23, as well as I Corinthians 11:4–5, for the command that women should cover their heads in church in order to show their subjection to men.

52. I Corinthians 11:7.

53. See also I Timothy 2:9–10, 13.

54. I Timothy 2:14.

55. For additional verses indicating the subjection of wives see I Timothy 2:11–12; Peter 3:5–7; Ephesians 5:22, 33.

56. I Timothy 2:11–12.

57. I Corinthians 14:34.

58. I Corinthians 14:35.

59. I Corinthians 7.

60. Ephesians 5. Titus 2:4–5.

61. I Timothy 3.

62. I Corinthians 7:9; see also Leslie, 177, who indicated that burning does not refer to the fires of hell but rather to the fires of passion.

63. See Queen and Habenstein, 184; Lawrence Stone, "The Rise of the Nuclear Family in Modern England: The Patriarchical Stage," in Charles E. Rosenberg (ed.), *The Family in History* (Philadelphia: University of Pennsylvania Press, 1975):53; Maurice Valency, *In Praise of Love* (New York: Macmillan, 1958):23.

64. I Corinthians 7:10.

65. R. Emerson Dobash and Russell P. Dobash, "Love, Honour, and Obey: Institutional Ideologies and the Struggle for Battered Women," *Contemporary Crises: Crime, Law, and Social Policy* Vol. 1 (June–July 1977a):403–415. For diverse reading on the patriarchy see Simone de Beauvoir, *The Second Sex*, trans. and ed. H. M. Parshley (Baltimore: Penguin, 1976):113–128; Janet S. Chafetz, *Masculine, Feminine, of Human? An Overview of the Sociology of Sex Roles* (Itasca: Peacock, 1974):19–27; Rosalind Delmar, "Looking Again at Engels's *Origins of the Family, Private Property, and the State,*" in Juliet Mitchell and Ann Oakley (eds.), *The Rights and Wrongs of Women* (Baltimore: Penguin, 1976):271–287; Friedrich Engels, "On the Origin of the Family, Private Property, and the State," 1st pub. 1884, in Karl Marx and Friedrich Engels, *Selected Works*, Vol. 2 (Moscow: Foreign Languages Publishing House, 1962); Eva Figes, *Patriarchal Attitudes: Women in Society* (London: Faber & Faber, 1970); Shulamith Firestone, *The Dialectic of Sex: The Case for Feminist Revolution* (London: Jonathan Cape, 1971); Evelyn Frankford and Ann Snitow, "The Trap of Domesticity: Notes on the Family," *Socialist Revolution* (July–August 1972):83–97; Charmie Guettel, *Marxism and Feminism* (Toronto: Hunter Rose, 1974); Roberta Hamilton, *The Liberation of Women: A Study of Patriarchy and Capitalism* (London: George Allen & Unwin, 1978); Millett, 23–73; Mitchell (1974); Woolf. Leon Trotsky, *Women and the Family* (New York: Pathfinder, 1970):9. It is stated that "czarist laws explicit permitted a man to beat his wife." See also Eli Zaretsky, *Capitalism, the Family, and Personal Life* (London: Pluto, 1976).

66. See Weber's classic statement about traditional, charismatic, and legalistic forms

of authority. Weber's analysis of these forms of authority is excellent and has had a profound impact upon sociological thinking. However, his emphasis, and that of many contemporary sociologists, upon the legal-ration form of authority is too great and tends to obscure much of the traditional patriarchal authority, which remains in the family as well as in all other social institutions. See H. H. Gerth and C. W. Mills (eds.), *From Max Weber: Essays in Sociology* (New York: Oxford University Press, 1946):224–229; Max Weber, *The Theory of Social and Economic Organizations*, trans. A. R. Henderson and Talcott Parsons (New York: Hodge 1947).

67. Although church and state have assumed many of the legal powers of the patriarch, and thus removed his absolute power and control, the basic principles of his superordinance, rightful control, and authority, etc., remain.

68. Randall Collins, "A Conflict Theory of Sexual Stratification," in H. P. Dreitzel (ed.), *Family, Marriage, and the Struggle of the Sexes* (London: Collier Macmillan, 1972):53–79; Queen and Habenstein, 225–228; Stone, 14, 16; Zaretsky, 26–28.

69. A household included all residents, including servants as well as relatives by blood and by marriage. See also Peter Laslett (ed.), *Household and Family in Past Time* (New York: Cambridge University Press, 1974):23, 27; Queen and Habenstein, 229–230.

70. Collins, 62–66. For a discussion of the medieval family see A. Abram, *English Life and Manners in the Later Middle Ages* (New York: Dutton, 1913), especially chaps. 4, 10; George E. Howard, *A History of Matrimonial Institutions*, 3 vols. (Chicago: University of Chicago Press, 1904), especially chaps. 7, 8; Leslie, 181–185; O'Faolain and Martines, 140–191; F. Pollock and F. W. Maitland, *The History of English Law before the Time of Edward I*, Vol. 2 (New York; Cambridge University Press, 1911); Eileen Power, "The Position of Women," in C. G. Crump and E. F. Jacobs (eds.), *The Legacy of the Middle Ages* (Oxford: Clarendon, 1926); Queen and Habenstein, 224–246.

71. Collins, 64–66; Queen and Habenstein, 225, 234–235.

72. Collins, 59–61, 65; O'Faolain and Martines, 109, 116, 149–156; Pollock and Maitland, 406, 432; Queen and Habenstein, 234–235, 243.

73. Leslie, 182; O'Faolain and Martines, 111; Queen and Habenstein, 234–235; Stone, 45; Trevelyan, 260–261.

74. For a discussion of romantic love see Hugo Beigel, "Romantic Love," *American Sociological Review* 16 (3) (1951):326–334; Collins, 67–71; William G. Dodd, *Courtly Love in Chaucer and Gower* (Boston: Ginn, 1913); Edgar Prestage (ed.), *Chivalry* (New York: Knopf, 1928); Queen and Habenstein, 225, 229, 231–233, 247–270; Valency.

75. Queen and Habenstein, 225, 229, 231–233.

76. Ibid., 232.

77. Ibid., 236–237; Valency, 14, 15, 23. Collins, 68, 71, presented two contradictory views about romantic love, that it is a woman's weapon against subordination and that it traps her and requires deference to males.

78. Collins, 71–74.

79. Leslie, 183; O'Faolain and Martines, 188; Queen and Habenstein, 238.

80. Fuero Jusgo, cited in O'Faolain and Martines, 191.
81. Statuti di Perugia, quoted in ibid.
82. Coutumes de Beauvaisis, cited in ibid., 188.
83. Ibid., 189.
84. L. Finkelstein, quoted in ibid.
85. Cherubino da Siena, Regole della vita Matrimoniale, quoted in ibid., 190, 191.
86. Jo Ann McNamara and Suzanne Wemple, "The Power of Women through the Family in Medieval Europe; 500–1100," *Feminist Studies* 1 (3–4) (1973):126–141.
87. Ibid.
88. Eisenberg and Micklow, 44; Hecker, 121, 238; Zaretsky, 44.

Chapter 4   The Nuclear Family and the Chastisement of Wives

1. Philippe Ariès, *Centuries of Childhood: A Social History of Family Life* (New York: Random House, Vintage Books, 1962):356; Stone, 13–57.
2. Ariès; McNamara and Wemple, 126–141; Zaretsky, 44–45.
3. P. Petiot, quoted in Ariès, 356.
4. Stone, 24–25.
5. Ibid.
6. Ibid., 55.
7. Ibid., 24–25, 55–56; see also Gordon J. Schochet, "Patriarchalism, Politics and Mass Attitudes in Stuart England," *The Historical Journal* 12(3) (1969):413–441.
8. C. H. McIlwain, cited in Stone, 54.
9. R. Filmer and C. Russell, both cited in ibid.
10. Ibid., 55; see also Ariès, 351.
11. Stone, 55.
12. Montesquieu, quoted in ibid., 55.
13. Ariès, 356.
14. Michel Foucault, *Madness and Civilization: A History of Insanity in the Age of Reason* (London: Social Science Paperback, 1967).
15. Zaretsky, 32.
16. Ibid., 23–35.
17. P. Laslett (1973):3.
18. Ibid.; P. Laslett (1974):23–27.
19. Marx (1970b):32, 438–442, 460, wrote about the transformation of labor from domestic industries to factory production.
20. See Barbara Laslett, "The Family as a Public and Private Institution: An Historical Perspective," *Journal of Marriage and the Family* 35 (0) (1973):480–492. In discussing the change from domestic to capitalist forms of production she wrote, "In brief, master and apprentice had stood in the rela-

tion of father and son; they now stood in the relation of employee and employer" (p. 435). See also Lenore Davidoff, "Mastered for Life: Servant and Wife in Victorian and Edwardian England," *Journal of Social History* 7 (4):406–428.

21. Wally Secombe, "The Housewife and Her Labour under Capitalism," *New Left Review* (January–February 1973):6; see also Zaretsky.

22. Of course, not all women are completely isolated within the home. Yet, even when they do go out to work, they are often segregated, such as being relegated to assembly line work or typing pools. This segregation also extends into other spheres outside the home. Some sections of cities are not open to women especially during certain times of the day. See Tove Stang Dahl and Annika Snare, "The Coercion of Privacy: A Feminist Perspective" (Paper presented to the Fourth Conference of the European Group for the Study of Deviance and Social Control, Vienna, September 1976).

23. We are not arguing that apprentices and other workers escaped oppression but rather that they became subject to other forms of oppression such as those of the factory system. This was also the age of the rise of institutions oriented to explicit forms of domination and control such as workhouses, bridewells, poorhouses, prisons, and asylums. See Michel Foucault, *Discipline and Punish: The Birth of the Prison*, trans. Allan Sheridan (London: Allen Lane, 1977).

24. Zaretsky, 34.

25. Stone, 13, 53.

26. Ariès, 356; Stone, 29–32.

27. Stone, 29–32.

28. Ibid., 27.

29. Martin Luther, quoted in O'Faolain and Martines, 209; see also Vera Bullough, *The Subordinate Sex* (Urbana; University of Illinois Press, 1973); Davidson, 14.

30. Vera Bullough, quoted in Davidson, 14.

31. Martin Luther, quoted in O'Faolain and Martines, 209.

32. Martin Luther, quoted in O'Faolain and Martines, 208–209.

33. See S. Goldberg, *The Inevitability of the Patriarchy* (London: Temple Smith, 1977).

34. Martin Luther, quoted in O'Faolain and Martines, 208.

35. Oscar C. Feucht and other members of the Family Life Committee of the Lutheran church (eds.), *Sex and the Church* (St. Louis: Concordia Publishing House, 1961):84. Cited in Bullough; Davidson, 14.

36. Stone, 26; see also John Calvin, cited in O'Faolain and Martines, 211–212.

37. Robert Cawdrey, quoted in Stone, 52.

38. Knox.

39. By the logic of stereotyping variations in behavior and skill can be defined in such a way as to retain the labels of superior and inferior groups despite the actions of particular members. If a man does something brilliant, then as an individual he is superior—but this is merely the expected outcome given the

superior nature of his sex; if he does something stupid or evil then he alone is at fault. When a woman does something brilliant it is because she is an exception and the stereotype of women as a group is unaffected. This style of argument was adopted by Joseph Swetnam, *The Araignment of Lewd, Idle, Froward and Unconstant Women* (London, 1616); Thomas Fuller, *Holy State* (London, 1642); Robert Cleaver, *A Godly Form of Household Government* (London, 1598); William Gouge, *Of Domesticall Duties: Eight Treatises* (London, 1634).

40. Knox, 25.
41. Basilius Magnus, cited in ibid.
42. Ibid., 29.
43. Ibid., 25.
44. Ibid., 20.
45. Ibid., 37–39.
46. Ibid., 27.
47. Ibid.
48. Stone, 52; Schochet, 415–421.
49. Cleaver.
50. Gouge.
51. Ibid., 270–271.
52. Ibid., 394–397.
53. Swetnam. Rebuttals included E. Sowernam, *Esther Hath Hanged Haman* (London, 1617); C. Munda, *The Worming of a Mad Dog* (London, 1617); R. Speght, *A Mouzell for Melastonmus* (London, 1617); no author, *J. Swetnam, The Womanhater Arraigned by Women* (London, 1620).
54. "Homily on Marriage" (1562), cited in Stone, 52–53.
55. Ibid.
56. Thomas Fuller, cited in ibid., 51.
57. John Smyth recorded this saying in *The History of the Hundred of Berkeley*, ed. J. MacLean (Gloucester, 1885):32.
58. Cleaver; Gouge, 397; Stone, 26. This is in opposition to the medieval theological decree that "a man must castigate his wife and beat her for her correction, for the Lord must punish his own as is written in Cratian's Decretum," quoted in G. G. Coulton (ed.), *Life in the Middle Ages*, Vol. 3 (New York: Macmillan, 1910):119.
59. Ariès, 258–264; John R. Gillis, *Youth and History* (New York: Academic Press, 1974); Stone, 37, 40.
60. Stone, 34–57.
61. D. Hunt, *Parents and Children in History: The Psychology of Family Life in Early Modern France* (New York: Basic Books, 1970):134.
62. Ariès, 258; Gillis; Stone, 40.
63. Nicole Castan, "Divers aspects de la constrainte maritale, d'après les documents judiciaires du XVIIIe siècle," trans. Kath Ryall (Paper presented to the American Sociological Association Convention, New York City, August 1976):5.

64. Ibid., 5.

65. Ibid., 6.

66. Ibid., 9.

67. Ibid., 5.

68. Ibid., 6.

69. Ibid., 11.

70. Cobbe, 56.

71. Ibid., 63.

72. Ibid., 64.

73. Reverend F. W. Harper, quoted in ibid. This also supported the principle of nonintervention in family matters.

74. See Natalie Zemon Davis, "The Reasons of Misrule: Youth Groups and Charivaris in Sixteenth Century France," *Past and Present* 50 (February 1971):41–75; Gillis; A contemporary practice that simulates this inversion of status is Sadie Hawkins Day, which is held once a year in some American schools. For this one day, the girls are allowed to chase the boys, ask them to go out, etc.

75. Edward Shorter, *The Making of the Modern Family* (Glasgow: Fontana/Collins, 1977):54, 71–72, 216–224; Rowbotham, 7.

76. Davis, 55–62; E. P. Thompson, *The Making of the English Working Class* (Baltimore: Penguin, Pelican Books, 1963):448, and "Rough Music: 'Le Charivari anglais,' " *Annales (Economics, Societies, Civilizations)* 27 (2) (1972):302.

77. Cobbe, notes on 56–57.

78. Ibid., 56.

79. Ibid., 57.

80. Shorter, 220.

81. Ibid. See also forthcoming work by Keith Thomas, Oxford historian, on the history of humor and charades.

82. As Shorter, 220–221, indicated, "Since men were seen as the natural bearers of authority, their abuses of authority were met with considerably greater tolerance than their failures to be in control." See also O'Faolain and Martines, 88; V. de Sola Pinto and A. E. Rodway (eds.), *The Common Muse* (Baltimore: Penguin, 1965):54.

83. Ariès; O'Faolain and Martines, 188; Shorter, 220–221.

84. Charles Rogers, cited in Jim Young, "Social Class and the National Question: Time Dialectics of Scottish History" (Department of History, University of Stirling, 1977).

85. Edward A. Parry, *The Law and the Woman* (London, 1916):100. Quoted in ibid. There is a branks displayed in John Knox's house in Edinburgh.

86. O'Faolain and Martines, 188.

87. Hecker; O'Faolain and Martines.

88. Hecker, 126; O'Faolain and Martines, 189.

89. Dobash and Dobash (1977a); Eisenberg and Micklow, 3; Hecker; Manchester.

90. O'Faolain and Martines, 356.

91. Ibid., 188.

92. Hecker, 126; Queen and Habenstein.

93. See Hecker, 120–139.

94. Sir William Blackstone, quoted in Manchester, 3.

95. Dobash and Dobash (1977a); Manchester, 5.

96. W. Wycherly, quoted in Stone, 50.

97. Hecker, 124–125.

98. Sir William Blackstone, quoted in Hecker, 125; see also Manchester, 4.

99. Hecker, 126. A further note illustrates how the law was prejudiced against women who might take the law that was denied them into their own hands. This discrimination was justified on the ground that women were precluded from having a place in the religious order: "By the Common Law, all women were denied the benefit of clergy; and till William and Mary they received sentence of death and might have been executed for the first offence in simple larceny, bigamy, manslaughter, etc., however learned they were, merely because their sex precluded the possibility of their taking holy orders; though a man who could read was for the same crime subject only to burning in the hand and a few months' imprisonment" (pp. 126–127). Truly a double bind of prejudices and discrimination supported by both church and state. For a summary of the common law with all its glaring injustices see Pollock and Maitland.

100. Hecker, 127.

101. Ibid., 125.

102. Blackstone, 444; Eisenberg and Micklow, 3; Hecker, 125.

103. Hecker, 125–126.

104. Sir Richard Steele, quoted in ibid., 126.

105. J. Prebble, *The Lion in the North: A Personal View of Scotland's History* (London: Secker & Warburg, 1971):298.

106. John Demos, *A Little Commonwealth* (New York: Oxford, 1970):93, cited in B. Laslett, 487; Edmund S. Morgan, *The Puritan Family* (New York: Harper, 1944):39–40.

107. *Bradley v. State* (1824), quoted in Eisenberg and Micklow, 4.

108. *Bread's Case* (Date) and *Adams v. Adams* cited in Eisenberg and Micklow, 4–5.

109. *State v. Rhodes*, 61 North Carolina, 349 (1868), quoted in Eisenberg and Micklow, 5.

110. Cobbe, 64.

111. Ibid., 76–77; Manchester, 12; Jim Young, "Wife-Beating in Britain: A Socio-historical Analysis, 1850–1914" (Paper presented to the American Sociological Association Convention, New York City, August 1976).

112. A. B. Chapman and M. W. Chapman, *The Status of Women under English Law: A Compendious Epitome of Legislative Enactment and Social and*

Political Events Arranged as a Continuous Narrative with References to Authorities and Acts of Parliament (London: Routledge and Sons, 1910):70.

113. For the cases defining cruelty see *Kelly v. Kelly* (1869) and *Russell v. Russell* (1897), cited in Manchester, 10–11, and in P. R. H. Webb, "Matrimonial Cruelty: A Lawyer's Guide for the Medical Profession," *Medicine, Science, and Law* 7 (1969):110–116. See also Chapman and Chapman, 71; E. M. Clive and V. G. Wilson, *The Law of Husband and Wife in Scotland* (Edinburgh: Green, 1974); Cobbe, 77; R. Emerson Dobash, Catherine Cavanagh, and Monica Wilson, "Violence against Wives: The Legislation of the 1960's and the Policies of Indifference" (Paper presented to the National Deviancy Conference, Sheffield, April 1977); Hecker, 133–135, 137.

114. *Reg. v. Jackson* (1891), cited in Hecker, 127; see also Manchester, 4.

115. *Fulgham v. State* (1871) and *Commonwealth v. McAfee* (1871), quoted in Eisenberg and Micklow, 6.

116. Eisenberg and Micklow, 4.

117. *Fulgham v. State* (1871) and *Poor v. Poor* quoted in ibid., 5–6.

118. Stedman, cited in Eisenberg and Micklow, 6. It should be noted that the wife's duty and subjection were still required, only it was not quite so acceptable to demand them through force. One cannot help but wonder why men no longer needed the assistance of the law to control their wives. Were women willing to submit without a struggle? Were the means of coercion becoming more subtle? Or was this mere legal chicanery? The parallels with the contemporary situation will become clear in Chapter 12.

119. South Carolina had no divorce; cruelty was not a ground for divorce in Arkansas, North Carolina, Texas, and Vermont; and only *limited* divorce, i.e. separation, on the ground of cruelty was allowed in West Virginia, New York, Tennessee, Virginia, Maryland, and New Jersey. For the status of women in each state at that time see Hecker, 174–235.

120. Vera Britten, *Lady into Woman* (New York: Macmillan, 1953):24; Hecker, 127; McLaren, 16–17; Nancy Tomes, "A 'Torrent of Abuse': Crimes of Violence Between Working-Class Men and Women in London, 1840–1875," *Journal of Social History* 11 (3) (1978):329–345.

121. Ronald Pearsall, *The Worm in the Bud* (London: Weidenfeld & Nicholson, 1969):79.

122. Albie Sachs and Joan Hoff Wilson, *Sexism and the Law: A Study of Male Beliefs and Judical Bias* (Oxford: Martin Robertson, 1978).

123. Wollstonecraft.

124. Ibid., 25; For discussions of Wollstonecraft (and other early feminists) see Figes, 102–107; Margaret Walters, "The Rights and Wrongs of Women: Mary Wollstonecraft, Harriet Martineau, Simone de Beauvior," and Juliet Mitchell, "Women and Equality," in Juliet Mitchell and Ann Oakley (eds.), *The Rights and Wrongs of Women* (Baltimore: Penguin, 1976):304–399; O'Faolain and Martines, 329–330; Alice S. Rossi (ed.), *The Feminist Papers: From Adams to de Beauvoir* (New York: Bantam, 1973):25–85; Rowbotham, 39–40.

125. H. W. V. Temperley, "Sale of Wives in England in 1823," in Jo Freeman (ed.),

Women: A Feminist Perspective (Palo Alto: Mayfield, 1975):419–420; see also Manchester, 1–2; Young (1976).

126. Cobbe.

127. Chapman and Chapman, 38.

128. Ibid., 39.

129. William Thompson, *Appeal of One Half of the Human Race, WOMEN, Against the Pretensions of the Other Half, MEN, to Retain Them in Political, and Thence in CIVIL AND DOMESTIC SLAVERY* (London, 1825). See also Chapman and Chapman, 28, 38, who indicated that this work was largely disregarded, and Rowbotham, 39–46, for a discussion.

130. Hecker, 157; for a discussion see Rossi (1975):86–117.

131. Judith Hole and Ellen Levine, "Rebirth of Feminism," in Freeman, 436–447.

132. Ibid., 439; Alice S. Rossi, "Social Roots of the Women's Movement in America," in Alice S. Rossi (ed.), *The Feminist Papers* (New York: Bantam Books 1976):241–281.

133. Hecker, 159–163.

134. Ibid., 161; for a partial list see Hole and Levine, 439–440.

135. Hole and Levine, 440; Rossi (1976):241. See also Elizabeth Cady Stanton, Susan B. Anthony, Matilda Joslyn Gage, and Ida Hustred Harper (eds.), *History of Women's Suffrage* (New York: Arno Press and the New York Times, 1969; first published in 6 vols. 1881–1922):73.

136. An Act Concerning the Rights and Liabilities of Husband and Wife (1860), cited in Hecker, 163.

137. For English laws see Chapman and Chapman, 49–57, and Hecker, 120–149. For American laws see Hecker, 150–235.

138. Chapman and Chapman, 51; Manchester, 7–8; Anthony Manchester, "Reform of the Ecclesiastical Courts," *American Journal of Legal History* 10 (51) (1966).

139. The 1858 Medical Act, which resulted in the exclusion of all women except Dr. Elizabeth Blackwell from the British Medical Register, the Contagious Diseases Act of 1866, and the Reform Acts, 1832 and 1835, cited in Chapman and Chapman, 38, 47–48, 52–54.

140. A. Dowling, *Reports of Cases Argued and Determined in the Queen's Bench Practice Courts* (London, 1841):630. In 1852 the opposite judgment was given in the case of *Rex v. Leggat*, cited in Manchester, 4, and O'Faolain and Martines, 330–331.

141. O'Faolain and Martines, 330–331.

142. Married Women's Property Act of 1857, quoted in Hecker, 132, and Chapman and Chapman, 51.

143. Chapman and Chapman, 63.

144. Wanda Neff, *Victorian Working Women* (New York: Columbia University Press, 1929):72. Another case, cited in Hecker, 132, and in Cobbe, 61, illustrates the extreme exploitation that had been legal until that time: "A lady whose husband had been unsuccessful in business established herself as a milliner in Manchester. After some years of toil she realised sufficient for the

family to live upon comfortably, the husband having done nothing mean-
while. They lived for a time in easy circumstances after she gave up business
and then the husband died, *bequeathing all his wife's earnings to his own illegitimate children.* At the age of 62 she was compelled, in order to gain her
bread, to return to business."

145. Henry Fitzroy, quoted in Manchester, 11. 124 Hansard's Parliamentary
Debates (3rd sec.) 1414, 1853. Fitzroy asked that Parliament extend to women
the same protection "as they already extended to poodle dogs and donkeys, for
cruelty to which a person subjected himself, under the Cruelty to Animals Act,
to three months imprisonment, with or without hard labor." See also Cobbe,
76–77; Dobash, Cavanagh, and Wilson, 4; Young (1976):9. In July 1975 Jack
Asheley, M.P., addressed the Commons in an almost identical fashion in support of the second reading of his Battered Wives (Rights to Possession of the
Matrimonial Home) Bill, which would have given the wife of a man convicted
of an act of violence against her possession of the matrimonial home if she applied for such an order. He maintained that about twenty-five thousand
women in Britain were habitually beaten up and yet there were only 30 refuges
for battered women. He stated: "I do not think society can view this situation
with anything but the most profound concern. . . . The purpose of the Bill is
to secure action for a section of the community which has suffered very
seriously from the worst possible kind of violence." The bill was about "great
brutality, beating, burning and battering, breaking bones and crushing
spirits." Asheley maintained that "what we need is a sanctuary for battered
wives in every town and city in this land." And speaking of a recent uproar
about the cruelty and inhumanity of using dogs for experiments with smoking,
he maintained, "It is really beyond comprehension how people can be more
concerned about beagles than about battered wives. Why do so many millions
of people become outraged at a couple of beagles smoking and no-one is concerned with battered wives? What has gone wrong with our values?" The Conservative M.P., Ronald Bell, opposed the bill because he said it referred to any
act of violence no matter how slight and because the possession order would be
made mandatory by the court and there would be complete right of possession
for the wife. *Slough* (Buckinghamshire) *Evening Mail,* July 14, 1975. The bill
was not passed at that time.

146. Cobbe, 76–77.
147. Chapman and Chapman, 51, see 1857 marriage laws.
148. Reverend W. M. Cooper, quoted in Young (1976):4.
149. Chapman and Chapman, 53–54.
150. Ibid.
151. Ibid., 44.
152. John Stuart Mill, *The Subjection of Women* (London: Dent, 1955; first
published 1869); for a discussion see Juliet Mitchell and Ann Oakley, *The
Rights and Wrongs of Women.* (Baltimore: Penguin, 1976):393–399.
153. Mill, 246–265.
154. Ibid., 295–296.
155. Cobbe, 78; 219 Hansard's Parliamentary Debates (3rd ser.) (1874):396. See
also Manchester, 12.

156. Computed from Parliamentary Papers (1875); see also Cobbe, 71–72.

157. Cobbe, 71.

158. Computed from Parliamentary Papers (1875).

159. The underreporting rate in our own study was 98%.

160. Cobbe, 79; Manchester, 13.

161. Parliamentary Papers (1875):130.

162. Ibid., 131.

163. *Transactions of the National Association for the Promotion of Social Science* (1876):345; Cobbe, 81.

164. Cobbe, 79.

165. Ibid.

166. Ibid., 73–76.

167. Ibid., 64, 65, 67, 70, 73, 75.

168. Ibid., 62–63.

169. Ibid., 7; Manchester, 15; Young (1976):6. Supposedly this clause was inspired by Frances Power Cobbe and pushed through the Commons by a friend of hers. Opposition was largely avoided because the vote was taken around midnight. Comments by Jim Young at the Conference of Socialist Economists, Stirling, Scotland, April 1978.

170. Britten, 24; Cobbe, 72; Tomes, 330.

171. Pearsall, 79.

172. Manchester, 8.

173. McLaren, 15–17, 70.

174. Ibid., 16, 70.

175. Young (1976):9; For an account of similar judicial opinion supporting the husband's authority and rights of chastisement and advocating leniency for wifebeaters see Edward W. Cox, *The Principles of Punishment, As Applied in the Administration of the Criminal Law, By Judges and Magistrates* (London: Law Times Office, 1877):90–106.

176. See Davidoff; Elizabeth Pleck, "Wife Beating in Nineteenth-Century America," Unpublished Paper, University of Michigan; Joan Scott and Louise Tilly, "Women's Work and the Family in Nineteenth-Century Europe," in Charles E. Rosenburg (ed.), *The Family in History* (Philadelphia: University of Pennsylvania Press, 1975); Tomes.

Chapter 5 Becoming a Wife

1. Norway and Australia recently introduced legislation that makes them the first countries which no longer support a husband's unquestioned right to exercise his conjugal rights against his wife's wishes. Under certain circumstances, husbands can now be charged with raping their wives.

2. This means that even those women who have highly skilled or professional jobs are still treated differently simply because their sex and marital status are seen as pivotal to their conditions of employment and advancement. See Cynthia Fuchs

Epstein, *Woman's Place: Options and Limits in Professional Careers* (Berkeley: University of California Press, 1970):31, 65, 92–100; Mirra Komarovsky, "Cultural Contradictions and Sex Roles," *American Journal of Sociology* 52 (Nov.) (1946):184–189; Ann Oakley, *Housewife* (London: Allen Lane, 1974a):80–90; Talcott Parsons, "Age and Sex in the Social Structure of the United States," *American Sociological Review* (1942):604–616; Alice S. Rossi, "Equality between the Sexes: An Immodest Proposal," *Daedalus* 93 (2) (Spring 1964):607–652, and "Women in Science: Why So Few?" *Science* 148 (3674) 1196–1202. This also means that men have considerable difficulties if they wish to remain at home and care for children.

3. Dahl and Snare; Frankford and Snitow; Secombe.

4. For an uncritical view of this concept see R. Blood and D. Wolfe, *Husbands and Wives* (New York: Free Press, 1960); Parsons; and most textbooks on the sociology of the family. For a critical view see Pauline B. Bart, "Sexism and Social Science: From the Gilded Cage to the Iron Cage, or the Perils of Pauline," *Journal of Marriage and the Family* 33 (4) (1971b):734–745; Chafetz; Beauvoir, 445–568, 689–724; Norman Dennis, Fernando Henriques, and Clifford Slaughter, *Coal Is Our Life: An Analysis of a Yorkshire Mining Community*, 2d ed. (London: Tavistock, 1969):171–245; Epstein; Komarovsky; Marcia Millman, "Observations on Sex Role Research," *Journal of Marriage and the Family* 33 (4) (1971):772–776; Oakley (1974a); Rossi, 1964; Julia Schwendinger and Herman Schwendinger, "Sociology's Founding Fathers: Sexist to a Man," *Journal of Marriage and the Family* 33 (4) (1971):783–799.

5. Studies of American, British, and French housewives conducted between 1929 and 1971 showed that most women spent between 51 and 82 hours a week performing domestic tasks with an average of 67 hours. Oakley (1974a):94. The Chase Manhattan Bank has estimated that housework takes 98 hours a week. The nature and extent of the commitment the woman is supposed to give to the domestic sphere of her life has been poignantly illustrated by MacLeod, who inverted the advice to a bride and made it the advice to a bridegroom. Jennifer MacLeod, cited in Bart (1971b):737–738.

6. E. H. Erikson, "Inner and Outer Space: Reflections on Womanhood," *Daedalus* 93 (1964). For a critical examination of this and other similar conceptions of women see Phyllis Chesler, "Women as Psychiatric and Psychotherapeutic Patients," *Journal of Marriage and the Family* 33 (4) (1971b):746–759. Research has shown the negative evaluation attached to those women who live up to this ideal image. Donald Broverman, Inge K. Broverman, F. E. Clarkson, P. S. Rosenkrantz, and S. R. Vogel, "Sex-Role Stereotypes and Clinical Judgements of Mental Health," *Journal of Consulting and Clinical Psychology* 34 (1970), showed that when therapists were asked to list the characteristics of a healthy, socially competent adult without specification of sex, they used similar terms to those they later used to describe a healthy adult male. Yet, their description of a healthy adult female contained characteristics that, had they been applied to males, would have been considered unhealthy, socially undesirable, and/or pathological.

7. Elena Belotti, *Little Girls: Social Conditioning and Its Effects on the Stereotyped*

Role of Women during Infancy (London: Writers and Readers Publishing Cooperative, 1975).

8. Ibid., 16.

9. Ibid., 15.

10. Ibid.

11. Ibid., 30–31.

12. Ibid., 26; see also Simon Dinitz, Russell R. Dynes, and Alfred C. Clarke, "Preferences for Male or Female Children: Traditional or Affectional?" *Marriage and Family Living* (May 1954):128–130; Amitai Etzioni, "Sex, Control, Science, and Society," *Science* (Sept. 13, 1968):1107–1112; Leslie, 279; John P. McKee and Alex C. Sherriffs, "The Differential Evaluation of Males and Females," *Journal of Personality* (March 1957):356–371.

13. Belotti, 22–23; Etzioni.

14. Belotti 32–40.

15. Ibid., 43–44.

16. On sex role socialization see David Aberle and Kasper Naegele, "Middle-Class Fathers' Occupational Role and Attitudes toward Children," *American Journal of Orthopsychiatry*, April (1952):366–378; Sandra L. Bem and Daryl J. Bem, "Case Study of a Nonconscious Ideology: Training the Woman to Know Her Place," in Daryl J. Bem (ed.), *Beliefs, Attitudes, and Human Affairs* (Belmont: Brooks/Cole, 1970):89–99; Urie Bronfenbrenner, "Socialization and Social Class through Time and Space," in Eleanor E. Maccoby et al. (eds.), *Readings in Social Psychology* (New York: Holt, Rinehart, 1958):400–425, "Freudian Theories of Identification and Their Derivatives," *Child Development* 31 (March 1960):15–40, and "Some Familial Antecedents of Responsibility and Leadership in Adolescents," in L. Petrullo and B. Bass (eds.), *Leadership and Interpersonal Behavior* (New York: Holt, Rinehart, 1961):267; Chafetz; Epstein, 50–85; Melvin Kohn, *Class and Conformity* (Homewood: Dorsey, 1969):52–59, 120–125; Komarovsky; Ann Oakley, *The Sociology of Housework* (London: Martin Robertson, 1974b):113–134; Talcott Parsons and Robert F. Bales, *Family, Socialization, and Interaction Process* (New York: Free Press, 1955):45; Talcott Parsons, "The Normal American Family," in Arlene Skolnick and Jerome Skolnick (eds.), *Family in Transition: Rethinking Marriage, Sexuality, Child Rearing, and Family Organization* (Boston: Little, Brown, 1971):397–402; Lenore J. Weitzman, "Sex-Role Socialization" (1975a), in Freeman, 105–144; William H. Whyte, "The Wife Problem," *Life*, January 7, 1952, reprinted in R. Winch, R. McGinnis, and H. Baringer (eds.), *Selected Studies in Marriage and Family* (New York: Holt, Rinehart & Winston, 1962).

17. Belotti, 35.

18. Ibid., 31.

19. Ibid., 27.

20. Ibid., 60–61.

21. Ibid., 14; see also Bem and Bem.

22. Belotti, 47, 66.

23. Ibid., 52; see also Daniel G. Brown, "Sex-Role Preference in Young Children,"

Psychological Monographs 70 (14) (1956):1–19; Ruth E. Hartley, "Sex-Role Pressures and the Socialization of the Male Child," *Psychological Reports* 5 (1959):457–468; Willard W. Hartup, "Some Correlates of Parental Imitation in Young Children," *Child Development* 33 (1962):85–96; Willard W. Hartup and Elsie A. Zook, "Sex-Role Preference in Three- and Four-year-old Children," *Journal of Consulting Psychology* 24 (December 1960):420–426; Alex Inkeles, "Society, Social Structure, and Child Socialization," in J. Clausen (ed.), *Socialization and Society* (Boston: Little, Brown, 1968):73–129; Meyer L. Rabban, "Sex-Role Identification in Young Children in Two Diverse Social Groups," *Genetic Psychological Monographs* 42 (1950):81–158; S. Smith, "Age and Sex Differences in Children's Opinions Concerning Sex Differences," *Journal of Genetic Psychology* 54 (1939):17–25; Godwin Watson, *Social Psychology: Issues and Insights* (Philadelphia: Lippincott, 1966):477; Weitzman (1975a).

24. Belotti, 70–72.

25. Marketing girls and young women for marriage is big business. Advertising, especially in bride, fashion, and housewife magazines, pushes makeup, clothing, slimming, athletics, etc., and this contributes to the image of the physically acceptable, beautiful, desirable female who can attract males.

26. Few girls are encouraged to think about what they are going to be as adults other than that they should get married and have children. For many, this successfully robs them of a conception of a future as an autonomous individual.

27. Conference of Socialist Economists, "On the Political Economy of Women" (1975), Pamphlet no. 2. (Available from 21 Theobalds Road, London, England); Department of Employment, *Women and Work: A Statistical Survey*, Manpower Paper no. 9 (London: HMSO, 1974); Epstein, 6; Freeman, 211–276; Audrey Hunt, *Survey of Women's Employment* (London: HMSO, 1968); Martin, 41–42; U.S. Department of Labor, Women's Bureau, "Twenty Facts on Women Workers" (Washington D.C.: U.S. Government Printing Office, June 1975); Zaretsky, 23–25.

28. John Bowlby, *Child Care and the Growth of Love* (Baltimore: Penguin, 1955).

29. For a critique of this and similar work see Rochelle Wortis, "The Acceptance of the Concept of the Maternal Role by Behavioral Scientists: Its Effects on Women," *American Journal of Orthopsychiatry* 41 (5) (1971):733–746.

30. Bruno Bettelheim, "The Commitment Required of a Woman Entering a Scientific Profession in Present Day American Society," in *Women and the Scientific Professions* (Westport: Greenwood, 1965).

31. *Basingstoke Gazette*, July 9, 1975.

32. R. Emerson Dobash and Russell P. Dobash, "Wife Beating: Still a Common Form of Violence," *Social Work Today* 9 (12) (1977b):14–17; Dobash and Dobash (1978).

33. Eisenberg and Micklow, 23.

34. Dobash and Dobash (1977b); Lenore J. Weitzman, "To Love, Honor, and Obey? Traditional Legal Marriage and Alternative Family Forms," *Family Coordinator* 24 (4) (1975b):543–547, and reprinted in Skolnick and Skolnick (2d ed.), 288–313.

Chapter 6 The Violent Event

1. See Eisenberg and Micklow; Gelles (1974); John R. Hepburn, "Violent Behavior in Interpersonal Relationships," *Sociological Quarterly* 14 (Summer 1973):419–429; Toch; David Luckenbill, "Criminal Homicide as a Situated Transaction," *Social Problems* 25 (2) (1977):176–186.

2. Hepburn.

3. Ibid., 420.

4. James McBeth, "The Agony of a Man Who Beats his Wife," *Daily Record*, March 24, 1977.

5. Dennis, Henriques, and Slaughter.

6. Eisenberg and Micklow.

7. Martin.

8. Quoted in Eisenberg and Micklow, 27.

9. Gelles (1974):139.

10. Toch, 144–145.

11. On this point also see Hepburn, 423.

12. Toch, 166.

13. Ibid., 167.

14. Hepburn, 423–425.

15. Ibid., 424.

16. Toch, 167; see also Jackson Toby, "Violence and the Masculine Ideal," *Annals of the American Academy of Political and Social Science* 364 (March 1966):20–27.

17. Gelles (1974):84.

18. Martin, 2.

19. Dennis, Henriques, and Slaughter, 230.

20. Toch, 174–175.

21. Tracy Johnston, "When He Stopped Beating His Wife," *San Francisco News Weekly*, July 6, 1975; also cited in Martin, 86.

22. Eisenberg and Micklow, 26.

23. Gelles (1974):52.

24. Kicking and standing on women was practiced with hobnail boots in Yorkshire during the late nineteenth century and was called "purring."

25. "Express Woman: The Other Side of the Battered Wife Syndrome," *Daily Express*, September 8, 1976.

26. Stuart Palmer, *The Violent Society* (New Haven: Yale University Press, 1972):46.

27. Eisenberg and Micklow, 27.

28. Gelles (1974):33.

29. Gelles goes on in the same chapter to discuss the presence of children during an assault.

30. See ibid.; Hepburn; Toch.

31. Faulkner's work on violence among ice hockey players illustrated a situation in which a supportive audience reinforced and indeed demanded the use of physical force.

32. Eisenberg and Micklow, 29.

33. Martin, 2.

34. Eisenberg and Micklow, 29.

35. Michele Kamisher, "Behind Closed Doors," *Real Paper*, November 2, 1976.

36. See Gelles (1974):113–118 for a discussion of the role of alcohol in violent events and C. H. McCaghy, "Drinking and Deviance Disavowal: The Case of Child Molesters," *Social Problems* 16 (1) (1968):43–49, for an example of the use of alcohol in disavowing responsibility for a socially unacceptable form of deviance.

37. G. W. Sykes and D. Matza, "Techniques of Neutralization: A Theory of Delinquency," *American Sociological Review* 22 (December 1957):667–670, considered several techniques that adolescents use in dealing with their feelings regarding delinquent acts; two of these are "denial of responsibility" and "denial of the victim," or blaming the victim.

38. Toch, 25–26.

39. Gay Search, "Notes from Abroad: London Battered Wives," *Ms.* 3 (June 1974):24–26.

40. Leghorn and Warrior.

41. Wolfgang.

42. Lynn A. Curtis, *Criminal Violence* (Lexington: Lexington Books, 1974).

43. Gelles (1974):95–107.

44. D. J. Pittman and W. Handy, "Patterns in Criminal Aggravated Assault," *Journal of Criminal Law, Criminology, and Police Science* 55 (4) (1964):462–470; McClintock (1963a).

45. Wolfgang; Pokornoy.

46. Gelles (1974):97.

47. The exception being the bathroom, though women did tell us about attacks while they were in the bath. The fact that violent attacks rarely occur in the bathroom substantiates our point. It is the one room in the house where husbands and wives very rarely come together.

48. Cf. Gelles (1974):95; Pittman and Handy, 465; Wolfgang, 378.

Chapter 7   The Violent Marriage

1. Dahl and Snare.

2. Anthony Storr, *Human Aggression* (Baltimore: Penguin, 1974):95.

3. Dennis Marsden and David Owen, "The Jekyll and Hyde Marriages," *New Society* 7 (May 1975):335.

4. Ibid., 333.

5. Gelles (1974):156.

6. Ibid., 157.

7. Ibid., 158.

8. Ibid., 160–161.

9. Ibid., 160.

10. Ibid., 163.

11. Storr.

12. M. Jobling, "Battered Wives: A Survey," *Social Service Quarterly* 47 (14) (1974):142–146.

13. See discussion of Rader's arguments in Letty Cottin Pogrebin, "Do Women Make Men Violent?" *Ms.* 3 (November 1974):49–55, 80.

14. Wolfgang; Curtis, 598.

15. Dobash and Dobash (1977a):403–415.

Chapter 8   Staying, Leaving, and Returning

1. See Elizabeth Truninger, "Marital Violence: The Legal Solutions," *Hastings Law Journal* 23 (1) (1971):259–276.

2. Ibid.

3. Ibid.

4. Ibid., 260–261.

5. Bonnie E. Carlson, "Battered Women and Their Assailants," *Social Work* 22 (6) (1977):455–460.

6. Maria Roy, "A Current Survey of 150 Cases," in Roy, 25–44.

7. Levinger.

8. O'Brien.

9. Richard Gelles, "Abused Wives: Why Do They Stay?" *Journal of Marriage and the Family* 38 (November 1976):659–668.

10. Cf. Gelles (1974):59–60; Murray A. Straus, "Leveling, Civility, and Violence in the Family," *Journal of Marriage and the Family* 36 (February 1974):13–15; Raymond Parnas, "The Police Response to Domestic Disturbance," *Wisconsin Law Review* (Fall 1967):952.

11. Cf. Schultz; Snell, Rosenwald, and Robey.

12. R. Emerson Dobash, "The Relationship between Violence Directed at Women and Violence Directed at Children within the Family Setting," Appendix 38, Parliamentary Select Committee on Violence in the Family (London: HMSO, 1976–1977):145. These cases include the 791 court cases appearing in Tables 4 & 5 as well as 142 additional cases from 1974; 169 which appeared in the police blotter but did not appear in the court records either because they went to another court or because there was no final disposal at the time of the above publication and 5 for which a disposals became available after the HMSO publication. The 933 cases referred to in the text represent the 791 court cases included in Tables 4 and 5 in Appendix B and 142 additional cases of wife assault. These additional cases were not included in the overall analysis of violent of-

fenses because technical problems regarding data collection made it impossible
to compare them directly to other violent offenses. However, these problems
did not preclude us from comparing them to other cases of wife assault.

13. Ibid., 144.
14. See Dahl and Snare; Epstein; Frankford and Snitow; Heidi Hartmann,
    "Capitalism, Patriarchy and Job Segregation by Sex," *Signs: Journal of Women
    in Culture and Society* 1 (3, 2) (1976):137–169; Secombe; Zaretsky.
15. Department of Employment, *Women and Work*; Hunt; Juanita Kreps, *Sex in
    the Marketplace: American Women at Work* (Baltimore: Johns Hopkins Press,
    1971); *Signs: Journal of Women in Culture and Society*, special issue on
    "Women and National Development," 3 (1) (1977); U.S. Department of Labor,
    "Twenty Facts"; J. A. Weiss, F. O. Ramirez and T. Tracy, "Female Participation
    in the Occupational System: A Comparative Institutional Analysis," *Social
    Problems* 23 (5) (1976):593–608.
16. Morris Finer, *Report of the Committee on One-Parent Families* (London:
    HMSO, 1975).
17. Martin, 39–43, 119–147, 188–192.
18. Veronica Beechey, "Some Notes on Female Wage Labour in Capitalist Produc-
    tion," *Capital and Class* (Autumn 1977):45–66; Francine D. Blau, "Women in
    the Labor Force: An Overview," in Freeman, 211–226; M. Blaxall and B. Reagan
    (eds.), *Women and the Workplace: The Implications of Occupational Segrega-
    tion*, Vol. 1 (Chicago: University of Chicago Press, 1976); Conference of
    Socialist Economists; Department of Employment, "Women and Work"; Ep-
    stein; Hunt; Kathleen Shortridge, "Working Poor Women," in Freeman,
    242–253.
19. Martin, 42.
20. Pizzey, 34–35, 42, 48, 51, 81, for accounts of women who were trapped at least
    partially because of a lack of money.
21. Eisenberg and Micklow, 30.
22. Martin, 84.
23. The Domestic Violence Act of 1977 (England) does allow for the eviction of a
    violent husband of cohabitant but this is only for a short period of time. See also
    community property laws in various states of America.
24. Gelles (1974):58–61; Parliamentary Select Committee on Violence in Marriage,
    Report from the Select Committee on Violence in Marriage, Vol. 2 (London:
    HMSO, 1975b):209.
25. Gayford (1975b); Select Committee on Violence in Marriage (1975b):173;
    Schultz; Snell, Rosenwald, and Robey; Storr. For other references to such ideas
    see Elliot Liebow, *Tally's Corner* (Boston: Little, Brown, 1966):78–83, 130–136;
    Mario Suárez, "Tucson, Arizona: Las Comadres," in Luis Valdez and Stan
    Steiner (eds.), *Aztlán: An Anthology of Mexican American Literature* (New
    York: Random House, Vintage Books, 1972):157–163. For women's objections
    to this conception see the section "Songs of Sorrow," which contains the poem
    "La Firolera." Chorus (pp. 264–265):

> My man has now died
> The devil has taken him
> Surely, he is paying
> For the kicks he gave me
> every day.

In fifteenth- and sixteenth-century Spanish literature there was a genre referred to as *la mal casada*, the badly married woman, which included the topic of battering. For this information we are grateful to Mac Malkowski.

26. See pp. 127–137, 193–200.

Chapter 9   Relatives, Friends, and Neighbors

1. *The Guardian*, April 27, 1977.

2. Ibid; *London Daily Telegraph*, April 23, 1977.

3. Eisenberg and Micklow, 126.

4. *St. Louis Globe-Democrat*, December 18 and 19, 1976.

5. Eisenberg and Micklow, 126–130.

6. James Bannon, "Law Enforcement Problems with Intra-Family Violence" (Paper presented to the American Bar Association Convention, August 1975):4.

7. See Bannon; Eisenberg and Micklow; Marjory Fields, "Wife-Beating: The Hidden Offense" (Available from Brooklyn Legal Services Corporation B, Matrimonial Unit, 152 Court Street, Brooklyn, New York 11201); Helene Pepe, "Wife Abuse: Does the American Legal System Offer Adequate Protection to the Abused Wife?" (Paper presented to the American Sociological Association Convention, New York City, August 1976); Wolfgang.

8. Gelles (1974):108.

9. Elston, Fuller, and Murch; Gelles (1974):58; Marsden and Owen, 333; Pepe, 1.

10. Catherine Cavanagh, "Battered Women and Social Control: A Study of the Help-Seeking Behaviour of Battered Women and the Help-Giving Behaviour of Those from Whom They Seek Help," Master's thesis, University of Stirling, 1978; Eisenberg and Micklow; Elston, Fuller, and Murch; Gayford (1975b):196.

11. Eleanor Kremen, "The 'Discovery' of Battered Wives: Considerations for the Development of a Social Service Network" (Paper presented to the American Sociological Association Convention, New York City, August 1976); Jan Pahl, *A Refuge for Battered Women: A Study of the Rôle of a Women's Centre*, London: HMSO, 1978; Suzanne Prescott and Carolyn Letko, "Battered Women: A Social Psychological Perspective," in Roy, 72–97.

12. Nick Miller, *Battered Spouses*, Social Administration Trust, Occasional Paper no. 57 (London: Bell and Sons, 1975):28–29.

13. For discussions of accommodation see Gayford (1975b); Marsden and Owen; and Miller.

14. Elizabeth Elston, Jane Fuller and Mervyn Murch, "Battered Wives: The Problem of Violence in Marriage as Experienced by a Group of Petitioners in Undefended

Divorce Cases." (Available from Department of Social Work, University of Bristol, Bristol, England, 1976):14.

15. See Metzger, 19.

16. Elston, Fuller, and Murch, 24.

17. Ibid., 23.

18. *Manchester Guardian*, May 17, 1977.

19. Ibid.

20. Ibid.

21. Gelles (1974):109.

22. Dobash (1976–1977):144–145.

23. It cannot be overlooked that about a quarter of police fatalities in America occur when police respond to domestic disputes. This statistic reflects, at least to some extent, the availability of firearms and the lack of training with such cases. Although this statistic is very serious it must be placed in perspective both in terms of the very large proportion of police work that involves domestic disputes and in terms of the behavior of police in other life-threatening situations, say, armed robberies, from which they do not flee.

Chapter 10   The Helping Professions

1. This is less likely in countries that have very expensive health care or private health insurance. Poor people and people on tight budgets may not seek medical treatment except for major illnesses or injuries and even the more affluent may not seek needed care because of the financial strain it imposes upon them. Health care is available to all British residents and is prepaid through a national health insurance system.

2. In 1974, the Nottingham Women's Aid group met with medical students working in the casualty ward of the local hospital in order to seek their assistance in determining the extent of casualties resulting from assaults on women in the home. The students agreed to help, and during a three-month period they recorded the number of women who *spontaneously* reported that they had received their injuries at the hands of their husbands. Two hundred cases of assaults on wives were recorded. During a subsequent three-month period, the students devoted additional time to interviewing each injured woman who sought treatment. When each woman was asked whether she had been assaulted by her husband, 600 answered yes, a threefold increase. This informal, unpublished study reveals the extraordinary reluctance of women to report the source of injury through fear of reprisal. We obtained this information from Jo Sutton, first national coordinator of the National Women's Aid Federation.

3. Patrick S. Byrne and Barrie E. Long, *Doctors Talking to Patients* (London: HMSO, 1976):137.

4. Ibid., 139.

5. Robert Chester, "Health and Marriage Breakdown," *British Journal of Preventive and Social Medicine* 25 (November 1971):231–235; Elston, Fuller, and

Murch, 17; Margaret Gregory, "Battered Wives," in Marie Borland (ed.), *Violence in the Family* (Manchester: Manchester University Press, 1976):107–128; Marsden and Owens, 335; Bruce J. Rounsaville, "Battered Wives: Barriers to Identification and Treatment," *American Journal of Orthopsychiatry* 48 (3) (1978):487–494.

6. See also Eisenberg and Micklow, 100; Gregory, 126; Kremen, 11; Miller, 31.

7. Eisenberg and Micklow, 100.

8. Ibid., 100–102.

9. Michael Balint, *The Doctor, His Patient, and the Illness*, 2d ed. (New York: Pitman Paperbacks, 1968):222–223.

10. Ibid.

11. Byrne and Long, 194.

12. Ibid.

13. P. A. Parrish, "The Prescribing of Psychotropic Drugs in General Practice," Pamphlet published by *Journal of Royal College of General Practitioners*, supp. 4, 21 (November 1971):58.

14. Byrne and Long, 144.

15. For a discussion of 55 of these techniques see ibid., 32–61.

16. They also found that 5% were distinctly negative, 21% were patient-centered, and 1.5% were collaborative. Ibid., 155. For a good patient-centered example see ibid., 91, 101–103, 106.

17. Ibid., 150.

18. Ibid., 76–77, 105, 116, 138–139.

19. Ibid., 117.

20. Ibid.

21. See S. Bloom, *The Doctor and His Patient* (New York: Russell Sage, 1963); Peter Barnet, David Metcalfe, and Barbara Hodgson, "Doctors and Counsellors: The Hull Experiment," *Marriage Guidance* (July 1970). Ann Cartwright, *Patients and Their Doctors* (London: Routledge & Kegan Paul, 1967); M. Goss, "Influence and Authority among Physicians in an Outpatient Clinic," *American Sociological Review* 26 (February 1961):39–50; Arnold I. Kisch and Leo G. Reeder, "Client Evaluation of Physician Performance," *Journal of Health and Social Behavior* 10 (March 1969):51–58; O. Peterson, "An Analytical Study of North Carolina General Practice, *Journal of Medical Education* 31 (December 1956):1–165; Thomas J. Scheff, "Negotiating Reality: Notes on Power in the Assessment of Responsibility," *Social Problems* 16 (Summer 1968):3–17; Charlotte Schwartz, "Strategies and Tactics of Mothers of Mentally Retarded Children for Dealing with the Medical Care System," in Norman Bernstein (ed.), *Diminished People: The Problems and Care of the Mentally Retarded* (Boston: Little, Brown, 1970); W. Stewart, "Promoting the Group Practice of Medicine," in *Report of the National Conference on Group Practice* (Washington D.C.: U.S. Government Printing Office, October 1967); Robert Weiss, "Helping Relationships: Relationships of Clients with Physicians, Social Workers, Priests, and Others," *Social Problems* 20 (3) (1973):319–328.

22. Byrne and Long, 122.

23. Select Committee on Violence in Marriage (1975b):209.

24. Ibid., 173.

25. It should be noted that this stance of nonintervention was also taken during the early 1960s in response to attempts to set up reporting and referral services for abused children.

26. Eisenberg and Micklow, 39.

27. Byrne and Long, 95.

28. Eisenberg and Micklow, 101. See also Rounsville, 491; when this researcher asked MD's about battered women a number of them said they must "like it."

29. On lack of motivation to seek additional help see Miller, 23.

30. See Borland, 126.

31. Lack of recording procedures has been noted by Eisenberg and Micklow, 102; Gregory, 126; Kremen, 11. The lack of referrals has also been noted by Kremen, 11, whose telephone survey of New York hospitals revealed that one large hospital had made only 2 referrals of battered women to social work departments during a six-month period in 1976 and that another had only made 25 referrals in seven years. See also Miller, 31; S. Smith and S. Noble, "Battered Children and Their Parents," *New Society*, November 15, 1973:393. In our own study there was a very low rate of referrals to other agencies; only six women were ever referred for any assault that had been reported to their doctors.

32. It has become axiomatic that we live in a society characterized by the use of both legal and illegal drugs. The prescribing of legal drugs is especially seen as a solution to problems of powerless groups such as women, prisoners, schoolchildren, and the aged.

33. Parrish, 16.

34. Ibid., 22.

35. Ibid., 29.

36. Ibid., 40.

37. Ibid., 30.

38. Ibid., 69.

39. Ibid., 1.

40. Ibid., 17, 19, 21.

41. Cf. Balint.

42. Elston, Fuller, and Murch, 18.

43. Ibid.; see also Jan Pahl, "The Role of a Women's Refuge in Assisting the Victims of Marital Violence" (1977a), and "Selected Tables from the Report on the Canterbury Women's Centre" (1977b): tables 13 and 14 (University of Kent at Canterbury), and *A Refuge for Battered Women: A Study of the Rôle of a Women's Centre* (London: HMSO, 1978).

44. Cf. Balint.

45. Parrish, 71.

46. Elston, Fuller, and Murch, 19.

47. Parrish, 1.

48. Ibid., 71.
49. See Pauline B. Bart, "The Myth of a Value Free Psychotherapy," in W. Bell and J. Mar (eds.), *Sociology and the Future* (New York: Russell Sage, 1971); C. R. Brown and M. L. Hellinger, "Therapists' Attitudes toward Women," *Social Work* (July 1975):266–270; Phyllis Chesler, "Marriage and Psychotherapy," *Radical Therapist* 1 (3) (Aug–Sept 1970); "Patient and Patriarch: Women in the Psychotherapeutic Relationship," in Vivian Gornick and Barbara K. Moran (eds.), *Women in Sexist Society: Studies in Power and Powerlessness* (New York: New American Library, Mentor Books, 1971a):362–392, and (1971b); Beauvoir, 69–83; Karen Horney, "The Flight from Womanhood," in H. Kelman (ed.), *Feminine Psychology* (New York: Norton, 1967); Millett, 176–220; Thomas J. Scheff, *Being Mentally Ill: A Sociological Theory* (Chicago: Aldine, 1966); T. T. Szasz, *The Myth of Mental Illness* (New York: Harper, 1961); Naomi Weisstein, "Psychology Constructs the Female," in Gornick and Moran, 207–224.
50. The literature on child abuse tends to be heavily oriented to an analysis of emotional problems of abuser and abused almost to the exclusion of any other factors (especially socioeconomic and cultural ones). Those who do use a wider analysis note the multiplicity of social, cultural, economic, and personal factors that contribute to child abuse. See especially David G. Gil, "Unraveling Child Abuse," *American Journal of Orthopsychiatry* 45 (3) (1975):346–356. Also Richard J. Gelles, "Child Abuse as Psychopathology: A Sociological Critique and Reformulation," *American Journal of Orthopsychiatry* 43 (July 1973):611–621; R. E. Helfer and C. H. Kempe (eds.), The Battered Child (2nd ed., 1st ed., 1968), Chicago: The University of Chicago Press, 1974; Ronald A. Jones, "Battering Families," *Health and Social Service Journal*, February 10, 1973:313; Samuel X. Radbill, "The History of Child Abuse and Infanticide," in Helfer and Kempe, 3–21; Brandt Steele and Carol B. Pollock, "A Psychiatric Study of Parents Who Abuse Infants and Small Children," in ibid., 89–133 (a much more mixed approach); Sidney Wasserman, "The Abused Parent of the Abused Child," in Suzanne K. Steinmetz and Murray A. Straus (eds.), *Violence in the Family* (New York: Dodd, Mead, 1974):222–229.
51. This view was put forward by Freud and his followers. See by S. Freud, "Three Contributions to the Theory of Sex" (first published 1908), in A. A. Brill (ed.), *Basic Writings of Sigmund Freud* (New York: Random House, 1938); "The Economic Problems of Masochism" and "Civilized Sexual Morality and Modern Nervousness," in *Collected Papers of Sigmund Freud*, Vol. 2, "Some Character Types Met in Psycho-analysis Work" (first published 1915), in J. Riviere (ed.), *Collected Papers of Sigmund Freud*, Vol. IV (New York: Basic Books, 1959); and "Femininity," *New Introductory Lectures in Psychoanalysis* trans. James Strachey (New York: Norton, 1933). See also Bettelheim; Broverman et al; Erikson; Joseph Rheingold, *The Fear of Being a Woman* (New York: Grune and Stratton, 1964).
52. Saul.
53. Ibid., 128.
54. Ibid., 128–129.
55. Ibid., 129–130.

Psychological Monographs 70 (14) (1956):1–19; Ruth E. Hartley, "Sex-Role Pressures and the Socialization of the Male Child," *Psychological Reports* 5 (1959):457–468; Willard W. Hartup, "Some Correlates of Parental Imitation in Young Children," *Child Development* 33 (1962):85–96; Willard W. Hartup and Elsie A. Zook, "Sex-Role Preference in Three- and Four-year-old Children," *Journal of Consulting Psychology* 24 (December 1960):420–426; Alex Inkeles, "Society, Social Structure, and Child Socialization," in J. Clausen (ed.), *Socialization and Society* (Boston: Little, Brown, 1968):73–129; Meyer L. Rabban, "Sex-Role Identification in Young Children in Two Diverse Social Groups," *Genetic Psychological Monographs* 42 (1950):81–158; S. Smith, "Age and Sex Differences in Children's Opinions Concerning Sex Differences," *Journal of Genetic Psychology* 54 (1939):17–25; Godwin Watson, *Social Psychology: Issues and Insights* (Philadelphia: Lippincott, 1966):477; Weitzman (1975a).

24. Belotti, 70–72.

25. Marketing girls and young women for marriage is big business. Advertising, especially in bride, fashion, and housewife magazines, pushes makeup, clothing, slimming, athletics, etc., and this contributes to the image of the physically acceptable, beautiful, desirable female who can attract males.

26. Few girls are encouraged to think about what they are going to be as adults other than that they should get married and have children. For many, this successfully robs them of a conception of a future as an autonomous individual.

27. Conference of Socialist Economists, "On the Political Economy of Women" (1975), Pamphlet no. 2. (Available from 21 Theobalds Road, London, England); Department of Employment, *Women and Work: A Statistical Survey*, Manpower Paper no. 9 (London: HMSO, 1974); Epstein, 6; Freeman, 211–276; Audrey Hunt, *Survey of Women's Employment* (London: HMSO, 1968); Martin, 41–42; U.S. Department of Labor, Women's Bureau, "Twenty Facts on Women Workers" (Washington D.C.: U.S. Government Printing Office, June 1975); Zaretsky, 23–25.

28. John Bowlby, *Child Care and the Growth of Love* (Baltimore: Penguin, 1955).

29. For a critique of this and similar work see Rochelle Wortis, "The Acceptance of the Concept of the Maternal Role by Behavioral Scientists: Its Effects on Women," *American Journal of Orthopsychiatry* 41 (5) (1971):733–746.

30. Bruno Bettelheim, "The Commitment Required of a Woman Entering a Scientific Profession in Present Day American Society," in *Women and the Scientific Professions* (Westport: Greenwood, 1965).

31. *Basingstoke Gazette*, July 9, 1975.

32. R. Emerson Dobash and Russell P. Dobash, "Wife Beating: Still a Common Form of Violence," *Social Work Today* 9 (12) (1977b):14–17; Dobash and Dobash (1978).

33. Eisenberg and Micklow, 23.

34. Dobash and Dobash (1977b); Lenore J. Weitzman, "To Love, Honor, and Obey? Traditional Legal Marriage and Alternative Family Forms," *Family Coordinator* 24 (4) (1975b):543–547, and reprinted in Skolnick and Skolnick (2d ed.), 288–313.

84. M. Faulk, "Men Who Assault Their Wives," *Medicine, Science, and the Law* 14 (1974):180–183.

85. Ibid., 181.

86. Dotson Rader, "The Sexual Nature of Violence," *New York Times* (1973), cited in Pogrebin, 49.

87. Ibid., 49–53, 80.

88. Ibid., 50.

89. Ibid.

90. John E. Mayer and Noel Timms, *The Client Speaks* (London: Routledge & Kegan Paul, 1970).

91. See Pauline Morris, Jennie Cooper, and Anthea Byles, "Public Attitudes to Problem Definition and Problem Solving: A Pilot Study," *British Journal of Social Work* 3 (3) (1973):301–320; Drew Reith, "I Wonder If You Can Help Me . . . ?" *Social Work Today* 6 (3) (1975):66–69.

92. On this point see Charles D. Bolton and Kenneth Kammeyer, "The Decision to Use a Family Service Agency," *Family Coordinator* 17 (January 1968):47–53; B. Glastonbury, H. Burdett, and R. Austin, "Community Perceptions and the Personal Social Services," *Policy and Politics* 1 (3) (1973):191–211; Ann McKay, E. Matilda Goldberg, and David F. Fruin, "Consumers and a Social Service Department," *Social Work Today* 4 (16) (1973):436–491; U. MacLean, "Sources of Help," *New Society*, April 5, 1973:16–18; Morris, Cooper, and Byles; A. M. Rees, "Access to the Personal and Health Welfare Services," *Social and Economic Administration* 6 (1) (1972):34–43; Stuart Rees, "No More Than Contact: An Outcome of Social Work," *British Journal of Social Work* 4 (3) (1974):255–279; Reith; Weiss.

93. Reith found that the people he interviewed were also apprehensive about the possibility of a judgmental and/or unsympathetic response from social workers.

94. Paul Mansfield and Jeff Smith, "What a Reception!" *Social Work Today*, 5 (12) (1974):354–356.

95. This problem of potential clients having inaccurate views of social service departments has been discovered in studies in America and Britain. See Bolton and Kammeyer; Glastonbury, Burdett, and Austin; McKay, Goldberg and Fruin; S. Rees.

96. On this point see Elizabeth Wilson, *Women and the Welfare State* (London: Tavistock, 1977):174.

97. Peggy C. Giordano, "The Client's Perspective in Agency Evaluation," *Social Work* 22 (January 1977):34–37; Mayer and Timms; S. Rees.

98. Howard S. Becker, *The Other Side* (New York: Free Press, 1974).

99. Beverely B. Nichols, "The Abused Wife Problem," *Social Casework* 57 (1) (1976):27–32.

100. See Eliot Friedson, "Specialities without Roots: The Utilization of New Services," *Human Organization* 18 (3) (1959):112–116. This observation was also made by Gregory.

101. Elston, Fuller, and Murch, 22.

102. See Kremen.

103. Psychoanalytic theories may not merely reflect conventional wisdom but actually create it. See Mannes Tidmarsh, "Violence in Marriage: The Relevance of Structural Factors," *Social Work Today* 7 (2) (1976):36–37, for a professional social worker's uncritical acceptance of the ideology of provocation.

104. Nichols, 27.

105. Select Committee on Violence in Marriage (1975b). The passages cited in the text appear on pp. 243, 268, and 280.

106. William Beveridge, *Report on Social Insurance and Allied Services* (London: HMSO, 1942); F. Seebohm, *Report of the Committee on Local Authority and Allied Personal Social Services* Cmnd. 3703, (London: HMSO, 1968).

107. Quoted in Elizabeth Wilson, "Battered Wives: A Social Worker's Viewpoint," *Royal Society of Health Journal* 95 (6) (1975):294–297.

108. See Seebohm; Social Work (Scotland) Act (London: HMSO, 1968); Children and Young Persons in Scotland Act (The Kilbrandon Report) (Edinburgh: HMSO, 1964). For a discussion of the impact of ideologies relating to the family on the structure of social service delivery see Gilbert Smith and Robert Harris, "Ideologies of Need and the Organization of Social Work Departments," *British Journal of Social Work* 2 (1) (1972):27–48.

109. John Bowlby, *Maternal Care and Mental Health* (Geneva: World Health Organization, 1951), and *Attachment and Loss*, Vol. 1 (London: Hogarth Press and the Institute of Psychoanalysis, 1969). For a scholarly and devastating critique of the research and arguments supporting the maternal deprivation thesis see Wortis.

110. See Wilson (1977) for an account of the way welfare policies in Britain have maintained and reinforced the traditional position of women through an emphasis on family stability and children. See also R. M. Moroney, *The Family and the Welfare State* (London: Longmans, Green, 1977).

111. The response of social workers may also reflect the problem of finding suitable accommodation; they may consider it better to have children at home with their mothers than in any other setting.

112. This type of response may reflect the statutory obligations of social service departments to protect children from violence—no such provision exists regarding women.

113. It has often been noted that social workers are part of the control network for society's deviants. Yet it is probably likely that they are much more successful in maintaining the traditional way of life and status of individuals in society, especially women. See Joel F. Handler, *The Coercive Social Worker* (Chicago: Rand McNally, 1973); A. M. Rees; S. Rees, 256; Peter Leonard, "Social Control, Class Values, and Social Work Practice," *Social Work* 22 (4) (1965):9–13; Weiss.

114. Other studies have shown that people feel degraded by their contacts with the helping professions and that the help they received was actually injurious to their self-esteem; see Weiss.

115. Nichols, 31.

Chapter 11 The Police and Judicial Response

1. The statuses relating to violent offenses in England, Wales, and Scotland are based on two separate legal and judicial systems. Assault is a common law offense in Scotland and an offender can be charged with assault, assault to severe injury, assault to the danger of life, culpable homicide, attempted murder, or murder. See Select Committee on Violence in Marriage (1975b):334. The laws in England and Wales are much more explicit regarding crimes of violence. The English legislation covering assaults dates from the Offences against the Person Act of 1861 and includes the following sections: section 18 (wounding with intent to do grievous bodily harm), section 20 (inflicting bodily injury), section 42 (common assault), section 43 (aggravated assault on women and children), and section 47 (assault occasioning bodily harm). Section 43 was intended to grant magistrates additional powers to enforce a separation order in cases of assaults against women (wives) and children but it carries no provision for arrest; that is, it can be enforced only by a magistrate and it is very rarely invoked. See ibid., 381. American statutes differ from state to state but Michigan law is exemplary. Under Michigan law a man may be charged with assault, assault and battery, assault and infliction of serious injury, felonious assault, assault with intent to commit murder, assault with intent to do great bodily harm less than murder, and assault with intent to maim. See Eisenberg and Micklow, 66–67. The primary distinction in the statutes in both the United States and Britain is between violence that does not result in physical injury, e.g., common or simple assault, and assault that results in physical harm. See Truninger for a discussion of California statutes relating to violence in the family.

2. See Donald Black, "The Social Organization of Arrest," *Stanford Law Review* 23 (June 1971):1087–1111; Michael Banton, *The Policeman in the Community* (London: Tavistock, 1964); Elaine Cumming, Ian Cumming, and Laura Edell, "Policeman as Philosopher, Guide, and Friend," *Social Problems* 12 (Winter 1965):276–286; Joseph Goldstein, "Police Discretion Not to Invoke the Legal Process: Low Visibility Decisions in the Administration of Justice," *Yale Law Journal* 69 (1960):543–594; Wayne LaFave, "Noninvocation of the Criminal Law by Police," in Donald R. Cressey and David Ward (eds.), *Delinquency, Crime, and Social Process* (New York: Harper & Row, 1969):154–184; Harold E. Pepinsky, "Police Patrolmen's Offense Reporting Behavior," *Journal of Research in Crime and Delinquency* 13 (1) (1976):33–47; Irving Piliavin and Scott Briar, "Police Encounters with Juveniles," in Cressey and Ward, 154–165; Carl Werthman and Irving Piliavin, "Gang Members and the Police," in David J. Bordua (ed.), *The Police* (New York: Wiley, 1967):56–98.

3. The mandatory application of the sanction of arrest is unwarranted especially when one considers the numerous offenses committed by youngsters, which if reacted to with immediate arrest and punishment would probably land over 90% of the population in jail during their teenage years. In making arrests police officers must judge the sense of morality and indignation of a community and enforce the law in that spirit. Unfortunately, they often misinterpret community ideals of right and wrong and/or enforce the norms and standards of only a narrow section of the community.

4. See LaFave; Werthman and Piliavin. The police may also not enforce the law relative to minority groups, for example, when they fail to arrest someone who commits a offense against a black immigrant in Britain.

5. Black, 1107, found that police officers were much more likely to arrest for a serious violent offense than for other offenses. LaFave, 190, found that police officers often used discretion in dealing with youthful offenders but "the chance of arrest is great when force or violence has been used against an innocent victim" especially if the victim is a woman (not a wife) (ibid., n. 19). Cumming, Cumming, and Edell, 281, indicated that calls regarding violence were very likely to result in an immediate police response.

6. Martha H. Field and Henry F. Field, "Marital Violence and the Criminal Process: Neither Justice nor Peace," *Social Service Review* 47 (2) (1973):221–240.

7. Black, 1097.

8. Lawrence Blum, "Crisis Intervention Demonstration Project: Mental Health and Police Collaboration and Consulation," cited in Eisenberg and Micklow, 113.

9. Field and Field, 224.

10. A husband's rights of control over the household were upheld as late as the early twentieth century in various court decisions in the United States and Britain and were embodied in the principles of "Matrimonial Domicile," "Wife's Duty to Render Services," and the "Husband's Right of Gentle Restraint." See James Schoulder, *Marriage, Divorce, Separation, and Domestic Relations*, Vol. 1, 6th ed. (New York: Matthew Bender, 1921):57–85. Often these laws gave the illusion of judicial neutrality but they actually favored the husband. Gradually these principles were eroded in Britain, especially through the introduction of the Matrimonial Causes Acts during the last quarter of the nineteenth century. See Webb; Manchester. For a brief discussion of historical developments in the American legal system see Truninger; Eisenberg and Micklow.

11. See Schoulder.

12. See Arthur S. Stinchcombe, "Institutions of Privacy in the Determination of Police Administrative Practice," *American Journal of Sociology* 69 (September 1963):150–160; Pepe.

13. Pepe, 4.

14. Ibid.; Eisenberg and Micklow.

15. Bannon, 2.

16. Maurice Punch and Trevor Naylor, "The Police: A Social Service," *New Society*, 17 May, 1973:328–330. This British research discovered that one-third of all the telephone calls received by three rural police forces in southern England involved "domestic occurrences." Cumming, Cumming, and Edell found that over one-half of the calls coming into the police department they studied involved personal and social problems. The President's Commission on Law Enforcement and Administration of Justice, *The Challenge of Crime in a Free Society* pointed out that family disputes are considered unimportant by the police, yet they occupy a great deal of the time of many policemen (p. 104). A special study conducted for the Parliamentary Select Committee on Marital Violence (1975b):362 revealed that 22% of all weekend emergency calls in a large British city were concerned with domestic violence. See also Parnas (1967) and "Police Discretion

and Diversion of Incidents of Intra-Family Violence," *Law and Contemporary Problems* 36 (4) (1971):539–565.

17. Parnas (1967).

18. Eisenberg and Micklow, 104.

19. Field and Field, 228. Field and Field also pointed out that police training emphasizes protective action. See Parnas (1967) for similar evidence.

20. Select Committee on Violence in Marriage (1975b):375–376.

21. International Association of Police Chiefs, *International Association of Chiefs of Police Training Key 16: Handling Disturbance Calls* (Gaithersberg, 1967).

22. Quoted in LaFave, 204.

23. A study of police responses to family disputes in Hamilton, Ontario, between summer 1974 and winter 1975 revealed that 98% of calls involved actual assaults (84%) or threatened assaults (14%) and 95% of the 619 violent incidents involved attacks on wives. Board of Directors, Home Intervention Team Project.

24. Quoted in Eisenberg and Micklow, 107, n. 17.

25. Field and Field, 239.

26. Quoted in Select Committee on Violence in Marriage (1975b):380.

27. One would imagine that most lawyers are willing to help women obtain a divorce, yet this may not be the case. For example, a Catholic lawyer may not consider divorce a legitimate alternative or other lawyers may emphasize reconciliation rather than divorce. The problem of cost may be solved for women able to obtain free legal assistance. Britain and the United States have established various agencies (Legal Aid and Citizen Advice Bureaus) to provide low cost or free legal assistance to the public. Services such as Legal Aid are very important but they are overburdened and many women do not qualify for their help or know such help is available.

28. Eisenberg and Micklow; Parnas (1971); Truninger, 265, found a similar pattern in California: "If the call for help comes from a wife against her husband, the [police] system is reluctant to intervene."

29. LaFave, 205, n. 70. It is interesting to consider the problematics of judging the potential for "excessive violence" in an assaultive situation over the telephone.

30. Quoted in Eisenberg and Micklow, 107, n.17. Parnas (1971):547 found that the Chicago police departments' telephone screening "guidelines specifically directed to 'family trouble' provide that such a situation 'is basically a civil matter. It is not a police function to arbitrate or undertake negotiations in marital difficulties.' "

31. The chief of police in Syracuse, where this incident took place, did tell Cumming, Cumming, and Edell, 281, n. 8, that this was "poor police practice."

32. Eisenberg and Micklow, 109, n. 18. Parnas (1971):546 noted, however, that even when a weapon is alleged the police may not respond: "From non-police sources, it was learned that although current responses were increasing, in recent years the police did not respond at all if the dispatcher knew it was a family dispute—even if the offender was said to have a gun."

33. Eisenberg and Micklow, 102, n. 18.

34. Lawrence Blum, cited in Eisenberg and Micklow, 113, n. 24.

35. See Steven Box, *Deviance, Reality, and Society* (New York: Holt, Rinehart & Winston, 1971); Black; LaFave; Werthman and Piliavin; and Piliavan and Brair.

36. Select Committee on Violence in Marriage (1975b):367–368. Guidelines of this nature are no more than orienting points since they may be interpreted in innumerable ways by individual police officers.

37. Police officers usually uphold rightful and legitimate authority in society regardless of the circumstances. See Martin Bard, "Family Intervention Police Teams as a Community Mental Health Resource," *Journal of Criminal Law, Criminology, and Police Science* 60 (2) (1969):247–250.

38. Individuals often justify violence by attributing undesirable characteristics to the victim(s). The public has justified violence against political radicals, students, and black people by reference to their perceived "immorality"—they must have deserved it. The use of violence may also be justified if the attacker is seen as defending cherished values and as having the authority to uphold these values. The clearest historical example of this form of justification is the doctrine of manifest destiny, which justified genocide against the American Indians. For a discussion and review of the literature relating to this evaluative process see Alan Jay Lincoln, "Justifications and Condemnations of Violence: A Typology of Response and a Research Review," *Sociological Symposium* 9 (Spring 1976):51–67; Monica D. Blumenthal, "Predicting Attitudes toward Violence," *Science* 179 4041 (June 1972):1296–1303. Westley also found the same sense of moral justification among police officers who used violence in subduing suspects.

39. James Bannon, quoted in Eisenberg and Micklow, 34.

40. Battered women testifying before the Select Committee on Violence in Marriage (1975b):16–31, 137–141, 220–226, 253–257 told of incidents in which police refused to act. This orientation was also clear in the memoranda submitted by various police associations and in police officials' oral evidence given to the Select Committee. For the American evidence see Parnas (1967) (1971); Truninger.

41. Bannon, 2, noted a similar pattern in Detroit. In dealing with violence against wives "[the police] reject the rule of law which makes it a crime to assault another person regardless of our relationship to them or degree of injury. We substitute in its stead an arbitrary determination usually based on irrelevant factors. Most frequently the factor which will cause police intervention is a family fight which disrupts the peace and tranquility of the neighborhood. Next most frequently the use of a deadly weapon and thirdly the degree of injury involved." Parnas (1971):548 concluded that the Chicago police employed the "following procedures: referral; threats of arrest or other forms of indirect sanctions; voluntary, temporary separation of the disputants; the threat of filing cross-complaints; and refusal to arrest except on a warrant. If the officers conclude, as is usually the case, that peace is at least temporarily restored through these actions, no further action will be taken."

42. The demeanor of the offender is a frequently reported reason for police action or inaction. See Black; Werthman and Piliavin; Piliavin and Briar.

43. Field and Field; Straus (1976); Select Committee on Violence in Marriage (1975b).

44. Many of the women we interviewed described incidents resulting in severe and visible injuries (which serve as corroborating evidence in Scotland and England) in which the police refused to take action unless the husband contested police authority, behaved in a belligerent manner, or caused enough noise to arouse the wrath of neighbors. The statutes of Britain and the United States specify that a police officer who witnesses an assault is empowered to arrest. In supporting his argument that the police will not apply the sanction of arrest when the victim is a member of the offender's family, LaFave, 204, cited a case that involved these exact circumstances: "Although the man was still hitting his wife when the officer arrived, the officer did not make an arrest but merely restored order and left."

45. On this point see Cumming, Cumming, and Edell, 276.

46. See Harvey A. Barocas, "Urban Policemen: Crisis Mediators or Crisis Creators?" *American Journal of Orthopsychiatry* 43 (4) (1973):632–639; Bard (1969) and "The Study and Modification of Intra-familial Violence," in J. Singer (ed.) *The Control of Aggression and Violence* (New York: Academic Press, 1971): 154–164; Martin Bard and Bernard Berkowitz, "Family Disturbance as a Police Function," in S. I. Cohen (ed.), *Law Enforcement Science and Technology*, Vol. 2 (Chicago: ITT Research Institute, 1969):565–568; Charles L. Newman, "Police and Families: Factors Affecting Police Intervention," *Police Chief* 39 (March 1972):25–30; Parnas (1971).

47. It is often the case that innocuous behaviors and property offenses result in stronger reaction than do violent acts, especially when the violence occurs within the home. We are not necessarily arguing for more stringent sanctions but in the context of the present judicial and law enforcement system arrest is the only sanction that strongly demonstrates social disapproval. Certainly, we agree with liberal proposals to decriminalize victimless crimes but the danger of these proposals is that the state will decriminalize only those offenses it considers unimportant. This allows the state to seem to be acting in a humane and reasonable fashion. It is very clear that the police and courts traditionally have seen violence against women as unimportant and have failed to apply criminal sanctions against men who beat their wives and in so doing have demonstrated lack of concern about this form of behavior.

48. The ending of this story is not altogether a happy one because the husband did continue to intimidate his wife for many years after this particular incident.

49. Scotland, unlike England and Wales and the United States, operates a system of public prosecution. This system seems to make it difficult for a citizen to seek redress regarding an offense directly from the courts but it also means that the state can pursue a charge even if the complainant does not wish to do so.

50. Field and Field.

51. Ibid.

52. Ibid.; Eisenberg and Micklow; Bannon.

53. The woman may become involved in a contradictory process in attempting to demonstrate her resolve since she is required to indicate her willingness to pur-

sue a divorce during the initial stages of judicial proceedings but then may be required to demonstrate her willingness to seek a reconciliation if the case comes before the bench.

54. Field and Field, 232.

55. Ibid., 233.

56. This powerful phrase appears in the title of Field and Field's work and reminds one of the historically significant *Gault* decision in which the U.S. Supreme Court decided that juveniles were receiving neither justice nor treatment as an outcome of the juvenile court process and ruled that they should at least receive some legal protection during juvenile court processing and proceedings.

57. Quoted in Eisenberg and Micklow, 124, n. 23.

58. James Bannon, cited in Eisenberg and Micklow. Only 366 of these cases were processed through the courts.

59. Truninger.

60. Manchester; Truninger.

61. Martin, 9–24; Fields, a New York city attorney who has represented innumerable battered women, concluded that "judges impose light or suspended sentences, even without the prosecutor's suggestions." See Marjory Fields, "Representing Battered Wives, or What to Do until the Police Arrive" (1977):2 (available from Brooklyn Legal Services, 152 Court Street, Brooklyn, New York 11201). Field and Field observed that the least likely outcome of judicial action in cases of domestic assault was the imposition of a jail sentence or fine.

62. These statistics were computed from Select Committee on Violence in Marriage (1975b):294 table.

63. On this point see Bannon.

64. Quoted in Eisenberg and Micklow, 124.

65. See the statements of police officials regarding the introduction of this new form of injunction in Select Committee on Violence in Marriage (1975b); see also Angela Singer, "The Strong Arm and the Law," *Manchester Guardian*, February 17, 1978.

66. Police official giving oral evidence to the Select Committee on Violence in Marriage (1975b):309. A police official from Manchester was also asked about the frequency of use of injunctions in that city; his response: "Very few" (p. 385).

67. Quoted in Singer.

68. Police evidence to the Select Committee on Violence in Marriage (1975b):275.

69. Ibid., 366.

70. See, for instance, the evidence of the police representative in ibid., 273.

71. It has been argued that the imposition of a fine will create a hardship for the woman since the family's resources will be depleted. This assumption may be correct, but it is just as likely that the husband was withholding his wages from his wife.

72. Select Committee on Violence in Marriage (1975b):381.

73. As James Bannon indicated in an interview quoted in Eisenberg and Micklow, 110, "When we further realize that our history of non-response has undoubtedly

had the effect of inhibiting future calls for help, we see ever greater potential demands for service which could exceed our capacity to serve."

74. According to Wolfgang (1958):336, "The facts suggest that homicide is the apex crime—a crescendo built upon previous assault crimes."

75. Field and Field, 234–235.

76. Ibid., 235.

Chapter 12: Refuges and Other Alternatives

1. Charlton.

2. Sutton.

3. For a fuller discussion of this split, see ibid.; Hilary Rose, "Up Against the Welfare State," Unit 30, DE206, *Social Work, Community Work and Society* (The Open University: Milton Keynes, 1978). Some North American observers who have only briefly visited Britain seem to have failed to appreciate the profound differences between Chiswick and the National Women's Aid Federation. See, for example, Lenore E. Walker, "Treatment Alternatives for Battered Women," in Jane Roberts Chapman and Margaret Gates (eds.), *The Victimization of women* (Beverly Hills: Sage, 1978):143–174.

4. The refuges and groups comprising the Scottish Women's Aid Federation were initially part of the NWAF. They formed their own separate but related organization because of unique legal and political problems in Scotland.

5. Anne Marcovitch, "Refuges for Battered Women," *Social Work Today* 7 (2) (1976):34–35.

6. Sutton, 577.

7. Ibid.

8. See Sutton; National Women's Aid Federation (1975) and "He's Got to Show Her Who's Boss: The National Women's Aid Federation Challenges a Man's Right to Batter," *Spare Rib* 69 (0) (1978):15–18.

9. Marcovitch, 35.

10. Glasgow Women's Aid, "Interval House: Report for the Year February 1976 to February 1977" (Glasgow, 1977).

11. See Dobash and Dobash (1977a); Jalna Hanmer, "Community Action, Women's Aid, and the Women's Liberation Movement," in Marjorie Mayo (ed.), *Women in the Community* (London: Routledge & Kegan Paul, 1977):91–108.

12. "Home for Battered Wives Opposed," *Guardian*, August 7, 1975.

13. "MP Attacks Aid for Battered Wives," *Glasgow Herald*, September 22, 1975.

14. See Hanmer, 102–103; Sutton.

15. In Glasgow the homeless family unit of the social work department, which deals almost exclusively with battered women, has worked out a quite amicable relationship with that city's Women's Aid group.

16. Northwest Region of the National Women's Aid Federation, "Battered Women and Social Work," in F. Martin (ed.), *Violence in the Family* (New York: Wiley, 1978).

17. National Women's Aid Federation (1975):10.

18. See Thomas Mathisen, *The Politics of Abolition* (London: Martin Robertson, 1974), for a discussion of the nature of contradictory and competing proposals.

19. This literature is available from the National Women's Aid Federation, 374 Gary's Inn Road, London, England; The Scottish Women's Aid Federation, Ainslie House, 11 St. Colme Street, Edinburgh, Scotland EH3 6AA; and the Welsh Women's Aid, 2 Coburn St., Cardiff.

20. Available from the sources listed in note 19 above.

21. Robert McCreadie, "Protection Against Domestic Violence," *SCOLAG: The Bulletin of the Scottish Legal Action Group* 22(July, 1978):145.

22. See ISIS, *International Bulletin* 4(July, 1977), which is devoted to a summary of the activities to aid battered women in various countries. See also Sara Haffner, "Wife Abuse in West Germany," *Victimology* 2(3–4) (1978):472–478; Elizabeth Kobus, "Founding 'Stay Away from My Body,' " ibid., 662–663.

23. NCN, *National Communication Network for the Elimination of Violence against Women* 1 (3) (1977). This publication is available from Transition House, c/o Women's Center, 46 Pleasant Street, Cambridge, Massachusetts 02139, and from Women's Advocates, 584 Grand Avenue, St. Paul, Minnesota 55102.

24. Ibid., 8.

25. Susan Naples and Sherry Jones, "Is There a Better Approach?" *Victimology* 2 (3–4) (1978):422–423.

26. Quoted in Warrior.

27. *Spare Rib* 69(1978):16.

28. Kobus; Nora Van Crevel, "But What about the Kids?" (Paper presented to the American Sociological Association Convention, New York City, August 1976); Ingerlise Slot-Anderson, "A Dutch Refuge for Battered Women: Who Comes?" (Paper presented to the American Sociological Association Convention, New York City, August 1976).

29. Kobus, 662.

30. Natalie Shainess, "Psychological Aspects of Wife-Battering," in Roy, 117.

31. Ibid., 118.

32. Field and Field labeled police action "irrelevant."

33. Bannon, 7.

34. Supreme Court of the State of New York, *Bruno v. Codd*, New York County, Index 21946/76(1976); Marjory D. Fields, "Wife Beating: Government Intervention Policies and Practices," (1978b). Available from Brooklyn Legal Services Corporation B, Matrimonial Unit, 152 Court Street, Brooklyn, New York 11201; Janet R. Wagner, "*Bruno v. Codd*: Battered Wives and the Police in the United States and Britain," (1978). Available from College of Law, University of Denver, Denver, Colorado.

35. Ibid; Rita Henley Jensen, "Battered Women and the Law," *Victimology* 2(3–4) (1978):585–590.

36. Field, 1978, 17.

37. *Bruno v. Codd*, 975–977.
38. Wagner, 1.
39. National Communication Network/Feminist Alliance Against Rape, *Aegis* (September/October 1978):22–27; (November/December 1978):42–44; (January/February 1979):16–18; *National Communication Network for the Elimination of Violence Against Women*, now *Aegis* 1 (3) (October, 1977):18–21.
40. Board of Directors, Home Intervention Team Project.
41. Martin, 179–180.
42. Truninger, 274–275.
43. Marjory Fields, "Wife Beating: Facts and Figures," *Victimology* 2 (3–4) (1978a):643–646.
44. Fields (1977):3.
45. Ibid., 9.
46. Northwest Region of the National Women's Aid Federation.
47. There are enough child care places for only 5% of the children under age five in Great Britain (1978).
48. Gregory J. Massell, "Law as an Instrument of Revolutionary Change in a Traditional Milieu: The Case of Soviet Central Asia," *Law and Society* 11 (2) (1968):186.
49. Ibid., 204.
50. Ibid., 213.
51. Leon Trotsky, *Women and the Family* (New York: Pathfinders, 1970):21.

Appendix C: The Study

1. Paul Feyerabend, *Against Method: Outline of an Anarchistic Theory of Knowledge* (London: New Left Books, 1975), especially chaps. 6–9.
2. Ibid.; Feyerabend (1970); Lakatos and Musgrave.
3. See Johan Galtung, *Theory and Methods of Social Research* (London: George Allen & Unwin, 1968); Eugene Webb, D. Campbell, R. D. Schwartz, and L. Sechrest, *Unobstrusive Measures: Nonreactive Research in the Social Sciences* (Chicago: Rand McNally, 1966). Both of these works recommend a broader conception of research methods and theory testing than is generally evident in social scientific work.
4. J. E. T. Eldridge (ed.), *Max Weber: The Interpretation of Social Reality* (London: Michael Joseph, 1971), especially part 1.
5. Ibid.
6. Ibid., 154.
7. Cicourel (1964):vii.
8. Paul F. Lazarsfeld and Allen H. Barton, "Qualitative Measurement in the Social Sciences: Classification, Typologies, and Indices," in David Lerner and H. D. Laswell (eds.), *The Policy Sciences* (Stanford: Stanford University Press, 1964). Lazarsfeld and Barton suggested that the process of moving back and forth from

the data to the literature should be a preliminary step to the development of more sophisticated theoretical classifications and concepts. However, most researchers probably engage in this two-way process throughout their research.

9. Barney G. Glaser and Anselm L. Strauss, *The Discovery of Grounded Theory* (Chicago: Aldine, 1967).

10. See W. S. Goode and P. K. Hatt, *Methods in Social Research* (New York: McGraw-Hill, 1955):176; Gideon Sjoberg and Robert Nett, *A Methodology for Social Research* (New York: Harper & Row, 1968):213–217.

11. The first public statement of our early position appeared in R. Emerson Dobash and Russell P. Dobash, "Violence between Men and Women within the Family Setting" (Paper presented to the Seventh World Congress of Sociology, Toronto, August 1974).

12. The Royal Scottish Society for the Prevention of Cruelty to Children (RSSPCC) is, of course, oriented primarily to the protection of children at risk. It also deals with, and attempts to help, women who have been assaulted by their husbands. The paper cited in note 11 above was partly a result of our collaboration with the RSSPCC on a small but interesting study it conducted on wife assault cases handled over a three-month period. We worked very closely with Daphne McQuaig on the analysis of the data from this study and we would like to thank her for her assistance.

13. See Galtung, 116; Cicourel (1974).

14. For examples of research on violence in the family that rely upon the use of standardized pencil and paper questionnaires see Gayford (1975b); Suzanne K. Steinmetz and Murray A. Straus, "The Family as a Cradle of Violence," *Society* 10 (September–October 1973):50–56; Murray A. Straus, "Leveling, Civility, and Violence in the Family," *Journal of Marriage and the Family* 36 (February 1974):13–29.

15. Galtung, 109.

16. Ibid., 120.

17. Cicourel (1964) (1974).

18. For a more complete transcription of one of our interviews with battered women see R. Emerson Dobash, Russell P. Dobash, Catherine Cavanagh, and Monica Wilson, "Wifebeating: The Victims Speak," *Victimology* 2 (3–4) (1978):608–622.

19. Abraham Kaplan, *The Conduct of Inquiry: Methodology for Behavioral Science* (San Francisco: Chandler, 1964).

20. All researchers agree on the necessity of gaining good rapport between interviewers and respondents. For discussions of this problem and others relating to interviewing see Cicourel (1964) (1974):84; Galtung, 109–161; Herbert Hyman, *Interviewing in Social Research*, rev. ed. (Chicago: University of Chicago Press, 1975); Sjoberg and Nett, 187–218; Bernard S. Phillips, *Social Research: Strategy and Tactics*, 2d ed. (New York: Macmillan, 1971).

21. See Galtung.

22. Although we were unable to interview men who had assaulted their wives, one of us (in another study relating to imprisonment) did interview a number of men

who had assaulted their wives and were imprisoned for this offense. The interviews in that study concerned issues more directly related to the prison experience but they provided important background knowledge for this study.

23. Gelles (1974); Whitehurst.

24. Toch, 22–23.

25. Boudouris; McClintock (1963a); Wolfgang (1958).

26. Toch; Ball-Rokeach.

27. Gelles (1974); Steinmetz and Straus (1973); Straus (1974).

28. Faulkner; Short and Strodtbeck; Westley.

29. For example, T. M. Kolb and M. A. Straus, "Marital Power and Marital Happiness in Relation to Problem Solving Ability," *Journal of Marriage and the Family* 36 (4) (1974):756–766. This article described an experimental study relating to power between husbands and wives. Straus used the findings of this study to make inferences about violence in the family. We also think it is unethical to use the records of social agencies (e.g., the police) to trace families in order to do research upon them without their full knowledge and consent. Cf. Gelles (1974):35–36.

30. Edinburgh and Glasgow are cities of very different socioeconomic complexions. Edinburgh is a city of approximately half a million people, the center of the Scottish civil service, the cultural and historical capital of Scotland. Glasgow, a city of over one million people, is a product of the industrial revolution. As one of the birthplaces of the industrial revolution it suffers from the withering away of heavy industry. A city with a particularly working-class character it has a high unemployment rate and poor housing, which is being replaced only gradually. The police district in which we examined police records is rather mixed in its socioeconomic composition since it includes a large working-class population as well as the university and its accompanying middle-class residences.

31. For example, Curtis; Gibson; Walter A. Lunden, "Crimes in London, England," *Police* 19 (1966):93–95; F. H. McClintock, "Crimes against the Person," *Proceedings of the Manchester Statistical Society* (February 1963a):1–32.

32. Such as Box, chaps. 3, 6; Leslie T. Wilkins, "The Measurement of Crime," *British Journal of Criminology* 3 (April 1963):321–341, and "New Thinking in Criminal Statistics," in Marvin E. Wolfgang, Leonard Savitz, and Norman Johnston, *The Sociology of Crime and Delinquency*, 2d ed. (New York: Wiley, 1970):63–73.

33. See Alan Booth, David R. Johnson, and Harvey M. Choldin, "Correlates of City Crime Rates: Victimization Surveys versus Official Statistics," *Social Problems* 24 (2) (1977):187–196. These researchers concluded that official statistics and victimization studies of crime are not a "satisfactory index of crime for purposes of explaining the causes of crime" (p. 196). See the following studies, which attempt to use official statistics to validate theories of violence: Boudouris; John D. McCarthy, Omer R. Galle, and William Zimmerman, "Population Density, Social Structure, and Interpersonal Violence: An Intermetropolitan Test of Competing Models," *American Behavioral Scientist* 18 (6) (1975):771–791; Pittman and Handy; Gastil.

310 VIOLENCE AGAINST WIVES

34. Donald Black and Albert J. Reiss, "Police Control of Juveniles," *American Sociological Review* 35 (1970):63–78; Box, chap. 6; William J. Chambliss and Richard Nagasawa, "On the Validity of Official Statistics," *Journal of Research in Crime and Delinquency* 6 (1969):71–77.

SELECTED REFERENCES

ABRAM, A.
1913   *English Life and Manners in the Later Middle Ages.* New York: Dutton.

ADLER, RUTH; HARRIS, LEA; AND WASOFF, FRAN
1975   "Edinburgh Women's Aid: A Review of the First Year." Available from Scottish Women's Aid, Ainslie House, 11 St. Colme Street, Edinburgh, Scotland.

ARIÈS, PHILIPPE
1962   *Centuries of Childhood: A Social History of Family Life.* Trans. Robert Baldick New York: Random House, Vintage Books.

BALINT, MICHAEL
1968   *The Doctor, His Patient, and the Illness* (2d ed.). London: Pitman Paperbacks.

BALL-ROKEACH, SANDRA J.
1973   "Values and Violence: A Test of the Subculture of Violence Thesis." *American Sociological Review* 38 (December):736–749.

BANDURA, A.
1973   *Aggression: A Social Learning Analysis.* Englewood Cliffs: Prentice-Hall.

BANNON, JAMES
1975   "Law Enforcement Problems with Intra-Family Violence." Paper presented to the American Bar Association Convention. August.

BANTON, MICHAEL
1964   *The Policemen in the Community.* London: Tavistock.

BARD, MARTIN
1969   "Family Intervention Police Teams as a Community Mental Health Resource." *Journal of Criminal Law, Criminology, and Police Science* 60 (2):247–250.
1971   "The Study and Modification of Intra-familial Violence." In J. Singer (ed.), *The Control of Aggression and Violence.* New York: Academic Press.

BARD, MARTIN, AND BERKOWITZ, BERNARD
1969   "Family Disturbance as a Police Function." In S. I. Cohen (ed.), *Law Enforcement Science and Technology.* Vol. 2. Chicago: ITT Research Institute.

BARDIS, PANOS D.
1964   "Family Forms and Variations Historically Considered." In Harold T.

311

Christensen (ed.), *Handbook of Marriage and the Family*. Chicago: Rand McNally.

BAROCAS, HARVEY A.
1973   "Urban Policemen: Crisis Mediators or Crisis Creators?" *American Journal of Orthopsychiatry* 43 (4):632–639.

BART, PAULINE B.
1971a   "The Myth of a Value Free Psychotherapy." In W. Bell and J. Mar (eds.), *Sociology and the Future*. New York: Russell Sage.
1971b   "Sexism and Social Science: From the Gilded Cage to the Iron Cage, or the Perils of Pauline." *Journal of Marriage and the Family* 33 (4):734–745.

BEAUVOIR, SIMONE DE
1976   *The Second Sex*. Translated and edited by H. M. Parshley. Middlesex, England: Penguin.

BECKER, ERNEST
1968   *The Structure of Evil*. New York: Free Press.

BECKER, HOWARD S.
1963   *Outsiders: Studies in the Sociology of Deviance*. New York: Free Press.

BEECHEY, VERONICA
1977   "Some Notes on Female Wage Labour in Capitalist Production." *Capital and Class* (Autumn):45–66.

BEIGEL, HUGO
1951   "Romantic Love." *American Sociological Review* 16 (3):326–334.

BELOTTI, ELENA
1975   *Little Girls: Social Conditioning and Its Effects on the Stereotyped Role of Women during Infancy*. Translated by L. Appignanesi, A. Fletcher, T. Shimura, S. Williams, and J. Wordsworth. London: Writers and Readers Publishing Cooperative.

BEM, SANDRA L., AND BEM, DARYL J.
1970   "Case Study of a Nonconscious Ideology: Training the Woman to Know Her Place." In Daryl J. Bem (ed.), *Beliefs, Attitudes, and Human Affairs*. Belmont, Calif.: Brooks/Cole.

BLACK, DONALD
1971   "The Social Organization of Arrest." *Stanford Law Review* 23: 1087–1111.

BLACK, DONALD, AND REISS, ALBERT J.
1970   "Police Control of Juveniles." *American Sociological Review* 35:63–78.

BLACKSTONE, SIR WILLIAM
1765   *Commentaries on the Laws of England*. Vol. 1. London.

BLAU, FRANCINE D.
1975   "Women in the Labor Force: An Overview." In Jo Freeman (ed.), *Women: A Feminist Perspective*. Palo Alto, Calif.: Mayfield.

BLAXHALL, M., AND REAGAN, B. (EDS.)
1976   *Women and the Workplace: The Implications of Occupational Segregation*. Vol. 1. Chicago: University of Chicago Press.

BLOOD, R., AND WOLFE, D.
   1960   *Husbands and Wives.* New York: Free Press.

BLUMENTHAL, MONICA D.
   1972   "Predicting Attitudes toward Violence." *Science* 179 (June):1296–1303.

BOARD OF DIRECTORS, HOME INTERVENTION TEAM PROJECT
   1976   "Proposal for Home Intervention Team Service: Hamilton–Westworth
          Region." November. Mimeographed paper, available from G. Gliva,
          Department of Psychiatry, MacMaster University, Hamilton, Ontario,
          Canada.

BOLTON, CHARLES D., AND KAMMEYER, KENNETH
   1968   "The Decision to Use a Family Service Agency." *Family Coordinator*
          (January):47–53.

BOOTH, ALAN; JOHNSON, DAVID R.; AND CHOLDIN, HARVEY M.
   1977   "Correlates of City Crime Rates: Victimization Surveys versus Official
          Statistics." *Social Problems* 24 (2):187–196.

BORLAND, MARIE (ED.)
   1976   *Violence in the Family.* Manchester: Manchester University Press.

BOUDOURIS, JAMES
   1971   "Homicide and the Family." *Journal of Marriage and the Family* 33
          (4):667–676.

BOWLBY, JOHN
   1955   *Child Care and the Growth of Love.* Hammondsworth: Penguin.

BOX, STEVEN
   1971   *Deviance, Reality, and Society.* New York: Holt, Rinehart & Winston.

BRITTEN, VERA
   1953   *Lady into Woman.* New York: Macmillan.

BRONFENBRENNER, URIE
   1958   "Socialization and Social Class through Time and Space." In Eleanor E.
          Maccoby et al. (eds.), *Readings in Social Psychology.* New York: Holt,
          Rinehart & Winston.
   1960   "Freudian Theories of Identification and Their Derivatives." *Child
          Development* 31 (March):15–40.

BROVERMAN, DONALD; BROVERMAN, INGE K.; CLARKSON, F. E.; ROSENKRANTZ, P. S.;
AND VOGEL, S. R.
   1970   "Sex-Role Stereotypes and Clinical Judgements of Mental Health." *Jour-
          nal of Consulting and Clinical Psychology* 34.

BROWNMILLER, SUSAN
   1975   *Against Our Will: Men, Women, and Rape.* London: Secker & War-
          burg.

BUCKLEY, WALTER
   1967   *Sociology and Modern Systems Theory.* Englewood Cliffs, N. J.:
          Prentice-Hall.

BYRNE, PATRICK S., AND LONG, BARRIE E.
   1976   *Doctors Talking to Patients.* London: HMSO.

CARLSON, BONNIE E.
   1977   "Battered Women and Their Assailants." *Social Work* 22 (6):445–460.

Castan, Nicole
  1976   Divers aspects de la constrainte maritale, d'après les documents judiciaires du XVIII è siècle." Translated by Kath Ryal for R. Emerson Dobash and Russell P. Dobash. Paper presented to the American Sociological Association Convention. August. New York City.

Cavanagh, Catherine
  1978   "Battered Women and Social Control: A Study of the Help-Seeking Behaviour of Battered Women and the Help-Giving Behaviour of those from Whom They Seek Help." Master's thesis. University of Stirling, Striling, Scotland.

Center for Women Policy Studies
  1978   "Response to Violence and Sexual Abuse in the Family." 2 (2). Available on a regular basis from CWPS, 2000 p Street N.W., Suite 508, Washington, D. C., 20036.

Chafetz, Janet S.
  1974   *Masculine, Feminine, or Human? An Overview of the Sociology of Sex Roles.* Itasca: Peacock.

Chapman, A. B., and Chapman, M. W.
  1910   *The Status of Women under English Law: A Compendious Epitome of Legislative Enactment and Social and Political Events Arranged as a Continuous Narrative with References to Authorities and Acts of Parliament.* London: Routledge and Sons.

Chapman, Jane Roberts, and Gates, Margaret (eds.)
  1978   *The Victimization of Women.* Beverly Hills: Sage.

Charlton, Caroline
  1972   "The First Cow on Chiswick High Road." *Spare Rib* 24:24–25.

Chesler, Phyllis
  1970   "Marriage and Psychotherapy." Radical Therapist 1 (3):16.
  1971a   "Patient and Patriarch: Women in the Psychotherapeutic Relationship." In Vivian Gornick and Barbara K. Moran (eds.), *Women in Sexist Society: Studies in Power and Powerlessness.* New York: New American Library, Mentor Books.
  1971b   "Women as Psychiatric and Psychotherapeutic Patients." *Journal of Marriage and the Family* 33 (4):746–759.

Chester, Robert, and Streather, Jane
  1972   "Cruelty in English Divorce: Some Empirical Findings." *Journal of Marriage and the Family* 34 (4):706–710.

Cicourel, Aaron V.
  1964   *Method and Measurement in Sociology.* New York: Free Press.
  1968   *The Social Organization of Juvenile Justice.* New York: Wiley.
  1974   *Theory and Method in a Study of Argentine Fertility.* New York: Wiley-Interscience.

Cleaver, Robert
  1598   *A Godly Form of Household Government.* London: Printed by R. Creede for T. Mann.

Cobbe, Francis Power
  1878   "Wife Torture in England." *Contemporary Review* (April):55–87.

COLLINS, RANDALL
1972 "A Conflict Theory of Sexual Stratification." In H. P. Dretizel (ed.), *Family, Marriage, and the Struggle of the Sexes.* London: Collier Macmillan.

CONFERENCE OF SOCIALIST ECONOMISTS
1975 "On the Political Economy of Woman." Pamphlet no. 2. Available from 21 Theobalds Road, London, England.

COX, EDWARD W.
1877 *The Principles of Punishment, As Applied in the Administration of the Criminal Law, By Judges and Magistrates.* London: Law Times Office.

CUMMING, ELAINE; CUMMING, IAN; AND EDELL, LAURA
1965 "Policeman as Philosopher, Guide, and Friend." *Social Problems* 12 (Winter):276–286.

CURTIS, LYNN A.
1974 *Criminal Violence.* Lexington: Lexington Books.

DAHL, TOVE STANG, AND SNARE, ANNIKA
1976 "The Coercion of Privacy: A Feminist Perspective." Paper presented to the fourth Conference of the European Group for the Study of Deviance and Social Control. September. Vienna.

DAVIDOFF, LEONORE
1974 "Mastered for Life: Servant and Wife in Victorian and Edwardian England." *Journal of Social History* 7 (4):406–428.

DAVIDSON, TERRY
1977 "Wifebeating: A Recurring Phenomenon throughout History." In Maria Roy (ed.), *Battered Women: A Psychosociological Study of Domestic Violence.* New York: Van Nostrand Reinhold.

DAVIS, ARTHUR K.
1957 "Social Theory and Social Problems." *Philosophy and Phenomenological Research* 18 (December):190–208.

DAVIS, NATALIE ZEMON
1971 "The Reasons of Misrule: Youth Groups and Charivaris in Sixteenth Century France." *Past and Present* 50 (February):41–75.

DELMAR, ROSALIND
1976 "Looking Again at Engels's *Origins of the Family, Private Property, and the State.*" In Juliet Mitchell and Ann Oakley (eds.), *The Rights and Wrongs of Women.* Aylesbury, England: Penguin.

DENNIS, NORMAN; HENRIQUES, FERNANDO; AND SLAUGHTER, CLIFFORD
1969 *Coal Is Our Life: An Analysis of a Yorkshire Mining Community* (2d ed.). London: Tavistock.

DEPAUW, LINDA GRANT, AND HUNT, CONOVER
1976 *Remember the Ladies: Women in America, 1750–1815.* New York: Viking.

DINITZ, SIMON; DYNES, RUSSELL R.; AND CLARKE, ALFRED C.
1954 "Preferences for Male or Female Children: Traditional or Affectional?" *Marriage and Family Living* (May):128–130.

DOBASH, R. EMERSON
1976–1977 "The Relationship between Violence directed at Women and Violence

directed at Children within the Family Setting." Appendix 38. Parliamentary Select Committee on Violence in the Family. London: HMSO.

Dobash, R. Emerson; Cavanagh, Catherine; and Wilson, Monica
1977   "Violence against Wives: The Legislation of the 1960's and the Policies of Indifference." Paper presented to the National Deviancy Conference meetings April. Sheffield, England.

Dobash, R. Emerson, and Dobash, Russell P.
1974   "Violence between Men and Women within the Family Setting." Paper presented to the Seventh World congress of Sociology. August. Toronto.
1975   "Wife Beating: Past and present." Paper presented to the First Meeting of the Anglo-French Exchange on Violence against Women. November. London.
1977a   Love, Honour, and Obey: Institutional Ideologies and the Struggle for Battered Women. Contemporary Crises: Crime, Law, and Social Policy 1 (June–July):403–415.
1977b   "Wife Beating Still a Common Form of Violence." Social Work Today 9 (12):14–17.
1978   "Wives: The 'Appropriate' Victims of Marital Violence." Victimology 2 (3–4):426–442.

Dobash, R. Emerson; Dobash, Russell P.; Cavanagh Catherine; and Wilson, Monica
1978   "Wifebeating: The Victims Speak." Victimology 2 (3–4):608–622.

Dobash, Russell P., and Dobash, R. Emerson
1975   "Battered Women: The Importance of Existing Perspectives." Paper presented to the British Sociological Association Study Group on Sexual Divisions in Society. November. London.

Domestic Violence Project, Inc.
1979   "Monthly Memo." Available from the National Technical Assistance Center on Family Violence, 1917 Washtenaw Avenue, Ann Arbor, Michigan 48104.

Dodd, William G.
1913   Courtly Love in Chaucer and Gower. Boston: Ginn.

Eisenberg, Sue, and Micklow, Patricia
1974   "The Assaulted Wife: Catch 22 Revisited. (An Exploratory Legal Study of Wifebeating in Michigan)." Mimeographed. University of Michigan Law School. Also available from Rutgers University School of Law, 180 University Avenue, Newark, N.J. 07102.

Eldridge, J. E. T. (ed.)
1971   Max Weber: The Interpretation of Social Reality. London: Michael Joseph.

Elston, Elizabeth; Fuller, Jane; and Murch, Mervyn
1976   "Battered Wives: The Problems of Violence in Marriage as Experienced by a Group of Petitioners in Undefended Divorce Cases." Mimeographed. Department of Social Work, University of Bristol, Bristol, England.

ENGELS, FRIEDRICH
   1962   "On the Origin of the Family, Private Property, and the State" (1st pub. 1884). In Karl Marx and Friedrich Engels, *Selected Works*. Vol. 2. Moscow: Foreign Languages Publishing House.

ENNIS, PHILIP H.
   1967   *Criminal Victimization in the United States: A Report of a National Survey*. National Opinion Research Center, University of Chicago, Washington D.C.: U.S. Government Printing Office.

EPSTEIN, CYNTHIA FUCHS
   1970   *Women's Place: Options and Limits in Professional Careers*. Berkeley: University of California Press.

ETZIONI, AMITAI
   1968   "Sex, Control, Science, and Society," *Science* (Sept. 13):1107–1112.

FAULK, M.
   1974   "Men Who Assault Their Wives." *Medicine, Science, and the Law* 14:180–183.

FAULKNER, ROBERT
   1973   "On Respect and Retribution: Toward an Ethnography of Violence." *Sociological Symposium* 9 (Spring):17–35.

FEIGEL, HERBERT
   1970   "The 'Orthodox' View of Theories: Remarks in Defense as Well as Critique." In Michael Rudner and Stephen Winokur (eds.), *Minnesota Studies in the Philosophy of Science*. Vol. 4: *Analyses of Theories and Methods of Physics and Psychology*. Minneapolis: University of Minnesota Press.

FEYERABEND, PAUL
   1970   "Against Method: Outline of an Anarchistic Theory of Knowledge." In Michael Radner and Stephen Winokur (eds.), *Minnesota Studies in the Philosophy of Science*. Vol. 4: *Analyses of Theories and Methods of Physics and Psychology*. Minneapolis: University of Minnesota Press.
   1975   *Against Method: Outline of an Anarchistic Theory of Knowledge*. London: New Left Books.

FIELD, MARTHA H., AND FIELD, HENRY F.
   1973   "Marital Violence and the Criminal Process: Neither Justice nor Peace." *Social Service Review* 47 (2):221–240.

FIELDS, MARJORY D.
   1976   "Wife-Beating: The Hidden Offense." Available from Brooklyn Legal Services Corporation B, Matrimonial Unit, 152 Court Street, Brooklyn, New York 11201.
   1977   "Representing Battered Wives, or What to Do until the Police Arrive." Available from Brooklyn Legal Services, 152 Court Street, Brooklyn, New York 11201.
   1978a "Wife Beating: Facts and Figures." *Victimology* 2 (3–4):643–646.
   1978b "Wife Beating: Government Intervention Policies and Practices." Available from Brooklyn Legal Services.

FIGES, EVA
   1970   *Patriarchal Attitudes: Women in Society*. London: Faber & Faber.

FINER, MORRIS
1975   *Report of the Committee on One-Parent Families.* London: HMSO.

FIRESTONE, SHULAMITH
1971   *The Dialectic of Sex: The Case for Feminist Revolution.* London: Jonathan Cape.

FOUCAULT, MICHEL
1967   *Madness and Civilization: A History of Insanity in the Age of Reason.* Translated by Richard Howard. London: Social Science Paperback.
1977   *Discipline and Punish: The Birth of the Prison.* Translated by Allan Sheridan. London: Allen Lane.

FRANKFORD, EVELYN, AND SNITOW, ANN
1972   "The Trap of Domesticity: Notes on the Family." *Socialist Revolution* (July–August):83–97.

FREEMAN, JO (ED.)
1975   *Women: A Feminist Perspective.* Palo Alto, Calif.: Mayfield.

FRIEDSON, ELIOT
1959   "Specialities without Roots: The Utilization of New Services." *Human Organization* 18 (3):112–116.

GALTUNG, JOHAN
1963   *Theory and Methods of Social Research.* London: George Allen & Unwin.

GASTIL, RAYMOND D.
1971   "Homicide and a Regional Culture of Violence." *American Sociological Review* 36 (June):412–427.

GAYFORD, J. J.
1975a "Battered Wives." *Medicine, Science, and the Law* 15 (4):237–245.
1975b "Wife Battering: A Preliminary Survey of 100 Cases." *British Medical Journal* 1 (January):194–197.
1976   "Ten Types of Battered Wives," *Welfare Officer* 1 (January):5–9.

GELLES, RICHARD J.
1974   *The Violent Home: A Study of Physical Aggression between Husbands and Wives.* Beverly Hills: Sage.
1976   "Abused Wives: Why Do They Stay?" *Journal of Marriage and the Family* 38 (November):659–668.

GERTH, H. H., AND MILLS, C. W.
1946   *From Max Weber: Essays in Sociology.* London: Oxford University Press.

GIBSON, EVELYN
1975   *Homicide in England and Wales, 1967–1971.* Home Office Research Study no. 31. London: HMSO.

GIBSON, EVELYN, AND KLEIN, S.
1969   *Murder, 1957 to 1968: A Home Office Statistical Division Report on Murder in England and Wales.* London: HMSO.

GIL, DAVID G.
1975   "Unraveling Child Abuse." *American Journal of Orthopsychiatry* 45 (3):346–356.

GILLIS, JOHN R.
1974   *Youth and History.* New York: Academic Press.

GIORDANO, PEGGY C.
1977   "The Client's Perspective in Agency Evaluations." *Social Work* 22 34–37.

GLASGOW WOMEN'S AID
1975   "Interval House: Report for the Year February 1974 to February 1975." Available from Scottish Women's Aid.
1977   "Interval House: Report for the Year February 1976 to February 1977." Available from Scottish Women's Aid.

GLASTONBURY, B; BURDETT, H.; AND AUSTIN, R.
1973   "Community Perceptions and the Personal Social Services." *Policy and Politics* 1 (3):191–211.

GOLDSTEIN, JOSEPH
1960   "Police Discretion Not to Invoke the Legal Process: Low Visibility Decisions in the Administration of Justice." *Yale Law Journal* 69:543–594.

GOODE, WILLIAM J.
1971   "Force and Violence in the Family." *Journal of Marriage and the Family* 33 (4):624–636.

GOODSELL, WILLYSTINE
1939   *A History of Marriage and the Family.* New York: Macmillan.

GORNICK, VIVIAN, AND MORAN, BARBARA K. (EDS.)
1971   *Women in Sexist Society: Studies in Power and Powerlessness.* New York: New American Library, Mentor Books.

GOUGE, WILLIAM
1634   *Of Domesticall Duties: Eight Treatises.* London: Printed by George Miller for Edward Brewster.

GREGORY, MARGARET
1976   "Battered Wives." In Marie Borland (ed.), *Violence in the Family.* Manchester: Manchester University Press.

GUETTEL, CHARMIE
1974   *Marxism and Feminism.* Toronto: Hunter Rose.

HAFFNER, SARA
1978   "Wife Abuse in West Germany." *Victimology* 2 (3–4):472–478.

HAMILTON, ROBERTA
1978   *The Liberation of Women: A Study of Patriarchy and Capitalism.* London: George Allen & Unwin.

HANKS, SUSAN E., AND ROSENBAUM, C. PETER
1977   "Battered Women: A Study of Women Who Live with Violent Alcohol-Abusing Men." *American Journal of Orthopsychiatry* 47 (2):291–306.

HANMER, JALNA
1977   "Community Action, Women's Aid, and the Women's Liberation Movement." In Marjorie Mayo (ed.), *Women in the Community.* London: Routledge & Kegan Paul.

HARTMANN, HEIDI
  1976 "Capitalism, Patriarchy, and Job Segregation by Sex." *Signs: Journal of Women in Culture and Society* 1 (3), pt. 2:137–169.
HECKER, EUGENE A.
  1910 *A Short History of Women's Rights: From the Days of Augustus to the Present Time.* London: Putnam.
HELFER, R. E., AND KEMPE, C. H. (EDS.)
  1974 *The Battered Child* (2d ed.). Chicago: University of Chicago Press.
HEPBURN, JOHN R.
  1973 "Violent Behavior in Interpersonal Relationships." *Sociological Quarterly* 14 (Summer):419–429.
HILL, REUBEN
  1971 "Modern Systems Theory and the Family: A Confrontation." *Social Science Information* 10 (5):7–26.
HOLE, JUDITH, AND LEVINE, ELLEN
  1973 "Rebirth of Feminism." In Jo Freeman (ed.), *Women: A Feminist Perspective.* Palo Alto: Mayfield, 1975.
HORNEY, KAREN
  1967 "The Flight from Womanhood." In H. Kelman (ed.), *Feminine Psychology.* New York: Norton.
HOWARD, GEORGE E.
  1904 *A History of Matrimonial Institutions.* 3 vols. Chicago: University of Chicago Press.
INKELES, ALEX
  1968 "Society, Social Structure, and Child Socialization." In J. Clausen (ed.), *Socialization and Society.* Boston: Little, Brown.
INTERNATIONAL ASSOCIATION OF POLICE CHIEFS
  1967 *International Association of Chiefs of Police Training Key 16: Handling Disturbance Calls.* Gaithersberg.
ISIS
  1977 *International Bulletin* 4 (July). Available from Case Postale 301, 1227 Carouge/Geneva, Switzerland.
JENSEN, RITA HENLEY
  1978 "Battered Women and the Law." *Victimology* 2 (3–4):585–590.
JOBLING, M.
  1974 "Battered Wives: A Survey." *Social Service Quarterly* 47 (14):142–146.
KAMISHER, MICHELE
  1976 "Behind Closed Doors." *Real Paper* (2 November).
KNOX, JOHN
  1558 *The First Blast of the Trumpet Against the Monstrous Regiment of Women.* London: Southgate.
KOBUS, ELIZABETH
  1978 "Founding 'Stay Away from My Body.' " *Victimology* 2 (3–4):662–663.
KOHN, MELVIN
  1969 *Class and Conformity.* Homewood: Dorsey.
KOLB, T. M., AND STRAUS, M. A.
  1974 "Marital Power and Marital Happiness in Relation to Problem Solving Ability." *Journal of Marriage and the Family* 36 (4):756–766.

KOMAROVSKY, MIRRA
  1946 "Cultural Contradictions and Sex Roles." *American Journal of Sociology* 52 (November):184–189.

KREMEN, ELEANOR
  1976 "The 'Discovery' of Battered wives: Considerations for the Development of a Social Service Network." Paper presented to the American Sociological Association Convention. August. New York City.

KREPS, JUANITA
  1971 *Sex in the Marketplace: American Women at Work.* London: The Johns Hopkins Press.

KUHN, THOMAS
  1962 *The Structure of Scientific Revolutions.* Chicago: University of Chicago Press.

LaFAVE, WAYNE
  1969 "Noninvocation of the Criminal Law by Police." In Donald R. Cressey and David Ward (eds.), *Delinquency, Crime, and Social Process.* New York: Harper & Row.

LAKATOS, IMRE, AND MUSGRAVE, ALAN (EDS.)
  1970 *Criticism and the Growth of Knowledge.* Cambridge: Cambridge University Press.

LASLETT, BARBARA
  1973 "The Family as a Public and Private Institution: An Historical Perspective." *Journal of Marriage and the Family* 35 (3):480–492.

LASLETT, PETER
  1973 *The World We Have Lost.* London: Methuen.

LASLETT, PETER (ED.)
  1974 *Household and Family in Past Time.* London: Cambridge University Press.

LAZARSFELD, PAUL F., AND BARTON, ALLEN H.
  1964 "Qualitative Measurement in the Social Sciences: Classification, Typologies, and Indices." In David Lerner and H. D. Laswell (eds.), *The Policy Sciences.* Stanford: Stanford University Press.

LEGHORN, LISA, AND WARRIOR, BETSY
  1974 *Houseworker's Handbook.* Somerville: New England Free Press.

LESLIE, GERALD
  1967 *The Family in Social Context.* New York: Oxford University Press.

LEVINGER, GEORGE
  1966 "Sources of Marital Dissatisfaction among Applicants for Divorce." *American Journal of Orthopsychiatry* 36 (October):803–807.

LIEBOW, ELLIOT
  1966 *Tally's Corner.* Boston: Little, Brown.

LINCOLN, ALLAN JAY
  1973 "Justifications and Condemnations of Violence: A Typology of Response and a Research Review." *Sociological Symposium* 9 (Spring):51–67.

LION, JOHN R.
   1977   "Clinical Aspects of Wifebattering." In Maria Roy (ed.), *Battered Women: A Psychosociological Study of Domestic Violence.* New York: Van Nostrand Reinhold.

LUCKENBILL, DAVID
   1977   "Criminal Homicide as a Situated Transaction." *Social Problems* 24 (2):176–186.

LUKÁCS, GEORG
   1971   *History and Class Consciousness: Studies in Marxist Dialectics.* Translated by Rodney Livingstone. London: Merlin.

LUNDEN, WALTER A.
   1966   "Crimes in London, England." *Police* 19:93–95.

LYSTAD, MARY HANEMANN
   1975   "Violence at Home: A Review of the Literature." *American Journal of Orthopsychiatry* 45 (5):328–345.

MACDONALD, ARTHUR
   1911   "Death penalty and Homicide." *American Journal of Sociology* 16:96–97.

MACLEAN, U.
   1973   "Sources of Help." *New Society* 5 (April):16–18.

MANCHESTER, ANTHONY
   1976   "The Legal History of Marital Violence in England and Wales, 1750–1976." Mimeographed. University of Birmingham Faculty of Law.

MANSFIELD, PAUL, AND SMITH, JEFF
   1974   "What a Reception!" *Social Work Today* 5 (12):354–356.

MARCOVITCH, ANNE
   1976   "Refuges for Battered Women." *Social Work Today* 7 (2):34–35.

MARSDEN, DENNIS, AND OWEN, DAVID
   1975   "The Jekyll and Hyde Marriages." *New Society* 7 (May):333–335.

MARTIN, DEL
   1976   *Battered Wives.* San Francisco: Glide.
   1978   "Battered Women: Society's Problem." In Jane Roberts Chapman and Margaret Gates (eds.), *The Victimization of Women.* Beverly Hills: Sage.

MARX, KARL
   1970a   *Capital.* Vol. 3: *Capitalist Production as a Whole.* (1st pub. 1909) London: Lawrence and Wishart.
   1970b   *Capital.* Vol. 1: *A Critical Analysis of Capitalist Production.* (1st pub. 1867) London: Lawrence and Wishart.
   1970c   *A Contribution to the Critique of Political Economy* (1st pub. 1859). Edited by Maurice Dobb. Moscow: Progress.

MASSELL, GREGORY J.
   1968   "Law as an Instrument of Revolutionary Change in a Traditional Milieu: The Case of Soviet Central Asia." *Law and Society* 11 (2): 170–228.

MATHISEN, THOMAS
1974   *The Politics of Abolition.* London: Martin Robertson.

MAYER, JOHN E., AND TIMMS, NOEL
1970   *The Client Speaks.* London: Routledge & Kegan Paul.

McCARTHY, JOHN D.; GALLE, OMER R.; AND ZIMMERMAN, WILLIAM
1975   "Population Density, Social Structure, and Interpersonal Violence: An Intermetropolitan Test of Competing Models." *American Behavioral Scientist* 18 (6):771–791.

McCLINTOCK, E. H.
1963a "Crimes against the Person." *Proceedings of the Manchester Statistical Society,* 1–32.
1963b *Crimes of Violence.* New York: St. Martin's.

McKAY, ANN; GOLDBERG, E. MATILDA; AND FRUIN, DAVID F.
1973   "Consumers and a Social Service Department." *Social Work Today* 4 (16):436–491.

McLAREN, LADY
1909   *The Women's Charter of Rights and Liberties.* London: Grosvenor.

McNAMARA, JO ANN, AND WEMPLE, SUZANNE
1973   "The Power of Woman through the Family in Medieval Europe; 500–1100." *Feminist Studies* 1 (3–4):126–141.

McCREADIE, ROBERT
1978   "Protection Against Domestic Violence," *SCOLAG* 22 (July):144–148.

MILL, JOHN STUART
1955   *The Subjection of Women.* Reprint of 1869 ed. London: Dent.

MILLER, NICK
1975   *Battered Spouses.* Social Administration Trust, Occasional Paper no. 57. London: Bell and Sons.

MILLETT, KATE
1972   *Sexual Politics.* London: Abacus.

MILLMAN, MARCIA
1971   "Observations on Sex Role Research." *Journal of Marriage and the Family* 33 (4):772–776.

MILLS, C. WRIGHT
1971   *The Sociological Imagination.* Middlesex, England: Penguin.

MITCHELL, JULIET
1974   *Woman's Estate.* Middlesex, England: Penguin.
1976   "Women and Equality." In Juliet Mitchell and Ann Oakley (eds.), *The Rights and Wrongs of Women.* Middlesex, England: Penguin.

MITCHELL, JULIET, AND OAKLEY ANN, (EDS.)
1976   *The Rights and Wrongs of Women.* Middlesex, England: Penguin.

MOORE, JEAN
1974   "Yo-yo Children: A Study of Twenty-three Violent Matrimonial Cases." Mimeographed. British Society for the Prevention of Cruelty to Children.

MORAN, RICHARD
    1971   "Criminal Homicide: External Restraint and Subculture of Violence."
            Criminology 8 (4):357–374.

MORRIS, PAULINE; COOPER, JENNIE; AND BYLES, ANTHEA
    1973   "Public Attitude to Problem Definition and Problem Solving: A Pilot
            Study." *British Journal of Social Work* 3 (3):301–320.

NATIONAL COMMUNICATION NETWORK
    1977   *National Communication Network for the Elimination of Violence
            against Women* 1 (3). Available from Transition House, c/o Women's
            Center, 46 Pleasant Street, Cambridge, Massachusetts 02139.

NATIONAL COMMUNICATIONS NETWORK/FEMINIST ALLIANCE AGAINST RAPE
    1979   "Aegis: Magazine On Ending Violence Against Women." (Jan-
            uary/February). Annual Subscription available from FAAR/NCN Box
            21033, Washington, D.C. 20009.

NATIONAL WOMEN'S AID FEDERATION
    1975   *Battered Women Need Refuges: A Report from the National Women's
            Aid Federation.* London: Rye.
    1978   "He's Got to Show Her Who's Boss: The National Women's Aid Federa-
            tion Challenges a Man's Right to Batter." *Spare Rib* 69:15–18.

NEFF, WANDA
    1929   *Victorian Working Women.* New York: Columbia University Press.

NEWMAN, CHARLES L.
    1972   "Police and Families: Factors Affecting Police Intervention." *Police Chief*
            (march):25–30.

NICHOLS, BEVERLY B.
    1976   "The Abused Wife Problem." *Social Casework* 57 (1):27–32.

NORTHWEST REGION OF THE NATIONAL WOMAN'S AID FEDERATION
    1978   "Battered Women and Social Work." In F. Martin (ed.), *Violence in the
            Family.* New York: Wiley.

OAKLEY, ANN
    1974a   *Housewife.* London: Allen Lane.
    1974b   *The Sociology of Housework.* London: Martin Robertson.

O'BRIEN, JOHN E.
    1971   "Violence in Divorce Prone Families." *Journal of Marriage and the Fam-
            ily* 33 (4):692–698.

O'FAOLAIN, JULIA, AND MARTINES, LAURO (EDS.)
    1974   *Not in God's Image: Women in History.* Glasgow: Fontana/Collins.
            (Reissued Spring 1979. London: Virago.)

PAGELOW, MILDRED DALEY
    1978   "Violence Against Women in the Family." Paper presented at the 9th
            World Congress of Sociology, Uppsala, Sweden, August.

PAHL, JAN
    1977a   "The Role of a Women's Refuge in Assisting the victims of Marital
            Violence." Mimeographed. University of Kent, Canterbury.
    1977b   "Selected Tables from the Report on the Canterbury Women's Centre."
            Mimeographed. University of Kent.

1978   *A Refuge for Battered Women: A Study of The Rôle of a Women's Cen-*
        tre. London: HMSO.

PALMER, STUART
1972   *The Violent Society.* New Haven: Yale University Press.

PARKER, HOWARD J.
1974   *View from the Boys.* London: David and Charles.

PARLIAMENTARY PAPERS
1875   "Reports of Chief Constables for the Years 1870–74 Pertaining to the
        Law Relating to Brutal Assaults." In Reports to the Secretary of State for
        the Home Department of the State of the Law Relating to Brutal
        Assaults, Cmnd. 1138.

PARLIAMENTARY SELECT COMMITTEE ON VIOLENCE IN MARRIAGE
1975a   *First Special Report from the Select Committee on Violence in Marriage*
        together with the Proceedings of the Committee. Vol. 1. Session
        1974–75. London: HMSO.
1975b   *Report from the Select Committee on Violence in Marriage together with*
        the Proceedings of the Committee. Vol. 2. Session 1974–75. London:
        HMSO.

PARNAS, RAYMOND
1967   "The Police Response to the Domestic Disturbance." *Wisconsin Law*
        Review (Fall) 914 (2).
1970   "Judicial Response to Intra-Family Violence." *Minnesota Law Review*
        54:585–644.
1971   "Police Discretion and Diversion of Incidents of Intra-Family Violence."
        Law and Contemporary Problems 36 (4):539–565.

PARRISH, P. A.
1971   *The Prescribing of Psychotropic Drugs in General Practice.* Pamphlet
        published by *Journal of Royal College of General Practitioners.* 4, 21
        (November).

PARSONS, TALCOTT
1942   "Age and Sex in the Social Structure of the United States." *American*
        Sociological Review 7 (5):604–616.
1971   "The Normal American Family." In Arlene Skolnick and Jerome
        Skolnick (eds.), *Family in Transition: Rethinking Marriage, Sexuality,*
        Child Rearing, and Family Organization Boston: Little, Brown.

PARSONS, TALCOTT, AND BALES, ROBERT F.
1955   *Family, Socialization, and Interaction Process.* Glencoe, Illinois: Free
        Press.

PEARSALL, RONALD
1969   *The Worm in the Bud.* London: Weidenfeld & Nicholson.

PEPE, HELENE
1976   "Wife Abuse: Does the American Legal System Offer Adequate Protec-
        tion to the Abused Wife?" Paper presented to the American Sociological
        Association Convention. August. New York City.

PEPINSKY, HAROLD E.
1976   "Police Patrolmen's Offense Reporting Behavior." *Journal of Research in*
        Crime and Delinquency 13 (1):33–47.

PITTMAN, D. J., AND HANDY, W.
    1964   "Patterns in Criminal Aggravated Assault." *Journal of Criminal Law, Criminology, and Police Science* 55 (4):462–470.

PIZZEY, ERIN
    1974   *Scream Quietly or the Neighbours Will Hear You.* London: Penguin.

PLECK, ELIZABETH
    1978   "Wife Beating in Nineteenth-Century America." Unpublished paper. History Department, University of Michigan. Ann Arbor, Michigan 48109.

PLECK, E.; PLECK, J.; GROSSMAN, M.; AND BART, P.
    1978   "The Battered Data Syndrome: A Reply to Steinmetz." *Victimology* 2 (3–4):680–683.

POGREBIN, LETTY COTTIN
    1974   "Do Women Make Men Violent?" *Ms.* 3 (November):49–55, 80.

POKORNY, ALEX D.
    1965   "Human Violence: A Comparison of Homicide, Aggravated Assault, Suicide, and Attempted Murder." *Journal of Criminal Law, Criminology, and Police Science* 56 (4):488–497.

POLLOCK, F., AND MAITLAND, F. W.
    1911   *The History of English Law before the Time of Edward I.* Vol. 2. London: Cambridge University Press.

POWER, EILEEN
    1926   "The Position of Women." In C. G. Crump and E. F. Jacobs (eds.), *The Legacy of the Middle Ages.* Oxford: Clarendon.

PRESCOTT, SUZANNE, AND LETKO, CAROLYN
    1977   "Battered Women: A Social Psychological Perspective." In Maria Roy (ed.), *Battered Women: A Psychosociological Study of Domestic Violence.* New York: Van Nostrand Reinhold.

PRESTAGE, EDGAR (ED.)
    1928   *Chivalry.* New York: Knopf.

PUNCH, MAURICE, AND NAYLOR, TREVOR
    1973   "The Police: A Social Service." *New Society* 5 (May):328–330.

QUEEN, STUART, AND HABENSTEIN, ROBERT W.
    1967   *The Family in Various Cultures* (3d ed.). Philadelphia: Lippincott.

RADBILL, SAMUEL X.
    1974   "The History of Child Abuse and Infanticide." In R. E. Helfer and C. H. Kempe (eds.), *The Battered Child* (2d ed.). Chicago: Univerisity of Chicago Press.

REES, A. M.
    1972   "Access to the Personal and Health Welfare Services." *Social and Economic Administration* 6 (1):34–43.

REES, STUART
    1974   "No More Than Contact: An Outcome of Social Work." *British Journal of Social Work* 4 (3):255–279.

REITH, DREW
    1975   "I Wonder If You Can Help Me . . . ?" *Social Work Today* 6 (3):66–69.

Rose, Hilary
1978   *Up Against The Welfare State.* Unit 30, DE206, Milton Keynes. The Open University.

Rosenberg, Charles E. (ed.)
1975   *The Family in History.* Philadelphia: University of Pennsylvania Press.

Rossi, Alice S.
1964   "Equality between the Sexes: An Immodest Proposal." *Daedalus* 93 (2) (Spring): 607–652.
1965   "Women in Science: Why So Few?" *Science* 148 (3674):1106–1202.
1976   "Social Roots of the Women's Movement in America." In Rossi (ed.), (First Pub. 1973) *The Feminist Papers.* New York: Bantam.

Rossi, Alice S. (ed.)
1976   *The Feminist Papers: From Adams to de Beauvoir.* (1st pub. 1973) New York: Bantam.

Rounsaville, Bruce J.
1978   "Battered Wives: Barriers to Identification and Treatment." *American Journal of Orthopsychiatry* 48 (3):487–494.

Rowbotham, Sheila
1973   *Hidden from History: Three Hundred Years of Women's Oppression and the Fight against It.* London: Pluto.

Roy, Maria
1977   "A Current Survey of 150 Cases." In Maria Roy (ed.), *Battered Women: A Psychosociological Study of Domestic Violence.* New York: Van Nostrand Reinhold.

Roy, Maria (ed.)
1977   *Battered Women: A Psychosociological Study of Domestic Violence.* New York: Van Nostrand Reinhold.

Russell, Bertrand
1935   "Rights Husbands Had Once." *Sunday Referee* (December 15):12.

Sachs, Albie, and Wilson, Joan Hoff
1978   *Sexism and the Law: A Study of Male Beliefs and Judical Bias.* Oxford: Martin Robertson.

Saul, Leon J.
1972   "Personal and Social Psychopathology and the Primary Prevention of Violence." *American Journal of Psychiatry* 128 (12):1578–1581.

Scheff, Thomas J.
1966   *Being Mentally Ill: A Sociological Theory.* Chicago: Aldine.
1968   "Negotiating Reality: Notes on Power in the Assessment of Responsibility." *Social Problems* 16 (Summer):3–17.

Schochet, Gordon J.
1969   "Patriarchalism, Politics and Mass Attitudes in Stuart England." *The Historical Journal* 12 (3):413–441.

Schoulder, James
1921   *Marriage, Divorce, Separation, and Domestic Relations.* Vol. 1. (6th ed.). New York: Matthew Bender.

Schultz, Leroy G.
1960   "The Wife Assaulter." *Journal of Social Therapy* 6 (2):103–112.

SCHWENDINGER, JULIA, AND SCHWENDINGER, HERMAN
  1971 "Sociology's Founding Fathers: Sexist to a Man." *Journal of Marriage and the Family* 33 (4):783–799.

SCOTT, JOAN, AND TILLY, LOUISE
  1975 "Women's Work and the Family in Nineteenth Century Europe." In Charles E. Rosenberg (ed.) *The Family in History.* Philadelphia: University of Pennsylvania Press.

SEARCH, GAY
  1974 "Notes from Abroad: London Battered Wives." *Ms.* 3 (June):24–26.

SECOMBE, WALLY
  1973 "The Housewife and Her Labour under Capitalism." *New Left Review* (January–February):3–27.

SELG, HERBERT (ED.)
  1975 *The Making of Human Aggression.* Translated by Arnold Pomerans. London: Quartet.

SHAINESS, NATALIE
  1977 "Psychological Aspects of Wife-Beating." In Maria Roy (ed.), *Battered Women: A Psychosoiological Study of Domestic Violence.* New York: Van Nostrand Reinhold.

SHORT, JAMES F., AND STRODTBECK, FRED L.
  1965 *Group Process and Gang Delinquency.* Chicago: University of Chicago Press.

SHORTER, EDWARD
  1977 *The Making of the Modern Family.* Glasgow: Fontana/Collins.

SKOLNICK, ARLENE, AND SKOLNICK, JEROME (EDS.)
  1971 *Family in Transition: Rethinking Marriage, Sexuality, Child Rearing, and Family Organization.* Boston: Little, Brown.

SLOT-ANDERSON, INGERLISE
  1976 "A Dutch Refuge for Battered Women: Who Comes?" Paper presented to the American Sociological Association Convention. August. New York City.

SMITH, GILBERT, AND HARRIS, ROBERT
  1972 "Ideologies of Need and the Organization of Social Work Departments." *British Journal of Social Work* 2 (1):27–48.

SNELL, JOHN E.; ROSENWALD, RICHARD; AND ROBEY, AMES
  1964 "The Wifebeater's Wife: A Study of Family Interaction." *Archives of General Psychiatry* 11 (August):107–112.

STEELE, BRANDT, AND POLLOCK, CAROL B.
  1974 "A Psychiatric Study of Parents Who Abuse Infants and Small Children." In R. E. Helfer and C. H. Kempe (eds.), *The Battered Child* (2d ed.). Chicago: University of Chicago Press.

STEINMETZ, SUZANNE K.
  1978 "The Battered Husband Syndrome." *Victimology* 2 (3–4):499–509.

STEINMETZ, SUZANNE K., AND STRAUS, MURRAY A.
  1973 "The Family as Cradle of Violence." *Society* 10 (September–October):50–56.

1974 *Violence in the Family.* New York: Dodd, Mead.

STINCHCOMBE, ARTHUR S.
1963 "Institutions of Privacy in the Determination of Police Administrative Practice." *American Journal of Sociology* 69 (September):150–160.

STONE, LAWRENCE
1975 "The Rise of the Nuclear Family in Early Modern England: The Patriarchical Stage." In Charles E. Rosenberg (ed.), *The Family in History.* Philadelphia: University of Pennsylvania Press.

STORR, ANTHONY
1974 *Human Aggression* (1st pub. 1968). Baltimore: Penguin.

STRAUS, MURRAY A.
1973 "A General Systems Approach to a Theory of Violence between Family Members." *Social Science Information* 12 (3):105–125.
1974 "Leveling, Civility, and Violence in the Family." *Journal of Marriage and the Family* 36 (February):13–29.
1976 "Sexual Inequality, Cultural Norms, and Wife-Beating." *Victimology* 1 (Spring):54–76.
1978 "Wife Beating: How Common and Why?" *Victimology* 2 (3–4):443–458.

STRAUS, MURRAY A.; GELLES, RICHARD J.; AND STEINMETZ, SUZANNE K.
1976 "Violence in the Family: An Assessment of Knowledge and Research Needs." Paper presented to the American Association for the Advancement of Science Convention. February. Boston.

SUPREME COURT OF NEW YORK
1976 *Bruno v. Codd.* Index 21946/76. New York County.

SUTTON, JO
1978 "The Growth of the British Movement for Battered Women." *Victimology* 2 (3–4):576–584.

SWETNAM, JOSEPH
1616 *The Araignment of Lewd, Idle, Froward and Unconstant Women.* London.

SZASZ, T. T.
1961 *The Myth of Mental Illness.* New York: Harper.

TEMPERLEY, H. W. V.
1975 "Sale of Wives in England in 1823" (1st pub. 1925). Reprinted in Jo Freeman (ed.), *Women: A Feminist Perspective.* Palo Alto: Mayfield.

THOMPSON, E. P.
1963 *The Making of the English Working Class.* Aylesbury, England: Pelican Books.
1972 "Rough Music: 'Le Charivari anglais,' " *Annales* (Economies, Societies, Civilizations) 27 (2):285–312.

THOMPSON, WILLIAM
1825 *Appeal of One Half of the Human Race, WOMEN, Against the Pretensions of the Other Half, MEN, to Retain Them in Political, and Thence in CIVIL AND DOMESTIC SLAVERY.* London.

Tidmarsh, Mannes
    1976   "Violence in Marriage: The Relevance of Structural Factors." *Social Work Today* 7 (2):36–37.

Tilly, Charles
    1966   "Chaos and Violence in the Living City." In Paul Meadows and Ephraim Mizruchi (ed.), *Urbanism, Urbanization, and Change: Comparative Perspectives.* Reading: Addison-Wesley.

Toby, Jackson
    1966   "Violence and the Masculine Ideal." *Annals of the American Academy of Political and Social Sciences* 364 (March):20–27.

Toch, Hans
    1969   *Violent Men: An Inquiry into the Psychology of Violence.* Chicago: Aldine.

Tomes, Nancy
    1978   "A 'Torrent of Abuse': Crimes of Violence Between Working-Class Men and Women in London, 1840–1875." *Journal of Social History* 11 (3):329–345.

Trevelyan, G. M.
    1966   *History of England* (3d ed., 1st pub. 1926). London: Longmans, Green.

Trotsky, Leon
    1970   *Women and the Family.* New York: Pathfinder.

Truninger, Elizabeth
    1971   "Marital Violence: The Legal Solutions." *Hastings Law Journal* 23 (1):259–276.

Valdez, Luis, and Steiner, Stan (eds.)
    1972   *Aztlan: An Anthology of Mexican American Literature.* New York: Random House, Vintage Books.

Valency, Maurice
    1958   *In Praise of Love.* New York: Macmillan.

Van Crevel, Nora
    1976   "But What about the Kids?" Paper presented to the American Sociological Association Convention. August. New York City.

Van den Berghe, Pierre
    1974   "Bringing Beasts Back In: Toward a Biosocial Theory of Aggression." *American Sociological Review* 39 (December):777–778.

Von Hentig, Hans
    1948   *The Criminal and His Victim.* New Haven: Yale University Press.

Voss, Harwin L., and Hepburn, John R.
    1968   "Patterns in Criminal Homicide in Chicago." *Journal of Criminal Law, Criminology, and Police Science* 59 (4):499–508.

Wagner, Janet R.
    1978   "*Bruno v. Codd:* Battered Wives and the Police in the United States and Britain." Mimeographed paper available from College of Law, University of Denver, Denver, Colorado.

Walker, Lenore E.
    1978   "Treatment Alternatives for Battered Women." In Jane Roberts Chap-

man and Margaret Gates (eds.), *The Victimization of Women*. Beverly Hills: Sage.

WALTERS, MARGARET
1976 "The Rights and Wrongs of Women: Mary Wollstonecraft, Harriet Martineau, Simone de Beauvoir." In Juliet Mitchell and Ann Oakley (eds.), *The Rights and Wrongs of Women*. Middlesex, England: Penguin.

WARRIOR, BETSY
1978 *Working on Wife Abuse* (6 ed., 1st Pub. 1976). Available from Transition House, Women's Center, 46 Pleasant Street, Cambridge, Massachusetts 02139.
1975 *Wifebeating*. Somerville: New England Free Press.

WEBB, P. R. H.
1969 "Matrimonial Cruelty: A Lawyer's Guide for the Medical Profession." *Medicine, Science, and Law* 7:110–116.

WEBER, MAX
1947 *The Theory of Social and Economic Organization*. Translated by A. R. Henderson and Talcott Parsons. New York: Hodge.
1949 *The Methodology of the Social Sciences*. Translated and edited by Edward Shils and Henry A. Finch. New York: Free Press.

WEGNER, ELDON
1975 "The Conception of Alienation: A Critique and Some Suggestions for a Context Specific Approach." *Pacific Sociological Review* 18 (2):171–193.

WEIR, ANGELA
1977 "Battered Women: Some Perspectives and Problems." In Marjorie Mayo (ed.) *Women in the Community*. London: Routledge & Kegan Paul.

WEISS, J. A.; RAMIREZ, F. O.; AND TRACY, T.
1976 "Female Participation in the Occupational System: A Comparative Institutional Analysis." *Social Problems* 23 (5):593–608.

WEISS, ROBERT
1973 "Helping Relationships: Relationships of Clients with Physicians, Social Workers, Priests, and Others." *Social Problems* 20 (3):319–328.

WEISSTEIN, NAOMI
1971 "Psychology Constructs the Female." In Vivian Gornick and Barbara K. Moran (eds.), *Women in Sexist Society: Studies in Power and Powerlessness*. New York: New American Library, Mentor Books.

WEITZMAN, LENORE J.
1975a "Sex-Role Socialization." In Jo Freeman (ed.), *Women: A Feminist Perspective*. Palo Alto: Mayfield.
1975b "To Love, Honor, and Obey? Traditional Legal Marriage and Alternative Family Forms." *Family Coordinator* 24 (4):543–547. Reprinted in Arlene Skolnick and Jerome Skolnick (eds.), *Family in Transition: Rethinking Marriage, Sexuality, Child Rearing, and Family Organization* Boston: Little, Brown, 1977.

WERTHMAN, CARL, AND PILIAVIN, IRVING
1967 "Gang Members and the Police." In David Bordura (ed.), *The Police*. New York: Wiley.

WESTLEY, WILLIAM A.
    1970   *Violence and the Police: A Sociological Study of Law, Custom, and Morality.* Cambridge: MIT Press.

WHITEHURST, ROBERT
    1971   "Violence Potential in Extra-marital Sexual Responses." *Journal of Marriage and the Family* 33 (4):683-691.

WHYTE, WILLIAM H.
    1962   "The Wife Problem." *Life,* January 7, 1952. Reprinted in R. Winch, R. McGinnis, and H. Baringer (eds.), *Selected Studies in Marriage and Family.* New York: Holt, Rinehart & Winston.

WILKINS, LESLIE
    1963   "The Measurement of Crime." *British Journal of Criminology* 3 (April):321-341.

WILSON, ELIZABETH
    1975   "Battered Wives: A Social Worker's Viewpoint." *Royal Society of Health Journal* 95 (6):294-297.
    1976   "Research into Battered Women: Why We Need Research and Why What Exists Is Potentially Dangerous: A Reply to Dr. Jasper Gayford." Available from the National Women's Aid Federation, 374 Gray's Inn Road, WC 1, London, England.
    1977   *Women and the Welfare State.* London: Tavistock.

WOLFGANG, MARVIN E.
    1958   *Patterns in Criminal Homicide.* New York: Wiley.

WOLFGANG, MARVIN E., AND FERRACUTI, FRANCO
    1967   *The Subculture of Violence: Towards an Integrated Theory in Criminology.* London: Tavistock.

WOLLSTONECRAFT, MARY
    1955   *A Vindication of the Rights of Women.* Reprint of 1792 ed. London: Dent.

WOMEN'S AID
    1973   "Battered Wives." Available from Women's Aid, 2 Belmont Terrace, London, W. 4., England.

WOOLF, VIRGINIA
    1974   *A Room of One's Own* (15th ed.) (1st pub. 1929). London: Hogarth.

WORTIS, ROCHELLE
    1971   "The Acceptance of the Concept of the Maternal Role by Behavioral Scientists: Its Effects on Women." *American Journal of Orthopsychiatry* 41 (5):733-746.

YOUNG, JIM
    1976   "Wife-Beating in Britain: A Socio-historical Analysis, 1850-1914." Paper presented to the American Sociological Association Convention. August. New York City.
    1977   "Social Class and the National Question: The Dialectics of Scottish History." Mimeographed. Department of History, University of Stirling.

ZARETSKY, ELI
    1976   *Capitalism, the Family, and Personal Life.* London: Pluto Press.

INDEX